DYNAMICS OF INDIAN BANKING

Views and Vistas

DYNAMICS OF INDIAN BANKING

Views and Vistas

Edited by

Manoranjan Sharma

ATLANTIC
PUBLISHERS & DISTRIBUTORS (P) LTD

Published by

ATLANTIC

PUBLISHERS & DISTRIBUTORS (P) LTD

7/22, Ansari Road, Darya Ganj,
New Delhi-110002
Phones : +91-11-23273880, 23275880, 23280451
Fax : +91-11-23285873
Web : www.atlanticbooks.com
E-mail : info@atlanticbooks.com

Branch Office
5, Nallathambi Street, Wallajah Road,
Chennai-600002
Phones : +91-44-64611085, 32413319
E-mail : chennai@atlanticbooks.com

ISBN 978-81-269-0998-8

Printed in India at Nice Printing Press, A-33/3A, Site-IV,
Industrial Area, Sahibabad, Ghaziabad, U.P.

Contents

Preface

In the present era of change and transformation, all elements are critically in ferment. Centuries of development are now telescoped into years of rapid growth and structural transformation—the kind of growth unprecedented in the annals of mankind. As the 21st century is characterised by rapid technological changes, blurring of geographical frontiers of countries and the revolution of 'rising expectations', a fundamental reorientation of the development strategies is necessary for high and sustained growth. Accordingly, the strategy to be adopted by banking and financial institutions needs to be redefined. These institutions can no longer afford to exist in cocoon or keep an ostrich like attitude and need to adopt new practices to adapt themselves to changing circumstances and the challenge of time.

The interaction of the real and monetary sectors is crucial for the stability of the financial system. A deep, liquid, vibrant and transparent financial market is the *sine qua non* for effective dissemination of monetary policy. There is limited depth in India's bond market because of narrow participation. In recent years, SEBI and Government of India have taken various steps to improve efficiency and transparency in the Indian bond market. However, there is an urgent need to remove 'government's captive market phenomenon' from the debt market. Greater participation of insurance and pension funds, harmonization of regulatory institutions and devising up of new financial architecture are imperative. Multiple regulators, though necessary because of multiple delivery channels, market segmentation and overlapping of regulatory functions, often provide wrong signals to market. Hence, there is a manifest need to examine the supervisory aspect of 'Financial Conglomeration' in an emerging market economy like India.

Winds of change have been sweeping the Indian banking system since the deregulation of the industry in 1991. Some of the important changes relate to growing competition from within and without, technological upgradation and enhanced supervision and monitoring. The transition from one phase to another has largely been influenced by the dynamics of three critical factors—the players, the playing fields and the regulator.

Given this overarching scenario, it is widely recognized that the banking sector reforms in India have transformed the face of banking. The saga of banking transformation is clearly reflected in terms of the steady improvement in Capital to Risk Assets Ratio (CRAR), the reduction in the level of both gross and net NPAs, the improvement in the operating profit to asset ratio, asset quality, return on assets (RoA), productivity, profitability, etc.

Banking System in India: The Challenge and the Response

New competitive realities have blurred industry boundaries, transformed standard management practices and rendered conventional models of strategy and growth obsolete. This is why, in conformity with the changing needs of the market, development of suitable products, has been a thrust area of the Banks. In bracing for tomorrow, contextual and socio-economic influences need to be borne in mind. Consequently, enterprise-wise quality improvement programmes must be assiduously pursued with an emphasis on customer service to create new, clearly differentiated values.

The significance of the banking sector reforms in fundamentally altering the banking system without any disruptive effects is not always realized. These changes need to be looked at against the broader macroeconomic canvas of the rapid expansion of the service sector, the growth of the external sector, the manifest need for enhancing investments in infrastructure to sustain higher growth and the critical role of agriculture and allied activities in providing livelihoods on a sustained basis. The evolving situation requires thrust on greater specialization by banks in different niches of the market such as retail, agriculture, export and the small-scale and corporate sector; greater reliance on non-fund businesses such as advisory and consultancy services, guarantee and custody services; greater overlap in product coverage between commercial banks and non-bank financial intermediaries; and greater financial disintermediation with large companies accessing securitised debt domestically and from financial markets abroad.

At this defining moment of history, the Indian banking system faces several challenges. Changes driven by globalization, internet, and technological developments are accelerating and thus transforming today's markets. As these changes intensify, the stakes rise higher necessitating a fundamental reorientation of strategies by banks to successfully meet the onslaughts of the progressive across the board liberalization. This stark reality check necessitates an attitudinal change, a paradigm shift from traditional process-oriented service to customer-oriented service. This requires developing alternative delivery channels through cost-effective technology platforms to sustain market leadership, retain customer base and improve customer service, besides widening business opportunities. Such challenges influencing the contemporary business environment relate to consolidation, capital adequacy, risk management and financial inclusion. Let me just briefly hit some of the high spots for a holistic assessment and perspective. This should not be taken to mean, in any way, that we can afford to rest on our laurels but to stress the significant distance traversed by us as also to highlight the road map for the future.

The banking sector in India has truly come of age in the contemporary Indian financial market. There have been several challenges on the road to the transformational journey, in the pursuit of making the banks stronger and vibrant. The strength of the Indian banking system is clearly reflected in their successful implementation of Basle-I norms and improved earning strength, sequential reform measures, maintenance of capital adequacy well above the international norm of 8 per cent, adoption of 90 days international norm of asset classification, expansion of the capital base with equity participation and diversification of ownership. Institutional and legal reforms have also been undertaken in the banking sector. Clearly, these are impressive achievements, particularly against the backdrop of the state of the Indian banking at the time of initiation of economic reforms. But there are mountains beyond mountains, peaks beyond peaks. And even when one reaches the peak, i.e. the summit, staying there is not all that easy. Goodhart justifiably maintained: "Setting standards is just the first step, maintaining them is the hard part." With globalization gaining force, Indian banks must move full steam with larger scale of operations—both within India and with enhanced footprints outside.

Relative Strength and Resilience of Indian Banks

Globalization impacts the banking industry through intensified competition, accent on efficiency, productivity and cost reduction, streamlined risk management systems and practices and strengthened service quality and delivery and cross-selling of products/services. Other important elements of business complexities include product innovation, technological automation on a much larger canvas, competency building and investment in human capital, mergers and acquisitions (M&A), transparency, disclosure and market discipline.

Compared to some Asian countries, the Indian financial sector, post-reforms, has been resilient to a great extent. However, a key concern of the financial system continues to be the fragility of some financial institutions. High government debt, stock market volatility, risk concentration and policy failure often distort the financial system. Given the serious damage a financial sector crisis can wreak on the economy, the stability of the financial sector should be the goal of the economy. Corporate governance, accounting disclosures, compliance with international accounting standards and regular off-site and on-site inspections will go a long way in enhancing financial stability. Financial stability can be improved by strengthening financial infrastructure, enhancing competition and restructuring weak segments of financial system.

Post-reforms, Indian banking is relatively much stronger *vis-à-vis* other Asian counterparts in terms of product range, range of investment and financial options for depositors and financial health of primary and secondary capital markets. But the banking sector now faces newer challenges, particularly in the context of Basle II norms, creating global brands, Anti Money Laundering, KYC Norms, changed role of regulators and entry of new players.

Sweeping changes have altered the market, increasing competition and stimulating the development of different models, products and methods of operating. Benchmarking product offering has rarely been so important and yet so difficult. This is why it is necessary to improve the understanding of how the market is evolving and, crucially, how operators are reacting to these changes with a focus on competition, service and marketing.

Apparently, the changes put in place may seem to be too far-reaching in their implications to achieve the desired results. "But successful companies", as Harvard Business School Professor Rosabeth Moss Kanter stressed, "develop a culture that just keeps moving all the time." It is this culture of moving all the time and long-term structural transformation that banks are now attempting. Long-term structural transformation has four characteristics: scale (the change affects all or most of the organizations), magnitude (it involves significant alterations of the status quo), duration (it lasts for months, if not years), and strategic importance. All the efforts must be focused on enhancing organizational capabilities.

This vision for a vibrant and internationally competitive banking sector in India is based on achievement of competitive advantage. Competitive advantage requires continued accent on efficiency, productivity and profitability and upscaling of technological upgradation on a much larger canvas, transition to greater capital account convertibility, while being consistent with continuing obligations under the WTO commitments. This would enable banks to emulate the international best practices and successfully weather the seemingly insurmountable challenges.

In view of recent developments and important issues germane to the healthy development of banks, including the emerging macroeconomic environment, the dialectics, dilemmas and challenges of banking development, the RBI's Stance on Regulation and Supervision has moved from 'micro-regulation' to 'macro-regulation'; from regulatory intervention to creating an enabling environment where banks can think freely and innovate; from rule-based to principles-oriented and from day-to-day monitoring to building a system of risk assessment and containment. In the future, given considerable autonomy granted to banks, the regulatory and supervisory role of RBI would not only be 'friendly and frank' but also be increasingly 'prompt and firm' in maintaining a balance between efficiency and stability while pursuing gradual economic integration with the rest of the world.

Indian Banking at an Inflexion Point

There has certainly been distinctly discernible improvement in performance indices. But the creation of a globally competitive size for the Indian banks remains a major challenge. Banks in Asia, particularly in China, are large in size compared to Indian banks. Indian banking industry needs larger amounts of capital to sustain growth in the future to effectively meet competition from the global banks. Basle II implementation is widely acknowledged as a significant challenge faced by both banks and the regulators internationally. But Basle II implementation is both a challenge and an opportunity.

The capital adequacy of banks will fall by 50 basis points in 2007-08 and by as much as 75 basis points each in the second and third year, after adopting the new capital adequacy norms. There would be a severe strain on capital due to the implementation of Basle II norms. The impact will, however, be spread over 3 years. Banks will have to adopt the new capital provisioning norms under Basle II from March 2008 onwards.

Transformed Ground Realities

Significant developments in the banking sector in the post-reforms phase have changed the face of Indian banking. The rapid growth of the banking sector in relation to the real economy enhanced the ratio of assets of scheduled commercial banks to GDP to 92.5% at end-March 2007. Financial performance of SCBs during 2006-07 was characterised by hardening of interest rates—both on the liability and the asset sides. Both net interest income and non-interest income of banks increased sharply in absolute terms, but declined in relation to total assets. With improved management capabilities, repositioned competitive strategies, enhanced IT architecture and sharper customer focus, profitability of commercial banks in India (as measured by Net Profits/Total Assets) rose sharply from 0.49% in 2000-01 to 0.90% in 2006-07. The intermediation cost (Operating Expenses/Total Assets) declined significantly from 2.64% in 2000-01 to 1.91% in 2006-07.

The overall capital adequacy ratio increased from 11.40% in 2000-01 to 12.28% in 2006-07. The increase in capital adequacy ratio needs to be looked at in the perspective of credit growth of 30% in the financial years 2005-06, 2006-07 and 2007-08. The latest Assessment Report on Indian Banking of Standard & Poor's maintains, "The outlook on the Indian banking and insurance industry is stable with strong growth likely to continue in 2008. In 2008, the Indian banking and insurance system, which has been unaffected by the US sub-prime markets, will continue to reap the benefits of strong economic growth."

The asset quality of the banking system improved significantly with the NPAs of SCBs, which stood at 7% of total assets in 1995-96, declining to 1.46% in 2006-07. The enabling architecture facilitated by initiatives like enactment of the Securitisation and Reconstruction of Financial Assets and Enforcement of Security Interest (SARFAESI) Act, empowerment of Asset Reconstruction Companies (ARCs), incorporation of the Credit Information Bureau (India) Limited (CIBIL) and Corporate Debt Restructuring (CDR) system have streamlined the recovery mechanism and brought about a greater sense of credit discipline.

A SWOT analysis reveals that despite altered ground realities, Public Sector Banks (PSBs) continue to hold sway with three-fourths of assets and income. While the share in net profit grew for both public and private sector banks, the share of PSBs in the overall profit of the banking sector increased. This suggests that with operational flexibility, PSBs are competing relatively effectively with private sector and foreign banks.

The ramifications of the large-scale transformation are significant not only for our banks but also the overall economy.

In the context of the steadily rising economy, the dynamics of banking development and the transforming macroeconomic landscape a new set of policies tailored to the specific needs is called for to foster a virtuous cycle of regenerative, broad-based growth. But there is no cause for alarm as the system is well equipped to meet them. What is needed is the pursuit of competitive advantage by achieving higher levels of efficiency and productivity and attain and maintain global benchmarks in terms of all identified parameters. Ever rising levels of efficiency in management of the man, machine, material and methods will help us to scale successively higher peaks of performance. Towards this end, slashing NPAs by streamlining credit delivery mechanism, enhanced organisational effectiveness by management of deregulated interest rates, market segmentation, asset-liability management (ALM) and technology upgradation are needed. Given the pressure on margins, the squeeze on profits and high stakeholder expectations, cross-selling of products, wealth management, marketing of mutual funds and insurance products and equity trading must constitute integral elements of the growth strategy. Generic customer acquisition and retention strategies such as technological upgradation, expansion of ATM network, use of new and innovative delivery channels would certainly be useful. But it is necessary to emphasise that the role of the staff at the customer touch points of the bank at the branches is of utmost importance. Little things such as a cherry smile to the customer and quality service at the counters would make the customer feel welcome and earn us his loyalty. This is important because it is not great things that make life; it is just the sum of little things. Such a proactive attitude would also have welcome spin-off effects of enhancing our customer base, volume and profitability. Word of mouth from a satisfied customer would bring in more business than a paid advertisement.

The spreads of the banks are under increasing pressure and the margins are being squeezed all the time. Hence, all out efforts with a sense of urgency need to be made to contain costs and increase yields. Success in the rapidly evolving environment requires customer orientation, market focus, innovativeness, efficient credit dispensation and monitoring, besides building up sound financials.

While it is important for a bank to closely monitor and conform to the needs and preferences of the customers, it is equally essential to build a quality culture within the organization. Accordingly, banks in India need to make quality a thrust area across functions. Sir Winston Churchill once quipped, "My tastes are simple. I am easily satisfied with the Best". This is the philosophy banks need to imbibe to survive and flourish in the present-day world.

In the rapidly changing present-day world, the banking industry landscape has been witnessing sweeping changes driven by cutting-edge technologies. Consequently, there has been a paradigm shift from traditional process-oriented service to customer-oriented service. Banks have been initiating a host of technology-driven products and services to sustain market leadership, retain customer base and improve customer service, besides widening business opportunities. Technology now needs to be increasingly leveraged by broad-basing the clientele, taking advantage of the booming economy. This requires thrust on low cost ATMs, kiosks as point of sales (PoS) that can provide financial services, PoS devices housed in the Post Offices or Gram Panchayats, biometric authentication and smart cards, credit scoring tools, end-to-end software supporting the credit cycle management including online management of loan repayment, loan processing fee, insurance fee, comprehensive MIS and portfolio analysis.

There has been a heightened consciousness of the strategic role of public sector banks, particularly the pioneering role of

PSBs in promotion of development in all its facets, including priority sector lending, commitment to government-sponsored schemes, branch expansion, technological upgradation and modernization. The PSBs have always gone the extra mile not just to enhance economic growth but also to bring about greater distributive equity through their focus on inclusive and broad-based growth, microfinance, doubling of agricultural credit in the last three years, and the like. All these are important areas, which are of considerable contextual significance to India.

The human resources of an institution constitute the basic determinant of success. Human resource issues challenging the banking sector include recruitment, compensation, evaluation and management (of performance), promotions, managing relations and planning. It is not bricks or mortar or even fancy interior decoration that makes an institution. But it is the quality of persons who work for it. This is why, it is necessary for the long-term objective of the individual and the institution to be in harmony, to be in sync for sustained growth of both the individual and the institution. Clearly, the issue of human resources management (HRM) has immense contextual significance because of the overarching context of the rapid growth of the Indian economy and the emergence of the banking and financial services sector as a key growth driver.

Adroit Risk Management

In line with global best practices, banks have put in place measures to comply with Basle II norms within the stipulated time frame. Banks have adequately integrated their risk management processes for effectively managing the entire gamut of risks, backed up by technological capabilities and requisite manpower expertise. Under the parallel run exercise, banks are on the threshold of implementing the basic approaches for credit and operational risks and standardized approach for arriving at capital charge for market risk. The overarching objective is to implement advanced approaches of risk management as prescribed in Basle II. Banks have also made considerable progress under risk-based internal audit of their branches, as part of the novel risk-based supervision system put in place by RBI.

Consolidation

Globally, mega-mergers in the financial sector have been taking place to leverage benefits of large size, expanding scope of business activities and harnessing core competencies. Competition is a driving force for banks to go for mergers to attain economies of scale and scope. Consolidation of players through mergers and acquisitions (M&As), globalization of operations, development of new technology and universalisation of banking have been the prime motives in going to scale. Product diversification, exploration of alternative revenue generating streams and customer convenient hi-tech/virtual banking services such as off-site and on-site ATMs, anywhere banking, internet and mobile banking, which have progressively made the need for brick and mortar banks almost redundant, also provide an impetus to the consolidation drive.

While financial sector reforms and prudent regulatory system have enhanced competitiveness and resilience of Indian banks, there is ample scope for banks in India to harness various core competencies and cost efficiencies through mergers and emerge world class banks. An analysis of the latest survey results of *The Banker* (July 2007) provides an opportunity to introspect and to chart out future road map. The analysis shows that the performance of Indian banks is mixed: while commercial banks in India compare well in terms of profitability and asset quality, they need to scale up in terms of size and efficiency. Among the top 100 banks in the world, there is only one Indian bank, SBI, at 70th position. Among the top 25 banks in Asia (ex-Japan), there are only two banks from India: SBI (11th place) and ICICI Bank (24th place). Among the top 25 Asian banks (ex-Japan) by Tier 1 capital, there are 7 banks from S. Korea, followed by 6 from China, 4 from Australia, 3 each from Singapore and Taiwan and 2 from India (SBI and ICICI). This is why, as repeatedly stressed by the Hon'ble FM, 3 Cs (competition, consolidation and convergence) are the need of the hour.

Mergers have appeared on the Indian banking horizon, though not on a scale comparable to that elsewhere in the world, to achieve efficiency and effectiveness in operations, productivity and cost reduction, superior risk management, diversification, upgradation of (a) technology, (b) infrastructure, and (c) competence building. Mergers ideally need to be synergy-driven and market-led with economies of scale and scope. However, market-driven consolidation is a relatively new phenomenon in India. Post-financial reforms, deregulation and globalization create large opportunities for the banks to optimally utilize their capacities to gain from a matrix of core competencies and efficiencies in several business lines. With reduced policy interventions in entry, exit and operations, greater absorption of IT advancements and thrust on competition and market mechanism, the financial system has expanded. Concomitantly, there is a strong drive towards consolidation through mergers with a view to exploiting core competence and for developing "niche" strategies. Several factors driving the forces of consolidation can be primarily categorized as market-driven and regulator-driven.

Increasing globalization and opening up of the financial sector worldwide have created many advantages for the local banks to expand worldwide through commercial presence abroad. Implementation of multilateral agreement on financial services under WTO will give further momentum to global mergers and acquisitions activities. These alliances can take various forms such as enhanced market share, augmented clientele base, increased geographical spread, technological upgradation and global reach for banks. The resolution of these interconnected issues is necessary for the Indian banking system to optimally utilize capacities to gain from a matrix of core competencies and efficiencies across business lines. This will create new avenues and opportunities for local banks in India to expand their global presence through self-expansion mode, strategic alliance among themselves and foreign-based banks.

Major drivers for attaining economies of size in India include need to invest in and continuously upgrade technology, rapid commoditisation of products leading to thinning operating spread, need to offer a comprehensive suite of products to both corporate and retail customers and recapitalisation of banks because of Basle II norms. Mergers, though at a nascent stage, are picking up in the private banking sector. Geographically well spread banks are customarily less vulnerable to economic shocks. Cost efficiency and profit efficiency depend significantly on volume of funds deployed and prudence in asset quality management. Similarly, size offers greater maneuverability in enhancing business volume and productivity.

Indian banks must strengthen their core competencies while exploring new vistas, increase size to achieve "critical mass" and substantially enhance their technological capabilities to surmount competition—both domestically and globally. But economies of scale envisaged through bank mergers may not markedly enhance margins in an increasingly competitive scenario. There are also other obstacles hampering successful consolidation. Consolidation is not a panacea for all ills of Indian banking and size has to be seen as a facilitator rather than an all-inclusive means to efficiency. Given such apprehensions, mergers may not be an unmixed blessing unless they are market-led and synergy-driven.

While PSBs have striking commonalties of policies and approaches, they and 'new generation' banks differ significantly in terms of operational issues, NPAs, organisational culture, mindset, attitude to work and HR issues—salary structure, role of trade unions, age-profile, promotions, transfers and postings. Mergers are now a matter of choice and no longer of compulsion. Size matters, but size alone does not matter. Successful mergers and acquisitions require a holistic perspective, from screening and due diligence to all aspects of the integration process.

Unfinished Development Agenda

The implementation of the development agenda requires development of the core competencies of banks while exploring new vistas, continuous development of new products, cultivation of the organisational culture and cooperation. In sum, the background developmental processes need not be taken as exogenously given. What is needed is a comprehensive strategy for defining strategic customer segments and value propositions, establishing enterprise wide customer guiding principles, identifying specific synergies, variations and gaps among business units and creating strategic customer initiatives to enhance the inherent strength and resilience of banks.

With this kind of vision of growth and structural transformation, India's banking system must stress transition from being largely domestic players to reaching global level with a combination of new technologies, strengthening of prudential norms, adoption of international benchmarks, consolidation within the financial system, management of organisational change, vastly improved processes of credit and risk appraisal, treasury management, etc. There are also important issues of innovation and product diversification and business process reengineering, streamlined internal control, upgradation of technological infrastructure of the financial system and human resources development and exploitation of latent "glocalisation" (think global, act local in the pursuit of global benchmarks without ever being oblivious of local realities) potential as the catalyst of transformation.

Inclusive Growth

The Indian economy is now on a high trajectory of sustained 8% growth. This growth is manifested in economic indicators across the development spectrum. But several developing countries—and not just China—are way ahead of India (126th among 177 countries) in terms of Human Development Index (HDI). Widespread financial exclusion emanates from deeply entrenched poverty, unemployment, skewed pattern of distribution of income and wealth. No wonder, then, the strategy of inclusiveness is all pervasive and now forms an integral part of the blueprint of the country's development planning to enhance economic benefits by raising the quality of work and the rate of employment.

The compelling case for inclusive and broad-based development is, by no means, new. Let me here quote from *The Declaration of Independence of America*: "We hold these truths to be self-evident, that all men are created equal, that they are endowed by their Creator with certain inalienable rights, that among these are Life, Liberty and the pursuit of Happiness." Given that 41% of the Indian population does not have access to bank account (with the North East, Eastern and Central regions being particularly affected) compared to 8% in the UK and 9% in the USA, 1% in Denmark, 4% in Germany, and 4% in France, there is a strategic need to 'connect people' with the banking system and not just credit dispensation; giving people access to the payments system; and portraying financial inclusion as a viable business model and opportunity. As C.K. Prahalad says in his seminal work *Fortune at the Bottom of the Pyramid*, "Doing more of the same, by refining the solutions—developmental aid, subsidies, governmental support, localized non-governmental organization (NGO)-based solutions, exclusive reliance on deregulation and privatization of public assets—is important and has a role to play, but has not redressed the problem of poverty". This is why there is an urgent need to think 'out-of-the-box' and provide revolutionary solutions that are also affordable, cost-effective, available and easily accessible. Towards this end, measures such as mobilization of 'no-frill accounts', simplified KYC norms for opening an account, one-time settlement scheme for borrowers with principal less than Rs. 25,000, General Purpose Credit Card in rural areas with a revolving credit facility upto Rs. 25,000, use of business facilitators and correspondents by the banks, launch of multilingual biometric voice-enabled ATMs, introduction of Gramin Vikas Vahini to spread financial literacy, start of Credit Counseling Centres are contextually relevant.

The excluded segments of the population require products which are customized, taking into consideration their varied savings, credit and insurance needs. The issues of affordability, accessibility, timeliness and appropriateness of credit and delivery of financial support to the vulnerable sections of society as also creation of an enabling environment for growth with distributive equity need to be examined seriously because of the changed ground realities. The World Bank's publications *World Development Indicators* (2006) and *Finance for All – Policies and Pitfalls in Expanding Access* (2008) clearly bring out that countries with large proportion of population excluded from the formal financial system also show higher poverty ratios and higher inequality. This requires modification of the formal credit delivery mechanism, enhanced credit absorption capacity especially amongst marginal and sub marginal farmers and poor non-cultivator households, new models for effective outreach and leveraging on technology-based solutions to create meaning and value in the lives of the poor and the vulnerable sections of society. India is poised to embark on a technology-led 'e-banking revolution' to swiftly expand cost-effective and affordable banking services for a larger section of under-banked and un-banked population in the pursuit of 'inclusive growth'.

Microfinance has proved successful because of risk spread and the group collateral as evidenced in the most successful model of microfinance, i.e. SHG Linkage Model. The recovery rate is quite amazing at above 95%. With the proposed inclusion strategy aiming for three-fold increase in formal banking reach within a span of 5 years, tracking of credit performance becomes crucial. Credit scoring in terms of payment history, length of credit history, types of credit used, delinquency record, etc. together with technological automation needs to be adopted for a healthy microfinance portfolio that is relatively risk-free and well managed.

The imperative need for streamlining rural financial institutions (RFIs) is also self-evident in the context of dynamics of Indian banking.

Going Forward

The transforming socio-economic milieu and the need to align with the fast-changing world necessitate a paradigm shift from product-society banking to knowledge-society banking. There have been changes because of internal factors relating to operations, prudent lending policies, risk management practices, effective recovery, etc. and external factors such as public policy, ownership, regulation, exacting norms of financial prudence, etc. Hence, suitable training, assessment of the recruitment strategies that help create future leaders and exploration of the benefits of organic growth are also necessary in managing flow and flux, reacting to market dynamics and changing needs of the industry. Since banks need to transform to be ahead of the learning curve, they must constantly reassess and adapt the business strategy to better reflect the changing workforce dynamics and the increasingly competitive banking environment.

Given the complexities of the rapidly evolving situation, a one-size-fits-all proposition is grossly inadequate in meeting the challenges of the present. This makes it necessary for each bank to find its own pace, space and scope. But some of the basic issues involved in raising the bar could be identified and isolated as Basle II norms, competition, consolidation and convergence (3 Cs), organic growth, closing the gap between economic and accounting valuations, streamlined risk management systems, enhanced transparency and market disclosures, improved management practices and corporate governance and effective management of the structural changes in the financial system.

The thrust on important areas such as financial inclusion; microfinance; bank efficiency and HR practices; payment and settlement systems; Basle II; governance, risk and compliance; risk management; Six Sigma and cost-efficiencies; rating and pricing mechanisms; rural financing, infrastructure; rural credit; Indian banks in International capital markets; trade finance; real estate and housing financing; technology, etc. can work as catalysts to rapid, sustained development. This requires an accent on synchronised measures across the development spectrum. But in strengthening the continuous cycle of competency and development, fostering a virtuous cycle of regenerative broad-based and higher growth, the focus has to be on technology, marketing, infrastructure and human resources.

While significant steps are being taken in the areas of capital reserves, credit deployment and labour laws, corporate governance, etc. much more needs to be done. Post-2009 banking sector scenario implies new competitive threats as well as new opportunities. The future will belong only to those, who acquire decent "size" by global standards, robust risk management capabilities and internal control systems, advanced technology, skilled manpower and sound marketing practices.

Tracking Growth Stimulants

Thrust on volume-led growth to competitive balance sheet size, migration from interest income to non-interest income and capital adequacy to capital efficiency are needed to maintain benchmarks of return on assets (>1%), return on owned funds (>18%), net non-performing loans (<1%), capital adequacy (9%), cost to income ratio (<40%), net interest margin (>3.5%) and intermediation cost (<1%).

The placing of banks on a higher and more sustainable growth trajectory assumes significance because of the banking sector metamorphosis in the post-reforms era. This metamorphosis has implications not only for the sustenance and growth of banks but also for the process and pattern of economic development. While banks have rapidly emerged as an important driver of economic growth and overall development, achievement of competitive advantage requires continued accent on efficiency, productivity and profitability and upscaling of technological upgradation on a much larger canvas, transition to greater capital account convertibility, greater penetration in terms of (a) financial products such as plastic money (credit and debit cards), (b) life insurance products (insurance premium is only 4% of GDP) and (c) mutual funds assets under management (AUM) (6% of GDP). Banking development is not a one-off effort; it is a constant process of growth and transformation to meet the evolving requirements making it imperative to revisit some of the conventional paradigms to attain and maintain benchmarks.

In bracing for tomorrow, a paradigm shift in bank financing through innovative mechanisms such as templates for assessing customer risk and pricing product offerings, credit scoring, availability and use of information are manifestly needed. Retail banking requires product development and differentiation, innovation and business process reengineering, micro-planning, marketing, prudent pricing, customisation, technological upgradation, home/electronic/mobile banking, cost reduction and cross-selling.

Mapping the Future of Indian Banking

The strategic planning must consist of the formulation of a clear objective and a series of identifiable, measurable action within a time scale. We need also to launch a host of sector-specific cutting edge initiatives in the field of information technology, forays into new areas, thrust on high growth segments, market segmentation and focus on marketing and other strategic business initiatives to succeed in this whole new ball game.

While banks have scaled new heights, set a platform for future growth and charted a path for sustenance of the onward journey towards excellence, the process of competition, convergence, consolidation, compliance and cost-efficiency needs to be carefully pursued through changes in products, technology, structure, processes, detection and elimination of "cost drivers" and introduction of advanced management concepts and practices to successfully introduce new financial instruments and strategies. The focus has to be on technology, marketing, infrastructure and human resources, which provide the cutting edge of development. The emerging order requires an accent on skill upgradation, capacity building, greater receptivity to technological automation so that Indian banks are fully prepared to face all challenges.

In pursuit of their "glocalisation" strategy, banks must respond quickly to opportunities and threats and embrace change across customer stimuli, competitive threats and technological automation. Success requires a threshold level of performance in terms of three key parameters—customer service, product innovation and operational excellence—and a clear leadership in one dimension. Development strategies must be broadened to incorporate all these three critical dimensions for secular dynamic change and structural transformation.

The papers in this book attempt to look at the entire spectrum of issues in the banking sector in a proper historical and comparative perspective and raise various questions about the process and pattern of banking development. While an attempt is also made to suggest the way forward, it is candidly admitted that the book raises several questions—questions, to which there may not be any easy answers. We do not claim to have all the answers. Far from it. But we do maintain that sometimes asking the right questions is even more important than indicating clear answers. I would be happy if this book provokes some debates and discussions on the emerging contours of banking development in India at this defining moment of history.

I express my deep gratitude to all the contributors, who have worked hard to present their papers. It is expected that the book would be useful to a wide cross-section of the reading public, including scholars and academics, the government officials, international institutions, business communities and planners and policymakers. I am grateful to Sri M.B.N. Rao, Chairman and Managing Director, Sri D.L. Rawal, Executive Director and Sri R.K. Madhukar, General Manager, Canara Bank, Bangalore for their blessings and good wishes, which have been a source of strength and inspiration to me. I am thankful to my friends and colleagues working in the Economic Research Section of Canara Bank for acting as a sounding board and providing help and assistance at all times.

I acknowledge the guidance received from my family members, for whom academic excellence is a way of life. I would particularly like to mention the role of my father, Professor D.D. Sharma (PhD) (Edinburgh), former Pro Vice-Chancellor, Lucknow University and my mother, late Dayamoyee Sharma, for instilling in me a passion for academic pursuits. I am thankful to my parents-in-law, Professor

J.C. Choudhary and Mrs. Usha Choudhary for their constant encouragement and advice.

I am deeply thankful to my wife, Archana Choudhary, IRS for her support to me in all my professional and academic endeavours. I am also thankful to my children Utkarsh and Upasana for bearing with me during this stressful period.

MANORANJAN SHARMA

Challenges and Implications of Basel II for Asia*

Y.V. Reddy

Basel I: Voluntarism and Gradualism in India

...Basel I framework for capital adequacy, was introduced in 1988. The Basel I framework was designed to establish minimum levels of capital for internationally active banks. However, its simplicity encouraged over 100 countries across the world to not only adopt the Basel I framework but also apply it across the entire banking segment without restricting it to the internationally active banks. Thus, the voluntary adoption of Basel I framework by several countries has made it, *de facto*, a globally accepted standard, though not all countries are fully compliant with all the aspects.

Adopting our general approach of gradualism, we in India have implemented the Basel I framework with effect from 1992-93 which was, however, spread over three years—banks with branches abroad were required to comply fully by end March 1994 while the other banks were required to comply by end March 1996. Further, India responded to the 1996 amendment to the Basel I framework, which required banks to maintain capital for market risk exposures, by initially prescribing various surrogate capital charges for these risks between 2000 and 2002. These were replaced with the capital charges as required under the Basel I framework in June 2004, which became effective from March 2005. We have gone a step further than the Basel I requirement and have required the banks in India to maintain

---

* Speech by Dr. Y.V. Reddy, Governor, Reserve Bank of India at the Seminar, as a part of the Asian Development Bank's 39th Annual Meeting of the Board of Governors in Hyderabad on May 3, 2006. Reproduced from June, 2006 issue of the Reserve Bank of India Bulletin.

capital charge for market risks on their 'Available for Sale' portfolio also with effect from March 2006. We continue to see considerable merit in pursuing a policy of gradualism in harmonising our regulations with the global standards.

Basel II: Benefits and Major Issues

The complexity of Basel II arises from several options available and these are well known. Consequently, many of the countries which have voluntarily adopted Basel I also view these issues with considerable caution. Compared to Basel I, the revised framework, namely Basel II, is considered to be highly complex, making its understanding and implementation a challenge to both the regulatory and the regulated community.

Dangers of Premature Adoption

Since the revised framework has been designed to provide options for banks and banking systems worldwide, the Basel Committee on Banking Supervision (BCBS) acknowledges that moving toward its adoption in the near future may not be the first priority for all non-G10 supervisory authorities in terms of what is needed to strengthen their supervision. Each national supervisor is expected to consider carefully the benefits of the revised framework in the context of its domestic banking system when developing a timetable and approach for implementation.

The views of the Executive Board of the International Monetary Fund clearly indicate that premature adoption of Basel II in countries with limited capacity could inappropriately divert resources from the more urgent priorities, ultimately weakening rather than strengthening supervision. They agreed that countries should give priority first to strengthening their financial systems comprising institutions, markets and infrastructure and focus on achieving greater level of compliance with the Basel Core Principles. Against this background, the IMF has cautioned that Fund staff should avoid conveying the perception that countries will be criticised for not moving to adopt the Basel II framework. They have urged staff to be completely candid when asked to assess countries' readiness to move to Basel II and to indicate clearly the risks of moving too quickly and too ambitiously.

Varying Implementation Plans Across Jurisdictions in Asia-Pacific

The implementation plans in regard to Basel II, as far as Asia-Pacific is concerned, may be broadly divided into three ranges—one, where the simplest approaches and the most advanced approaches are available at the time of first implementation (Australia, Korea, Singapore, New Zealand); second, where the simplest approaches are available initially and at least one of the most advanced approaches is available within a year or two thereafter (Hong Kong, Japan, Indonesia, Thailand); and third, where the simplest approaches are allowed initially and the date of availability of the most advanced approaches is yet to be announced or are available after more than two years (China, India, Malaysia, and Philippines). Further, one might be able to link the choice of the above broad ranges to the extent of share of foreign banks in the respective banking sectors.

It is observed that the banking systems where foreign banks account for a significant share in the banking assets (Singapore, Hong Kong) are reflecting a desire to adopt the advanced approaches ahead of those territories where the foreign bank share is not significant (India). Onc might also see a similar trend in respect of countries which might remain on Basel I for a longer period before migrating to Basel II (China).

Implementation in India

The policy approach to financial sector in India is that the ultimate goal should be to conform to the best international standards and in the process, the emphasis is on gradual harmonisation with the international best practices. Consistent with this approach, for Basel II also, currently all commercial banks in India are expected to start implementing Basel II with effect from March 31, 2007—though a marginal stretching beyond this date should not be ruled out in view of the latest indications on the state of preparedness. While considering implementation of Basel II, special attention was given to the differences in degrees of sophistication and development of the banking system and it was decided that they will initially adopt the Standardised Approach for credit risk and the Basic Indicator

Approach for operational risk. After adequate skills are developed, both by the banks and also by the supervisors, some of the banks may be allowed to migrate to the Internal Rating Based (IRB) Approach.

As per normal practice in regard to all changes in financial sector, and with a view to ensuring a particularly smooth migration to Basel II, a consultative and participative approach has been adopted for both—designing and implementing Basel II.

On current indications, implementation of Basel II will require more capital for banks in India due to the fact that operational risk is not captured under Basel I, and the capital charge for market risk was not prescribed until recently. The cushion available in the system, which at present has a Capital to Risk Assets Ratio (CRAR) of over 12 per cent, provides for some comfort but the banks are exploring various avenues for meeting the capital requirements under Basel II. The Reserve Bank has, for its part, issued policy guidelines enabling issuance of several instruments by the banks, *viz.* innovative perpetual debt instruments, perpetual non-cumulative preference shares, redeemable cumulative preference shares and hybrid debt instruments so as to enhance their capital raising options.

Three-track Approach for Implementation in India

In India, we have 85 commercial banks, which account for about 78 per cent (total assets) of the financial sector; over 3000 cooperative banks, which account for 9 per cent; and 196 Regional Rural Banks, which account for 3 per cent. Taking into account the size, complexity of operations, relevance to the financial sector, need to ensure greater financial inclusion and the need for having an efficient delivery mechanism, the capital adequacy norms applicable to these entities have been maintained at varying levels of stringency. One might say that we are adopting a three-track approach with regard to capital adequacy rules. Given the differential risk appetite across banks and their business philosophies, it is likely that banks would 'self select' their own approach, which in turn, is likely to engender a stabilising influence on the system as a whole.

On the first track, the commercial banks are required to maintain capital for both credit and market risks as per Basel I framework; the cooperative banks, on the second track, are required to maintain capital for credit risk as per Basel I framework and through surrogates for market risk; the Regional Rural Banks, on the third track, have a minimum capital requirement which is, however, not on par with the Basel I framework. Consequently, we have a major segment of systemic importance on a full Basel I framework, a portion of the minor segment partly on Basel I framework, and a smaller segment on a non-Basel framework.

It is for the same reasons that, at least initially, a similar diversity may be visible in the Indian banking segment even after the commercial banks begin implementing Basel II framework in March 2007. In the post-March 2007 scenario we may witness Basel II, Basel I and non-Basel entities operating simultaneously in the Indian banking system. It is useful to note that a somewhat similar choice has been exercised even in the USA where one is likely to see at least Basel II and Basel I-A entities operating simultaneously. Similarly, even amongst the Basel II entities, it is likely that banks will be implementing various combinations of the multiple options available for computing capital requirements for the three major risks. Consequently, we may see Basel II implementation as a part of a *spectrum* of frameworks within which there can be progressive enhancement of quality amongst different categories.

It is likely that on implementation of Basel II, some banks might adopt the IRB Approach for credit risk while some other banks in the same jurisdiction, might adopt the Standardised Approach. Since the IRB Approach is more risk sensitive *vis-à-vis* the Standardised Approach, a small change in the degree of risk could result in a large additional capital requirement for the banks following the IRB approach—which would dissuade such banks from assuming high-risk exposures. From a systemic point of view, therefore, the banks adopting the Standardised Approach, and consequently, having a greater concentration of high-risk assets in their portfolio, could perhaps become vulnerable in times of economic downturns. These issues would need to be appropriately taken into account while deciding on the implementation of the Basel II.

Implementation Challenges in Developing Countries

Even though it has been mentioned in several places that over 100 countries had implemented Basel I, the assessments done in 71 countries as a part of Financial Sector Assessment Program (FSAP) have revealed many deficiencies in the areas of risk management, consolidated supervision and corrective action for undercapitalised institutions, which are considered to be crucial to sound supervision and proper Basel II implementation. While a supervisory system which is fully or largely compliant with Basel Core Principle 6, which incorporates Basel I as the capital adequacy standard, is considered necessary for moving to Basel II, the assessments reveal that about 37 per cent of these countries had not complied with this Core Principle. The remaining countries were at various stages of compliance. Given this level of compliance, the challenges that are likely to be faced by the developing economies in implementing the Basel II framework, will be daunting.

As acknowledged by the IMF, they do not have adequate internal expertise to assess and assist Basel II implementation in various jurisdictions. Given the complexities of financial regulation and the added complexities of the Basel II framework, which will have to be specifically tailored to suit the domestic economies and the domestic banking systems, the regulators are right in insisting on the freedom and flexibility for adopting and implementing an appropriate roadmap without being constrained by any external pressures, direct or indirect. The ideal solution for managing a complex task of this nature is through mutual cooperation and assistance amongst the central banks.

Dangers of Asymmetry in Financial Intermediation

A likely scenario, which might arise post-Basel II implementation, is the asymmetry in regulatory regime amongst the competing broad segments of the financial sector, *viz.* banking, securities and insurance sectors. While the commercial banking sector is expected to migrate to the Basel II regimen soon, the other segments are not likely to be subjected to the same or similar discipline unless they are a part of a banking group, where Basel II regimen would apply indirectly through the parent bank. Hence, we are likely to see some scope for regulatory arbitrage amongst the three broad segments unless the regulators of these segments also recognise the need and relevance of a comparable prescription for those segments. The Joint Forum has taken some initiatives in this direction, which may have to be pursued further to achieve parity in the level of regulatory burden across the three sectors, which compete amongst themselves for the business of financial intermediation.

Basel II and Social Dimensions

The three-track theme to Basel II implementation, as mentioned earlier, might give rise to scope for regulatory arbitrage within the banking system. This would, however, not be of much concern in the Indian context on account of the relatively insignificant size of the non-Basel II entities and their relevance from the systemic perspective. While the desire would be to reduce the scope for regulatory arbitrage, we may have to strike a delicate balance to ensure that this desire does not constrain the non-Basel II entities from discharging their respective specified roles in the national economies, *viz.* achieving greater financial inclusion, playing a developmental role, and acting as conduits for credit delivery to the neglected sectors. I think, the multi-track theme for Basel II implementation and the consequent handling of regulatory arbitrage and stability issues may be reflected in other similarly placed emerging market economies as well.

A Roadmap Approach for Implementation of Basel II

In the light of experience gained by us, it appears that the balance of advantage would lie in favour of encouraging the central banks/banking sector regulators to implement Basel II framework at their own pace and in a manner as appropriate to their economies, banking systems and supervisory mechanisms. It is also possible that the multilateral development agencies are yet to get fully equipped to assist in Basel II implementation. Ideally each country may devise a road map to be implemented flexibly taking account of the country context....

Reforms, Productivity and Efficiency in Banking: The Indian Experience*

Rakesh Mohan

2

...Issues of productivity and efficiency have been at the centre-stage of discussions in recent years. Nowhere is this truer than the financial sector, which is perceived to be the 'brain' of the economy (Stiglitz, 1998). Even within the financial sector, given the dominance of bank-based financial systems in most emerging markets including ours and the systemic importance of banks in the financial system, the banking sector continues to be the centre of attention for academia and policy-makers alike. Not surprisingly therefore, performance of the banking sector has repercussions across the length and breadth of the economy....

The objective of reforms in general is to accelerate the growth momentum of the economy, defined in terms of per capita income. Typically, improvements in the growth rate can be effected through three, not necessarily mutually exclusive channels: improving productivity of capital, through investments in human capital and raising total factor productivity (TFP).

The quality of functioning of the financial sector can be expected to affect the functioning and productivity of all sectors of the economy. Efficient financial intermediation should help in improving economy-wide resource allocation thereby promoting productivity growth all round. Thus, discussion on

* Address delivered by Dr. Rakesh Mohan, Deputy Governor, Reserve Bank of India at the 21st Annual General Meeting and Conference of the Pakistan Society of Development Economists at Islamabad in December 2005. The assistance of Abhiman Das, Saibal Ghosh and Partha Ray in the preparation of the paper is gratefully acknowledged. Reproduced from March, 2006 issue of the Reserve Bank of India Bulletin.

economic efficiency and productivity should involve analysis of developments in the financial sector. Improvements in the financing of physical and human capital, both in terms of increasing magnitudes, and in terms of allocative efficiency, should raise efficiency and productivity across the economy....

Financial intermediation is essential to the promotion of both extensive and intensive growth. The efficient intermediation of funds from savers to users enables the application of available resources to their most productive uses. The more efficient a financial system is in such resource generation and in its allocation, the greater is its contribution to productivity and economic growth. As resource allocation improves and real returns increase, savings would presumably respond and higher resource generation should result. Thus, development of the financial system is essential to the generation of higher productivity and economic growth.

...First, I will explore in brief the impact of banking sector productivity on the rest of the economy. This is relevant in view of the fact that any discussion on productivity and efficiency issues in banking would need to be judged in conjunction with the level of financial development and other country-specific features. This will be followed by a brief review of banking sector reforms in India. The subsequent section will examine, in some detail, the trends in productivity and efficiency in Indian banking. My concluding remarks will be in the nature of the way ahead on areas germane to this sector at the present juncture.

1. How does Productivity in Banking Influence the Rest of the Economy?

Economic history provides support for the fact that financial development makes a fundamental contribution to growth. Financial development helped in thc promotion of industrialisation in developed countries by facilitating the mobilisation of capital for large investments. Well-functioning banks or other financial intermediaries such as venture capital funds also spur technological innovation by identifying and funding entrepreneurs who are perceived to have the best chances of developing new products successfully and for implementing innovative production processes.

Recent research has provided robust evidence supporting the view that financial development contributes to economic growth.

- At the cross-country level, various measures of financial development (including measures of financial sector assets, domestic credit to private sectors and stock market capitalisation) are found to be positively related to economic growth.
- Other studies establish a positive relationship between financial development and growth at the industry level (Rajan and Zingales, 1998).
- Similarly, at the firm level, firms in countries with deeper financial development are able to obtain more external funds and thereby enabled to grow faster (Demirgúc-Kunt and Maksimovic, 1998).

A basic indicator of financial development is the contribution of finance-related activities to GDP. The share of real GDP originating from finance-related activities in India tripled from just around 2 per cent during the 1970s to around 6 per cent during the 1990s and further to 7 per cent during the first half of this decade. Within the services sector, the share of finance rose from less than 5 per cent to more than 12 per cent over the same period (Table 1).

Table 1: Share of Real GDP Originating in Banking and Insurance

(per cent)

Period	Share of banking and insurance in GDP	Share of banking and insurance in services
1970-71 to 1974-75	1.8	4.6
1975-76 to 1979-80	2.2	5.4
1980-81 to 1984-85	2.5	5.9
1985-86 to 1992-93	3.9	8.5
1993-94 to 1998-99	5.8	11.8
1999-2000 to 2003-04	6.7	12.3

Source: Computed from *National Accounts Statistics*, Central Statistical Organisation.

The broad-based indicators of financial development, as culled from the flow-of-funds accounts, are also testimony to gradual widening and deepening of the economy. Most of the commonly tracked ratios exhibited an upward trend during the 1970s and 1980s, while moderate fluctuations in these ratios were observed during the 1990s (Table 2). What is of interest is that the Finance Ratio, a proxy for financial deepening, witnessed remarkable improvement over this period.

Table 2: Flow of Funds-based Indicators of Financial Development

Period	FR	FIR	NIR	IR
1970-71 to 1974-75	0.2	1.4	0.8	0.8
1975-76 to 1979-80	0.3	1.8	1.0	0.7
1980-81 to 1984-85	0.3	2.4	1.4	0.7
1985-86 to 1989-90	0.4	2.4	1.4	0.7
1991-92	0.5	2.9	1.6	0.8
1994-95	0.5	2.4	1.2	0.9
1995-96	0.5	2.3	1.3	0.7

FR = Finance ratio = Total issues/National income (net national product at current prices);
FIR = Financial interrelations ratio = Total issues/Net domestic capital formation;
NIR = New issue ratio = Primary issues/ Net domestic capital formation;
IR = Interrelations ratio = secondary issues (i.e. issues by banks and other financial institutions)/Primary issues.
Source: Reserve Bank of India.

When we move away from these broad-based indicators to more specific liquidity and credit-based indicators, a similar picture emerges. Illustratively, the ratio of aggregate deposits to GDP exceeded 50 per cent during the first half of the current decade; M3/GDP has averaged around 50 per cent since the 1990s. At a slightly more disaggregated level, while bank credit to government has witnessed some tapering off in the second half of the 1990s, credit to the commercial sector averaged over 30 per cent of GDP during the first half of the current decade (Table 3). These observations are particularly relevant from the standpoint of the role of banks in the intermediation process. Juxtaposed with the financial sector reforms, this suggests that the enhanced freedom of banks since the liberalisation process has provided them with the flexibility in resource mobilisation and deployment, which has manifested itself in the uptrend in these ratios. Thus, financial deepening has been taking place continuously in India and is still in progress.

Table 3: Liquidity and Credit-based Indicators of Financial Development (as per cent of GDP at current market prices)

Period	Aggregate deposits	M3	Bank credit to Government	Bank credit to commercial sector
1970-71 to 1974-75	16.4	25.9	13.3	15.6
1975-76 to 1979-80	24.1	33.0	14.0	21.8
1980-81 to 1984-85	30.0	39.1	18.7	26.9
1985-86 to 1989-90	36.1	45.4	22.9	30.3
1990-91 to 1994-95	39.6	49.3	23.6	29.0
1995-96 to 1999-2000	43.8	53.8	21.9	28.6
2000-01 to 2004-05	54.7	65.3	24.9	33.5

Source: Reserve Bank of India.

Studies by the Reserve Bank (RBI, 2000) on the association between finance and growth for an extended time span from 1971-72 to 1999-2000 find that the causality between finance (proxied by real M3 growth) and growth (proxied by real GDP growth) is bi-directional. However, in the absence of any structural model underlying such relationships, these 'causality' estimates can only be interpreted in terms of the predictive content of each of the variables. Subsequent research on the interlinkage between finance and growth in India has veered around to the view that the Indian growth process has essentially been 'finance-led': expansion in the financial sector played an enabling role in promoting capital accumulation, which, in turn, engendered higher growth (Bell and Rousseau, 2001). Typically however, studies of this genre tend to be susceptible to the time period and choice of variables, so that a different period with another set of variables could possibly lead to different conclusions. What is, however, accepted is that finance did play a role in influencing the growth process in India, although such observations related to financial deepening have little to say about efficiency and productivity growth.

The aforesaid observations do not take into account the changing dynamics of the financial system. The traditional classification of the financial system as bank or market-based often tends to be static; in contrast, financial systems evolve and develop over time in response to changes in the institutional environment, legal set up and other country-specific features. This has been the case in India as well. Many of you would be aware that, cross-country classifications of financial system have typically classified India as a 'bank-based' system. This is not surprising, since banks have traditionally been the dominant financial intermediaries. However, the relative share of banks in total financial sector assets, which was nearly three-fourths in the early 1980s, came down gradually over a period of time and has hovered around the two-thirds mark since the 1990s (Ray & Sengupta, 2004).

More importantly however, following the rapid growth of stock markets since the 1990s, the role of 'market-based' finance has been on the rise. The most commonly employed measure of financial system orientation—the ratio of market capitalisation to bank assets—supports this observation (Table 4). This suggests that not only have financial institutions gained in terms of financial assets, but there is also considerable potential for market financing to develop. However, the magnitude of market capitalisation is obviously dependent on the vagaries of the stock market: it is not expected to exhibit a consistent increase as a ratio of GDP, whereas the growth in bank assets/GDP ratio is much more regular.

Table 4: Financial System Orientation
(as per cent of GDP at current market prices)

As at end (1)	Assets of scheduled commercial banks (2)	Market capitalisation at BSE (3)	Financial system orientation (4) = (3)/(2)x100
December 1970	17.9	3.8	21.3
December 1975	21.0	2.6	11.0
December 1980	40.0	3.8	9.3
December 1985	46.8	7.4	15.2
March 1991	56.3	16.0	28.4
March 1995	51.6	43.1	83.5
March 2000	59.1	46.8	79.3
March 2003	69.0	23.2	33.7
March 2004	71.6	43.5	60.8
March 2005	75.9	54.7	72.1

BSE: The National Stock Exchange, Mumbai.
Source: Computed from *Handbook of Statistics on the Indian Economy*, RBI.

Whereas financial deepening is easier to measure, analysing productivity and efficiency changes in banking is more complex and needs to be viewed in relation to the changing contours of the banking industry in India.

2. Contours of Indian Banking Sector Reforms

The transformation of the banking sector in India needs to be viewed in light of the overall economic reforms process along with the rapid changes that have been taking place in the global environment within which banks operate. The global forces of change include technological innovation, the deregulation of financial services internationally, our own increasing exposure to international competition and, equally important, changes in corporate behaviour such as growing disintermediation and increasing emphasis on shareholder value. Recent banking crises in Asia, Latin America and elsewhere have accentuated these pressures.

...India embarked on a strategy of economic reforms in the wake of a serious balance-of-payments crisis in 1991; a central plank of the reforms was reform in the financial sector and, with banks being the mainstay of financial intermediation, the banking sector. The objective of the banking sector reforms was to promote a diversified, efficient and competitive financial system with the ultimate objective of improving the allocative efficiency of resources through operational flexibility, improved financial viability and institutional strengthening. A summary profile of the banking industry over the last 15 years is presented in Table 5.

Table 5: Summary Profile of the Banking Industry: 1990-91 to 2004-05

Year/Bank Group	1990-91			1995-96			2004-05		
	PSB	Private	Foreign	PSB	Private	Foreign	PSB	Private	Foreign
1. No. of banks	28	25	23	27	35(8)	29	28	29(9)	31
(a) Listed	None	None	NA	2	9(3)	NA	20	18(7)	NA
(b) Non-listed				25	26(5)	NA	8	11(2)	NA
2. Share (in per cent) of									
(a) Assets	91.4	3.7	4.9	84.5	6.5(1.5)	7.9	75.3	18.2(12.5)	6.5
(b) Deposits	92.0	4.0	4.0	85.4	6.6(1.3)	6.7	78.0	17.3(10.9)	4.7
(c) Credit	93.0	4.0	3.0	82.4	6.8(1.9)	8.9	73.2	20.0(13.9)	6.8
(d) Income	89.4	3.3	7.3	82.5	8.2	9.4	76.4	16.9	6.7
(e) Expenses	90.0	3.3	6.8	84.1	7.5	8.4	76.7	16.9	6.4
(f) Profit	68.5	4.1	27.4	-33.3	55.6	77.8	74.2	16.4	9.4
3. Memo Bank asset / GDP (per cent)	56.3	50.4	80.4						

PSB: Public sector banks; NA: Not applicable; Listed: Banks listed on recognised stock exchanges.
Figures in bracket under Private pertain to *de novo* private banks.
Source: Reserve Bank of India.

...The financial system in India by the late 1980s was characterized by dominant government ownership of banks and financial institutions, widespread use of administered and variegated interest rates, and financial repression through forced financing of government fiscal deficits by banks and through monetisation. Thus, although a great degree of financial deepening had indeed taken place and financial savings had increased continuously, financial markets were not really functioning, and there was little price discovery in terms of the cost of money, i.e. interest rates. The efficiency and productivity enhancing function of the financial system was severely handicapped. Hence, a widespread financial sector reform effort has been underway since 1991.

Let me briefly sum up the major areas of banking sector reforms:

- Financial repression through statutory preemptions has been reduced, while stepping up prudential regulations at the same time.
- Interest rates have been progressively deregulated on both the deposit and lending sides (Box I).

Restoration of the health of the banking system has involved:

- Restoration of public sector banks' net worth achieved through recapitalisation where needed (total cost less than one per cent of GDP).
- Competition increased through entry of new private sector banks and foreign banks.
- Higher levels and standards of disclosure achieved to enhance market transparency.
- Bank regulation and supervision strengthened towards international best practice.
- Micro prudential measures instituted.
- Supervision process streamlined with combination of on-site and off-site surveillance along with external auditing.
- Risk based supervision introduced.

- Process of structured and discretionary intervention introduced for problem banks through a prompt corrective action mechanism.
- Ownership of public sector banks has been broadened through disinvestment up to 49 per cent, and banks have been listed (Table 6).
- Mechanism for greater regulatory coordination instituted for regulation and supervision of financial conglomerates.
- Measures taken to strengthen creditor rights (still in process).

Box I: Interest Rate Deregulation

Deposit Rate Deregulation

- April 1992:
  - Interest rates freed between 46 days and 3 years and over, but ceiling prescribed,
  - October 1995: Ceiling removed for deposits over 2 years.
- July 1996: Ceiling removed for deposits over 1 year.
- October 1997: Interest rates on Term Deposits completely deregulated.
- 2004: Minimum maturity for Term Deposits reduced to 7 days.

Lending Rate Deregulation

- 1992-93: Six categories of lending rates:
  - 5 slabs for below Rs. 2 lakh,
  - Minimum lending rate above Rs. 2 lakh.
- October 1994: Lending rate freed for loans above Rs. 2 lakh & minimum rate abolished.
- October 1996: Banks to specify maximum spread over PLR.
- 1997-98: Separate PLRs permitted for cash credit/demand loans and term loans above 3 years. Floating rate permitted.
- 1998-99: PLR made ceiling for loans up to Rs. 2 lakh.
- 1999-2000: Tenor linked PLR introduced.
- 2001-02: PLR made benchmark rate; sub PLR permitted for loans above Rs. 2 lakh.
- 2002-03: Bank-wise PLRs made transparent on RBI website.
- 2003-04: Computation of benchmark PLR rationalized, tenor linked PLRs abolished.

Table 6: Private Shareholding in Public Sector Banks (as on March 31, 2005)

Shareholding (in per cent)	Number of banks*
Up to 10	4
More than 10 and up to 20	-
More than 20 and up to 30	5
More than 30 and up to 40	6
More than 40 and up to 49	6

* Comprising 19 nationalised banks, State Bank of India and IDBI Ltd.

Source: *Trend and Progress of Banking in India, 2004-05*, RBI.

As the banking system has been liberalised and has become increasingly market-oriented and financial markets have developed concurrently, the conduct of monetary policy has also been tailored to take into account the realities of the changing environment (switch from direct to indirect instruments).

This macro-approach to financial monitoring has enabled policy-makers to fine-tune their regulatory stance in consonance with the changing market and institutional dynamics so as to balance growth and stability concerns. For instance, despite the gradual tightening of prudential norms, the ratio of non-performing loans (NPL) to total loans, which was at a high of 15.7 per cent for scheduled commercial banks (SCBs) at end-March 1997, has declined by more than two-thirds to 5.2 per cent at end-March 2005 (Table 7). Net NPLs also witnessed a significant decline, driven by the improvements in loan loss provisioning and improved recovery management, which comprises over half of the total provisions and contingencies. Capital adequacy of the banking sector also recorded a marked improvement and reached 12.8 per cent at end-March 2005, well above the stipulated level of 9 per cent. Banks have also been sensitised to develop robust risk management systems for credit and operational risks and focus on their asset-liability maturity profile to withstand adverse movements in market risk parameters such as interest rates and take corrective measures.

Table 7: Non-performing Loans of Different Bank Groups: 1994—2005

(per cent to total advances)

Year (end-March)	PSB	Old Private Banks	New Private Banks	Foreign Banks	*Memo*: NPL/total loans (per cent) - 2004
1994	24.8	NC	NC	NC	China: 15.6
1995	19.5	NC	NC	NC	Indonesia: 13.4
1996	18.0	NC	NC	NC	Korea: 1.7
1997	17.8	10.7	2.6	4.3	Malaysia: 11.6@
1998	16.0	10.9	3.5	6.4	Argentina: 17.5@
1999	15.9	13.1	6.2	7.6	Brazil: 3.9
2000	14.0	10.8	4.1	7.0	US: 0.8
2001	12.4	10.9	5.1	6.8	UK: 2.2
2002	11.1	11.0	8.9	5.4	Japan: 2.9
2003	9.4	8.9	6.7	5.3	
2004	7.8	7.6	5.0	4.6	
2005	5.5	6.0	3.6	2.8	*Global range: [0.3 to 30.0]*

@: relates to 2005. NC: Not compiled.

Source: Computed from *Statistical Tables relating to Banks in !ndia*, RBI, various years.

Another heartening development in banks' balance sheets, driven by the twin forces of international accounting irregularities and regulatory initiatives, has been the increasing focus on corporate governance. As part of their Annual Report, banks presently disclose, under the head 'Report on corporate governance', details of their boards of directors, number of board meetings attended by members, details of the various sub-committees of the boards and provided the banks are listed, information on their stock price movements. This is complemented with the banks' philosophy on corporate governance and the enabling mechanisms undertaken by the banks to achieve their philosophy.... Such listing is an important component of the process of 'market discipline', which complements the regulatory initiatives undertaken by the authorities. To take the governance process in banks a step further, we had some time back issued guidelines laying down transparent criteria for determining the 'fit and proper' status of owners and directors in private banks. Given our focus on a consultative approach to policy formulation, the document was posted on the RBI website for encouraging a debate on this issue. Based on the feedback received, the draft is being reviewed before final guidelines can be issued to banks.

The whole policy reform process has been designed to make the banking system more market oriented to enable efficient price discovery and to induce greater internal efficiency in the resource allocation process. Thus, whereas the efforts in the 1960s, 1970s and 1980s were essentially devoted to financial deepening, the focus of reforms in the past decade and a half has been engendering greater efficiency and productivity in the banking system in particular, and in the financial sector as a whole. How well have we succeeded?

3. Efficiency and Productivity Analysis in Banking

In recent times, a significant body of literature has evolved which explores the performance of financial institutions in the wake of financial liberalisation. These studies are essentially micro-economic in nature and seek to analyse the efficiency and productivity of banking systems. Such analysis is of relevance from the policy standpoint, because as the finance-growth literature suggests, if banks become better-functioning entities, this is expected to be reflected in safety and soundness of the financial system and ultimately, lead to increases in the rate of economic growth. More importantly, such analysis is useful in enabling policy-makers to identify the success or failure of policy initiatives or, alternatively, highlight different strategies undertaken by banking firms which contribute to their successes.

A priori, deregulation is expected to unleash competitive forces. Such competition would, in turn, enable banks to alter their input and output mix, which when combined with technological developments facilitates increase in output that raises overall bank productivity and efficiency. Second, liberal entry of *de novo* private and foreign banks as a part of the deregulation process is expected to raise bank efficiency, productivity and technology levels, because *de novo* private/foreign banks are associated with superior management practices and technology, which can be fruitfully imbibed by those which are not. A third strand of thinking, borrowing from the public choice framework, contends that different ownership structures may engender different efficiency levels. The theoretical argument is straightforward: lack of capital market discipline weakens owners' control over management, enabling the latter to pursue their own interests, and provides fewer incentives for them to be efficient. Finally, as banking in the current world is technology driven and technological progress itself is scale augmenting, the relationship between bank size and efficiency becomes important. Skeptics, on the contrary, argue that deregulation is, in general, accompanied by an increase in banks' operational cost and could induce financial fragility due to over-expansion of banking activity. Thus, productivity gains after deregulation could be temporary and not sustainable in the long run. As a result, evidence in support of a unidirectional relationship between deregulation and efficiency/productivity is not conclusive.

Besides various methods of estimation, the efficiency and productivity studies in banking are constrained by the absence of precise definitions of inputs and outputs of banks. As a result, several approaches exist and the appropriateness of each approach varies according to the circumstances (Box II).

Box II: Inputs and Outputs of Commercial Banks

Banks are typically multi-input and multi-output firms. As a result, defining what constitutes 'input' and 'output' is fraught with difficulties, since many of the financial services are jointly produced and prices are typically assigned to a bundle of financial services. Additionally, banks may not be homogeneous with respect to the types of outputs actually produced. In view of these complexities, four approaches have come to dominate the literature on banking output: the *production approach*, the *intermediation approach*, the *operating (income-based) approach* and more recently, the *modern approach*.

Under the *production approach*, banks are primarily viewed as providers of services to customers. The input set under this approach includes physical variables (e.g., labour, material, space or information systems) and the outputs represent the services provided to customers and are best measured by the number of deposit and loan accounts.

Under the *intermediation approach*, financial institutions are viewed as intermediating funds between savers and investors. Banks produce intermediation services through the collection of deposits and other liabilities and their application in interest-earning assets, such as loans, securities and other investments. This approach includes both operating and interest expenses as inputs, whereas loans and other major assets count as outputs. In principle, there are three variant of intermediation approach, viz. the *asset approach*, the *user cost approach* and *value-added approach*. The *asset approach* is a reduced form modelling of the banking activity, focusing exclusively on the role of banks as financial intermediaries between depositors and final uses of bank assets. Deposits and other liabilities, together with real resources (labour and physical capital) are defined as inputs, whereas the output set includes earning assets such as loans and investments. The *user cost approach* determines whether a financial product is an input or an output on the basis of its net contribution to bank revenue. If the financial returns on an asset exceed the opportunity cost of the funds or alternately, if the financial costs of a liability are less than the opportunity cost, they are considered as outputs; otherwise, they are considered as inputs. The *value-added approach* identifies major categories of produced deposits and loans as outputs because they form a significant proportion of value added.

The *operating approach* (or *income-based approach)* views banks as business units with the final objective of generating revenue from the total cost incurred for running the business. Accordingly, it defines banks' output as the total revenue (interest and non-interest) and inputs as the total expenses (interest and operating expenses).

Finally, the *modern approach* seeks to integrate some measure for risk, agency costs and quality of bank services. In this approach, the individual components of CAMEL are derived from the financial tables of the banks and are used as variables in the performance analysis.

Source: Adapted from Berger and Humphrey (1992) and Frexias and Rochet (1997).

Competition and Profitability of Indian Banks

Beginning from 1992, Indian banks were gradually exposed to the rigours of domestic and international competition. Newly opened banks from the private sector and entry and expansion of several foreign banks resulted in greater competition in both deposit and credit markets. Consequent to these developments, there has been a consistent decline in the share of public sector banks in total assets of commercial banks. The evidence of competitive pressure is well supported from the declining trend of Herfindahl's concentration index (Table 8). Notwithstanding such transformation, the public sector banks still remain the mainstay, accounting for nearly three-fourths of assets and income. It is also important to note that public sector banks have responded to the new challenges of competition, as reflected in the increase in the share of these banks in the overall profit of the banking sector. From the position of net loss in the mid-1990s, in recent years the share of public sector banks in the profit of the commercial banking system has become broadly commensurate with their share in assets, indicating a broad convergence of profitability across various bank groups. This suggests that, with operational flexibility, public sector banks are competing relatively effectively with private sector and foreign banks. The 'market discipline' imposed by the listing of most public sector banks has also probably contributed to this improved performance. Public sector bank managements are now probably more attuned to the market consequences of their activities (Mohan, 2005).

Table 8: Herfindahl's Index of Concentration on Deposits and Credit of Scheduled Commercial Banks: 1992—2004

Year (end-March)	Deposit	Credit
1992	8.1	10.4
1993	7.6	10.1
1994	7.4	8.6
1995	7.0	7.9
1996	6.9	7.8
1997	6.7	7.3
1998	6.6	7.4
1999	7.1	7.2
2000	6.9	6.9
2001	7.3	6.7
2002	7.1	6.0
2003	6.9	6.0
2004	6.3	5.8

Source: Author's calculations.

Since the late1990s, in line with the benign interest rate regime, both interest income and interest expenditure of banks as proportions of total assets have declined. However, interest expenditure declined faster than interest income, resulting in an increase in net interest income. However, non-interest income, which emanates mostly from fee-based activities, has been increasing consistently in the post-reform period. For example, non-interest income as a proportion of total assets of the banking sector increased from 1.2 per cent in 1993 to more than 2 per cent in 2004 (Table 9). In this context, it is also appropriate to mention that Indian banks, in particular the public sector banks, are yet to catch-up fully with their foreign counterparts.

Table 9: Non-interest Income of Scheduled Commercial Banks: 1992—2004

(as percentage to total asset)

Year (end-March)	Public Sector Banks	Indian Private Banks	Foreign Banks	All Scheduled Commercial Banks
1992	1.22	1.03	3.40	1.38
1993	1.19	1.13	0.99	1.17
1994	1.26	1.34	2.22	1.34
1995	1.26	1.43	2.46	1.36
1996	1.39	1.68	2.35	1.49
1997	1.32	1.64	2.54	1.45
1998	1.33	1.94	2.96	1.52
1999	1.22	1.36	2.46	1.33
2000	1.28	1.67	2.60	1.43
2001	1.22	1.28	2.47	1.32
2002	1.43	1.59	2.91	1.57
2003	1.66	2.45	2.64	1.86
2004	1.91	2.08	2.98	2.01

Source: Computed from *Statistical Tables relating to Banks in India*, RBI, various years.

Efficiency of Indian Banks

Improvements in efficiency of the banking system are expected to be reflected, *inter alia*, in a reduction in operating expenditure, interest spread and cost of intermediation in general. Several indicators have been employed in the literature to compare banking production costs across time. Illustratively, intermediation cost, defined as the ratio of operating expense to total assets, witnessed a gradual reduction in the post-reform period across various bank groups barring foreign banks (Table 10). This decline in intermediation cost needs to be weighed against the large expenditures incurred in upgradation of information technology and institution of 'core banking' solutions. Admittedly, intermediation costs of banks in India still tend to be higher than those in developed banking markets.

Table 10: Intermediation Cost* of Scheduled Commercial Banks: 1992—2004

(as percentage to total asset)

Year (end-March)	Public sector banks	Indian private banks	Foreign banks	All scheduled commercial banks
1992	2.60	2.97	2.26	2.59
1993	2.64	2.71	2.70	2.65
1994	2.65	2.49	2.65	2.64
1995	2.83	2.35	2.73	2.79
1996	2.99	2.47	2.78	2.94
1997	2.88	2.36	3.04	2.85
1998	2.66	2.14	2.99	2.63
1999	2.65	2.04	3.40	2.65
2000	2.52	1.85	3.12	2.48
2001	2.72	1.87	3.05	2.64
2002	2.29	1.45	3.03	2.19
2003	2.25	1.99	2.79	2.24
2004	2.20	2.01	2.76	2.20

*Intermediation cost = Operating expenses.

Source: Computed from *Statistical Tables relating to Banks in India*, RBI, various years.

At a more disaggregated level, it is evident that Indian banks have improved their efficiency in the post-reform period as evidenced from the declining trend in per unit cost of output, irrespective of the choice of outputs (Table 11). The operating cost per unit of earning assets declined from 2.1 per cent in 1992 to 1.8 per cent in 2004; similarly, operating cost per unit of total volume of business declined from 3.4 per cent to 2.6 per cent during the same period. Among the components of operating expenses, employee cost per unit of output witnessed a noticeable decline in the post-reform period. This decline is discernible across all bank groups, and especially for public sector banks in the post-2001 period consequent to the voluntary retirement scheme across several nationalised banks. On the other hand, the change in physical capital cost per unit of output has been marginal, reflecting the fact that Indian banks maintained a steady flow of investments towards physical capital formation, especially on automation and information technology.

Table 11: Operating Expense and its Components of Scheduled Commercial Banks: 1992—2004

(per cent)

Year (end-March)	Operating expense/ earning assets@	Labour cost/ earning assets@	Non-labour cost/ earning assets@	Operating expense/ total business*	Labour cost/ total business*	Non-labour cost/ total business*
1992	2.08	1.40	0.68	3.42	2.30	1.12
1993	2.14	1.43	0.72	3.51	2.34	1.17
1994	2.22	1.44	0.78	3.56	2.31	1.25
1995	2.32	1.54	0.78	3.74	2.48	1.26
1996	2.48	1.73	0.75	4.01	2.80	1.22
1997	2.36	1.60	0.76	3.84	2.60	1.24
1998	2.16	1.46	0.70	3.51	2.37	1.14
1999	2.21	1.47	0.74	3.55	2.35	1.20
2000	2.05	1.37	0.68	3.22	2.15	1.06
2001	2.16	1.47	0.69	3.36	2.28	1.07
2002	1.82	1.18	0.64	2.73	1.77	0.96
2003	1.81	1.13	0.69	2.65	1.65	1.00
2004	1.78	1.08	0.71	2.61	1.58	1.03

@ Earning assets = credit + investment.
* Total business = deposit + credit.
Source: Computed from *Statistical Tables relating to Banks in India*, RBI, various years.

From the efficiency standpoint, the intermediation cost needs to be viewed in conjunction with non-interest income. Till 2001, the burden (the excess of non-interest expenditure over non-interest income as a percentage to total assets) of commercial banks hovered around 1 to 1.5 per cent (Table 12). This gap between intermediation cost and income from fee-based activities has narrowed considerably in recent years. For example, the burden of Indian commercial banks declined from 1.2 per cent in 1992 to 0.2 per cent in 2004. Moreover, there has been a lowering of the burden across bank groups in recent years. The improvement in respect of Indian private banks has been remarkable; their non-interest income in recent years has surpassed their intermediation cost and has resulted in a negative burden.

Table 12: Burden* of Scheduled Commercial Banks: 1992—2004 (as percentage to total asset)

Year (end-March)	Public sector banks	Indian private banks	Foreign banks	All scheduled commercial banks
1992	1.37	1.94	-1.14	1.21
1993	1.45	1.57	1.70	1.48
1994	1.39	1.16	0.42	1.30
1995	1.57	0.92	0.27	1.43
1996	1.60	0.78	0.43	1.44
1997	1.56	0.72	0.50	1.40
1998	1.33	0.19	0.03	1.11
1999	1.44	0.69	0.94	1.32
2000	1.24	0.18	0.53	1.05
2001	1.51	0.59	0.59	1.32
2002	0.86	-0.14	0.12	0.63
2003	0.59	-0.46	0.15	0.38
2004	0.29	-0.07	-0.22	0.19

*Burden=Non-interest expense *less* non-interest income. It reflects the extent to which non-interest expenses are recovered through non-interest income.
Source: Computed from *Statistical Tables relating to Banks in India*, RBI, various years.

The cost income-ratio (defined as the ratio of operating expenses to total income less interest expense) of Indian banks showed a declining trend during the post-reform period. For example, Indian banks paid roughly 45 per cent of their net income towards managing labour and physical capital in 2004 as against nearly 72 per cent in 1993 (Table 13). In other words, Indian banks recorded a net cost saving of nearly 27 per cent of their net income during the post-reform period. According to the data reported in *The Banker 2004*, the cost-income ratio of world's largest banks varied markedly from a low of 48 per cent to a high of 116 per cent and the ratio around 60 per cent is an indicative benchmark (RBI, 2005). In that respect, the cost-income ratio of Indian banks is now comparable internationally. Among various ownership patterns, public sector banks have tended to have relatively higher cost-income ratio as against private banks and foreign banks.

This explanation needs to be viewed in conjunction with the differential ownership profile of banks. Early studies (Sarkar *et al.*, 1998) found somewhat weak evidence to suggest that ownership was an important determinant of performance. More recent studies exhibit mixed evidence: while certain studies (Keova, 2003) suggest ownership to have some effect on bank performance, others (e.g., Bhaumik and Dimova, 2004) veer around the view that competition induced public sector banks to eliminate the performance gap that existed between them and both domestic and foreign and private sector banks. More recent research reported differences in the efficiency of Indian commercial banks with different ownership status, level of non-performing loans, size and asset quality (Das and Ghosh, 2006). More importantly, their study uncovered evidence that public sector banks (PSBs) recorded higher efficiency gains in the post-reform period. Clearly, the evidence here is not conclusive, because comparisons are beset with several difficulties. Given the size and variety of PSBs, it is possible to find banks that could equal the good private sector banks as well as bad ones. In addition, PSBs have to reckon with 'legacy' problems, such as many of the non-performing assets that they have been saddled with. Some PSBs operate in relatively backward areas with limited discretion to pull out from such areas. The question still remains: whether there is a better pay-off in enabling PSBs to improve their performance while promoting private sector banks, as compared with an alternative policy that provides for transfer of ownership and control from the public to the private sector. Will greater scope for mergers and acquisitions within and between public and private sector add to greater efficiency?

Table 13: Cost-income Ratio of Scheduled Commercial Banks: 1992—2004

(per cent)

Year (end-March)	Public Sector Banks	Indian Private Banks	Foreign Banks	All Scheduled Commercial Banks
1992	58.4	58.9	30.9	55.3
1993	73.7	66.8	59.2	71.9
1994	73.1	57.3	41.2	68.1
1995	67.6	52.2	40.6	63.5
1996	66.7	51.5	45.6	63.3
1997	64.3	51.3	45.6	61.0
1998	62.7	48.5	43.1	58.9
1999	65.9	58.9	56.9	64.3
2000	63.2	48.6	48.5	59.9
2001	67.0	51.8	50.0	63.4
2002	54.9	45.6	49.1	53.1
2003	47.8	45.1	46.5	47.2
2004	45.1	46.6	42.8	45.1

Cost-income ratio= Ratio of operating expenses to total income *less* interest expense. It measures the extent to which non-interest expense devours net total income.

Source: Computed from *Statistical Tables relating to Banks in India*, RBI, various years.

Another important indicator of efficiency of banks is net interest margin (NIM), defined as the excess of interest income over interest expense, scaled by total bank assets. Broadly speaking, this ratio reflects the allocative efficiency of financial intermediation, a lower ratio being indicative of higher efficiency. It is quite reasonable to believe that the decline in deposit rates ushered by the deregulation process will be manifested in the lending behaviour of banks. In practice, however, lending rates have tended to be sticky downwards and seem to operate with a time lag. Historically, the NIM of Indian banks is rather high. Around the onset of the reform process in 1992, the NIM of Indian banks was about 3.3 per cent (Table 14). Thereafter, it recorded a relatively modest decline to around 3 per cent in recent years. And traditionally, it is the foreign banks, which by virtue of their ability to mobilise low-cost deposits, have the highest NIMs, whereas those for private banks have been the lowest in recent years. These comparisons are not watertight: typically, small and medium banks had high NIM until 1997. Thereafter, NIM for big banks recorded a rise. Contextually, it may be mentioned that banks in most developed countries and several emerging economies have NIM (as a percentage to total assets) of around 2 per cent. This provides some indication that competition in banking still has some way to go in India.

Table 14: Spread[@] of Scheduled Commercial Banks: 1992—2004

(as percentage to total asset)

Year (end-March)	Public Sector Banks	Indian Private Banks	Foreign Banks	All Scheduled Commercial Banks
1992	3.22	4.01	3.90	3.30
1993	2.39	2.92	3.57	2.51
1994	2.36	3.01	4.20	2.54
1995	2.92	3.07	4.27	3.03
1996	3.10	3.10	3.76	3.15
1997	3.16	2.95	4.13	3.22
1998	2.91	2.46	3.97	2.95
1999	2.81	2.11	3.51	2.79
2000	2.70	2.13	3.85	2.72
2001	2.84	2.33	3.64	2.84
2002	2.73	1.58	3.25	2.57
2003	2.52	1.96	3.36	2.48
2004	2.97	2.24	3.47	2.87

[@]Spread = Interest earned – interest paid.

Source: *Report on Trend and Progress of Banking in India*, RBI, various years.

Productivity

Studies on productivity in Indian banking have only begun to emanate of late. A recent study found that total factor productivity growth has improved marginally in the post-deregulation period, but there was little evidence of narrowing of productivity differentials across ownership categories following deregulation (Kumbhakar and Sarkar, 2003). Among various productivity indicators, labour productivity indicators like business per employee and profit per employee are most commonly used. In addition, business per branch is also used to judge branch-level productivity. The business per employee of Indian banks increased over threefold in real terms from Rs. 5.4 million in 1992 to Rs. 16.3 million in 2004, exhibiting an annual compound growth rate of nearly 9 per cent (Table 15). At the same time, the profit per employee increased more than fivefold: from Rs. 20,000 to Rs. 150,000 over the same period, implying a compound growth of around 17 per cent. Branch productivity also recorded concomitant improvements. Overall, the balance of evidence suggests distinctive productivity improvements in the banking sector over the reform period. The extant literature suggests that such improvements could be driven by two factors: *technological improvement*, which expands the range of production possibilities and a *catching-up effect*, as peer pressure amongst banks compels them to raise productivity levels. In the context of gradual deregulation of financial sector, several factors could have been at work: a significant shift of the best-practice frontier, driven by a combination of technological advances, financial innovation and different strategies pursued by banks suited to their business philosophy and risk-return profile, changing composition of banks' input-output, and reduction in total cost due to improvements in overall efficiency. While it is difficult to pinpoint the relative mix of these factors in raising productivity, the bottomline is clear: Indian banks witnessed significant productivity improvements, post-reforms.

Table 15: Select Productivity Indicators of Scheduled Commercial Banks

(Rs. million at 1993-94 prices)

Year	Business per employee	Profit per employee	Business per branch
1992	5.4	0.02	109.9
1993	5.4	-0.05	110.4
1994	5.4	-0.04	109.2
1995	5.6	0.02	113.0
1996	6.0	0.01	119.6
1997	6.6	0.04	129.0
1998	7.5	0.05	144.9
1999	8.4	0.03	158.7
2000	9.7	0.05	179.4
2001	11.5	0.05	196.2
2002	13.7	0.09	214.9
2003	15.0	0.12	234.8
2004	16.3	0.15	254.5

Source: *Statistical Tables relating to Banks in India*.

In a wider framework, cross-country studies of deregulation and productivity growth of banks report divergent views. Typically, cross-country comparisons are often fraught with difficulties, not only because of the different regulatory and economic regimes encountered by financial entities, but also owing to the differential quality of services associated with deposits and loans in different countries. Maudos and Pastor (2001) analysed the cost and profit efficiency across 14 EU economies, as well as Japan and the USA. The results uncovered the evidence that, since the start of the 1990s increasing competition has led to gains in profit efficiency in the USA and Europe but not so in the Japanese banking system. Their results also show that the variance in profitability between countries would be considerably reduced if inefficiencies were eliminated, efficiency gains thus being a very important source of improvement in profitability. A recent study in the Asian context analysed various efficiency measures of South-East Asian (Indonesia, Korea, Malaysia, Philippines and Thailand) banks in the context of corporate governance (Williams and Nguyen, 2005). Although the motivation of the study was different, their empirical results found economic justification for the policy of bank privatisation.

Let me encapsulate this section by making some general comments on the efficiency and productivity growth of Indian banks *vis-à-vis* leading Asian nations like China and Korea. As far as real growth (adjusted for price movement and exchange rate fluctuations) in banking business is concerned, Indian banks are favourably placed. In recent years, the real growth of deposits and of loans of Indian banks were noticeably higher than those of other Asian countries such as China and Korea. At the same time, profitability of Indian banks, as determined by the return on assets, is also much higher (Tables 16, 17, 18 and 19). The intermediation cost of Indian banks seems to be relatively higher

Table 16: Spread (net interest margin) of Banks of Major Asian Countries

(as percentage to total asset)

Year	China	Indonesia	Korea	Malaysia	Philippines	Thailand	India
1996	1.86	2.92	1.70	2.91	4.07	2.57	3.07
1997	2.27	2.76	1.80	2.94	4.21	3.00	2.83
1998	2.16	-9.38	1.69	3.32	4.52	0.74	2.66
1999	1.83	-3.11	2.03	2.67	3.16	0.69	2.56
2000	1.76	2.21	2.06	3.02	2.54	1.43	2.74
2001	1.78	3.16	2.12	2.83	2.60	1.69	2.54
2002	1.78	3.61	2.33	2.70	2.29	1.84	2.74
2003	1.87	4.22	2.50	2.61	2.30	1.99	2.84

Source: BankScope.

Table 17: Intermediation Cost (operating expense) of Banks of Major Asian Countries

(as percentage to total asset)

Year	China	Indonesia	Korea	Malaysia	Philippines	Thailand	India
1996	1.23	2.39	2.24	1.42	3.52	1.50	2.77
1997	1.24	4.50	2.55	1.49	3.28	2.05	2.60
1998	1.40	4.04	2.53	1.68	3.67	2.54	2.58
1999	1.18	2.83	1.53	1.50	3.38	2.20	2.41
2000	1.12	2.72	1.46	1.70	3.32	1.98	2.57
2001	1.10	2.36	1.42	1.80	3.30	2.01	2.21
2002	1.05	2.73	1.39	1.73	3.16	1.78	2.22
2003	1.01	2.94	1.38	1.61	3.00	1.71	2.19

Source: BankScope.

than that of Korea and China. Nonetheless, higher operating cost in India is well compensated by the higher non-interest income, as compared to other Asian countries. Finally, the labour productivity of the top 4 banks in India (which includes one *de novo* private bank) and the four state-owned Chinese banks indicate that except the private bank, the top three public sector banks in India recorded much lower employee productivity. However, in the absence of data on employment for banks in other countries, it is difficult to ascertain the degree of labour productivity differentials across countries.

Table 18: Non-interest Income of Banks of Major Asian Countries

(as percentage to total asset)

Year	China	Indonesia	Korea	Malaysia	Philippines	Thailand	India
1996	0.26	0.99	1.06	0.98	2.12	0.68	1.44
1997	0.24	2.97	0.93	1.10	1.73	1.00	1.49
1998	0.13	1.31	0.20	1.16	1.96	1.03	1.38
1999	0.17	1.96	0.99	1.00	1.95	0.97	1.47
2000	0.22	1.51	0.74	1.01	1.59	0.62	1.33
2001	0.22	1.08	1.28	1.15	1.73	0.73	1.49
2002	0.25	1.30	0.91	1.11	2.11	0.93	1.83
2003	0.25	1.46	0.80	0.94	2.16	0.95	1.97

Source: BankScope.

Table 19: Net Profit of Banks of Major Asian Countries

(as percentage to total asset)

Year	China	Indonesia	Korea	Malaysia	Philippines	Thailand	India
1996	0.29	1.01	0.17	1.40	2.06	-0.56	0.71
1997	0.30	-0.39	-0.84	1.03	1.63	-1.17	0.90
1998	0.20	-46.92	-3.10	0.04	0.85	-5.57	0.54
1999	0.17	-9.20	-1.40	0.96	0.10	-5.88	0.70
2000	0.21	0.46	-0.37	1.29	-0.03	-0.15	0.48
2001	0.20	0.87	0.76	0.68	0.48	1.46	0.69
2002	0.20	1.30	0.60	1.03	0.60	0.21	0.97
2003	0.12	1.61	0.15	1.08	1.08	0.63	1.14

Source: BankScope.

A clear message emanating from these findings is the role of technology in driving productivity and efficiency improvements. In today's world of banking, technology is considered as the basic tool of the 'process engineers' of the organisation. It is crucial for the design, control, and execution of service delivery in banks. Therefore, a key driver of efficiency and productivity in the banking industry today is the effective use of technology. This is a crucial prerequisite for capitalising on future opportunities for the banking sector. In effect, it has become the key to servicing all customer segments—offering convenience to retail customer, corporates and government clients. The increasing sophistication, flexibility and complexity of products and servicing offerings makes the effective use of technology critical for managing the risks associated with banking business. However, the 'technological penetration' in India has been quite modest. According to data reported in the *World Development Indicators* database, as of 2002, the number of computers per 1000 persons was about 7 in India compared to anywhere between 70-500 in most emerging markets and even higher in most developed economies. Wide disparities exist within the banking sector as far as technological capabilities are concerned: the percentage of 'computer literate' employees as percentage of total staff in 2000 was around 20 per cent in public sector banks compared with 100 per cent in new private and around 90 per cent in foreign banks (Reserve Bank of India, 2002). Data reported by the RBI suggest that nearly 71 per cent of branches of public sector banks are fully computerized. However, computerization needs to go beyond the mere 'arithmeticals', to borrow a term from the Report of the Committee on Banking Sector Reforms (Government of India, 1998), and instead, needs to be leveraged optimally to achieve and maintain high service and efficiency standards. In fact, recent research on the role of technology in driving productivity improvements in banking demonstrates that computer employees and IT capital exhibit higher productivities than their respective non-computer employees and non-IT capital, respectively (Huang, 2005). The challenge, therefore, remains threefold: acquiring the 'right' technology, deploying it optimally and remaining cost-effective whilst delivering sustainable returns to shareholders. In effect, 'managing' technology so as to reap the maximum benefits remains a key challenge for the Indian banks.

4. Way Ahead

How do we see the future? In this context, I would like to share some of the issues that need to be kept in view while discussing productivity and efficiency in banks. Needless to state, these issues remain relevant, in varying degrees, in economies that share similar features in the banking sector, as ours.

First, ...small and medium enterprises (SMEs) constitute an important segment of the industrial and services sectors in India in view of their significant contributions to employment generation as also exports. With the emergence of new activities in the rural segment such as agri-clinics, contract farming and rural housing with forward and backward linkages to SMEs, lending to SMEs has become a viable revenue proposition for banks. The Reserve Bank has also initiated several measures to streamline the flow of credit and address structural bottlenecks in credit delivery to this segment. Salient among these include fixing of self-set targets for financing, rationalisation of cost of loans, expanding the outreach of formal credit, and formulation of comprehensive and more liberal policies for credit extension. Public sector banks have also been advised to constitute specialized SME branches in identified clusters/centers with preponderance of small and medium enterprises. A noteworthy development in this context has been the passage of the Credit Information Companies (Regulation) Act, 2005 in the Parliament. The Act is expected to encourage setting up of credit information companies and thereby, improve exchange of information on credit histories of borrowers. Coupled with appropriate risk assessment models and mechanisms, this is expected to lower transactions costs of banks. The overall effect of this process is likely to be reflected in a lowering of the risk premium embedded in interest rates charged to SMEs with positive spillovers for bank lending to the SME sector.

Although liberalisation of financial services and competition has improved customer services, experience shows that customers' interests are not always accorded priority. More importantly, concerns have been raised with regard to banking practices that tend to exclude vast segments of the population. In this context, the Reserve Bank has announced its intention to implement policies to incentivise banks to provide extensive services responsive to the needs of the underprivileged. As part of the process, the Reserve Bank has recently advised all banks to make available a basic banking 'no frills' account either with 'nil' or very low minimum balances as well as charges that would make such accounts accessible to vast sections of population. The nature and number of transactions in such accounts could be restricted, but made known to the customer in advance in a transparent manner. Banks have been urged to give wide publicity to this facility so as to ensure greater financial inclusion.

The growth performance of the Indian economy during the last few years indicates a possible ratcheting up of the trend rate of growth from around 6 per cent to around 8 per cent per year. Yet, there is a need to undertake significant efforts to achieve higher rates of growth in a sustained manner. The current levels of investment might not be adequate to achieve such growth rates, even after accounting for reductions in the existing incremental capital-output ratios. Looking beyond the aspect of fiscal consolidation, action on several fronts needs to be pursued vigorously to step up growth rates. First is the issue of investment in agriculture and allied activities, a sector that produces 21 per cent of GDP, but supports nearly 60 per cent of the population. There is often substantial loss of output owing to inadequate storage and transport facilities and paucity of adequate food processing capacities. This necessitates greater public and private investment on these post-harvest facilities to not only increase value addition, but also to improve the agriculture-industry linkage. The second issue of importance is the simplification of procedures. Cumbersome procedural formalities introduce delays and results in significant output losses. Added to these, the de-reservation of items from exclusive production under SSI units is likely to permit the sector reap economies of scale and scope and enhance competitiveness. The third is the issue of finances. The incipient investment boom in infrastructure, industry and services will yield best results only if enormous resource flows are successfully intermediated at a low cost. This will depend on the ability of the financial sector to process information properly and to intermediate the extant savings into optimal investment by specific firms and sectors. The fourth aspect of stepping up investment is to address the deficiencies in infrastructure. The decline in public spending on infrastructure has not been adequately compensated by the private sector, possibly owing to difficulties in the regulatory environment. Therefore, nurturing an appropriate policy framework, with a conducive environment for public-private participation, remains the key to accelerating investment in infrastructure. The final aspect is the need to complement domestic investment with higher foreign investment, primarily in the form of FDI. Such investment is likely to trigger technology spillovers, assist human capital formation and more generally, improve the efficiency of resource use.

Over the reform period, more and more banks have begun to get listed on the stock exchange, which, in its wake, has led to greater market discipline and concomitantly, to an improvement in their governance aspects as well. This has led to a broadbasing of the ownership of PSBs. Such diversification of ownership has also led to a qualitative difference in their functioning, since there is induction of private shareholding as well as attendant issues of shareholder's value, as reflected by the market capitalisation, board representation and interests of minority shareholders (Reddy, 2002). The issue of mixed ownership as an institutional structure where government has controlling interest is a salient feature of bank governance in India. Such aspects of corporate governance in PSBs is important, not only because PSBs dominate the banking industry, but also because, it is likely that they would continue to remain in banking business. To the extent there is public ownership of PSBs, the multiple objectives of the government as owner and the complex principal-agent relationships needs to be taken on board. Given the increased technical complexity of most business activities including banking and the rapid pace of change in financial markets and practices, PSBs would need to devise imaginative ways of responding to the evolving challenges within the context of mixed ownership. All in all, this is an exciting phase for PSBs to grow and prosper, and it is up to these banks to respond to the challenges.

Let me conclude: the discussion has have traversed a modest terrain, focusing on the efficiency and productivity changes in Indian banking. The patterns of efficiency and technological change witnessed in Indian banking can be viewed as consistent with expectations in an industry undergoing rapid change in response to the forces of deregulation. In reaction to evolving market prospects, a few pioneering banks might adjust quickly to seize the emerging opportunities, while others respond cautiously. As deregulation gathers momentum, commercial banks would need to devise imaginative ways of augmenting their incomes and more importantly their fee-incomes so as to raise efficiency and productivity levels.

REFERENCES

Bell, C. and Rousseau, P. (2001): "Post-Independence India: A Case of Finance-led Industrialization?", *Journal of Development Economics*, 65: 153-75.

Berger, A.N and Humphrey, D.B. (1992): "Measurement and Efficiency Issues in Commercial Banking", Z. Griliches (Ed.): *Output Measurement in the Services Sector*, Chicago: University of Chicago Press, 245-79.

Bhaumik, S.K. and Dimova, R. (2004): "How Important is Ownership in a Market with Level-Playing Field? The Indian Banking Sector Revisited", *Journal of Comparative Economics*, 32: 165-80.

Bhide, M.G., Prasad, A. and Ghosh, S. (2001): "Emerging Challenges in Indian Banking", *Working Paper No.103*, Centre for Research in Economic Development and Policy Reform, Stanford University.

Das, A. and Ghosh, S. (2006): "Financial Deregulation and Efficiency: An Empirical Analysis of Indian Banks during the Post-Reform Period", *Review of Financial Economics* (forthcoming).

Demirgúc-Kunt, A., & Maksimovic, V. (1998): "Law, Finance and Firm Growth", *Journal of Finance*, 53: 2107-37.

Frexias, X and Rochet, J.C. (1997): *Microeconomics of Banking*, Cambridge MA: MIT Press.

Government of India (1998): *Report of the Committee on Banking Sector Reforms* (Chairman: Shri M. Narasimham), New Delhi.

Huang Tai-Hsin (2005): "A Study on the Productivities of IT Capital and Computer Labor: Firm-level Evidence from Taiwan's Banking Industry", *Journal of Productivity Analysis*, 24: 241–57.

Koeva, P. (2003): "The Performance of Indian Banks During Financial Liberalization", *IMF Working Paper No.150*, Washington DC.

Kumbhakar, S. and Sarkar, S. (2003): "Deregulation, Ownership and Efficiency Change in Indian Banking: Evidence from India", *Journal of Money, Credit and Banking*, 35: 403-14.

Maudos, J. and Pastor, J.M. (2001): "Cost and Profit Efficiency in Banking: An International Comparison of Europe, Japan and USA", *Applied Economics Letters*, 8: 383-87.

Mohan, R. (2005): "Financial Sector Reforms: Policies and Performance Analysis", *Economic Political Weekly, Special Issue on Money, Banking and Finance* (March), 40: 1106-21.

Rajan, R.G. and Zingales, L. (1998): "Financial Dependence and Growth", *American Economic Review*, 88: 559-86.

Rangarajan, C. and Jadhav, N. (1992): "Issues in Financial Sector Reforms", B. Jalan (Ed.): *The Indian Economy*, Delhi: Penguin Books India.

Ray, P. and Sen Gupta, I. (2004): "Systemic Restructuring of Banks: The Indian Experience", *Journal of the Indian Bankers Association.*

Reddy, Y.V. (2002): "Public Sector Banks and the Governance Challenge: Indian Experience", Lecture Delivered at the World Bank, IMF and Brookings Institutions Conference, April.

Reserve Bank of India (2000): *Report on Currency and Finance 1999-2000*, RBI: Mumbai.

Reserve Bank of India (2002): "Expenditure Pattern and IT Initiatives of Banks", *RBI Bulletin*, December.

Reserve Bank of India (2005): *Report on Trend and Progress of Banking in India 2004-2005*, RBI: Mumbai.

Sarkar, J., Sarkar, S. and Bhaumik, S.K. (1998): "Does Ownership Always Matter? Evidence from the Indian Banking Industry", *Journal of Comparative Economics*, 26: 262-81.

Stiglitz, J.E. (1998): "More Instruments and Broader Goals: Moving Towards the Post-Washington Consensus", WIDER Annual Lecture, Helsinki.

Williams, J. and Nguyen, N. (2005): "Financial Liberalization, Crisis, and Restructuring: A Comparative Study of Bank Performance and Bank Governance in South East Asia", *Journal of Banking and Finance*, 29: 2119–54.

Bank Efficiency in India since the Reforms: An Assessment

Rajesh Chakrabarti and *Gaurav Chawla*

1. Introduction

With deposits of over $385 billion dollars, the Indian banking sector accounts for three-quarters of the country's financial assets. Over the decades, the sector has grown steadily in size, measured in terms of total deposits, at a fairly uniform average annual growth rate of about 18 per cent. In the years since liberalization, several significant changes have occurred in the structure and character of the banking sector—the most visible being perhaps the emergence of new private sector banks as well as the entry of several new foreign banks. The spirit of competition and the emphasis on profitability are also driving the public sector banks towards greater profit-orientation in a departure from the socialistic approach followed for decades. In general, it seems that the emergence of the new private banks and the increased participation of foreign banks have increased professionalism in the banking sector. Competition has clearly increased with the Herfindahl index (a measure of concentration) for advances and assets dropping by over 28 per cent and about 20 per cent respectively between 1991-1992 and 2000-2001.[1] Over the period, SBI, the largest Indian bank, witnessed a decline in asset market share from 28 per cent to 24 per cent while its loan market share dropped from 27 per cent to 22 per cent. The deposit share, on the other hand, stayed pretty much the same at 23 per cent. The asset, loan and deposit shares of the top 10 banks all fell from close to 70 per cent to below 60 per cent. Nevertheless, the public sector banks still enjoy a pre-eminent position in Indian banking today, accounting for over 80 per cent of deposits and credit (see Figures 1 and 2). There is, however, a noticeable trend of private banks gradually eroding the market share of the public sector.

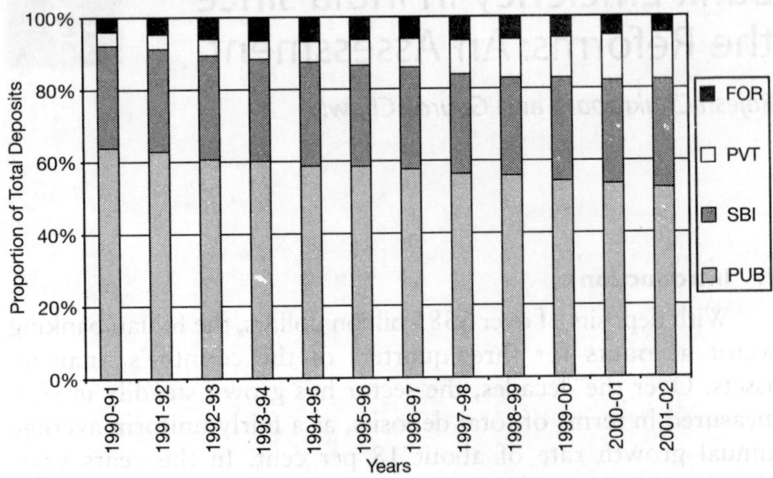

Figure 1: Share of Deposits

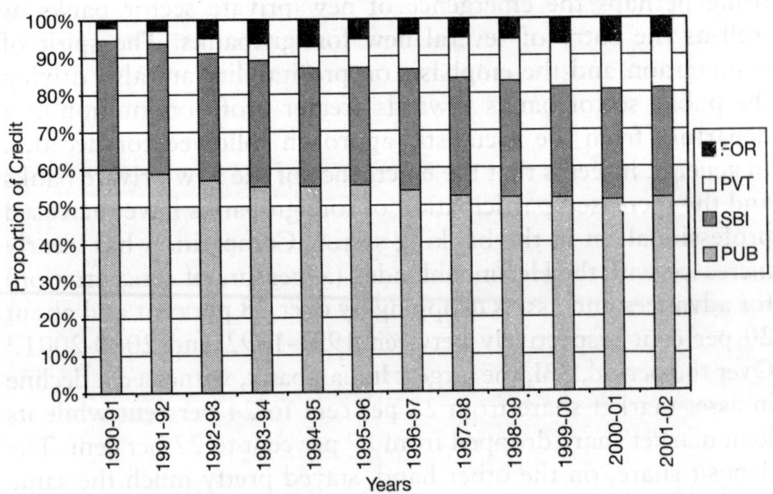

Figure 2: Share of Credit

Performance and efficiency of commercial banks are key elements of the efficiency and efficacy of a country's financial sector. It is not surprising then, that considerable attention has been focused on the performance of commercial banks in India in recent years. According to the general perception as well as on several metrics, the "new" private sector banks and the foreign banks have led the way in terms of efficiency. Public sector banks, still not entirely free from the old bureaucratic mode of functioning and constrained by certain "developmental" lending objectives, are often thought to be lagging behind in the race to efficiency. Bank privatization and further liberalization of the banking sector including allowing bank mergers are frequently discussed as remedies for the situation. In this paper, we investigate the relative performance of banks in India for over a decade since liberalization, using the Data Envelopment Analysis (DEA) approach.

We find that on a "value" or profitability basis (in the specific sense of our second DEA model as well as the more general Return on Assets sense), the foreign banks, as a group, have been considerably more efficient than all other bank groups, followed by the Indian private banks. From a "quantity" perspective or on the basis of volume of deposits and credit created with given input levels, however, Indian private banks have been the best performers while the foreign banks are the *worst* performers. This suggests that the foreign banks have been "cherry-picking"—focusing on more lucrative segments of banking.

The rest of the paper is arranged as follows. The next section gives a background discussion of bank performance in India. The third section discusses the Data Envelopment Analysis (DEA) approach and summarizes the findings of prior studies of Indian banking using the DEA methodology. The fourth section describes our study and discusses our findings. The fifth and final section draws conclusions and provides pointers for future research.

2. Performance of Commercial Banks in Recent Years—A Brief Background

The performance of commercial banks in India has been under policy and academic spotlight for a while now with the public sector bank performance receiving the greatest attention.

The performance of several public sector banks (PSBs) has been so poor that many have called for a complete overhaul of these banks and privatization as a solution.

Performance evaluation of banks, particularly in an economy that is dominated by public sector banks that are not driven purely by profit motive, however, is not a simple task. Profitability is definitely a key measure of performance, but its use as the *sole* measure is disputed by many and several alternative measures of efficiency have been used in the literature. Here we take a look at a few of these measures to evaluate the performance of banks in the post-reforms era.

A caveat is in order here. A key issue in judging bank efficiency is the link between management objectives and the selected measure of efficiency. As in any business, banks too seek to maximize shareholder value as well as pursue strategic objectives. Banks at different levels of market share frequently set differing objectives, so any measure other than Return on Assets is fraught with comparability problems. In addition, more than in many other businesses, risk management plays a crucial role in banking and it is, indeed, a difficult task to figure out the riskiness of a bank's operations without going through a detailed analysis of its investments and loan portfolio. A cross-sectional comparison of relative bank performance, as presented here, abstracts in a large measure from these considerations, which are doubtless limitations of such analysis.

Panel A of Figure 3 shows the Return on Asset (Profit/Asset) for different bank groups. It is evident that foreign banks are, by far, the most profitable bank category in India. The non-SBI public sector banks have consistently been the worst performers. There appears to have been a mild improvement in the efficiency of the banking sector in general during the decade[2] much of which has been driven by improvements in performance of the private and foreign banks. Within the private sector banks, the "new" private sector banks, those that came up in the post-reforms era, seem to have driven the efficiency gains.

It is however, imperative to consider risk in evaluating a bank's performance. The riskiness of banking is not wholly

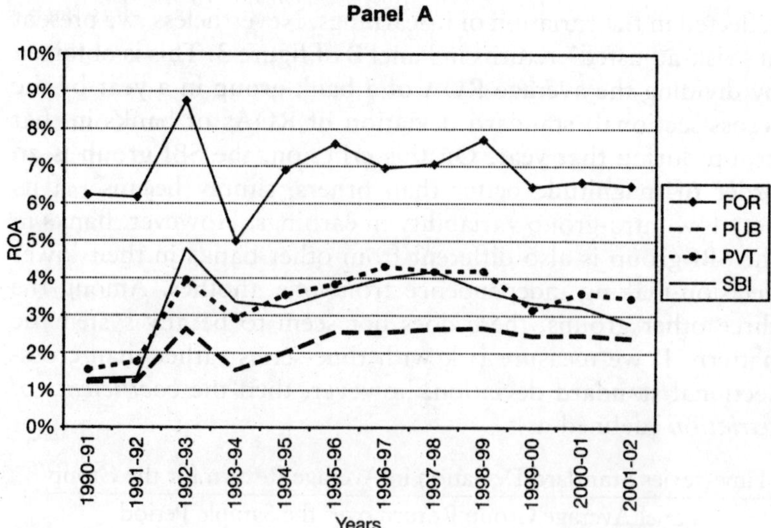

Source: Reserve Bank of India.

Figure 3: Return on Assets (Group-wise)

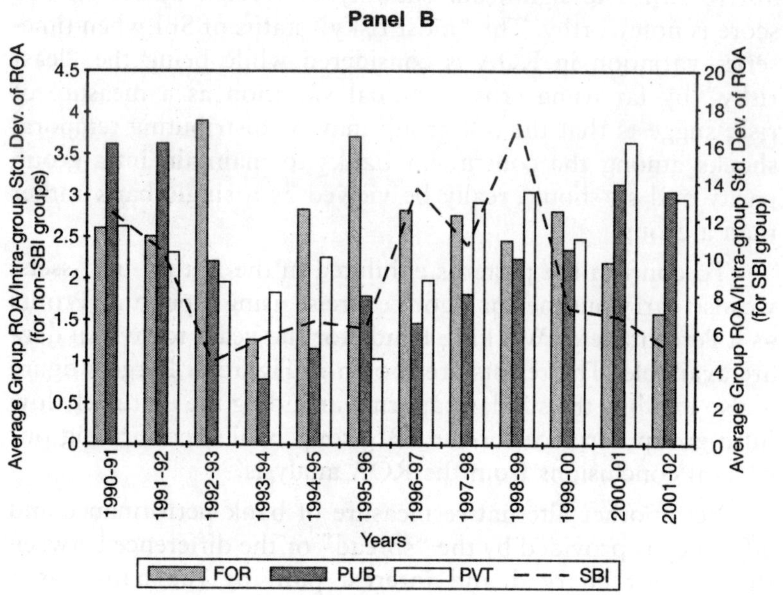

Figure 3: Risk-adjusted ROA (Group-wise)

reflected in the variation of its earnings. Nevertheless, we present at "risk-adjusted" returns in Panel B of figure 3. This is obtained by dividing the average ROA of a bank group in a year by the (cross-sectional) standard deviation of ROAs of banks in that group during that year. On this criterion, the SBI group is an order of magnitude better than others, simply because of its very low intra-group variability in earnings. However, banks in the SBI group is also different from other banks in their lower decision-making independence from one another. Among the three other groups, there does not seem to be any systematic pattern. If we measure risk with time-series rather than cross-sectional standard deviation, however, then the *coefficients of variation* (defined as)

$$\frac{\text{Time-series Standard Deviation in Average Return for the Group}}{\text{Panel Average Group Return over the Sample Period}}$$

provide the following ranking of the four bank groups (least to most risky): foreign banks (0.14), public (0.25), private (0.27), SBI (0.32). The significant stability of foreign banks on this score is noteworthy. The "most risky" status of SBI when time-series variation in ROA is considered while being the "least risky" by far using cross-sectional variation as a measure of risk, suggests that the SBI group may be distributing temporal shocks among the constituent banks to maintain intra-group parity and so should really be viewed as a single bank rather than a group.

To confirm the patterns exhibited in the Return on Assets, we also carry out the analogous exercise using Operating Profits as a Percentage of Working Funds for the years for which data are available. The results are shown in Figure 4. Largely figure 4 also exhibits the similar patterns (including the extremely low intra-group variance for the SBI group banks) confirming our general conclusions from the ROA analysis.

Yet another alternative measure of bank performance and efficiency is provided by the "spread" or the difference between the interest charged and interest paid by the banks as a proportion of total assets of the banks—the Net Interest Margin

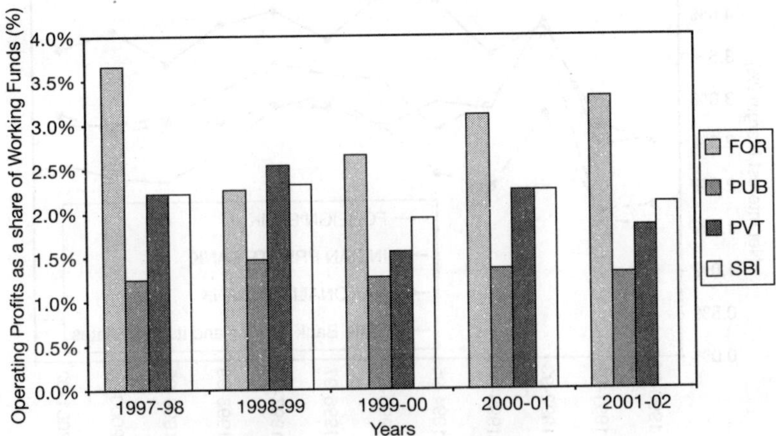

Source: Reserve Bank of India.

Figure 4: Operating Profits as a fraction of Working Funds

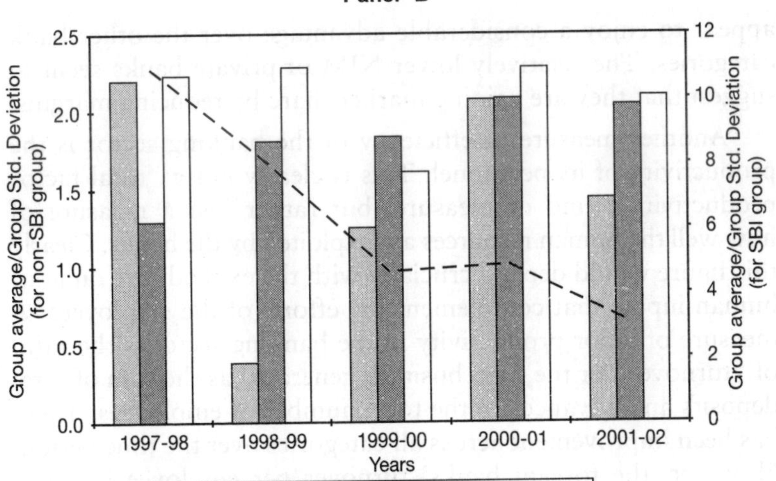

Figure 4: Operating Profits as a share of Working Funds (Group Level — Risk-adjusted)

(NIM). Figure 5 shows the variation of this metric for different categories of banks during the 90s. Once again, foreign banks

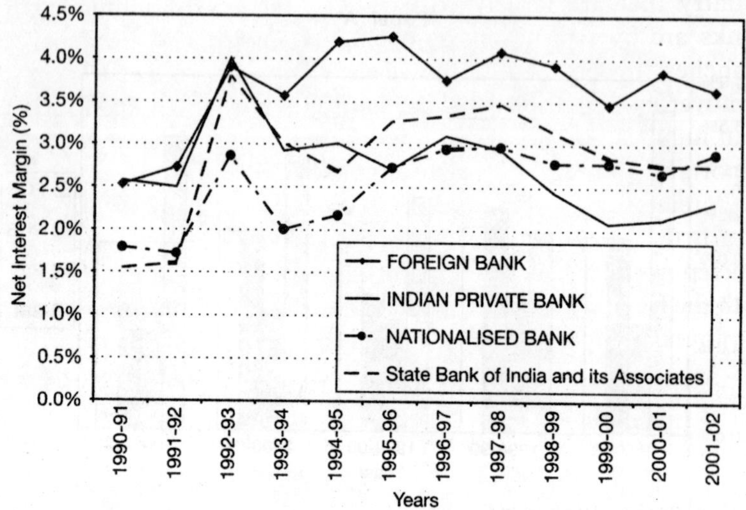

Source: Reserve Bank of India.

Figure 5: Net Interest Margin of Indian Banks (Group-wise)

appear to enjoy a considerable advantage over the other bank categories. The relatively lower NIM of private banks seem to suggest that they are gaining market share by reducing margins.

Another measure of efficiency of the banking sector is the productivity of its personnel. This is clearly not a "total factor productivity" kind of measure, but rather just a measure of how well the human resources are exploited by the banks. Clearly this figure would depend crucially with the expenditure on non-human inputs that complement the efforts of the employees. A measure of labor productivity in the banking sector is the ratio of "turnover" or the total business generated as the sum of total deposits and advances to the total number of employees. There has been improvement across all categories over the time period. However, the foreign banks' turnover per employee is about *five* times that of the nationalized banks.[3] Equally impressive has been the relative surge of the private banks on this metric, from below par when compared to the public sector banks at the beginning of the decade to over twice as efficient as the nationalized banks in later years. Much of the relative poor performance of the public sector banks stem from the fact that they are required to have branches in rural areas all over the country that are largely cost centers. However, public sector banks are overstaffed even when their metro and urban area branches are considered.[4] However, when we look at the banks' turnover as a multiple of their employee *cost* (Figure 6), rather than number of employees, the difference is less marked. More importantly the Indian private banks appear to have trounced the foreign banks on this score in the latter half of the decade. Clearly the "new" private sector banks have been more successful in keeping their employee costs down while raising turnover. Both the foreign and private banks hire fewer but more expensive employees than their public sector counterparts.

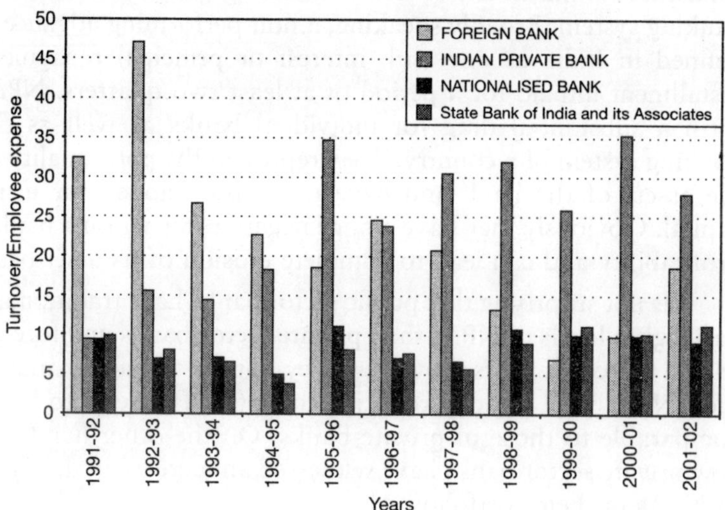

Source: Reserve Bank of India.

Figure 6: Turnover per Rupee of Employee Expense

Foreign banks tend to use information technology more intensively and practice niche banking. As for private banks, their climb of the efficiency ladder has been driven almost exclusively by the new private banks—ICICI Bank, UTI Bank, HDFC Bank, etc. that have followed the foreign bank-type staffing practices and business model with lower clerical and subordinate staff strength. All these features have important policy implications for the debate concerning restructuring and privatizing of public sector banks. There is also the view,[5] however, that ownership *per se* does not affect the operational efficiency of banks—it is the discipline of stock markets that make the *traded* private companies more efficient than public sector banks.[6]

While the regulatory mechanism is frequently blamed for the lackluster performance of public sector banks, till 1996, deregulation had not resulted in productivity surge in public sector banks, though private banks improved performance through expansion.[7]

Perhaps the best measure of a country's financial health and robustness is the extent of non-performing assets (NPAs) in its banking system. Broadly speaking, a non-performing advance is defined in India as one with interest or principal repayment installment unpaid for a period of at least two quarters. NPAs form a substantial drag for individual banks as well as the banking system of a country. They represent the poor quality of the assets of the bank and have to be provisioned for using capital. Obviously they have a huge negative impact on a bank's profitability and can lead to complete erosion of its asset base.

It is not surprising that public sector banks have traditionally had higher levels of NPAs than private sector banks and foreign banks. In recent years, however, they appear to have managed their NPAs well, steadily reducing them (see Figure 7) to levels comparable to those of private banks. On the other hand, the new private sector banks have witnessed an increase in the share of NPAs in their portfolios.

A closer look at the cross-sectional distribution of NPAs among the different banks (Figure 8), however, suggest that as a group, public sector banks have a tighter distribution than other categories, particularly foreign banks which show considerably larger skewness in the ratio of net NPAs to net advances.

There is, however, skepticism in some quarters about the definition and measurement of NPAs in Indian banks. Banks often indulge in creative accounting and loan rollovers—"ever-greening"—to keep the NPA figures artificially low.[8] The share

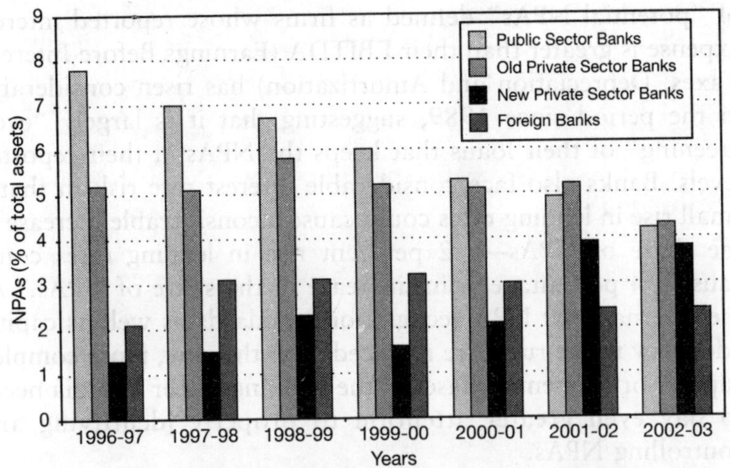

Source: Reserve Bank of India.

Figure 7: Gross NPAs as a Percentage of Total Assets

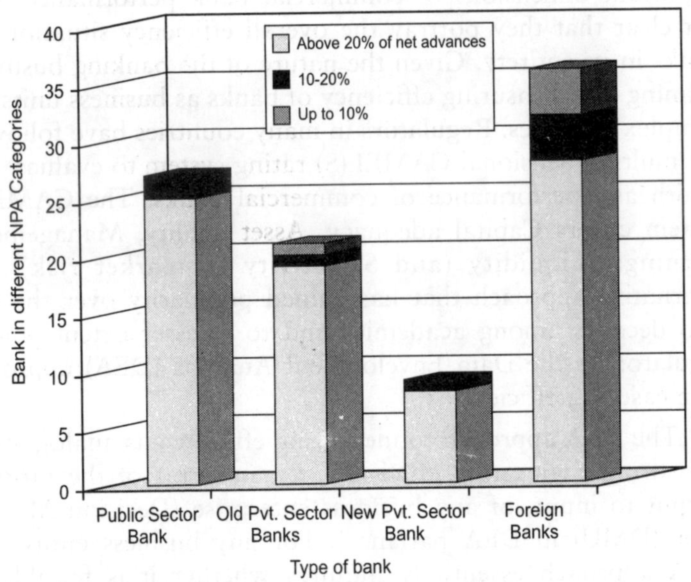

Source: *Trend and Progress of Banking in India, 2002-03*, Reserve Bank of India.

Figure 8: NPA Category-wise Breakdown of Banks in March 2003

of "potential NPAs" defined as firms whose reported interest expense is greater than their EBITDA (Earnings Before Interest, Taxes, Depreciation and Amortization) has risen considerably in the period since 1989, suggesting that it is largely "ever-greening" of their loans that keeps the NPAs at their reported levels. Banks also face considerable interest rate risk in that a small rise in lending rates could cause a considerable increase in the share of NPAs—a 2 per cent rise in lending rates could cause a 4 percentage point increase in the share of NPAs.[9] As the international NPA recognition standards as well as capital adequacy ratios rules are replaced with the new, more complex supervisory system of Basel II, the banking sector in India needs to pay even greater attention to properly identifying and controlling NPAs.

3. The DEA approach

While the measures discussed in Section 2 above capture important dimensions of commercial bank performance, it is not clear that they portray the overall efficiency situation for banks in its entirety. Given the nature of the banking business, defining and measuring efficiency of banks as business units are complex exercises. Regulators in many countries have followed the multi-dimensional CAMEL(S) rating system to evaluate the health and performance of commercial banks. The CAMELS system covers Capital adequacy, Asset quality, Management, Earnings, Liquidity (and Sensitivity to market risk). An alternative approach that has gained popularity over the last two decades among academics and to a lesser extent among regulators is the Data Envelopment Analysis (DEA) approach to measuring efficiency.

The DEA approach to measuring efficiency is analogous to measuring engineering efficiency, i.e. in terms of the ratio of output to input, of any business enterprise (Decision Making Unit (DMU) in DEA parlance). For any business entity, the DEA approach essentially inquires whether it is feasible to produce the same output using less input than the enterprise is currently employing or if the output level can be raised while keeping the level of input the same. If the answer to either of these questions is in the affirmative, then the DMU is "inefficient." The exercise is clearly a relative one, since the feasibility in question can only be evidenced by the production function of some other DMU in the sample. So efficiency, or lack thereof, can only be established in comparison with other units in question. Therefore, the DEA approach essentially consists of estimating an "efficiency frontier" in the input-output space consisting of the "efficient" DMUs and finding out whether the DMU of interest lies on the frontier (efficient) or inside it (inefficient). The extent of inefficiency can also be measured from the distance of the DMU in question from the frontier. The exact mechanics of the DEA approach is explained in greater details in Box 1.

Box 1: Data Envelopment Analysis

The idea behind Data Envelopment Analysis (DEA) is to compare the input-output matrix of different decision making units (DMUs)—banks in our analysis. Efficiency is essentially defined by the ratio of output to input, a concept akin to that of engineering efficiency. The central challenge, however, is to implement this in the context of multiple inputs and outputs—in a multi-dimensional hyperspace. If bank A uses more of input 1 but less of input 2 than bank B to produce more of output 1 but less of output 2, how do we compare the efficiency of the two banks? Any such comparison would involve taking an "average" of outputs and an "average" of inputs to compare the efficiencies, but the weighting system chosen in the averaging exercise may tilt the verdict in favor of either bank.

The DEA approach, therefore, consists of generating an "efficiency frontier" from the input-output matrix of the DMUs. For instance in the example above, both banks may be situated on the frontier and a third bank C which uses more of either input to produce no more than any one of the other two banks would be positioned "inside the frontier". (For multiple inputs and outputs, the frontier takes the shape of a polyhedron.) The efficient units, located on the "frontier", are assigned an efficiency score of 1 (maximum possible) while those inside get scores between zero and one. The further away they are from the frontier, the lower the score.

Since this is a relative "benchmarking" technique, the resulting efficiency scores of a bank cannot be compared over time. If a particularly efficient bank starts business in a year it will depress the scores of many other banks with no change in actual efficiency levels in the latter.

While this basic principle of DEA is intuitive and straightforward, implementing it for business enterprises, particularly commercial banks, involves some judgment and subjectivity. A fundamental question arises in the definition of inputs and outputs. The role of deposits is particularly vexing. Should we consider them an input or an output for a bank? The answer to this depends upon the view we adopt on the nature of a bank's business. If we think of banks as financial "intermediaries" transforming deposits to loans, then deposits should be considered an input. If, alternatively, we view banks as financial institutions using capital and labor to produce financial products like loans and deposit account services, then deposits should figure as output. Both approaches have been used in the literature.

Even after taking a position on deposits, there remain considerable degrees of freedom in the selection of inputs and outputs and the results of the analysis are, indeed, sensitive to the choice of inputs and outputs.

This room for judgment in specification notwithstanding, the DEA methodology has become very common in evaluating operational efficiencies of commercial banks around the world.[10] A few studies have already applied the DEA approach to the Indian context sometimes reaching surprising conclusions.[11] These studies seem to indicate that, contrary to the general perception, efficiency in public sector banks were higher than those in private sector banks in India both before the reforms[12] as well as after it.[13] In the post-1995 period, the public sector banks appear to have gained in efficiency while the private sector banks seem to have undergone a decline in efficiency.[14] The present paper covers a longer time-frame (1990—2002) than these studies and looks at the four main types of banks—the SBI group banks, other public sector banks, private banks and foreign banks—together, providing a comparative picture of bank efficiency among these bank categories and refutes the broad findings of these studies.

4. Analysis of Commercial Bank Efficiency in India

While there are over 100 commercial banks operating in India, our DEA analysis covers a total of 70 banks over a time period ranging from 1990 to 2002. To avoid including banks with insignificant or nominal operations, we exclude the bottom quartile of all banks in each year from our analysis. Most of the banks excluded were foreign banks with rudimentary or insignificant operations in India. We also excluded banks that were present for less than 5 years in our sample period. Table 1 lists the banks included in our study. We cover 8 banks of the SBI group, 19 other public sector banks, 28 private banks and 15 foreign banks. All our data are drawn from the Reserve Bank of India website. Of course, not all of these 70 banks have been operational in every year of our sample period, but they have been functional for at least five years during this interval.

Table 1: Banks Included in the Analysis

SBI Group
State Bank of Bikaner & Jaipur
State Bank of Hyderabad
State Bank of India
State Bank of Indore
State Bank of Mysore
State Bank of Patiala
State Bank of Saurashtra
State Bank of Travancore

Other Public Sector
Allahabad Bank
Andhra Bank
Bank of Baroda
Bank of India
Bank of Maharastra
Canara Bank
Central Bank of India
Corporation Bank
Dena Bank
Indian Bank
Indian Overseas Bank
Oriental Bank of Commerce
Punjab & Sind Bank
Punjab National Bank
Syndicate Bank
UCO Bank
Union Bank of India
United Bank of India
Vijaya Bank

Private
Baharat Overseas Bank
Bank of Madura
Bank of Punjab
Bank of Rajasthan
Benares State Bank
Catholic Syrian Bank
Centurion Bank
City Union Bank
Development Credit Bank
Federal Bank
Global Trust Bank
HDFC Bank
ICICI Bank
IDBI Bank
Indusind Bank
Jammu & Kashmir Bank
Karnataka Bank
Karur Vysya Bank
Lakshmi Vilas Bank
Lord Krishna Bank

Nedungadi Bank
Sangli Bank
South Indian Bank
Tamilnad Mercantile Bank
United Western Bank
UTI Bank
Vysya Bank

Foreign
ABN Amro Bank
Abu-Dhabi Commercial Bank
Bank of Nova Scotia
Bank of America
Bank of Tokyo
BNP Paribas
British Bank of Middle East
Citibank
Credit Agricole Indosuez
Credit Lyonnais
Deutsche Bank
Hongkong & Shanghai Bank
Societe Generale
Standard Chartered Bank
Grindlays Bank

We use two alternative model specifications for our analysis. The first model[15] uses interest expenses and operating expense as inputs and advances, investments and deposits as outputs.[16] In using deposits as an output variable, this model uses the "production" view of banking. An issue here is that bank management may not always explicitly consider deposits as an output as it is a source of expense rather than revenue. However, given that a bank's ability to lend and invest is restricted by its level of deposits, the approach is not wholly without merit.

The second model[17] is closer to measuring financial performance in its approach. It uses interest and non-interest expenses as inputs and studies interest income and non-interest income as outputs. Thus the first model takes more of a "quantity" approach to performance measurement while the second looks more at "value created". It is important to emphasize, however, that the "value created" captured here does not directly measure returns to shareholders.

The "Quantity" Approach

As a group, the foreign banks perform significantly *worse* than the other bank groups in this metric, though their relative performance has somewhat improved over the years. This relatively poor performance, however, may well be by design. Foreign banks may be selectively choosing high-value business niches trading off quantity. Private banks, on the other hand have performed the best on average over the sample period. We present the annual distribution of average efficiency scores for the different bank groups for the different years in Figure 9. We use the "distribution" perspective to emphasize that the scores are not comparable over time and are only *relative* in their nature. Thus a larger area in a particular bar signifies greater efficiency.

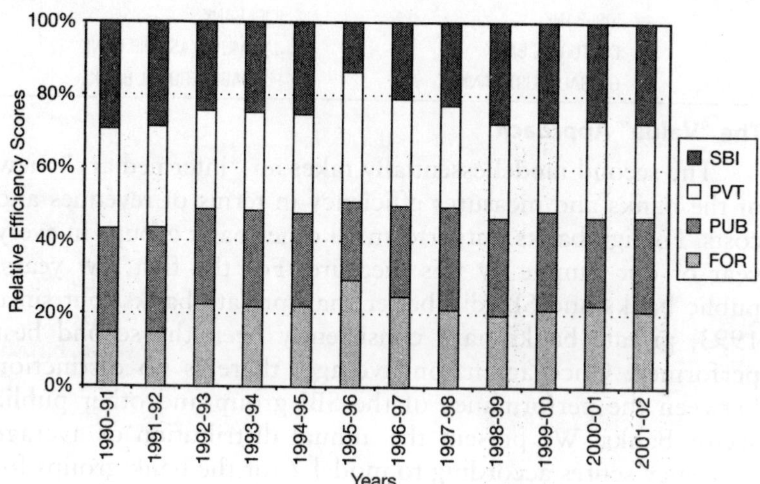

Figure 9: Distribution of Average Efficiency Scores (Model 1)

At the individual bank level, of course, there is considerable variation in relative performance both within each bank category as well as for the same individual bank over time. In order to capture the relative "best" performers, therefore, we use the following approach. We calculate the ranks of all banks in terms of their efficiency scores in each year. Next we find the average rank of each bank over the period, adjusting the averaging for varying total number of banks over the years. A final ranking based on these average ranks then gives us a list of banks ordered by their operational efficiency. Table 2 shows the ten "best" performing banks on this criterion during our period of study after excluding banks with less than six years of existence in our data (to minimize the effects of abnormal years or events). With the exception of Punjab National Bank at rank 10, all the banks in the list are "new" private sector banks. Somewhat surprisingly, Global Trust Bank, that went under just a few years later, features in this list. This is perhaps because the troubles at GTB started after 2001-02, when our data ends.

Table 2: The Best Performers (Model 1)

INDUSIND BANK	HDFC BANK
UTI BANK	BANK OF PUNJAB
IDBI BANK	ICICI BANK
CENTURION BANK	JAMMU & KASHMIR BANK
GLOBAL TRUST BANK	PUNJAB NATIONAL BANK

The "Value" Approach

The second model essentially takes an "intermediary" view of the banks and measures efficiency in terms of revenues and costs. Foreign banks outperform all other bank groups in every year of our sample by this measure. For the first few years, public banks and SBI did better than private banks, but since 1993, private banks have consistently been the second best performer. Once again, on average, there is no distinction between the performance of the SBI group and other public sector banks. We present the annual distribution of average efficiency scores according to model 2 for the bank groups for the different years in Figure 10. Once again we use the "distribution" perspective to emphasize the lack of comparability over time and the *relative* nature of the efficiency scores.

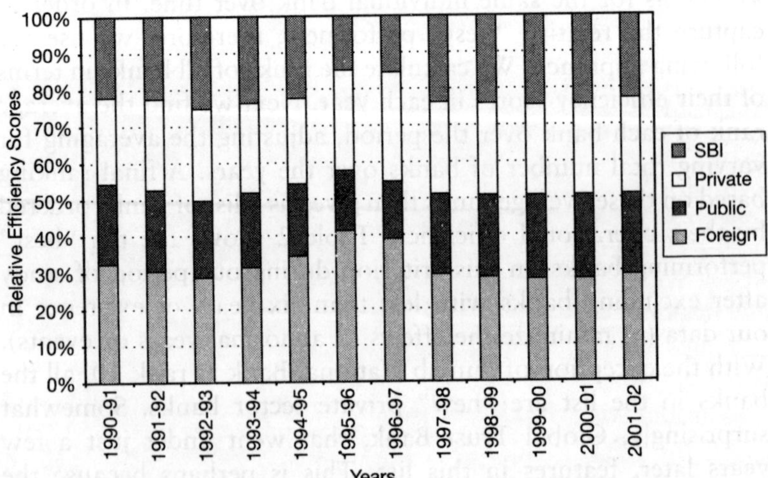

Figure 10: Distribution of Average Efficiency Scores (Model 2)

Within the bank groups, again, there is considerable variation. As a group, the private sector banks exhibit maximum variance followed by foreign banks. The SBI group is the most homogeneous. The ten "best" banks according to this criterion are shown in Table 3. This time there are more major foreign banks in the list.

Table 3: The Best Performers (Model 2)

Indusind Bank	Global Trust Bank
Centurion Bank	Bank of Punjab
Deutsche Bank	Citibank
HDFC Bank	Bank of Tokyo
Credit Lyonnais	IDBI Bank

The undisputed superiority of foreign banks according to the second model, given the dominance of private banks according to the first model seems to suggest that foreign banks in India are, relatively speaking, "cherry pickers", choosing higher value-added businesses rather than volume, while the "new" private sector banks appear to have successfully pushed volume with the best among them doing well on value creation as well.

The exclusion of risk analysis poses a limitation for our study as it does for most DEA studies in the literature. The explicit treatment of risk in the DEA model remains a challenge. Annual financial results may fail to give a correct impression of a bank's performance if its assets are not marked to market and its assets are inordinately risky. This is perhaps best illustrated by Global Trust Bank being present on the "best performers" list for both models and yet going under soon after.

5. Conclusion

We apply the increasingly popular methodology of Data Envelopment Analysis to evaluate the relative efficiency of Indian banks during the 1990—2002 period. Our results suggest that on a "value" basis, the foreign banks, as a group, have been considerably more efficient than all other bank groups, followed by the Indian private banks. From a "quantity" perspective however, the Indian private banks dominate with foreign banks coming up last.

It is important to bear in mind that the relatively lackluster efficiency of public sector banks is doubtless explained in part by their responsibility to serve small depositors, a group generally ignored by foreign banks as well as many "new" private sector banks; as well as by the provision of low-paid services like tax collection, maintaining and supervising pension and provident fund accounts. Also the smaller scale of foreign banks allows them to deploy a larger share of funds in advances rather than government securities.

Future research should probe into the nature and sources of the efficiency advantages in the different bank groups, as well as those at the individual bank level. Our analysis has abstracted from risk management issues as well as an explicit consideration of Government rules and directives that drive a wedge between the functioning of public sector banks and the private banks. It would be instructive to see to what extent such regulations determine the difference in efficiency between bank groups. A clearer understanding of the relationship between bank efficiency and overall social benefits would help us better evaluate these regulations. A better identification of the drivers of bank efficiency is essential for policy-makers, regulators and managers to improve standards in this most important sector of India's financial system.

NOTES

1. Koeva (2003). The Herfindahl index is a measure of industry concentration and is computed as the sum of the squared market shares of the firms in an industry. Ranging between 0 and 10,000, a lower Herfindahl index represents less concentration and greater competition.
2. A conclusion also supported by Koeva (2003).
3. D'Souza (2002).
4. D'Souza (2002).
5. See Sarkar, *et al.* (1998).
6. While *a priori* one would expect the threat of takeovers, rather than trading of shares *per se* to improve efficiency, recent evidence [see

Gupta (2005)] suggests that Indian public sector companies listing only a non-controlling part of the equity have experienced profitability and productivity enhancements.

7. See Kumbhakar and Sarkar (2003).
8. See Banerjee, *et al.* (2004) and Topalova (2004).
9. Topalova (2004).
10. See Berger and Humphrey (1997) for a survey of the literature and Mukherjee, *et al.* (2001), Casu, *et al.* (2004) and Kao and Liu (2004) for more recent applications of the DEA method to US, European and Korean banking sectors respectively.
11. See, for instance, Bhattacharya, *et al.* (1997), Saha and Ravishankar (2000), Das (2002), Sathye (2003), Bhaumik and Piesse (2003) and Galagedera and Edirisuriya (2004).
12. Bhattacharya, *et al.* (1997).
13. Sathye (2003).
14. Galagedera and Edirisuriya (2003).
15. This is the approach used in Bhattacharya, *et al.* (1997).
16. Changes rather than levels of these variables could also be used. It can also be argued that such a measure would be less affected by historical size differences among bank groups. However, given the fact that negative values cannot be used in the analysis, leading to a large loss in observations, the result would not be unbiased.
17. One of the models used in Sathye (2003).

REFERENCES

Banerjee Abhijit V., Shawn Cole and Esther Duflo, (2004). Banking Reform in India, *MIMEO*, MIT.

Berger, A.N. and Humphrey, D.B. (1997). "Efficiency of Financial Institutions: International Survey and Directions for Future Research", *European Journal of Operational Research*, 98, 175-212.

Bhattacharyya, A., Lovell, C.A.K. and Sahay, P. (1997). "The Impact of Liberalization on the Productive Efficiency of Indian Commercial Banks", *European Journal of Operational Research*, 98, 332-345.

Bhaumik, Sumon K. and Jenifer Piesse, (2003). "Are Foreign Banks Active in Emerging Credit Markets? Evidence From the Indian Banking Industry", *Working Paper*, Queen's University, Belfast.

Casu, Barbara, Claudia Girardone and Philip Molyneux, (2004). "Productivity Change in European Banking: A Comparison of Parametric and Non-parametric Approaches", *Journal of Banking & Finance,* Vol. 28, Issue 10, 2521-40.

D'Souza, Errol, (2002). How well have public sector banks done? A note. *Economic and Political Weekly*, March 2, 2002.

Das, Abhiman, (2002). Risk and productivity change of public sector banks, *Political Weekly*, February 2, 2002.

Galagadera, Don U.A. and Edirisuriya, P. (2004). Performance of Indian commercial banks (1995—2002): An application of data envelopment analysis and Malmquist productivity index, *Working Paper*, Monash University.

Gupta, Nandini, (2005). Partial privatization and firm performance, *The Journal of Finance,* Vol. LX, No. 2, 987-1015.

Kao, Chiang and Shiang-Tai Liu, (2004). Predicting bank performance with financial forecasts: A case of Taiwan commercial banks, *Journal of Banking & Finance,* Vol. 28, Issue 10, 2353-68.

Koeva, Petya, (2003). The performance of Indian banks during financial liberalization, *IMF Working Paper No.* 03/150.

Kumbhakar, S.C. and Sarkar, S. (2003). Deregulation, ownership, and productivity growth in the banking industry: Evidence from India, *Journal of Money, Credit, and Banking*, 35, 403-24.

Mukherjee, K., S.C. Ray and Miller, S.M. (2001). Productivity growth in large US commercial banks: The initial post-deregulation experience, *Journal of Banking & Finance,* Vol. 25, Issue 5, 913-39.

Saha, A. and Ravisankar, T.S. (2000). Rating of Indian commercial banks: A DEA approach, *European Journal of Operational Research*, 124, 187-203.

Sarkar, Subrata, Jayati Sarkar and Sumon K. Bhaumik, (1998). Does ownership always matter? Evidence from the Indian banking industry, *Journal of Comparative Economics*, Vol. 26, 262-81.

Sathye, Milind, (2003). Efficiency of banks in a developing economy: The case of India, *European Journal of Operational Research,* Vol. 148, Issue 3, 662-71.

Topalova, Petia, (2004). Overview of the Indian corporate sector: 1989—2002. *IMF Working Paper No.* 04/64.

Corporate Governance in Banks in India*

4

Y.V. Reddy

General Observations

... corporate governance, as a subject of significance for both public policy and markets, is of recent origin. It is useful to recognise that it is a dynamic concept, in terms of scope, thrust and relevance. For example, the issue is approached very differently today compared to original view of the Cadbury Committee on the subject. East-Asian crisis gave a new dimension to corporate governance in the context of financial stability. In U.S.A., the regulatory regimes, post-corporate scandals, are very different from those of the early 1990s. The OECD set out its corporate governance principles in 1999 but revised them in 2004. Basel Committee on Banking Supervision (under the aegis of the BIS) published guidelines on corporate governance in banks in 1999. As an update, in July 2005, the Basel Committee has issued a Consultative Document on enhancing corporate governance for banking organisations, seeking comments by end October 2005. I would advise that this document for now and the final document when released by BIS, should be a compulsory reading for all the regulators concerned and all the directors on the boards of the banks. The point to be noted is that corporate governance should be viewed as an ongoing process subject to rapid changes based on experiences, developments and policy-setting.

---

* Speech by Dr. Y.V. Reddy, Governor, Reserve Bank of India, at the Seminar on Corporate Governance for Bank Directors organized by the Indian Institute of Management, Bangalore; International Institute of Finance, Washington and the Indian Banks' Association on December 16, 2005 at Hotel Taj Palace, Mumbai. Reproduced from January 2006 issue of the Reserve Bank of India Bulletin.

There is considerable divergence in the understanding and practice of corporate governance in general, and in respect of banks, in particular, but there is also an increasing tendency towards convergence. The cultural context may be difficult to capture but the legal, institutional and attitudinal contexts do vary perceptibly across countries. Differences can be noticed even amongst the industrialised countries—say between Anglo-Saxon, European and Japanese situations. At the same time, the trend towards greater convergence is for several reasons. The corporates are getting listed in multiple stock exchanges in different countries and carry out corporate operations in several jurisdictions while the cross-border financial flows seek an assurance of some commonly understood standards of governance, which have a mutually reinforcing tendency. Banks, in particular, have been a subject of special interest for governance, especially in view of their fiduciary role. The cross-border operations of banks provide an added impetus for convergence in such standards.

Public policy framework in regard to corporate governance typically involves multiplicity of agencies in all countries. For instance, in India, these are Department of Company Affairs; Securities and Exchange Board of India in respect of listed entities apart from the banking regulator in respect of banks. Harmonising their policies in a dynamic setting is a daunting task for policy-makers and adds to the complexities of the corporates or banks concerned to ensure compliance.

In regard to sectors such as banking in India where ownership of government is dominant, there are additional issues. Government, as an owner, is accountable to political institutions in terms of broader socio-economic objectives and hence, its goals may not necessarily be compatible with purely economic incentives. Mixed ownership, with the government as a major shareholder, brings into sharper focus the possible divergent objectives of share-ownership in a corporate or a bank and issues relating to the rights of minority shareholders. The problem gets more complex if public ownership is exercised through separate legislation and not under the Company Law, normally applicable to other competing entities. The role of directors in such divergent organisational settings, therefore, needs a nuanced appreciation.

Let me end these general observations with an anecdote. When I was working in the World Bank in late 1970s, I joined the George Washington University for getting a taste of education in a foreign university. I took a course in management services. The Professor emphasised various aspects of organisational behaviour. I found that the best interest of the organisation that one serves was missing in the analysis. When I queried, he said: "It is your boss who interprets to you, what is good for the organisation." When I persisted, he added, "We deal with the corporate behaviour in the context of north American male in the U.S.A." I must confess that I continue to be old-fashioned. Any institution has, and in any case, should have a character, culture and interest that are worth pursuing even if they appear to be at variance from the sum of the interests of the individual, or the minority or the majority stakeholders....

Reserve Bank's Approach

The formal policy announcement in regard to corporate governance was first made by Dr. Bimal Jalan in the Mid-Term Review of the Monetary and Credit Policy on October 21, 2001. Pursuant to this announcement, a Consultative Group was constituted in November 2001 under the Chairmanship of Dr. A.S. Ganguly: basically, with a view to strengthen the internal supervisory role of the Boards. An Advisory Group on Corporate Governance under the chairmanship of Dr. R.H. Patil had earlier submitted its report in March 2001 which examined the issues relating to corporate governance in banks in India including the public sector banks and made recommendations to bring the governance standards in India on par with the best international standards. There were also some relevant observations by the Advisory Group on Banking Supervision under the chairmanship, Shri M.S. Verma which submitted its report in January 2003. Keeping all these recommendations in view and the cross-country experience, the Reserve Bank initiated several measures to strengthen the corporate governance in the Indian banking sector.

In June 2002, the report of the Ganguly Group was transmitted to all the banks for their consideration while simultaneously transmitting it to the Government of India for appropriate consideration. It may be noted here that there is a basic difference between the private sector banks and public sector banks as far as the Reserve Bank's role in governance matters relevant to banking is concerned. The current regulatory framework ensures, by and large, uniform treatment of private and public sector banks by the Reserve Bank in so far as prudential aspects are concerned. However, some of the governance aspects of public sector banks, though they have a bearing on prudential aspects, are exempted from applicability of the relevant provisions of the B.R. Act, as they are governed by the respective legislations under which various public sector banks were set up. In brief, therefore, the approach of RBI has been to ensure, to the extent possible, uniform treatment of the public sector and the private sector banks in regard to prudential regulations. In regard to governance aspects relevant to banking, the Reserve Bank prescribes its policy framework for the private sector banks while suggesting to the Government the same framework for adoption, as appropriate, consistent with the legal and policy imperatives.

As a follow-up of the Ganguly Committee report, in Mid-Term Review of the Monetary and Credit Policy in November 2003, the concept of 'fit and proper' criteria for directors of banks was formally enunciated, and it included the process of collecting information, exercising due diligence and constitution of a Nomination Committee of the board to scrutinise the declarations made by the bank directors. In this regard, it will be useful to refer to the RBI guidelines on ownership and governance in the private sector banks released recently.

It is heartening to note that based on the guidelines issued by RBI, all the banks in the private sector have carried out, through their nomination committees, the exercise of due diligence in respect of the directors on their Boards. In some cases, where the track record of the directors was not considered satisfactory, the directors vacated their positions. In regard to some others, there is an on-going process to ensure 'fit and proper' status of the directors.

In this regard, it may be useful to distinguish the issue of the composition of the Board from the 'fit and proper' status of individual non-executive directors and chief executives. The first relates to collective expertise on the Board available to meet the competitive challenges before the bank to ensure commercial activity while maintaining soundness. The existing legal provisions in regard to banks stipulate specific areas of background that a director should be drawn from such as accountancy, banking, economics, finance, agriculture, etc., but do not specify the extent or degree of professionalism or expertise required in regard to that area. Hence, it is left to the good faith of the shareholders to elect directors from the various specified areas with qualifications and experience that is appropriate to the bank. In regard to public sector banks, such good faith is expected when directors are nominated by government.

However, when the issue of 'fit and proper' status of non-executive directors comes up, the norms only seek to ensure that the candidate should not have come to the adverse notice of the law and regulations or any professional body so that there is no objection from the RBI. In the case of non-executive directors not satisfying the 'fit and proper' criteria, there is a prescribed due process to be followed by the RBI to disqualify such directors, which includes opportunities to be heard. The position in regard to the CEOs of the private sector banks is on a different footing where the Reserve Bank is in a position to exercise its judgement on the suitability of the candidates proposed, in as much as the approval of the Reserve Bank is required for the appointment and the RBI may seek removal also. These provisions are broadly consistent with global best practices though there is scope for enhancing effective implementation.

There is no legal provision as of now for the Reserve Bank to insist on the 'fit and proper' status of the directors nominated by the government or elected by the shareholders to the Boards of the public sector banks. The appointment of the CEOs in the public sector banks, as well as their removal, is also a matter to be decided only by the Government of India. There is, however, active consultation with the Reserve Bank in regard to appointment of CEOs. Thus, by and large, there is *de facto* compliance with many governance requirements in public sector banks.

Way Forward

As a step towards distancing the regulator from the functioning of the Boards, the Reserve Bank has withdrawn its nominee directors from almost all the private sector banks. Observers have been appointed as a transitional measures mostly in respect of those banks which are yet to fully comply with the Reserve Bank's guidelines of ownership of governance. It is hoped that the need for observers also will diminish as the quality of governance improves.

Second, legislative amendments have been proposed in regard to the public sector banks to remove the provisions for mandatory nomination of RBI officers on their boards and thus, to bring them on par with the private sector banks in this regard.

Third, the Government has been requested to keep in view the policy framework for governance in private sector banks while deciding on the appointments of the directors on the Boards of public sector banks and constitution of various committees of the Board.

Fourth, the RBI, as far as possible, has recently been refraining from issuing circulars or instructions specifically addressed to the public sector banks. It is expected that all the existing instructions specifically applicable to the public sector banks will be reviewed by the Reserve Bank so that uniformity in regulatory framework between different categories of banks is formally established.

Fifth, several amendments to the Banking Regulation Act have been proposed which would enhance RBI's capacity to ensure sound governance specially relevant to the banks, consistent with global best practices.

In regard to urban cooperative banks (UCBs), there are unique problems which need to be addressed. Since all the governance aspects of urban cooperative banks fall entirely within the jurisdiction of the State Governments, while only prudential aspects are in the RBI's domain, it has been difficult to ensure effective coordination owing to the problems of dual control in the matters of governance which have a bearing on prudential regulation. Further, the market discipline in terms of shareholders' influence on governance does not exist in regard to urban cooperative banks since they do not depend on equity markets for their funds. Moreover, the governance structure in the UCBs seems to be tilted in favour of the borrowers from the UCBs, thus, possibly undermining the interest of the depositors. Currently, to avoid problems of dual control, a mechanism of Memorandum of Understanding (MoU) with the State Governments, is being attempted. RBI has entered into such MoUs with Andhra Pradesh, Gujarat and Karnataka and is providing facilities for upgrading the skills of the members of the Board and the management of the UCBs, in these States.

The problem of dual control is even more acute in regard to the rural cooperative credit structure. However, these are being currently addressed by the Government of India in the light of the recommendations of the Vaidyanathan Committee.

The RRBs are yet another category of banks which are actually owned, in a pre-determined pattern, by the State, Centre and the sponsor banks. The sponsor banks are virtually managing the RRBs and the issues of governance of these institutions are yet to be addressed. Deposit taking NBFCs and, perhaps, NBFCs with systemic implications may also need to be considered for a careful review of their current governance practices in view of their unique role and expanding importance in our financial sector.

Conclusion

Let me conclude with a reiteration that the Reserve Bank is continuously striving to ensure compliance with international standards and best practices of corporate governance in banks as relevant to India. RBI is also interacting closely with the

Government and the SEBI in this regard. Increasing regulatory comfort in regard to standards of governance in banks gives greater confidence to shift from external regulation to internal systems of controls and risk-management. Each of the directors of the banks has a role in continually enhancing the standards of governance in banks through a combination of appropriate knowledge and values....

Central Banks and Risk Management: Pursuing Financial Stability*

5

Rakesh Mohan

...Although financial stability has always been of concern to central banks, it is a relatively new concept in terms of the widespread attention being given to it in recent years.... Achieving this understanding would also help in explaining some of the behaviour of central banks.

Financial Stability: What Is It?

What is financial stability? Despite widespread usage of the term, there is no widespread agreement on a useful working definition of the term. Some define financial stability in terms of what it is not—the absence of financial instability. Others take a more macro-prudential view and specify financial stability in terms of limitation of risks of significant real output losses in the presence of episodes of system wide financial distress.

In the absence of a widely accepted definition it is useful to discuss what we expect a financial system to do.

The primary function of the financial system is to smoothly and efficiently facilitate inter-temporal allocation of resources from savers to the ultimate users. This process of intermediation of funds enables the utilisation of available resources to their most productive uses. Such a process implies management of financial risk on an inter-temporal basis. In doing so however, the financial system is expected to absorb real economic surprises and shocks. If for some reason this is not done well, it could impair the efficient functioning of the financial system as a whole and engender financial instability.

But we need to be careful in thinking about financial instability. Disturbances in financial markets or at individual

* Reproduced from December 2006 issue of the Reserve Bank of India Bulletin.

financial institutions need not constitute financial instability if they do not impair overall economic functioning. Illustratively, a closure of a small financial institution, or for that matter, movement in asset prices within certain limits or even minor corrections in financial markets need not necessarily hamper stability. On the contrary, fluctuations in asset and other prices in financial markets may actually be good for overall financial stability as adjustment mechanisms. Such market adjustments also help to keep authorities alert and sensitive to incipient developments and can enable them to identify and monitor newer risks. What are important from the macroeconomic standpoint are issues related to contagion and systemic risk, which can lead to economy-wide upheavals and would, therefore, need to be monitored on an on-going basis.

The point of making these observations is that unlike price stability, which can be easily quantified, financial stability cannot be easily summarised into a single measure. As a consequence, monitoring financial stability needs to encompass not only financial institutions and markets, but also the state of financial infrastructure: a stable financial system depends as much on the health of financial institutions as it does on the complex inter-linkages between those institutions and the interplay between the financial system, the financial markets and the associated financial infrastructure. The integrity of the payment system is at the core of the financial system, and confidence in the use of money as a unit of account is essential to maintenance of financial stability. While central bankers have always been concerned with addressing these aforesaid aspects, the issue therefore remains: why is there an overt concern with financial stability in modern-day financial systems?

Historical Background

To understand the current outbreak of concerns, let us review a little bit of history. It would be useful to start of with salient developments in the world economy since the early 1900s in order to understand the relevance of financial stability in modern day financial systems.

Until World War I, the international experience had broadly been of long run price and monetary stability. A great degree of turbulence followed after the conclusion of World War I: the German hyper-inflation, the Great Depression, World War II itself, the Korean war, and later the Vietnam war. It is not surprising that in the presence of such economic and political dislocation, price and financial stability also suffered during this period. The financing of wars led to fiscal expansionism usually financed by money creation. Thus a period of relatively high inflation ensued in the 1960s and 1970s, culminating in double digit inflation in the US and Western Europe in the late 1970s, spiked by severe oil shocks of the 1970s. Thus, after this long tumultuous period of fluctuating inflation during the 1960s and 1970s, aggressive disinflationary policies of the early 1980s brought international inflation down to tolerable levels.

Prior to World War I, the gold standard was, in some sense, the anchor of monetary, price and financial stability. Central Banks' commitment to ensuring the convertibility of their currency into gold at fixed prices did much to engender confidence in the system. There was also a significant degree of cooperation among the central banks and governments of major economies, which helped to lubricate the system in its functions in times of financial imbalances (Eichengreen, 1992). The gold standard, however, came under severe strain after World War I in the wake of the breakdown in cooperation between countries. The consequence was the depression, competitive devaluations, beggar thy neighbour policies, decline in world trade and high unemployment, at different times in different countries during the inter war period. Overall, there was a great degree of instability during this period.

The quest for a new international economic order that would restore economic and financial stability in the world gave rise to the Bretton Woods institutions and the Bretton Woods Currency System. It was not until 1958 that most European currencies became convertible and many currency adjustments took place after the end of World War II. The anchor now was essentially the US dollar as the reserve currency and the commitment to its convertibility to gold. The International

Monetary Fund was to act as the lender of last resort in case of balance of payment crises. But even this fixed exchange rate system lasted only till 1971. The over-financing of exports, the economic pick up in hitherto war torn countries led to the glut of the dollar; and the American inflation of the 1960s; all contributed to the cessation of dollar convertibility to gold. The fixed exchange rate system got abandoned after the Smithsonian agreement. The floating exchange rates that then followed meant that the world was left without an easily understood, credible monetary anchor. Hence the increasing quest for methodologies promoting financial stability.

The other major feature of global financial markets has been the trends in capital flows. A major surge in capital flows started around the 1870s and continued till World War I. This era, which coincided with the operation of the gold standard, has been regarded until recently as the golden era of capital mobility. Open trade and open labour markets also characterized this period. In retrospect, there was an effective system shut down after World War I, almost until the 1970s. During the inter war period, the world economic system got characterized by increasing trade restrictions, high tariffs, curbs on capital flows, fixed exchange rates and other rigidities. Post World War II it has taken a long time to open up international trade through the successive GATT rounds and now through the WTO.

The period after 1973 has been characterized by floating exchange rates and gradually increasing international capital flows, along with increasing volumes of international trade. The geographical demarcation of national borders gradually became less of a constraint for both trade and capital flows. By the 1990s, open trade and open capital accounts led to a phenomenal growth cross border flows, including to developing countries and the emerging economies in Eastern Europe.

All this entailed a phenomenal expansion of financial activity. This was partly in response to the demographically-driven increase in the amount of investible wealth, but also reflected the increased need for markets and institutions to channel funds between an increasingly active and diverse range of borrowers and lenders.

At the same time, domestic financial liberalization led to the removal of constraints on the activities of financial institutions of different kinds within a given national market in many countries. The liberalization of cross-border capital movements and rights of market access meant that a broader range of domestic and foreign institutions were able to provide banking and other financial services in a given market. The range of services on offer also expanded; and an increasing number of both markets and institutions became active across national boundaries. While this entailed lower costs of products and services for consumers, this also entailed the possibility of contagion with ramifications extending well beyond national borders particularly in the context of inadequate development of financial markets in some countries.

On the flip side, however, this transformation of the financial marketplace extended and tightened linkages across markets and institutions, increasing the uniformity of the information sets available to economic agents and encouraging greater similarity in the assessment of information, driven to a large extent by advances in information technology and communications networking. This, in effect, meant that weaknesses in the financial system could engender serious and far more disruptive economic consequences than was previously the case, and could increasingly engender contagion effects extending well beyond national boundaries. The Mexican crisis of 1994-95, the East Asian crises of 1997-98 and the more recent crises in Argentina and Turkey are ample testimony to this fact. At the national level, the banking crises in Nordic countries in the 1980s and 1990s, the problems in the Philippines and Korean banking systems in the 1990s (and the near panic at the time of the LTCM affair), and the financial bubble in Japan whose costs are felt even at present, deserve mention.

During the 1980s and 1990s, nearly one hundred national banking systems collapsed, many more than in any comparable previous period. The range of movements in exchange rates and the extent of deviations in market exchange rates from real exchange rates—the magnitude of undershooting and overshooting—were larger than in any previous period. There were also massive asset price bubbles in some countries: Japan, Sweden, Thailand, South East Asian countries like, Malaysia and finally in the United States.

All this meant that the sources of crises, which were earlier traced primarily to weaknesses in banking systems, became manifold, and could emanate from any segment of the financial sector with possibilities of spillovers to other sectors and countries. More importantly, as the Asian crises amply demonstrated, such crises could even affect economies with sound real sector fundamentals. The deficiencies in the international financial architecture meant that the IMF was no longer large enough to take care of the crises. The earlier concerns on banking stability therefore become much larger in scope and content, to assume the term 'financial stability'.

These developments have had several consequences for the institutional and systemic structure. Among the most important of these from the point of view of systemic significance has been disintermediation. Credit-worthy firms are relying increasingly on capital markets, rather than bank loans, to finance investment projects. This has led to the deepening of capital markets of various kinds, as well as to a more important role for the institutions that deal in traded securities.

A second important structural change is the emergence of markets for risks of different kinds, in which exposures to specific market or credit risk can be bought and sold separately from financial assets. This has provided economic agents the leeway to reduce or increase their exposure to specific categories of risk.

A third key trend has been changes in the business profile of financial institutions. In many countries, services traditionally associated with "banking" are now offered by institutions not legally characterized as banks, while banks are increasingly engaged in para-banking activities.

These fundamental changes—deregulation, liberalization and disintermediation—have, not surprisingly, made financial systems far more interconnected, with possible ramifications for contagion in the event of an exigency in any country. As a consequence, central banks, which were traditionally focused on monetary and banking stability, have increasingly come to focus on financial stability as a key concern in the conduct of monetary policy.

How are Central Banks Responding to This Development?

Avoiding crises becomes ultimately a national responsibility. The impact of instability in times of crisis typically tends to be borne by domestic taxpayers rather than the global private entities. The burden of such an asymmetric adjustment means that there is a need to institute domestic mechanisms that could focus on the aspect of financial stability on an ongoing basis. As institutions traditionally mandated with the task of price stability, central banks became the natural choice for governments to be entrusted with oversight of financial stability.

Given that financial stability has become a paramount focus of central banks, the key question therefore arises is: how are central banks responding to the challenge? Interestingly, new legislations explicitly provide mandates for financial stability; illustratively, Hungary passed such legislation in 2001, the Netherlands in 1993, Spain in 1994 and the UK in 1997.

So, the question is why have the central banks become interested in financial stability? Central banks are clearly responsible for issue of currency, maintaining its value as a means of exchange and unit of account. They are also responsible for maintaining the efficiency and integrity of payment systems. Ultimately, they are the lenders of last resort. Notwithstanding the complexity involved, evidence suggests that involvement in financial stability can be broadly categorised into five types of activities. Being a key fulcrum of the policy apparatus responsible for financial stability, central banks might be involved in several of these tasks.

First, *oversight of the financial infrastructure*: This involves the operation as well as oversight of the payments and settlement systems and securities clearing system. It might also involve oversight of financial disclosures, market conduct and the like. It is important to note that all at the markets need the payment system, including the capital market.

Second, *regulation and supervision of financial entities*: This involves the formulation of prudential guidelines (capital adequacy and reserve requirements, provisioning norms, risk management standards), the monitoring of compliance with those rules (on-site inspection and off-site surveillance) and the imposition of sanctions in case of non-compliance.

Third, *safety net provisions*: This involves decisions to restructure troubled banks as well as 'honest brokering'. It also involves the operation of financial safety net in the form of deposit insurance.

Fourth, *liquidity*: The response to a crisis may necessitate judicious use of the emergency liquidity assistance facilities in order to avoid disruptions from disorderly failures and to contain contagious strain. Only central banks can inject liquidity.

Fifth, *market surveillance*: Central banks are often involved in the regulation and surveillance of markets. The three markets that are primarily the focus of surveillance by central banks are the money, bond and foreign exchange markets.

In addition, central banks are typically concerned with *macro financial stability*. This encompasses monitoring the behaviour of all important players in the financial sector, the health of non-financial sector balance sheets as well as assessment of systemic vulnerabilities. This analysis is accompanied by communication policy on financial stability issues, either through dedicated financial stability reports or disclosure of information on financial stability as part of regular reports (Annex 1). The basic motive behind such reports is to communicate to the markets and the public at large and thereby express the commitment of the central bank for achieving its objectives. This is accompanied by a process of structured communication among the various bodies involved in the pursuit of financial stability.

In their quest for financial stability, central banks worldwide have exhibited a variety of responses. On the one hand, several central banks have been given an explicit mandate to promote financial stability (Annex 2). Another broad category of response has been the constitution of independent departments to oversee financial stability. Illustratively, at the Reserve Bank of New Zealand, the supervisory and financial market departments were merged into a Financial Stability Department. At the ECB, the area concerned with financial stability matters (Prudential Supervision Division) was upgraded to a Directorate (Financial Stability and Supervision), which reports to a member of the Executive Board, and plays a coordination role for euro area/EU financial stability monitoring. Finally, the Bank of England has also constituted a dedicated Financial Stability Department for oversight of financial stability matters, headed by a Deputy Governor. The transfer of supervisory responsibilities outside the central bank in several countries has also led central banks to focus their attention on systemic issues as reflected in a reorientation of organisational arrangements.

The crux of these observations is that financial stability has been a prime locus of change in central banks and increasingly, central banks are taking a pro-active stance to address the threats posed by financial instability. The *Financial Stability Forum*, for instance, was created in the aftermath of the Asian financial crisis, comprising members as major countries, international financial institutions such as BIS and IMF and the international standard setters such as International Organisation of Securities Commissions (IOSCO) and International Association of Insurance Supervisors (IAIS).

Having traced the broad contours of the growing importance of financial stability worldwide and the role played by central banks in the process, let us see how the Reserve Bank has been responding to the challenge.

Indian Experience on Financial Stability—An Overview

Till the onset of reforms in the early 1990s, India was a relatively closed economy, being largely insulated from the vicissitudes of global markets. It was not, of course, totally insulated from exogenous shocks. The severe drought of 1965 to 1967, the oil shocks of 1973, 1979 and 1989, and wars all had significant effects including the emergence of external payments crises. However, the financial system was effectively controlled, particularly in the 1970s and 1980s and the risk of financial contagion was therefore not high.

The gradual opening up of the economy since the 1990s raised several important challenges for central bankers. The opening of the external sector meant that developments in India came to be increasingly influenced by developments abroad. It is interesting to look at some numbers. Contrary to various perceptions, the Indian economy is now substantively open. As the Finance Minister observed in a lecture at Yale University, whereas India's GDP in 2004-05 was roughly US $700 billion, the gross flows on the current account and the capital account, put together, came to US $500 billion. This is despite the fact that trade tariffs are still higher than in most other countries in the world, and that capital account controls still exist. The large capital inflows, despite the cautious approach to liberalization, meant that such flows can engender volatility in exchange rate movements. The speed of capital flows, both inward and outward, is much higher than current account flows and can therefore destabilize the exchange rate, and operation of financial and capital markets, possibly in response to external events unconnected with the domestic economy (Jalan, 2003). Consequently, we have to be concerned with exchange rate instability, as distinguished from mere fluctuation, for its potential to affect other markets, both goods and capital markets. Exchange rate instability arising from external events can give rise to domestic instability in the operation of the stock market, government securities markets, and the money markets, along with their attendant effects. For emerging economies such as India, it therefore becomes necessary to institute special defenses for ensuring financial stability. Furthermore, with the interest rate emerging as a key channel of monetary policy signals, the efficacy of monetary transmission is predicated on the health of the financial sector. The gradual liberalization of the financial sector has also witnessed the emergence of conglomerates, with attendant systemic implications.

More broadly however, the period since the 1990s has been testimony to several shocks impinging on the economy. Illustratively, nuclear sanctions and the border tensions in the late 1990s, the monsoon vagaries in the recent past, most recently in 2003, the crises in East Asia in 1997 and 1998, the upheaval in domestic stock markets in May 2004 coupled with the recurrent oil price fluctuations, has meant that the economy has been susceptible to intermittent shocks. And unlike the shocks of earlier decades, the economy has been able to withstand these disruptions with limited impact on the financial sector. The role of central banks in such a milieu is not hard to foresee. The response of the Reserve Bank in May 2004 is a case in point. Judged thus, the role of Reserve Bank in its task of monitoring financial stability can hardly be over-emphasized.

Financial stability has, therefore, emerged as a key consideration in the conduct of monetary policy. In this process, the Reserve Bank has adopted a two-track approach in the pursuit of financial stability. First, by ensuring monetary stability through lowering of inflation, it has lowered inflationary expectations, thereby fostering financial stability. Second, the Reserve Bank has adopted a multi-pronged strategy, with suitable country-specific adaptations, to promote stability of financial institutions, financial markets and the financial infrastructure. The stable economic regime combined with the macro financial oversight of the financial system has imparted confidence to market players to conduct their business in an orderly manner.

In general, it is possible to discern two broad sets of instruments by which the Reserve Bank has been addressing the financial stability concerns: preventive instruments, comprising micro and macro-prudential measure and reactive instruments, comprising liquidity support measures and public intervention tools aimed at safeguarding depositors' interests.

With regard to *institutions*, the Reserve Bank founded the Board of Financial Supervision in 1994 to upgrade its practice of financial supervision. A set of prudential norms for the commercial banking sector had been instituted as early as 1994 with regard to capital adequacy, income recognition and asset classification (IRAC), provisioning, exposure norms and more recently, in respect of their investment portfolio. The approach adopted here was one of gradual convergence with international best practices, while internalizing it to suit country-specific requirements. In tandem with the gradual opening up of the economy, the regulatory and supervisory framework was spruced up comprising of a three-pronged strategy of regular on-site inspections, technology-driven off-site surveillance and extensive use of external auditors. As a result of improvements in the regulatory and supervisory framework, the degree of compliance with the Basel *Core Principles* has gradually improved. The supervisory framework has been further upgraded with the institution of a framework of Risk-based Supervision (RBS) for intensified monitoring of vulnerabilities. A scheme of Prompt Corrective Action (PCA) was effected in December 2002 to undertake mandatory and discretionary intervention against troubled banks based on well-defined financial/prudential parameters. In view of the growing emergence of financial conglomerates and the possibility of systemic risks arising therefrom, a system of consolidated accounting has been instituted. A half-yearly review based on financial soundness indicators is being undertaken to assess the health of individual institutions and macro-prudential indicators associated with financial system soundness. The findings arising thereof are disseminated to the public through its various Reports. In fact, in 2003 the Reserve Bank published a chapter titled 'Financial Stability' in its Report on *Currency and Finance* in that year, highlighting its challenges and problems in the pursuit of stability. Subsequently, with effect from 2004, the annual statutory Report of Trend and Progress of Banking in India has began to publish a dedicated chapter on financial stability. This is in addition to the Monetary and Credit Policy Review where the Governor highlights the threats and challenges to the financial environment before announcing policy measures.

Given the multi-faceted nature of financial stability, no one body might be in a position to monitor it in its entirety. Keeping this in view, the Ministry of Finance has constituted a High-Level Coordination Committee on Financial and Capital Markets with the Governor, RBI, Chairman, Securities and Exchange Board of India (SEBI) and Chairman, Insurance Regulatory and Development Authority (IRDA) along with the Finance Secretary,

Government of India as members to address policy gaps and overlaps.

An important aspect of the financial stability process has been the growing emphasis on the role of market discipline. As part of the process, the Reserve Bank has laid strong emphasis on the levels of transparency and standards of disclosure in banks' balance sheets. These disclosures, presently supplemented as 'Notes on Accounts' not only encompasses prudential ratio pertaining to capital adequacy (tier-I and tier-II separately) ratio, non-performing loans, exposure to sensitive sectors (capital market, real estate and commodities), but also financial ratios such as interest and non-interest income as percentage of working funds, return on average assets and net profit per employee. These disclosures have been gradually expanded over time and presently include maturity pattern of assets and liabilities (both Rupee and FC), movements in non-performing loans, issuer composition of non-SLR investment, assets subject to corporate debt restructuring as well as details of assets sold to Securitisation/ Reconstruction company.

....The performance of the non-financial sector has an important bearing on financial stability. Keeping this in view, the Reserve Bank has also been closely monitoring the stability ratios of the non-financial sector. In the corporate sector for instance, the reduction in debt liabilities following corporate restructuring and reduced interest expenses in an environment of low interest rates has improved the financial stability indicators in manufacturing. Available indications are that both consumption and investment demand are currently buoyant. Business surveys also point to high levels of both business confidence and capacity utilisation. The improved investment sentiment and business confidence, as reflected in the increasing number of firms incurring capital expenditure, suggests the prospects for buoyant manufacturing growth in 2005-06.

....Issues of governance in banks has assumed relevance worldwide in the wake of accounting irregularities in the US and elsewhere. Problems in governance can derail even the best efforts on the part of regulators to ensure financial stability. To address this aspect, the Reserve Bank issued guidelines on ownership and governance based on well-defined principles, *viz.* a well-diversified ownership and control; important shareholders being 'fit and proper'; directors and CEO being 'fit and proper' and observation of sound corporate governance principles.

An important hallmark of the pursuit of financial stability in India has been the adoption of a consultative approach to policy formulation, taking on board the various stakeholders in the financial system. Such an approach has had the merit of providing useful lead time to market participants to adjust their behavior in conformity to the regulatory guidelines.

Evidence suggests that no two crises are exactly alike. As a result, in addition to preventative instruments just discussed, the Reserve Bank had also resorted to reactive instruments.

One such instrument is *emergency liquidity support*. Thus, in very rare and unusual circumstances, when a bank faces a sudden and unforeseen liquidity problem, the Reserve Bank has, on an earlier occasion, at its discretion, extended liquidity support to the bank.

A second such instrument is the *provision of safety net* in the form of deposit insurance (DI). In India, DI is mandatory and covers all banks (commercial/cooperative/RRBs/LABs). All deposits except (a) deposits of foreign governments, (b) deposits of Central/ State Governments, (c) inter-bank deposits and (d) deposits held abroad are covered by DICGC. The amount of coverage is presently Rs. 1 lakh (Rs. 100,000), and is provided to deposits held in the same right and in the same capacity. Given the present limit, as much as 95 per cent of deposit accounts and 66 per cent of assessable deposits are fully protected. Given the level of per capita GDP at constant prices (Rs. 15017 in 2004), this implies that the coverage limit is roughly 6 times the per capita GDP (Annex 3). The premium is charged on a flat rate basis, which is presently 8 paise per Rs. 100 of assessable deposits for the year 2004-05 and 10 paise from 2005-06 (earlier it was 5 paise per Rs. 100 of assessable deposits).

A third instrument is *treatment of insolvent banks* (winding down). The Reserve Bank, rather than closing them down, has shown a preference for merging such banks with healthy banks.

The rationale behind such an approach has been dictated by two considerations. First, given the dominance of commercial banks, their closure can raise systemic concerns. Second, given that a significant portion of bank depositors in India are small, it is imperative to safeguard their interests, while dealing with insolvent banks (Mohan, 2004).

The second broad element of strategy has been the development of financial markets. Ensuring orderly conditions in *financial markets* has been an important component of the Reserve Bank's approach towards financial stability. The cornerstone of the process has been to widen, deepen and integrate various segments of financial markets to enable the price discovery process, lower transactions costs and enhance market liquidity. Accordingly, the operating procedures of monetary policy have been continuously fine-tuned to attune it to the realities of market dynamics.

In the *money market*, the focus has been on developing a deep and liquid money market, supplanted by a wide array of instruments to modulate monetary conditions with a relative emphasis on indirect policy instruments to enable swift responses to changing market conditions. In the face of large capital flows, a new facility in the form of Market Stabilisation Scheme (MSS) was instituted in April 2004. The MSS essentially seeks to differentiate the liquidity absorption of a more enduring nature by way of sterilisation from the day-to-day normal liquidity management operations.

In the *foreign exchange market*, the exchange rate policy adopted by India has been one of managing volatility with no fixed target, while allowing the underlying demand and supply conditions to determine the exchange rate movements over a period in an orderly way. Market players are also enabled to manage risk through various designated hedging instruments. Prudent management of the external sector coupled with a calibrated approach to capital account liberalization has been an important component of macroeconomic policy to ensure financial stability.

In the *government bond market*, the major objectives of reforms were to impart liquidity and depth to the market by broadening the investor base and ensuring market-clearing interest rate mechanism. The important initiatives introduced included a market-related government borrowing and consequently, a phased elimination of automatic monetisation of Central Government budget deficits. This, in turn, enabled the shift from direct to indirect tools of monetary regulation—activating open market operations and the development of secondary market. The entire range of changes necessitated developments in (a) instruments, (b) institutions and (c) technology, along with concomitant improvements in (d) transparency and (e) the legal framework. As of April 1, 2006 the FRBM Act now prohibits the Reserve Bank from subscribing to government securities in the primary market. This has necessitated the further development of techniques and instruments to ensure stability in the G-securities market.

Developing a robust and secure *financial infrastructure* has been a key component of financial stability. Towards this end, the Reserve Bank undertook several initiatives to upgrade the payment and settlement system in the country. Salient among these included Electronic Clearing Service, Electronic Funds Transfer, establishment of a secured private network which serves as a private gateway to the financial system. Based on the framework prevalent in developed financial markets, a Real Time Gross Settlement (RTGS) system has been operationalised. The RTGS provides for an electronic-based settlement of inter-bank and customer-based transactions with intra-day collateralised liquidity support from the Reserve Bank. Side by side, in its quest for benchmarking with international best practices, the Reserve Bank has benchmarked its conformity with the *Core Principles for Systematically Important Payment System* (*CPSS*). The degree of compliance with these *Principles* is presently on par with those prevailing internationally.

Challenges to Financial Stability

Given the inherent dynamic nature of financial stability, its operationalization raises several challenges.

First, the changing structure of the financial system with the blurring of boundaries between financial institutions and markets raises significant policy challenges. As I remarked earlier, services traditionally associated with 'banking' are presently being offered by institutions not legally characterized as banks, while banks are increasingly engaged in para-banking activities. Such 'conglomerisation' of financial activity raises the possibility of systemic risk with attendant implications for financial contagion, which lies at the very root of financial instability.

Second, in this context coordination between the regulators assumes paramount importance. In recognition of these concerns, the Reserve Bank has taken a structured approach to their surveillance by instituting a coordinated monitoring mechanism with other domestic regulators (SEBI and IRDA) on matters of supervision of financial conglomerates. In addition, the Reserve Bank has been holding half-yearly discussions with the Chief Executive Officers of the conglomerate in association with other principal regulators to address outstanding issues and supervisory concerns. This process is working well at present. However, as financial development takes place in India we can expect further blurring of distinction between different types of financial intermediaries. We can also expect greater presence of large financial conglomerates, including foreign ones. Hence, we need to consider the development of a more organized approach to the regulation and oversight of the emerging financial conglomerates as has been done in other countries. In the United States, for example, the Federal Reserve Board has been designed as the lead umbrella supervisor of financial holding companies (FHCs). Pending such developments, as a workable measure, there could be need to execute general/specific memoranda of understanding (MoU) as part of the process of supervisory co-ordination towards furtherance of financial stability.

Third, another significant feature of the Indian economy post-reforms has been the greater opening up of the economy. The size of merchandise, as well as services trade, has been increasing steadily in recent years, reflecting greater integration of the economy with the rest of the world. The recent experience also suggests subtle shifts in international comparative advantage with software, business and commercial services gaining prominence. Overall capital flows have also been buoyant, given the positive outlook on the economy. The large capital flows have, in turn, resulted in accumulation of reserves, rendering the reserve position comfortable according to various indicators of reserve adequacy. While these developments have resulted in benefits, it has also made the economy much less quarantined from global developments and the task of central bankers that much more difficult than in the erstwhile autarkic regime. As a result, central bankers have to be continuously alert and watchful not only to domestic but also global developments because, as the Asian crises testifies, developments abroad can have significant domestic ramifications even for an economy with perfectly sound fundamentals.

Fourth, the spread of the financial system with growing liberalization of the economy and the increasing reach of formal finance has gradually expanded to cover larger segments of the population. The 'demographic dividend' of a larger and younger labour force has meant that banks have been able to expand their loan portfolio quite rapidly, enabling consumers to satisfy their lifestyle aspirations at a relatively young age with an optimal combination of equity and debt to finance consumption and asset creation. On the other side, such opening up has also meant that interest rates have become a much more potent tool of monetary policy, affecting consumption and investment decisions of the population in a fashion much more rapidly than was the case earlier. With a sizeable proportion of the population having limited ability to insure themselves against unforeseen contingencies, there is merit in considering the need to devise 'shock absorbers' in order to insulate the economy from contagion effects. Continuous and pro-active efforts towards developing a robust financial system and instituting appropriate market surveillance mechanisms that can throw up 'early warning signals' of financial distress are important parameters of such resilience.

The fifth challenge to the maintenance of financial stability lies in the increasing growth of the economy. The traditional measure of national accounting does not take cognizance of the knowledge flows that create value in the medium to long run. This phenomenal growth of the knowledge economy and its value-enhancing effect are only recently being addressed for the US economy. Judged from this standpoint, it seems that central banks would not only need to keep track of traditional measures of consumption and investment, but in addition, have a hang of the knowledge flows across borders in order to assess the impact of its decisions on the real economy. This is easier said than done and moving ahead from the traditional accounting framework to a more 'realistic' one incorporating 'knowledge flows' is a challenging task that central bankers will have to deal with sometime sooner than later.

Another challenge relates to the issue of coordination policy-making bodies. Instabilities can arise in any segment of the financial system and not necessarily in segments which are under the domain of the Reserve Bank, although through contagion effects, their effects are likely to be felt across the entire financial sector. This calls for closer and continuous coordination among the various policy-making bodies, including an even broader set of players such as accounting standard setters, legislators and tax authorities. The multiplicity of policy actors emphasizes the need for a cooperative organization of policy efforts in this regard.

The opening of trade has meant the death of commodity inflation. The expectations of financial market participants on financial variables are different from the market expectations of commodity prices. The recent surge in the stock market is likely to engender the 'wealth effect', which through multiplier process, is likely to spillover into prices and more particularly, into asset prices. Although such a phenomenon is widely acknowledged, attempting to precisely quantify the spillover from commodity to asset prices and the magnitude of such over-extension remains a challenge. There is a need in this context for serious analytical work that can explore the link in the movements between commodity prices and asset prices.

Concluding Thoughts

Over the last few years, the global financial system has been buffeted by a number of pressures and some unprecedented shocks. Nonetheless, the system has continued to prove resilient and financial stability has been maintained. Potential fault lines that have emerged in the process, *viz.* those pertaining to corporate governance, auditing and accounting standards and prudential norms have been receiving close scrutiny from policy-makers.

The Indian financial system is not quarantined from global developments, but our judgment is that it remains robust, underpinned by the continued expansion of the Indian economy. The task for all of us is therefore to remain alert and proactive, identify and address newer risks, eschew harmful incentives and adjust the regulatory environment to address any unforeseen contingency in the economic environment.

REFERENCES

Eichengreen, Berry (1992): *Golden Fetters: The Gold Standard and the Great Depression, 1919—1939*. New York: Oxford University Press.

Jalan, Bimal (2003): "Exchange Rate Management: An Emerging Consensus?" Address the 14th National Assembly of Forex Association of India on August 14, 2003, *RBI Bulletin*, September 2003.

Manded, Michael (2006): "Why the Economy is a Lot Stronger than you Think: In a knowledge-Based World, the Traditional Measures Don't Tell the Story", *Business Week*, February 13, 2006, 63-70.

Mohan, Rakesh (2004): "Financial Sector Reforms: Policies and Performance Analysis", *RBI Bulletin*, November 2004.

Annex 1: Financial Stability Reports published by central banks

Central bank / Monetary authority	Name of periodical	Frequency of publication	Languages
Dedicated financial stability reports			
Australia	Financial Stability Review	Bi-annual	English
Austria	Financial Stability Report	Once/twice a year	English, German
Belgium	Financial Stability Review	Annual	English (excerpts in Dutch and French)
Brazil	Financial Stability Review	Bi-annual	English, Portuguese
Canada	Financial System Review	Bi-annual	English, French
France	Financial Stability Review	Bi-annual	English, French
Hungary	Report on Financial Stability	Bi-annual	English, Hungarian
Norway	Financial Stability Report	Bi-annual	English, Norwegian
Spain	Financial Stability Report	Bi-annual	English, Spanish
Sweden	Financial Stability Report	Bi-annual	English, Swedish
UK	Financial Stability Review	Bi-annual	English
Financial stability articles by other central banks			
European Central Bank	Financial stability and Supervision (section in Annual Report)	Annual	English, other EU languages
Germany	Report on the Stability of German Financial System (section in Bundesbank monthly report)		English, German
Hong Kong SAR	Half-yearly Monetary and Financial Stability Report (section in Quarterly bulletin)	Bi-annual	English, Chinese
India	Reinforcing Financial stability (published as a Chapter of Report on Currency and Finance, 1999-2000)*		English, Hindi
Netherlands	Financial Stability (section of Quarterly bulletin)	Quarterly	English, Dutch

* A regular chapter titled Financial Stability has been introduced in the statutory Report on Trend and Progress of Banking in India from the year 2003-04.

Annex 2: Legal basis for financial stability function

Central bank	Legal basis for the financial stability function
Australia	The RBA Board should use its monetary and banking policy so as to best continue to (i) the stability of the currency, (ii) the maintenance of full employment and (iii) the economic prosperity and welfare of the people of Australia.
Austria	Article 79(l) of the Austrain Banking Act, 1993 (as amended in 2001) observes 'observations and findings of a fundamental nature or of particular importance in the area of banking…' should be exchanged between the OeNB, the Financial Market Authority and the Federal Ministry of Finance. Moreover, Article 13(l) of the Financial Market Authority Law explicitly states that 'A Financial Market Committee shall be established at the Federal Ministry of Finance in order to promote the cooperation and exchange of opinions as a platform by the institutions jointly responsible for the stability of the financial markets'.
Belgium	The amended National Bank of Belgium Act, 1988 (Article 8) states that 'the Bank contributes to the stability of the financial system'.
Canada	According to Section 19 (g.l) of the Bank of Canada Act, the Bank may purchase or sell a wider than normally allowable range of securities for the 'purpose of promoting the stability of the Canadian financial system'.
European Central Bank	"The primary objective of the ESCB shall be to maintain price stability. Without prejudice to the objective of price stability, it shall support the general economic policies in the Community with a view to contributing to the achievement of the objectives of the Community." *"the basic tasks to be carried out through the ECSB shall be….to promote the smooth operation of the payment systems."* "The ECSB shall contribute to the smooth conduct of policies pursued by the competent authorities relating to the prudential supervision of credit institutions and the stability of the financial system."
France	According to the Banking Act of 1984, the Governor of the Banque de France chairs the Commission Bancaire, which is responsible for the supervision of credit institutions and investment firms.
Germany	The German Banking Act stipulates that the supervisory authority 'shall counteract undesirable developments in the banking and financial sector which…involve serious disadvantages for the national economy.'
Hungary	The Central Banking Act, of 2001 states: 'The NBB shall promote the stability of the financial system and shall contribute to the development and smooth conduct of policies related to the prudential supervision of the financial system.'
Netherlands	The Bank Act, 1998 (Section 3) states that 'in implementation of the (EU-) Treaty, the Bank shall, within the framework of the ESCB, contribute to the smooth conduct of policies pursued by the competent authorities relating to the prudential supervision of credit institutions and the stability of the financial system.'
Norway	Section I of the Norges Bank Act states that the Bank shall…'promote efficient payment system domestically as well as vis-à-vis other countries, and monitor developments in the money, credit and foreign exchange markets.'
Spain	The law that granted independence to the Banco de Espana (Law on Autonomy of the Banco de Espana 1994) includes as one of its objectives to promote financial stability.

Sweden	The Riksbank Act states that it is the mission of the Bank to promote a safe and efficient payment system.
UK	The Bank was formally charged with the responsibility for the 'overall stability of the financial system as a whole' by the Chancellor in a letter to the Governor in May 1997 and subsequently in the Memorandum of Understanding between HM Treasury, the Bank of England and the FSA, published in October 1997.

Annex 3: Features of Deposit Insurance Scheme

Feature	India	European Union	US	World Average
Explicit	Yes	Yes	Yes	68 countries
Coverage limit	US $ 2,288*	US $ 25,823**	US $ 1,00,000	3 times per capita GDP
Co-insurance	No	10 per cent	No	17 out of 68 countries
Coverage of foreign currency deposits	Yes	Can be excluded	Yes	48 out of 68 countries
Coverage of inter-bank deposits	No	No	Yes	18 out of 68 countries
Source of Funding	Joint (public *plus* private)	Not regulated	Joint	Joint: 51 Private: 15 Public:1 Not available for 1 country
Administration	Public	Not regulated	Public	Joint: 24 Public: 33 Private: 11
Membership	Compulsory	Compulsory	Compulsory	55 out of 68 countries have compulsory membership
Premium levied (% of deposits)	0.08	Varies markedly	0.00-0.27	58 countries regularly levy premium
Risk-adjusted premium	No	Not regulated	Yes	31 out of 68 countries

* US $ 1=Rs. 43.7; ** US $ 1= Euro 0.7745.

Economic Growth, Financial Deepening and Financial Inclusion*

6

Rakesh Mohan

1. Introduction

....What is the big change that has taken place in India since 2004? The Indian growth story has been steadily coming of age and the performance of the Indian economy has attracted worldwide attention. The Indian growth story is now mentioned in the same breath as that of China. The economy has been averaging a growth rate of more than 8.0 per cent during the last three years. The recently released numbers from CSO have placed the first quarter growth (April to June, 2006) at 8.9 per cent, more than the overall growth rate of 8.0 per cent reiterated recently by the Reserve Bank in its Mid-Term Review.

...non-food credit growth from 2002-03 to 2005-06 averaged 28.8 per cent. This growth shows little sign of abating in the current year when it has recorded a growth of over 30.0 per cent. The growth in broad money since 2002-03 has averaged 16.2 per cent, which during the present year has been of the order of 19.0 per cent. These trends signal further that India is on a high economic growth path accompanied by financial deepening.

A new concern has emerged in the process: that of financial inclusion. Moreover, the Government of India has also expressed its explicit concern on the issue of overall inclusion in the development process through its various initiatives such as the Rural Employment Guarantee Scheme, the *Bharat Nirman*

---

* Address by Dr. Rakesh Mohan at the Annual Bankers' Conference 2006, at Hyderabad on Nov 3, 2006. This draws heavily on my earlier lecture on a similar subject at the FICCI-IBA Conference in Mumbai on Sep. 26, 2006. Address at Annual Bankers' Conference 2006 at Hyderabad on November 03, 2006.

programme, the *Sarva Shiksha Abhiyan*, and the like. A committee on financial inclusion (Chairman: Dr. C. Rangarajan) has also been constituted by the Government of India in June 2006 to recommend a strategy to achieve higher financial inclusion in the country.

Likewise, enabling access to a greater number of the population to the structured and organised financial system has explicitly been on the agenda of the Reserve Bank since 2004. Unlike several central banks, which focus solely on inflation, many developed and emerging economies, including ours, focus also on growth. There is currently a clear perception that there are a vast number of people, potential entrepreneurs, small enterprises and others, who are excluded from the financial sector, which leads to their marginalisation and denial of opportunity for them to grow and prosper. The Reserve Bank has therefore introduced various new measures to encourage the expansion of financial coverage in the country. Not only is financial inclusion essential because of its implications for the welfare of citizens but it needs to be stressed that it has to be an explicit strategy for fostering faster economic growth in a more inclusive fashion. It is in this context that I thought it would be appropriate to place the strategy of financial inclusion in the wider context of economic growth and financial deepening.

My ideas on this topic are organised along the following lines. To begin with, I shall dwell upon the process of growth and financial deepening in India. This will be followed by definitional aspects and some evidence from the experience of other countries, with regard to financial inclusion. Thereafter, the focus would be on interlinking the relevance of financial inclusion in our economy, which has entered a high growth orbit, with the rural economy. The penultimate section focuses on the role being played by the Reserve Bank in this regard.

2. Economic Growth

The growth trend of the Indian economy over the last few years appears to indicate the beginning of a new phase of higher growth. From an average growth rate of around 6.0 per cent for a quarter of a century, the growth rate has accelerated to

8.1 per cent over the last few years. Along with declining population growth, this suggests high growth in per capita income in excess of 6 per cent in recent years, and perhaps approaching 7 per cent, which would lead to doubling of per capita income every ten years. Most importantly, the current growth process is not a flash in the pan and is exhibiting signs of sustainability along with financial stability, notwithstanding the pressures from unforeseen external shocks.

On the savings front, the increasing trend in gross domestic saving as a proportion of GDP witnessed since the early 2000s has also continued unabated. The gross domestic savings rate has improved from 23.6 per cent of GDP in 2001-02 to 29.1 per cent in 2004-05, led by a turnaround of 4.2 per cent in public saving, from a dis-saving of 2.2 per cent of GDP in 2001-02 to a saving of 2.0 per cent in 2004-05, mainly reflecting the fiscal consolidation process. Household savings continue to grow and increased corporate savings reflect their healthy growth in profitability. The encouraging sign of a pick up in investment has also strengthened unhindered. Along with the improvements in savings and investment rates, there has also been a marked lowering of inflation from 7.8 per cent in the 1990s to 4.7 per cent in recent years. With such healthy increases in savings and investment rates financial intermediation is assuming increasing importance (Annex Table 1).

Alongside these improvements there has also been a resurgence of manufacturing activity. There had been noted stagnation in manufacturing during 1997—2003. Overall industrial recovery set in during 2002-03 and this has been sustained since then on the back of healthy growth in domestic demand, along with that of exports supported by high world economic growth, increasing capacity utilisation, augmentation of capacity, and positive business and consumer confidence. But there is little evidence of significant growth in manufacturing employment leading to emerging doubts in the inclusive nature of this growth.

The current high industrial growth is reflected in the acceleration in growth of bank credit in recent years. Average growth in non-food credit between 1970 and 2000 had been

16.9 per cent, which had been seen as evidence of finance led industrialisation by some (Bell, 2001). In the period of industrial slowdown, 1998 to 2002, annual growth in non-food credit had also slowed to 14.5 per cent.... In recent years, during 2002-03 to 2005-06, this growth has accelerated significantly to 28.8 per cent, possibly signalling financial deepening of the system.

Much of this recent expansion in non-food credit has been fuelled by an increase in retail credit. During the same period, 2002-03 to 2005-06 annual growth in retail credit was 46 per cent: its share in overall bank credit consequently increased from 6.4 per cent in 1990-91 to 25.5 per cent in 2005-2006. Earlier, most of bank credit had gone to the industrial corporate sector. Hence this shift to retail credit can also be seen as a move toward financial deepening, and one that itself fuels industrial and overall economic growth through expansion of greater demand for consumer goods.

The high industrial growth is also corroborated by the record of very healthy performance of the corporate sector, which has recorded unusually high profit growth over the past three years: over 40 per cent growth in profit after tax for 11 successive quarters from Q_3 2002-03 to Q_1 2005-06. Although this growth has slowed somewhat in the last four quarters, it continues to be high, between 25 and 35 per cent. Corporate sector savings have grown from 4.4 per cent of GDP in 1999-2002 to 5.3 per cent in 2004-05. Hence, the probability of continued high corporate growth in terms of output is made more likely by the availability of high retained earnings, burgeoning valuations, and continued productivity growth.

All these developments point to overall financial deepening but, once again, one has to ask the question whether such performance extends to small and medium enterprises also and, whether there has also been extension of financial intermediation for such enterprises, raising issues of financial inclusion.

The high industrial and credit growth of recent years has also been supported by high trade growth in both merchandise goods and services. Merchandise exports have grown from 5.8 per cent of GDP in 1990-91 to about 13.1 per cent in

2005-06; and gross invisible receipts have grown from 2.4 per cent to 11.5 per cent of GDP. If we take gross trade, the sum of both current account receipts and payments, as a proportion of GDP as an index of the openness of the economy, this has increased from 19.2 per cent in 1990-91 to 49.5 per cent in 2005-06. Since all such receipts and payments pass through the banking system, this increasing openness of the economy has also added to financial deepening, while aiding the acceleration in economic growth (Annex Table 2).

The high credit growth witnessed in recent years has, however, not been matched by adequate deposit growth. The growth in deposits since 2001-02 has been far lower than that required to support overall credit expansion (Graph 1). Banks have been financing much of the incremental credit expansion by unwinding their surplus investments in government securities. What deposit growth that has been observed is, moreover, concentrated in the larger cities: presumably it has been helped by the high corporate profitability leading to high corporate cash balances. The trend therefore indicates that while banks may have been proactive in credit deployment, their focus on deposit mobilisation may have been less than adequate. The indication that deposit growth in non-metro areas has been slow

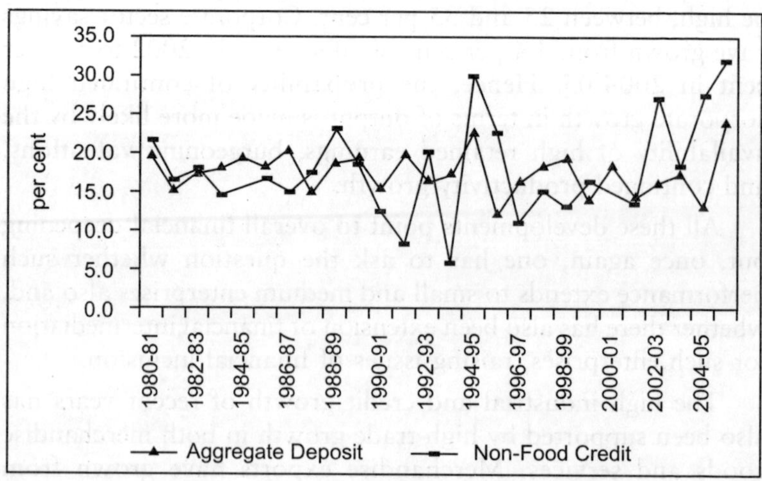

Graph 1: Growth in Aggregate Deposits and Credit

could also mean that financial inclusion may have suffered. We also need to understand that if deposit growth does not match credit growth, excess demand would inevitably lead to increases in real interest rates leading to further possibility of financial exclusion.

Overall, it is clear from the recent performance of the economy and that of the financial sector that a good deal of financial sector growth has accompanied the recent acceleration of economic growth. We also observe that a good part of credit growth has gone towards financing consumption and housing which suggests widening of the financial system. But deposit growth has been slow, particularly outside metro areas, leading to questions concerning financial deepening and inclusion.

3. Financial Deepening

There is a general consensus among economists that financial development spurs economic growth. Theoretically, financial development creates enabling conditions for growth through either a supply-leading (financial development spurs growth) or a demand-following (growth generates demand for financial products) channel. A large body of empirical research supports the view that development of the financial system contributes to economic growth (Rajan and Zingales, 2003). Empirical evidence consistently emphasises the nexus between finance and growth, though the issue of direction of causality is more difficult to determine. At the cross-country level, evidence indicates that various measures of financial development (including assets of the financial intermediaries, liquid liabilities of financial institutions, domestic credit to private sector, stock and bond market capitalisation) are robustly and positively related to economic growth (King and Levine, 1993; Levine and Zervos, 1998). Other studies establish a positive relationship between financial development and growth at the industry level (Rajan and Zingales, 1998). Even the recent endogenous growth literature, building on 'learning by doing' processes, assigns a special role to finance (Aghion and Hewitt, 1998 and 2005).

A developed financial system broadens access to funds; conversely, in an underdeveloped financial system, access to funds is limited and people are constrained by the availability of their own funds and have to resort to high cost informal sources such as money lenders. Lower the availability of funds and higher their cost, fewer would be the economic activities that can be financed and hence lower the resulting economic growth.

Some of the recent concerns on financial inclusion have emanated from the results of the All-India Debt and Investment Survey (AIDIS), 2002. Over a period of 40 years, the share of non-institutional sources of credit in sources of credit for cultivator households had declined sharply from about 93 per cent in 1951 to about 30 per cent in 1991, with the share of money lenders having declined from 69.7 per cent to 17.5 per cent. In 2002, the AIDIS revealed, however, that the share of money lenders had again increased to 27 per cent, while that of non-institutional sources overall rose to 39 per cent (Table 1). In other words, notwithstanding the outreach of banking, the formal credit system has not been able to adequately penetrate the informal financial markets; rather it seems to have shrunk in some respects in recent years.

Table 1: Relative Share of Borrowing of Cultivator Households*

(per cent)

Sources of Credit	1951	1961	1971	1981	1991	2002$
1	2	3	4	5	6	7
Non-institutional	**92.7**	**81.3**	**68.3**	**36.8**	**30.6**	**38.9**
of which:						
Money lenders	69.7	49.2	36.1	16.1	17.5	26.8
Institutional	**7.3**	**18.7**	**31.7**	**63.2**	**66.3**	**61.1**
of which:						
Co-operative societies, *etc.*	3.3	2.6	22.0	29.8	30.0	30.2
Commercial banks	0.9	0.6	2.4	28.8	35.2	26.3
Unspecified	-	-	-	-	3.1	-
Total	**100.0**	**100.0**	**100.0**	**100.0**	**100.0**	**100.0**

* : Borrowing refers to outstanding cash dues.
$: AIDIS, NSSO, 59th Round, 2003.
Source: All India Debt and Investment Surveys.

Coincidentally, it is also true that the rate of agricultural growth during the last decade has slowed down and it is particularly striking in respect of foodgrains production. Since the green revolution, banks have been mainly focused on financing crop loans connected largely with food grains. There is, therefore, reason to believe that financial exclusion may actually have increased in the rural areas over the last 10-15 years.

One of the key features of financial deepening is that it accelerates economic growth through the expansion of access to those who do not have adequate finance themselves. Typically, in an underdeveloped financial system, it is the incumbents who have better access to financial services through relationship banking. Moreover, incumbents also finance their growth through internal resource generation. Thus, in an underdeveloped financial system, growth is constrained to the expansion potential of incumbents. In mature financial systems on the other hand, financial institutions develop appraisal techniques, and information gathering and sharing mechanisms, which then enable banks to even finance those activities or firms that are at the margin, thereby leading to their growth-inducing productive activities in addition to the incumbents. It is this availability of external finance to budding entrepreneurs and small firms that enables new entry, while also providing competition to incumbents and consequently encouraging entrepreneurship and productivity.

What has been the case in India? ... the incredible corporate profit growth, in excess of 40 per cent for almost three years consecutively, would suggest that there should have been massive new entry to whittle down profitability to more moderate levels. This, however, does not seem to be the case on the ground yet with corporate profitability still growing at an annual rate of around 35 per cent during April-June 2006. That entry of new firms has possibly been limited is also indicated by the fact that among the different categories of credit growth, lending to SMEs has been the lowest, though there are some signs of higher growth in recent months.

There are, however, other signs of financial deepening (Mohan, 2004). According to one indicator of financial deepening, the ratio of bank assets to GDP, financial depth in India was among the lowest in the world (Barth, Caprio and Levine, 2001). Comparable cross-country data indicated that in

2001, this ratio, at 48 per cent for India, was lower than those prevalent in Asian economies such as Indonesia (101 per cent), Korea (98 per cent), Philippines (91 per cent), Malaysia (166 per cent) and much lower than developed economies, such as UK (311 per cent), France (147 per cent) and Germany (313 per cent). In India, while the ratio of bank assets to GDP has increased significantly to a shade over 80 per cent in 2005-06—obviously a consequence of the high credit growth in recent years—it is still lower than other emerging countries. In absolute terms, the annual expansion in non-food credit has increased from Rs. 64,302 crore in 2001-02 to Rs. 3,54,193 crore in 2005-06, while retail credit has increased from around Rs. 16,000 crore to Rs. 1,09,129 crore. So, it needs to be recognised that financial deepening has been taking place on an accelerated pace on a macro basis in recent years, that banking productivity has improved significantly, and that bankers have clearly been very busy.

An important question that arises logically is: has commensurate financial deepening been taking place at the micro-level? There is sufficient anecdotal evidence to suggest that the poor or less well-off people find it difficult to open a bank account in any area—rural, urban or semi-urban. Thus, not only is the common individual deprived of access to banks for generating savings or availing credit, but so is the financial system of resources commensurate with the burgeoning growth of incomes all over the country. It is this very feature that the process of financial inclusion seeks to address....

4. Financial Inclusion

.... Broadly defined, financial exclusion signifies the lack of access by certain segments of the society to appropriate, low-cost, fair and safe financial products and services from mainstream providers. Financial exclusion is thus a key policy concern, because the options for operating a household budget, or a micro/small enterprise, without mainstream financial services can often be expensive. This process becomes self-reinforcing and can often be an important factor in social exclusion, especially for communities with limited access to financial products, particularly in rural areas.

Two major factors have often been cited as the consequences of financial exclusion. First, it complicates day-to-day cash flow management—being financially excluded means households, and micro and small enterprises deal entirely in cash and are susceptible to irregular cash flows. Second, lack of financial planning and security in the absence of access to bank accounts and other saving opportunities for people in the unorganised sector limit their options for providing for themselves for their old age. From the macroeconomic standpoint, being without formal savings can be problematic in two respects. First, people who save by informal means rarely benefit from the interest rate and tax advantages that people using formal methods of savings enjoy. Second, informal saving channels are much less secure than formal saving facilities. Those who can afford it least suffer the highest risk. The resultant lack of savings and saving avenues means recourse to non-formal lenders, like money lenders. This, in turn, could lead to two adverse consequences—(a) exposure to higher interest rates charged by formal lenders; and (b) the inability of customers to service the loans or to repay them. As loans from non-formal lenders are often secured against the borrower's property, this raises the problem of inter-linkage between two apparently separate markets. Judged in this specific context, financial exclusion is a serious concern among low-income households, mainly located in rural areas.

Once access to financial institutions improves, inclusion affords several benefits to the consumer, regulator and the economy alike. Establishment of an account relationship can pave the way for the customer to avail the benefits of a variety of financial products, which are not only standardised, but are also provided by institutions that are regulated and supervised by credible regulators, and are hence safer. The bank accounts can also be used for multiple purposes, such as, making small value remittances at low cost and making purchases on credit. Furthermore, the regulator benefits, as the audit trail is available and transactions are conducted transparently in a medium that can be monitored. The economy benefits, as greater financial resources become transparently available for efficient intermediation and allocation, for uses that have the highest returns. In other words, the single gateway of a banking account can be used for several purposes and represents a beneficial situation for all the economic units in the country.

In addition, I would like to flag an important perspective. Improvements in rural infrastructure in terms of availability of electricity, improvement in connectivity through provision of rural roads and telecommunications, and construction of warehouses, are expected to lead to better overall supply chain management, enhance productivity of physical resources in the rural areas and greater addition in agriculture. These developments would lead to much greater demand for banking activity in rural areas. The twofold implications of these developments for the banking sector are apparent. First, with higher financing needs of such new activities *vis-a-vis* traditional ones, the overall financing intensity of agriculture is likely to experience a manifold rise. Second, along with growth in rural infrastructure, there is also likely to be an increase in rural non-farm activities, such as repair activities, education, housing, restaurants and medical services. These activities, both traditional and emerging ventures, would be available for financing by the banking sector.

Thus, as the economy begins to grow rapidly, the rate of financial intermediation is expected to increase further. In other words, the banking system will be expected to increasingly provide larger quantum of funds to existing and emerging enterprises. And without adequate deposit growth, however, credit expansion might not be sustainable over the medium-term, without putting immense pressure on real interest rates and impacting the overall stability of the financial system.

International Experience

Typically, countries with low levels of income inequality tend to have lower levels of financial exclusion, while high levels of exclusion are associated with the least equal ones. In Sweden, for example, lower than two per cent of adults did not have an account in 2000 and in Germany, the figure was around three per cent (Kempson, 2006). In comparison, less than four per cent of adults in Canada and five per cent in Belgium, lacked a bank account (Buckland *et al.* 2005). Countries with high levels of inequality record higher levels of banking exclusion. To illustrate, in Portugal, about 17 per cent of the adult population had no account of any kind in 2000 (Kempson, 2006).

The policy responses to such exclusion have been varied (Box 1). In Sweden, for example, banks cannot refuse to open a saving or deposit account under Section 2 of the Banking Business Act of 1987; in France, Article 58 of the Banking Act, 1984

Box 1: Policy Response to Financial Exclusion—Country Experiences

Two major kinds of policy responses have been implemented by central banks in response to financial exclusion: codes of practice and specific legislation. First, countries such as France and Belgium have undertaken initiatives to committing banks to open an affordable account with bare minimum facilities. Termed 'call deposit account' in Belgium, it offers three basic types of transactions: money transfers, deposits and withdrawals, and bank statements. However, individual banks may opt to offer other services if they wish. In Germany, a voluntary code was introduced by the German Bankers Association in 1996. This makes provision for an 'everyman' current account, offering basic banking transactions, without an overdraft facility. Likewise, access to basic banking in the United Kingdom and Australia has been achieved through voluntary arrangements with banks and has not involved formal charters. In the United Kingdom, for instance, a Banking Code has been drafted, which requires banks to inform customers about their basic bank account and its suitability for their needs. A Financial Inclusion Taskforce, instituted in April 2005, monitors access to basic banking services.

Several countries have also introduced specific legislation that gives both, a universal right to a bank account and, spells out the precise nature of banking services to be provided. In France, the law on exclusion of July 1998 reiterated the right to an account first set out in the 1984 law and has since then simplified the process of exercising the right to an account. In Belgium, a banking bill was enacted which has been implemented since October 2003. In addition to setting out the minimum standards for basic bank accounts, it also specifies the ceiling on charges and a minimum number of free face-to-face transactions. In many ways, the policy response in Canada combines the best of developments in other countries. The relevant legislation, enacted in June 2001, requires all banks to provide accounts without minimum opening balances to all Canadians, regardless of employment or credit history, with minimum identification requirements. A Financial Consumer Agency of Canada has been established to monitor whether financial institutions adhere to their public commitments.

Sources: Kempson, E. (2006). Policy Level Response to Financial Exclusion in Developed Economies: Lessons for Developing Countries, paper presented at the conference, Access to Finance: Building Inclusive Financial Systems, World Bank, Washington, D.C.

Connolly, C., and K.Hajaj (2001). Financial Services and Social Exclusion, Financial Services Consumer Policy Center, University of New South Wales. HM Treasury (1999). Access to Financial services. London: HM Treasury.

recognised the principle of the right to a bank account; in the US, federal Government introduced the Community Reinvestment Act in 1997, partly in response to concerns about bank branch closures in low-income neighbourhoods. Under this legislation, federal bank regulatory agencies rate banks on their efforts to serve low-income communities. These early legislations were designed to ensure access to a deposit account but did not spell out the nature of banking services that should be on offer. Refinements in this area have actually taken place in the latter half of the 1990s, resulting partly from a wider concern regarding social exclusion (Caskey *et al.* 2006, Kempson *et al.* 2000). It may, thus, be noted that financial inclusion is a concern even in developed countries and legislative or regulatory measure to achieve it are a common feature.

Present Situation in India

....The share of deposits and credit in rural and semi-urban areas is on the decline. In contrast, the share in metropolitan areas is rising. The share of credit is lower than that of deposits in all regions except metropolitan, implying that resources get intermediated into metropolitan areas (Table 2). This in itself may not necessarily be undesirable or unexpected if resources are being intermediated to their best uses. However, they do provide some indication for concern and for the need for more investigation.

Table 2: Spatial Distribution of Banking Services

(per cent)

	Offices			Deposits			Credit		
	1969	1996	2005	1969	1996	2005	1969	1996	2005
1	2	3	4	5	6	7	8	9	10
Rural	22.2	51.2	45.7	6.4	14.4	12.2	3.3	11.4	9.5
Semi-urban	40.4	21.3	22.3	21.8	19.5	16.9	13.1	13.1	11.3
Urban	19.2	15.2	17.6	26.5	22.4	21.5	21.8	17.7	16.4
Metropolitan	18.2	12.3	14.4	45.3	43.7	49.4	61.8	57.8	62.7
Total	100.0	100.0	100.0	100.0	100.0	100.0	100.0	100.0	100.0

Source: Reserve Bank of India.

The total number of saving accounts, considered to be a better indicator of banking penetration than other deposit accounts, as per cent of number of households, was 137 in rural areas and 244 in the urban areas on the eve of reforms in 1991. By 2005, despite the reforms, the differential continues to be similar. In the case of credit accounts, the situation has deteriorated for rural households while showing significant improvement in the urban areas (Table 3), corroborating the very significant increase in retail credit.

Table 3: Number of Deposit and Credit Accounts in Scheduled Commercial Banks

(Per cent of Number of Households)

		1981	1991	1996	2001	2004	2005
1	2	3	4	5	6	7	8
Deposit Accounts							
Current Accounts	Rural	3.6	5.5	4.7	4.9	4.4	4.6
	Urban	15.0	23.4	24.1	19.2	17.5	18.3
Savings Accounts	Rural	59.6	137.0	129.8	123.3	126.8	131.5
	Urban	135.5	243.7	249.7	197.4	206.5	213.1
Current and Saving Accounts	Rural	63.2	142.6	134.5	128.2	131.1	136.1
	Urban	150.5	267.2	273.7	216.6	224.0	231.4
Term Deposits Accounts	Rural	22.9	41.8	45.5	52.0	48.3	45.7
	Urban	74.6	96.9	105.0	105.6	113.4	104.0
Total Deposits Accounts	**Rural**	**86.1**	**184.4**	**180.0**	**180.1**	**179.4**	**181.8**
	Urban	**225.1**	**364.1**	**378.7**	**322.2**	**337.4**	**335.4**
Credit Accounts	**Rural**	**18.0**	**44.3**	**36.0**	**26.5**	**28.7**	**32.2**
	Urban	**15.1**	**29.9**	**27.1**	**28.4**	**42.5**	**50.2**

Notes:

1. The census population groups are 'rural' and 'urban', whereas the population groups used in BSR data are 'rural', 'semi-urban', 'urban' and 'metropolitan'. There is no unique relationship between the two. For comparison purpose and simplicity, 'Rural' and 'Semi-Urban' are taken as 'rural', and 'urban' and 'metropolitan' are combined as 'urban'.
2. For three new formed States, number of households, in 1991 have been estimated based on 2001 data. Population is as per 1981, 1991 and 2001 census. For 1996, 2004 and 2005 projected population has been used, and rural and urban proportion of past census is applied.

Sources: 1. Reserve Bank of India. 2. Census, 2001.

Total deposits, as per cent of GDP, increased from 32.2 in 1991 to 47.1 in 2005 in rural areas and from 37.3 to 61.2 in urban areas. Similarly, credit extended, as per cent of GDP, increased from 17.3 to 22.3 in rural and from 24.8 to 45.0 in urban areas (Table 4). In terms of banking penetration, the number of deposit and credit accounts of scheduled commercial banks as per cent of adult population are significantly lower in the rural areas as compared with the urban areas (Table 5).

Table 4: Deposits and Credit Amounts in Scheduled Commercial Banks

(per cent of GDP)

		1981	1991	1996	2001	2005
1	2	3	4	5	6	7
Deposit Accounts						
1. Current Accounts	Rural	2.6	2.7	2.4	2.9	3.3
	Urban	5.5	7.1	7.0	7.0	8.7
2. Savings Accounts	Rural	9.8	11.2	10.5	13.6	18.6
	Urban	7.2	9.0	7.9	9.8	13.3
3. Current and Saving Accounts	Rural	12.4	13.9	12.8	16.4	21.9
(1 + 2)	Urban	12.7	16.1	14.9	16.8	22.0
4. Term Deposits Accounts	Rural	13.8	18.3	20.5	27.9	25.2
	Urban	16.6	21.2	22.4	29.2	39.1
5. Total Deposits Accounts	**Rural**	**26.3**	**32.2**	**33.3**	**44.4**	**47.1**
(3 + 4)	**Urban**	**29.3**	**37.3**	**37.3**	**46.0**	**61.2**
6. Credit Accounts	**Rural**	**13.0**	**17.3**	**14.4**	**15.8**	**22.3**
	Urban	**20.0**	**24.8**	**25.5**	**31.1**	**45.0**

Notes:

1. GDP at Market Prices (current prices) is used. The rural and urban figures of GDP are based on ratio of monthly per capita Total Consumer Expenditure, NSSO.
2. Same as in Table 3.

Source: Same as in Table 3.

Table 5: Number of Deposit and Credit Accounts in Scheduled Commercial Banks

(per cent of Adult Population, Age 15+)

		1981	1991	1996	2001	2005
1	2	3	4	5	6	7
Deposit Accounts						
Current Accounts	Rural	1.0	1.6	1.4	1.4	1.4
	Urban	4.5	6.6	6.8	5.4	5.2
Savings Accounts	Rural	16.1	39.6	37.6	36.5	39.0
	Urban	40.3	69.2	70.9	55.8	60.2
Current and Saving Accounts	Rural	17.1	41.3	38.9	38.0	40.3
	Urban	44.8	75.8	77.7	61.2	65.4
Term Deposits Accounts	Rural	6.2	12.1	13.2	15.4	13.6
	Urban	22.2	27.5	29.8	29.8	29.4
Total Deposits Accounts	**Rural**	**23.3**	**53.4**	**52.1**	**53.4**	**53.9**
	Urban	**67.0**	**103.4**	**107.5**	**91.0**	**94.7**
Credit Accounts	**Rural**	**4.9**	**7.7**	**8.0**	**7.9**	**9.5**
	Urban	**4.5**	**12.8**	**10.4**	**8.0**	**14.2**

Note: Same as in Table 3.

Source: Same as in Table 3.

Even in terms of financial widening, the scope for improvement remains. In terms of regional dis-aggregation since 1991, population per bank office has increased in rural areas from 13,462 in 1991 to 16,650 in 2005 and, as expected, declined in the urban areas from 14,484 to 13,619 over the period. Three regions, North-Eastern, Eastern and Central have higher population per office than the all-India average and it has increased significantly in the rural areas in 2005 over 1991 (Table 6). Consequently, compared to an all-India average of 29.9 savings accounts per 100 persons in 1991, virtually all of the states in the Eastern and North-Eastern regions and several pockets in the Central region had figures lower than this average. In the rural areas, Northern and Southern region are above the all-India average while in the urban areas, Northern and Western region dominate. In terms of number of credit accounts per 100 persons, the Southern States, both in rural and urban areas perform above the all-India average.

Table 6: Regional Level Indicators of Scheduled Commercial Banks

	1991	2005	1991	2005	1991	2005
	Total		Rural		Urban	
1	2	3	4	5	6	7
Population per Office						
Northern	11,002	12,257	10,771	13,043	11,571	10,941
North-East	16,870	26,227	16,335	22,158	21,169	20,318
Eastern	16,441	19,913	16,402	21,208	16,614	15,759
Central	15,786	19,518	15,153	20,264	18,745	17,297
Western	12,771	14,618	12,579	15,526	13,108	13,472
Southern	11,932	12,328	11,276	12,372	13,811	12,243
All-India	**13,711**	**15,680**	**13,462**	**16,650**	**14,484**	**13,619**
Deposits: Number of Savings Accounts per 100 persons						
Northern	40.0	38.3	30.1	29.7	62.6	55.4
North-East	17.8	17.6	16.1	16.4	28.4	24.2
Eastern	21.8	20.5	17.7	16.9	40.0	36.1
Central	23.8	24.5	21.0	22.1	34.7	32.9
Western	35.5	32.5	24.7	23.8	53.8	45.2
Southern	37.0	37.6	34.6	35.5	42.7	41.8
All-India	**29.9**	**29.2**	**24.5**	**24.4**	**45.6**	**41.6**
Credit: Number of Credit Accounts per 100 persons						
Northern	6.4	5.7	6.6	5.1	5.9	6.7
North-East	4.4	3.3	4.4	3.2	4.4	3.9
Eastern	6.6	4.2	7.2	4.2	4.3	4.3
Central	5.5	4.3	5.8	4.2	4.4	4.5
Western	5.7	7.5	6.2	4.2	4.8	12.2
Southern	11.8	14.2	13.6	12.7	7.6	17.4
All-India	**7.3**	**7.0**	**7.9**	**6.0**	**5.5**	**9.8**

Notes: Same as in Tables 3 and 4.

Source: Same as in Table 3.

Thus, the apparent implication emerging from the above data reveals that the rural areas are not being served adequately by banks. This suggests that banks need to make efforts to mobilise resources from the rural sector, whereas discussed earlier, scope for increase in business is emerging. Further, if the banks are to balance their overall deposit mobilisation and credit extension, as generally robust banking practice would imply, then they would need to devise imaginative ways to mop up the resources, particularly in rural areas.

5. Rural Economy—Growth, Production Patterns and Credit Extension

It is instructive to examine the rural economy in a bit more detail. Although the share of agriculture in overall GDP has declined from around 35.8 per cent in 1980-81 to less than 19.9 per cent at present, the fall in the proportion of population dependent on the sector has been limited (Table 7). In other words, a majority of the workforce is still dependent on agriculture, while the GDP growth due to agriculture is marginally above the rate of growth of the population, in contrast to a strong growth rate in the non-agriculture sector.

Table 7: Components of Gross Domestic Products*

(per cent)

Year/Sector	Agriculture and Allied	Of which: Agriculture	Industry	Services	Total
1	2	3	4	5	6
1970-71 to 1979-80	42.8	37.7	16.9	40.3	100.0
1980-81 to 1989-90	36.4	33.1	19.5	44.0	100.0
1990-91 to 1999-2000	29.1	26.7	21.9	49.0	100.0
2000-01 to 2005-06	21.9	20.8	21.4	56.7	100.0

*: Annual averages.
Source: National Account Statistics.

The slowdown in agriculture in recent years is characterised by the stagnation in domestic production in case of commodities like wheat, sugar and pulses. There has been a marked deceleration in the share of cereals in total production (agriculture and allied) from 31.7 per cent in 1960-61 to 24.1 per cent in 2004-05 (Table 8). On the other hand, the share of other segments such as livestock and fishing, and non-cereals are recording a significant increase. There has been a silent revolution over the last 20 years, unnoticed by researchers and policy-makers alike. The value of output of non-cereal vegetarian food and of non-vegetarian food (livestock and fishing) is each higher than that of cereals. In principle, these activities should be more credit intensive. It is, therefore, of utmost importance that our image of what is agriculture, changes from that of simple rice and wheat to a more complex structure, so that policy-makers can assign due importance to the sector and respond accordingly (Mohan, 2006).

Table 8: Changing Pattern of Agricultural Production

Year	Cereals and pulses	Non-cereals food	Cash crops	Livestock and fishing	Forestry and logging	Ag. and allied (Rs. crore)
	Sectoral shares: as per cent of agriculture and allied					
1	2	3	4	5	6	7
1960-61	31.7	33.6	4.9	20.3	9.5	1,32,292
1970-71	31.4	34.9	4.8	20.1	8.8	1,69,066
1980-81	30.3	36.2	4.4	23.4	5.7	2,26,719
1990-91	28.6	36.4	4.5	26.2	4.3	3,10,165
2000-01	25.4	37.6	3.9	28.0	3.9	5,68,990
2004-05	24.1	n.a	n.a	29.2	3.8	6,22,183

Source: National Accounts Statistics.

Apart from non-cereal food production, service and manufacturing activities have also been growing faster in rural areas. There are new supply chain activities: sorting, grading, storage, cold storage, transportation, food processing, and the like. All are in the cash economy and potentially in need of credit. In fact, it is estimated that agriculture now accounts for less than half of rural GDP: an epochal change that took place some time in the late 1990s. So "rural" can no longer be equated with agriculture. The consequence is that rural per capita income has probably been growing at a rate similar to that of urban per capita income.

There is also good evidence (NCAER) of the dramatic changes in consumption and income growth and distribution patterns in the rural economy. As classified consistently by NCAER, keeping real income cut-offs constant, the proportion of households classified as "low income" in rural areas has fallen from about two-thirds in the early 1990s to only about a quarter now. At the same time, those classified as middle income households have risen from a third to almost 70 per cent now (NCAER, 2003). Hence, there should have been a surge in financial savings in rural areas: but we do not see evidence of this in the number or proportion of households that have bank accounts.

The banking system needs to adjust to the realities in the rural sector. There is evidence they are finding it difficult. As the ratio of agricultural GDP to total GDP declines, agricultural credit to total GDP would also decline. However, this is not observed from the data (Table 9). In recent years a concern over the falling share of agricultural credit as a proportion of total credit has been expressed. The data reveal that agriculture credit as a ratio of total credit has also been rising in the recent years but is still below the level of 1970s.

Table 9: Ratio of Direct Agricultural Credit to Agricultural GDP, Total GDP and total Credit

Year	Ag. Credit/Ag. GDP	Ag. Credit/Total GDP	Ag. Credit/CS
1	2	3	4
1970s	5.4	2.1	10.8
1980s	8.3	2.6	8.5
1990s	7.4	2.0	6.4
1999-2000	10.0	2.6	8.1
2000-01	11.3	2.8	7.9
2001-02	14.0	3.0	8.2
2002-03	16.6	3.1	7.7
2003-04	18.0	3.4	8.6
2004-05	25.0	4.4	9.8
2005-06	25.9	4.9	9.3

Notes:

1. Agricultural credit; direct credit for agricultural and allied activities extended by co-operatives, commercial banks and regional rural banks.
2. Total GDP and Agricultural GDP are at factor cost and at current prices.
3. CS—other banks' credit to commercial sector (outstanding) proxy for total credit.

Source: RBI and NABARD.

The existing agricultural credit system, as indicated earlier, is geared to the needs of foodgrain production. It is gratifying to note that agriculture credit has not fallen as a proportion of agricultural GDP despite the share of foodgrain production declining as a proportion of total agricultural production. In fact, according to available data, agricultural credit has been rising in recent years as a share of both the value of inputs and the value of outputs (Table 10).

Moreover, long-term credit as a share of private investment has also been rising in the 1990s (Table 11). The balance of evidence also suggests that non-performing loans (NPLs) in agriculture are not higher than in other sectors, more specifically those in small-scale industries (SSIs). To illustrate, NPLs in agriculture—both for public as well as private banks—were lower than those in the SSIs as at end-March 2005 (Mohan, 2006).

Table 10: Gross Value of Output, Value of Input and Short-Term Credit

(Rs. crore at current prices)

Year	Gross value of output	Value of input	Short-term credit	Short-term credit as percentage of	
				Value of output	Value of input
1	2	3	4	5	6
1993-94	2,71,839	55,401	5,424	2.0	9.8
1998-99	4,88,731	93,416	10,821	2.2	11.6
1999-2000	5,26,658	1,21,878	12,610	2.4	10.3
2000-01	5,29,800	1,26,773	15,442	2.9	12.2
2001-02	5,66,563	1,37,802	18,882	3.3	13
2002-03	5,56,121	1,51,437	23,324	4.2	15.[illegible]
2003-04	6,25,121	1,53,770	31,972	5.1	20.8
2004-05	6,48,096	1,59,658	—	—	—

—: Not available.

Source: National Accounts Statistics.

Table 11: Private Capital Formation and Share of Long-Term Credit

(Rs. crore)

Decade/Year	Private Sector Capital Formation	Investment Credit	Per cent (Col 3 over Col 2))
1	2	3	4
1980-81 to 1989-90	7,840	2,603	33.2
1990-91 to 1999-2000	12,299	7,794	63.4
2000-01	15,374	11,707	76.2
2001-02	15,823	11,992	75.8

Source: Reserve Bank of India (2004).

In addition to the above data analysis, ... non-institutional agricultural credit has declined from over 92.7 per cent in 1950s to 38.9 per cent in 2002. Thus, nationalisation of banks and their increased geographical expansion into rural areas certainly made a difference but there is scope for improvement.

The rising economic activity in rural areas driven by the growth of newer activities such as horticulture, floriculture, organic farming, genetic engineering, food processing and packaging—all of which are cash intensive—would necessitate increased banking facilities. In view of the evidence of a pick-up in consumer financing in rural areas, there is also a need to streamline the supply chain to deliver credit at the lowest cost to the ultimate user in the rural areas, to the benefit of both the bank and the borrower. And, as is the case for most developing countries, bank credit will be the key driver towards financing emerging activities.

6. Strategy for Bank Credit

There has been a long history of concern regarding agricultural credit. The increase in share of institutional credit to agriculture has been rather slow. It has clearly been found difficult to extend institutional credit in rural areas. Some of the important reasons pertained to risk perception, costs of its assessment and management, lack of rural infrastructure, and vast geographical spread of the rural areas with more than half a million villages, some sparsely populated.

Lending to small borrowers dispersed over vast expenses of geographical areas naturally involve high transaction costs. The strategy that evolved after considerable experimentation was to provide for directed credit to priority sectors that have primarily included agriculture and small scale industries. This was also the key reason for nationalisation of banks. That this strategy has been relatively successful is borne out by the data (Table 1), but it may have reached its limit, as also demonstrated by the deterioration in the reach of formal credit in the 1990s.

The key issue now is how to mainstream rural credit from institutional sources so as to achieve wider coverage, expand financial inclusion and promote economic growth. Increasingly, banks and other financial intermediaries have to see the extension of rural credit as a business opportunity and not as an obligation to do forced directed lending.

One strategy that is achieving great popularity and wide acceptance is that of microfinance, as best exemplified by the success of the Bangladesh Grameen Bank, which has now also achieved even greater recognition through the award of the Nobel Peace Prize to Mohammad Yunus. But most microfinance is not only for crops, but for other lending, in both rural and urban areas. The main issue is that of reducing transaction costs for both the lender and the borrower.

For banks, microfinance agencies and other financial intermediaries to look at rural lending as business opportunities, much more information generation has to be done so that they recognise and understand the many different activities that take place in the rural economy in addition to crop agriculture. Non-cereal foods, non-food agriculture, service activities, construction and housing, rural retail activities, will all increase levels of formal financing channels that are easy to access. This will need innovation in risk assessment, reduction in transaction costs, the search for new credit channels, and the use of cheaper information technology for delivery and collection systems.

The task of policy-makers in designing an appropriate package of measures becomes more challenging considering the fact that the new growth areas of agriculture are characterised by a high degree of heterogeneity, unlike in the case of traditional crops such as rice and wheat. There is a multiplicity of varieties that can be produced in each of these product groups; production is often regionally concentrated; the production and marketing conditions differ significantly; and the input requirements are equally heterogeneous. Hence, policies and programmes that are to be attuned to support higher productivity and production in these areas need to be much more regionally disaggregated and knowledge intensive. A key difference in approach would have to be the much greater involvement of region-specific market participants, and of private sector suppliers in all these activities, and credit suppliers ranging from public sector banks, co-operative banks, the new private sector banks and micro-credit suppliers, especially self-help groups.

To finance all these new activities, which will aid and accelerate economic growth tremendously, banks will clearly need to step up their efforts in generating deposits as well from the many currently underserved households and small businesses.

7. Role of RBI

Historically, the Reserve Bank and the Government of India have been making efforts to increase banking penetration in the country. Some of these measures include the creation of State Bank of India in 1955; nationalisation of commercial banks in 1969 and 1980; initiating the Lead Bank Scheme in 1970; establishing regional rural banks (RRBs) in 1975; introducing a Self-help Group (SHG)-Bank Linkage Programme in 1992 and formulating the *Kisan* Credit Card scheme in 2001. Notwithstanding these improvements, financial inclusion found a place in policy documents only very recently. In the Annual Policy of the Reserve Bank for 2004-05, the Governor, Dr. Reddy observed ....

> There has been expansion, greater competition and diversification of ownership of banks leading to both enhanced efficiency and systemic resilience in the banking sector. However, there are legitimate concerns in regard to the banking practices that tend to exclude rather than attract vast sections of population, in particular pensioners, self-employed and those employed in unorganised sector. While commercial considerations are no doubt important, the banks have been bestowed with several privileges, especially of seeking public deposits on a highly leveraged basis, and consequently they should be obliged to provide banking services to all segments of the population, on equitable basis.

Pursuant to this, the Reserve Bank has undertaken a number of measures with the objective of attracting the financially excluded population into the structured financial system. These measures, mainly, are in the nature of code of ethics and voluntary charters to promote greater financial access (Box 2).

Box 2: Measures undertaken by Reserve Bank towards Financial Inclusion

In November 2005, banks were advised to make available a basic banking 'no-frills' account with low or nil minimum stipulated balances as well as charges to expand the outreach of such accounts to vast sections of the population. Several banks have since introduced such 'no-frills' account with and without value-added features. According to the information available with the Reserve Bank, about five lakh no-frill accounts have been opened until March 31, 2006, of which about two-third are with the public sector and one-third with the private sector banks.

In order to ensure that persons belonging to low income group, both in urban and rural areas do not encounter difficulties in opening bank accounts owing to procedural hassles, the know your customer (KYC) procedures for opening accounts has been simplified. The Reserve Bank has directed banks to make available all printed material used by retail customers in English, Hindi and the concerned regional language. More recently, in January 2006, banks were permitted to utilise the services of non-governmental organisations (NGOs/SHGs), microfinance institutions and other civil society organisations as intermediaries in providing financial and banking services through the use of business facilitator and business correspondent models.

To extend hassle-free credit to bank customers in rural areas, the guidelines on general credit card (GCC) schemes were simplified to enable customers' access credit on simplified terms and conditions, without insistence on security, purpose or end-use of credit. With a view of providing hassle-free credit to customers, banks were allowed to issue general credit cards akin to *Kisan* credit cards. A simplified mechanism for one-time settlement of loans with principal amount up to Rs. 25,000 which have become doubtful and loss assets as on September 30, 2005 was suggested for adoption. In case of loans granted under Government-sponsored schemes, banks were advised to frame separate guidelines following a state-specific approach to be evolved by the State-Level Bankers' Committee (SLBC). Banks have been specifically advised that borrowers with loans settled under the one time settlement scheme will be eligible to re-access the formal financial system for fresh credit. Banks were advised to give effect to these measures at all branches for achieving greater financial inclusion. Initiatives have also been undertaken towards achieving greater financial inclusion in the North-Eastern region, which had perennially remained under-banked.

The Reserve Bank considers that IT-enabled services can meet the challenges which need to be addressed for increasing the scope and coverage of financial inclusion such as lack of adequate infrastructure, higher transaction costs and low volumes of transactions. The Reserve Bank has already initiated action in the North-Eastern region.

Source: Reserve Bank of India.

The Reserve Bank has also been periodically issuing guidelines on public grievance redressal mechanism in banks, including constitution of customer service centers. Based on the recommendations of a Committee on Procedures and Performance Audit of Public Services for ensuring improvements in quality of service rendered, banks were advised to constitute a Customer Service Committee of the Board. In the Reserve Bank, the Customer Service Department has recently been constituted to, *inter alia*, serve as the interface between customers and banks.

On a broader plane, the Reserve Bank has been adopting a two-pronged strategy to generate greater awareness and expand the reach of banking services—which can be termed as empowerment and protection. As regards the former, financial inclusion is the first stage of the process. This is strengthened by inculcating awareness among the masses through financial education. Concurrently, an advisory mechanism in the form of credit counseling is being encouraged to help distressed borrowers and bring them within the fold of formal finance. As regards protection, a Banking Codes and Standards Board of India has been established recently to ensure a comprehensive code of conduct for minimum standards of banking services to be offered by banks. The revised Banking Ombudsman Scheme has been put in place to redress deficiencies in customer service by banks.

8. Concluding Remarks

The economy is presently in a phase of rapidly rising incomes, rural and urban, arising from an expansion of extant economic activities as well as the creation of new activities. Corporate profitability has exhibited sustainable trends and consumer incomes are increasing rapidly, riding on the growth momentum. All of these developments suggest that the demand for financial services, both for savings as well as production purposes, will be greater than has been the case in the past, and there will be many new entrants in need of financial services who have not hitherto been served. At present our financial depth is much lower than that of other Asian countries, though it has picked up in the recent past. While there is evidence of an increase in financial deepening, particularly during the present decade, the increase in the breadth and coverage of formal finance has been less than adequate. Deepening the financial system and widening its reach is crucial for both accelerating growth and for equitable distribution, given the present stage of development of our country.

There has been a burst of entrepreneurship across the country, spanning rural, semi-urban and urban areas. This has to be nurtured and financed. It is only through growth of enterprises across all sizes that competition will be fostered. A small entrepreneur today will be a big entrepreneur tomorrow, and might well become a multinational enterprise eventually if given the comfort of financial support. But we also have to understand that there will be failures as well as successes. Banks will therefore have to tone up their risk assessment and risk management capacities, and provide for these failures as part of their risk management. Despite the risk, financing of first time entrepreneurs is a must for financial inclusion and growth.

The Parliament passed the Credit Information Bureau Act.... This should enable, over time, the availability of credit histories of both individuals and small businesses, which will help significantly in reducing transactions and information costs for banks. It will also help in spreading the credit culture among borrowers. It should help banks greatly in assessing and managing risk at low cost.

As poverty levels decline and households have greater levels of discretionary incomes, they will be first time financial savers. They will, therefore, need to have easy access to formal financial systems to get into the banking habit. Banks will need to innovate and devise newer methods of including such customers into their fold. The importance of 'no-frills' account and expanding the range of identity documents that is acceptable to open an account without sacrificing objectivity of the process in this milieu can never be over-emphasised. Banks will need to go to their customers, rather than the other way around.

The micro-credit and the Self Help Group movements are in their infancy but are gathering force. More innovation in the form of business facilitators and correspondents will be needed for banks to increase their outreach for banks to ensure financial inclusion. New entrants to the banking system need households at their doorstep.

To conclude, ... increasing liberalisation and higher economic growth, the role of banking sector is poised to increase in the financing pattern of economic activities within the country. To meet the growing credit demand, the banks need to mobilise resources from a wider deposit base and extend credit to activities hitherto not financed by banks. The trend of increasing commercialisation of agriculture and rural activities should generate greener pastures, and banks should examine the benefits of increasing penetration therein. Financial inclusion will strengthen financial deepening and provide resources to the banks to expand credit delivery. Thus, financial inclusion will lead to financial development in our country which will help to accelerate economic growth.

REFERENCES

Aghion, P. and Howitt, P. (1998): *Endogenous Growth Theory,* MIT Press.

Aghion, P. and Howitt, P. (2005): *Appropriate Growth Policy: A Unifying Framework*, The 2005 Joseph Schumpeter Lecture, European Economic Association, Amsterdam.

Barth, J., Caprio, G. and Levine, R. (2001): *The Regulation and Supervision of Banks around the World: A New Database*, World Bank Policy Research Working Paper No. 2588, Washington DC.

Bell, C. (2001): "Post-independence India: A Case of Finance-led Industrialisation", *Journal of Development Economics,* 65, 153-75.

Buckland, J. and Guenther, B. (2005): 'There Are No Banks Here, Financial and Insurance Exclusion in Winnipeg North End', *Social Sciences and Humanities Research Council of Canada* (September).

Caskey, J.P., Duran, C.R., and Solo, T.M. (2006): "The Urban Unbanked in Mexico and the United States', World Bank Policy Research Working Paper 3835.

Connolly, C. and Hajaj, K. (2001): "Financial Services and Social Exclusion", Financial Services Consumer Policy Center, University of New South Wales.

Government of India: *Economic Survey* (various years), Government of India, New Delhi.

HM Treasury (1999): *Access to Financial Services*. London: HM Treasury.

Kempson, E. (2006): "Policy Level Response to Financial Exclusion in Developed Economies: Lessons for Developing Countries", Paper Presented at the Conference, Access to Finance: Building Inclusive Financial Systems, World Bank, Washington, D.C.

Kempson, E., Caskey, J., Whyley, C. and Collard, S. (2000): *In or Out?* London: Financial Services Authority.

King, R.G. and Levine, R. (1993): "Finance and Growth: Schumpeter Might Be Right", *Quarterly Journal of Economics,* 108, 717-37.

Levine, R. and Zervos, S. (1998): "Stock Markets, Banks and Economic Growth," *American Economic Review,* 88, 537-58.

Mohan, R. (2002): "Transforming Indian Banking: In Search of a Better Tomorrow", *RBI Bulletin* (January).

Mohan, R. (2004): "Financial Sector Reforms in India: Policies and Performance Analysis", *RBI Bulletin* (October).

Mohan, R. (2006): "Agricultural Credit in India: Status, Issues and Future Agenda", *Economic and Political Weekly* (March), 1013-23.

NCAER (2003): *India Market Demographics Report 2002*, New Delhi: NCAER.

Rajan, R.G. and Zingales, L. (1998): "Financial Dependence and Growth", *American Economic Review,* 88, 559-86.

Rajan, R.G. and Zingales, L. (2003): *Saving Capitalism from Capitalists,* Crown Business, New York.

Reserve Bank of India (2004): *Report of the Advisory Committee on Flow of Credit to Agriculture and Related Activities from Banking System* (Chairman: V. S. Vyas), RBI, Mumbai.

Annex Table 1: Select Macro Economic Indicators—Annual Average Growth Rate

(per cent)

	1970-71 to 1990-91	1991-92 to 2000-01	2001-02 to 2005-06
1	2	3	4
1. Per capita income*	2.0	3.5	5.3
2. Population	2.2	2.0	1.7
3. GDP (constant prices)	4.4	5.7	6.7
Agriculture	2.9	2.6	2.5
Industry	5.9	5.9	6.2
of which:			
Manufacturing	5.7	6.1	6.8
Services	5.3	7.4	8.6
4. Gross Domestic Savings (as per cent of GDP)	18.7	23.2	27
Household	13.7	18.7	22.7
Corporate	1.7	3.9	4.2
Public	3.3	0.7	0.1
5. Gross Domestic Investment (as per cent of GDP)	19.8	24.3	26.4
6. Inflation (WPI)	8.7	7.8	4.7

*: NNP (factor cost)
Source: National Accounts Statistics, CSO.

Annex Table 2: Index of Openness of the Indian Economy

(per cent of GDP)

	1991-96	1996-2001	2001-06
1	2	3	4
1. Merchandise Exports	8.0	8.8	11.3
2. Merchandise Imports	10.1	12.4	14.9
3. Gross Invisible Receipts*	4.1	6.1	9.2
4. Gross Invisible Payments	3.1	3.8	5.1
5. Index of opening (1+2+3+4)	25.3	31.1	40.5

* Less official transfers.
Source: Reserve Bank of India.

Agro-Business: In Search of New Frontiers Global Perspectives in Agricultural Finance

M.B.N. Rao

PREAMBLE

Our country's transition from the position as food importing country to the present position of self-sufficiency in food production is, by any standards, remarkable. In 1950-51, the food production was 50.83 million tonnes. With the ushering in of "Green Revolution" which started in 1965-66, the food production increased to 211.17 million tonnes by 2001-02. The food production has been more or less stagnant thereafter. With Agriculture sector contributing substantially to our GDP—both directly and indirectly, the time has come to kick-start the second round of "Green Revolution". Agribusiness and Agriprocessing should be the main driver of the second round of Green Revolution with crop diversification as one of the main strategies. Banks in the country had contributed well in the first round of Green Revolution. The second Green Revolution offers a much greater role for banks.

If the history of Agricultural development of the developed nations is put on a scanner, one could see that after a phase of rapid increase in productivity and efficiency in Agricultural sector, they all have graduated into Agriprocessing and Agribusiness. Today, agriculture is being perceived as a business proposition, rather than a way of life for the rural people in the developing world.

We are presently in the transitional stage of converting agriculture into Agribusiness. This involves several policy initiatives and huge investment and introduction of latest technology.

The food habits within the country are changing. The growing middle-class is prepared to accept the changes. The ever increasing disposable income of middle-class with availability of cheap credit is driving every business and it is quite natural that the Agribusiness is also likely to be driven by this changing consumption pattern. The demand for processed/ semi-processed food in urban centre is certainly on the rise and now it is being mostly met by imports.

The huge domestic market and large international market throw open great avenues for financing this sector. By international market here, I mean not only the developed nations, but also the developing economies of East and Middle-East and Africa. India has all the advantages, viz. varied agro-climatic conditions to produce every product of demand, cheap and strong labour, abundant natural resources and largest agriculture extension/research institutions. Still the share of agriculture in Indian exports is only 15%. What is required is the initiative to make huge investments coupled with strong policy support.

Need for Diversification and Value Addition in Agriculture

Diversification of agriculture and developing processing industry with high level of sophistication to meet strict international standards would have major multiplier effects on employment and equitable income growth. Agribusiness has a significant role in rural and economic development, and agro-enterprises can be a major source of non-farm employment and income.

It is to be recognized that a strong and dynamic food processing industry can play a vital role in diversification and commercialization of agriculture, ensure value addition to agricultural produce, generate employment, enhance income levels and create quality products for export.

Value addition is constrained by the long value chain, with too many intermediaries making scale efficiencies difficult.

In recognition of the Tenth Five-Year Plan's priorities for public sector investment, the Government of India has identified Agribusiness development as a strategic priority. Government of India has initiated several steps to develop Agribusiness both for domestic and export markets. Some of the steps initiated/ proposed include:

(i) Promoting direct marketing.
(ii) Improving credit flow to the agriculture sector.
(iii) Improving credit delivery supported by a system of negotiable warehouse receipts.
(iv) Enabling forward and future trading in commodities.
(v) Promoting the use of information technology in agricultural marketing.
(vi) Improving extension services.

The National Horticulture Board has estimated the current domestic fruit production at about 46 million tonnes (almost 10% of global production) and vegetable production at almost 90 million tonnes (about 15% of global production). Production of fruits and vegetables has been growing at compounded annual rate of around 5% over the past decade. Although we are the world's second largest producer of fruit and vegetables, only 2–4% of this production is commercially processed, in contrast to 83% in Malaysia, 78% in Philippines and 30% in Thailand.

The best of international technology has to come to India in this field. Tremendous changes are to be brought in the area of processing, packaging, marketing covering the entire value chain. To kick-start the process of adopting the best technology, there is an urgent need to establish a technology bank and incubation centres. Small units cannot bring this change. The food processing industry has to be driven by corporates as the capital investment is huge.

Financing Opportunities in Agribusiness

Strength of Indian Banking

Immediately the nationalization of major banks in 1969 induced Commercial Banks in India to spread their branch network to every nook and corner of the country. Later in 1976 Regional Rural Banks, a set of new banks with focus on rural areas, were established. Commercial Banks and Regional Rural

Banks have today a branch network of 68,116 (as in March 2005) with an average population of 16,000 per bank branch (as in March 2005). This phenomenal outreach of banks in the country is a great strength and it could be leveraged well to transform the traditional agriculture into Agribusiness.

With domestic savings growing at 28.1% of GDP, resources available for lending does not pose a major constraint. (*Economic Survey*, 2004-05).

Since early '90s, Indian agriculture has made forays into commercial and hi-tech agriculture, high value crops, etc., both for domestic and export markets. These require larger investments. A large number of corporates, technocrats, new generation entrepreneurs, etc., are venturing into this area. For banks and financial institutions, Agribusiness offers a huge potential whose annual growth rate is likely to exceed that of other sectors. With newer and newer areas under Agribusiness emerging, for Commercial Banks a huge opportunity for lending is slowly opening up.

Role of Banks in Bringing Out New Credit Products

As a financial intermediary, banks can play a major role in promotion of Agribusiness ventures. Banks should be prepared to offer products to suit the changing needs. A credit product for a banker is not static but it is a dynamic one and has to be responsive to emerging situations and changes. Therefore, credit products cannot be viewed from a narrow prism. The present credit products of the Commercial Banks in India for the producer, i.e. the farmers are well-known and do not need elaboration. However, it would be apt to look into some of the new areas which can drastically diversify agriculture in the country and where banks can play a stellar role in the position.

Indian Agriculture in the Global Context—Financing Opportunities

New Frontiers

1. **Post-Harvest Management**

(a) *Cold Storages*

Post-Harvest Management holds the key for value addition to agriculture products. Post-Harvest Management includes grading, packaging of the produce and storing with end to end market focused approach. There is a need to develop cold chains and establishment of large and sophisticated "controlled atmosphere cold storages" in strategic locations for long storage of fruits and vegetables. This provides a good avenue for the banks for lending, as huge investments are needed for creating such a large infrastructure.

(b) *Milk—Value Chain*

Even a partial upgradation of animal population has created surplus milk production in India. The future in this area is extremely promising, but the potential needs to be harnessed to produce high quality dairy products conforming to best global standards. Investment in this area needs to be made from end to end.

Establishing innumerable number of privately owned milk chilling plants under contract with large players in dairy, like Amul, State/District Co-operatives, etc., in every village is the key for further leap. This offers tremendous scope for the vastly networked banking system of the country with huge financing opportunities.

(c) *Logistics*

The upscaling of quality in preservation, demands availability of a large number of refrigerated vehicles and containers to carry the produce like fruits, vegetables and milk from farms to plants. This again needs large investments providing scope for financing opportunities.

(d) *Establishment of Marketing Infrastructure, Grading and Standardization*

With the modifications in the APMC Act permitting setting up of agricultural markets in private and co-operative sector and allowing direct marketing, the need for establishing of marketing infrastructure is felt. The expert committee set up by Ministry of Agriculture has estimated that an investment requirement of Rs. 11,172 crores in the next ten years would be required for establishing infrastructure in agricultural marketing. Infrastructure includes:

- construction of market yards, platforms for loading, assembling and auctioning, weighing and mechanical handling equipments, etc.,
- assembling, grading, standardization, quality certification, labeling, packing,
- infrastructure for e-trading,
- mobile infrastructure for post-harvest operations such as grading, packaging, quality testing, etc.

Understanding the vitality, Government of India has recently come out with a scheme which offers subsidy benefits also. The present focus for market yards is only for handling dry crops that have high shelf life. Focus needs to be shifted to market yards/auctioning centres that can handle perishable commodities including flowers. Again this needs huge investments. This provides the Commercial Banks with yet another avenue for extending finance.

2. Other Infrastructure and Spread of IT in Rural Centres

Recent trend is that rural India always tries to emulate the urban counterparts when it comes to comfort and convenience.

Today, shopping malls are the pride of metros and large urban centres. Parts of rural India with improved income levels also have developed to accept similar exclusive agricultural malls that have a trade ambience suiting the local needs. These complexes or rural malls could offer diversity of agriculture related goods and services including expert advice, in addition to usual white goods and other essential home needs. The corporate sector has already sown the first seeds in rural technology participation in this line. Some of the notable corporate initiatives in this direction include ITC's e-choupals, Hindustan Lever's I–Shakthi, Amul's IS-Kiosks. Banks have tremendous opportunities to develop credit products to suit such initiatives.

3. Agro-based Industries

The Agro Processing Industry provides vital link between industry and agriculture. It aims at reducing the wastage of the produce and mops up surplus at farm level, thereby ensuring higher income to the farmers and make available good quality and hygienic food/produce to the consumers. Worldwide, agro-processing industry is emerging as a strong economic activity in view of development of new technological capabilities in processing, storage, etc. The potential of agro-processing in India is vast due to relative abundance of diversified crops and availability of man power.

Agro-processing industries provide a huge potential for Banks to lend. The finance for agro-processing can be in the form of project lending, term loans, working capital finance. Extending timely and adequate working capital to processing units is of paramount importance considering the seasonal and perishable nature of the produce.

Another area of opportunity for lending is modernization of existing facilities. Apart from exports to developed countries/ better infrastructure and processing, conforming to HACCP or Euro-Gap Standard, we need to extend term loan facilities to the existing units quickly conforming to these standards.

The present efforts in this area are sporadic. Stand alone small units are not viable and their failure rate is high. They cannot afford high cost of technology, machinery and total quality management.

4. Contract Farming

Contract farming of various types is already in practice for certain commercial crops. There are many success stories on contract farming such as Amul, Sugarcane cultivation in Maharashtra, Pepsico India in respect of potato, tomato, groundnut, etc., seed production contracts by Hybrid Seed Companies, poultry integration through contract farming, etc. On the other side of the coin, for a banker, financing under contract farming has many advantages. Contract farming provides good framework for flow of credit to marginal/small farmers, tenant cultivators/oral lessees, etc., at a reduced transaction cost. They can also be organized into Self Help Groups. However, there are certain grey areas such as security comfort for the banker, transparency in contracts, legal protection to the contracting parties, etc., which need to be addressed to. However, in the days to come, as more and more agroprocessing units get established, contract farming would become a buzzword and offer a good potential for the bankers to lend.

Only through contract farming, the stringent international quality standards can be complied. Specific product of a standard specific quality needs to be produced in sufficient quantity. Several products including gherkin, pineapple and even flowers are in great demand world over. But we are not able to provide the required quantity in standardized uniform quality. Contract farming is the right answer for this.

5. Collateral Management Services

A Collateral Manager is one who has a chain of warehouses for storing of commodities and provide end-to-end solution in warehousing. A Collateral Manager identifies and accredits warehouses, evolves commodity specific warehouse standards, accepts commodities and issues warehouse receipts (also in electronic form) and delivers the commodities on instructions. Utilizing the services of the Collateral Manager will mitigate the risks involved in commodity backed financing. Canara Bank has recently launched a scheme to extend finance against the warehouse receipts issued by National Collateral Management Services Limited, a company promoted by National Commodities and Derivatives Exchange Limited (NCDEX) and financial institutions. This kind of arrangement provides a comfort zone for the Banks and also the much needed liquidity for the producer. It is expected that in the days to come, financing against commodities would expand, with wider acceptance of the services of Collateral Managers.

6. Price Risk Mitigation Products

With commodity exchanges in India now spreading far and wide covering a large number of commodities, it is time to make the benefit of commodities markets available to the farmers. The commodity exchanges need to be permitted to trade in derivatives with put and call option. Commercial banks in India with a wide network of branches in the rural areas can act as aggregators and act as an intermediary between the exchanges and farmers and thus make available the benefits of risk price insurance to large sections of the farmers through put option contract. This can be a win-win situation for both farmers and the banks, as banks can also use this to derive fee-based income for their intervention and reduce risk of extending crop loans.

7. Agri Export Zones

Agri Export Zones are set up by Government of India in various States for promoting specific produce/products in a contiguous area with an objective of providing remunerative returns on a sustained basis. The establishment of AEZs provides scope for credit, both under production and processing of agricultural produce.

A co-ordinated attempt to develop AEZ is yet to happen, except for a few sporadic initiatives. AEZs have been declared after careful study on the potential. Involvement and special focus by everyone concerned would only lead to the success of at least some of these AEZs. Banks, I am sure, would be more than willing to participate in the development of AEZs.

8. Food Parks

It is a concept where there will be a decentralized system of production and centralized system of processing and marketing. In many countries, the concept has been found viable. The concept could be another avenue for lending by the banks.

9. Bio-Fertilizers and Pesticides

With organic farming gaining popularity both within the country and abroad, there is good demand for bio-fertilizers and organic manure manufactured through anaerobic processes. Similarly, bio-pesticides and biological control (trichogramma for example) throws up other investment opportunities.

10. Other New Products/Avenues

One area, banks can provide liquidity to farmers, is to develop products to discount bills/Bill of Exchange of farmers on their supply of produce to corporates under contract farming or otherwise.

The transition from traditional agriculture to Agribusiness would also throw up opportunities for financing the ancillary units like packaging material industries, service centres, etc. Further, improved opportunities under channel financing and distributors of corporates are available to banks.

To make sustained success in Agribusiness a reality, product specific approach needs to be created. These product specific approaches are to be driven by the respective promotional agencies, for example, Amul or NDDB for dairy products, Spices Board for spices, Commodity Boards for various other specific commodities. If proper direction is given by the agencies, there is a good possibility of the products becoming popular. One recent example is the promotion of vanilla plantation by Spices Board. Huge quantity of vanilla is now produced and many farmers have shifted to vanilla cultivation during the last few years. Here again, as all of us know, the value addition on processing with proper technology is 50–100 times.

Constraints

Apart from the infrastructure bottlenecks and the economy of size, one major problem we face is the outdated APMC Act. Though a few states have amended, still it comes in the way of units/corporates going in for contract farming as they cannot directly procure the produce from farmer producers. Government can think of providing incentives to states to amend the APMC Act to enable the fruits of technology to reach the masses, in tune with the other reforms undertaken.

Conclusion

Agricultural credit from the banking sector has played a vital role in supporting improved agricultural production in the country during the "Green Revolution". The transformation to a successful technology oriented "Agribusiness" could really take off only when large corporates of the country appreciate the enormous business opportunities and enter this arena. Smaller units cannot bring about the transition as they have limitations to bringing in the best of technology and make huge investments.

Agribusiness financing too needs to undergo a metamorphosis to bring about the transition and banks need to come out with innovative financing products. Commercial banks in the country are today ready to support the second Agrirevolution in India in full measure.

Indian Banks and the Global Challenges*

8

V. Leeladhar

It gives me great pleasure and privilege to participate in the seminar jointly hosted by Indian Merchants' Chamber and IBA at a juncture when financial services sector across jurisdictions is going through a strong phase of increasing globalisation. Integration of economies leads to integration of financial markets catalyzing the globalisation process. The growing role of the financial sector in allocation of resources has significant potential advantages for the efficiency with which our economy functions. Consequently, the adverse consequences of malfunction of the financial system are likely to be more severe than they used to be in the past. Hence, all our efforts today are focused at ensuring greater financial stability. Given the significance of the Indian banking system, one cannot afford to underplay the importance of a robust and resilient banking system.

The enhanced role of the banking sector in the Indian economy, the increasing levels of deregulation along with the increasing levels of competition have facilitated globalisation of the Indian banking system and placed numerous demands on banks. Operating in this demanding environment has exposed banks to various challenges. The last decade has witnessed major changes in the financial sector—new banks, new financial institutions, new instruments, new windows, and new opportunities—and, along with all this, new challenges. While

---

* Inaugural address by Shri V. Leeladhar, Deputy Governor, Reserve Bank of India, at the seminar on "Indian Banks and the Global Challenges" organised jointly by the Indian Merchants' Chamber and the Indian Banks' Association in Mumbai on January 31, 2006. Reproduced from December 2005 issue of the Reserve Bank of India Bulletin.

deregulation has opened up new vistas for banks to augment revenues, it has entailed greater competition and consequently greater risks. Demand for new products, particularly derivatives, has required banks to diversify their product mix and also effect rapid changes in their processes and operations in order to remain competitive in the globalised environment.

Globalisation—A Challenge as well as an Opportunity

The benefits of globalisation have been well-documented and are being increasingly recognised. Globalisation of domestic banks has also been facilitated by tremendous advancement in information and communications technology. Globalisation has thrown up lot of opportunities but accompanied by concomitant risks. There is a growing realisation that the ability of countries to conduct business across national borders and the ability to cope with the possible downside risks would depend, *inter alia*, on the soundness of the financial system and the strength of the individual participants. Adoption of appropriate prudential, regulatory, supervisory, and technological framework on par with international best practices enables strengthening of the domestic banking system, which would help in fortifying it against the risks that might arise out of globalisation. In India, we had strengthened the banking sector to face the pressures that may arise out of globalisation by adopting the banking sector reforms in a calibrated manner, which followed the twin governing principles of non-disruptive progress and consultative process.[1]

Global Challenges in Banking

...A few broad challenges faced by the Indian banks have been identified in the following areas, *viz.* enhancement of customer service; application of technology; implementation of Basel II; improvement of risk management systems; implementation of new accounting standards; enhancement of transparency and disclosures; and compliance with KYC aspects. An overview of the global challenges would include the following: Basel II implementation; enhancing corporate governance; alignment of regulatory and accounting requirements; outsourcing risks; and application of advanced technology. I propose to cover these aspects now.

Basel II Implementation

Basel II implementation is widely acknowledged as a significant challenge faced by both banks and the regulators internationally. It is true that Basel II implementation may be seen as a compliance challenge. While it may be so for some banks,...Basel II implementation has another dimension which offers considerable opportunities to banks....two opportunities that are offered to banks, *viz.* refinement of risk management systems; and improvement in capital efficiency

Comprehensive risk management: Under Basel I banks were focused on credit and market risks. Basel II has brought into focus a larger number of risks requiring banks to focus on a larger canvas. Besides the increase in the number of risks, banks are now beginning to focus on their interlinkages with a view to achieve a more comprehensive risk management framework. Basel II implementation, therefore, is being increasingly seen as a medium through which banks constantly endeavour to upgrade the risk management systems to address the changing environment. Further, in the initial stages, banks were managing each risk in isolation. It is no longer adequate to manage each risk independently. Enterprises worldwide are, therefore, now putting in place an integrated framework for risk management which is proactive, systematic and spans across the entire organisation. Banks in India are also moving from the individual silo system to an enterprise wide risk management system. While the first milestone would be risk integration across the entity, banks are also aware of the desirability of risk aggregation across the group both in the specific risk areas as also across the risks. Banks would, therefore, be required to allocate significant resources towards this endeavour.

Capital efficiency: Basel II prescriptions have ushered in a transition from the traditional regulatory measure of capital adequacy to an evaluation of whether a bank has found the most efficient use of its capital to support its business, i.e. a transition from capital adequacy to capital efficiency. In this transition, how effectively capital is used will determine return on equity and a consequent enhancement of shareholder value. In effect, banks may adopt a more dynamic approach to use of capital, in which capital will flow quickly to its most efficient use. This revised efficiency approach is expected to guide the return-on-equity strategy and influence banks' business plans. With the extension of capital charge for market risks to the AFS portfolio this year, banks would need to shore up the capital levels not only for complying with these requirements but also for supporting the balance sheet growth. With a view to enhancing the options available to banks for augmenting their capital levels, the Reserve Bank has recently permitted banks to issue new capital instruments, including perpetual instruments. A notable feature of these instruments is that these are designed to help banks in not only managing their capital effectively but also efficiently.

Enhancing Corporate Governance

The issues related to corporate governance have continued to attract considerable national and international attention in light of a number of high-profile breakdowns in corporate governance. This becomes all the more relevant for banks since they not only accept and deploy large amount of uncollateralized public funds in fiduciary capacity, but also leverage such funds through credit creation. Banks are also important participants in the payment and settlement systems. In view of the above, legal prescriptions for ownership and governance of banks in Banking Regulation Act, 1949 have been supplemented by regulatory prescriptions issued by RBI from time to time.

In view of the importance of the banking system for financial stability, sound corporate governance is not only relevant at the level of the individual bank, but is also a critical ingredient at the system level. Effective risk management systems determine the health of the financial system and its ability to survive economic shocks. To a large extent, many risk management failures reflect a breakdown in corporate governance which arise due to poor management of conflicts of interest, inadequate understanding of key banking risks, and poor Board oversight of the mechanisms for risk management and internal audit. Corporate governance is, therefore, the foundation for effective risk managements in banks and thus the foundation for a sound financial system.[2] Therefore, the choices which banks make when they establish their risk management and corporate governance systems have important ramifications for financial stability. These systems can affect how the institution functions and how others perceive it in the marketplace.[3]

A good "governance culture" is crucial for financial stability but since it is 'intangible', rules may not be able to capture its essence effectively. Therefore, banks may have to cultivate a good governance culture building in appropriate checks and balances in their operations. There are four important forms of oversight that should be included in the organisational structure of any bank in order to ensure appropriate checks and balances: (1) oversight by the board of directors or supervisory board; (2) oversight by individuals not involved in the day-to-day running of the various business areas; (3) direct line supervision of different business areas; and (4) independent risk management, compliance and audit functions. In addition, it is important that key personnel are fit and proper for their jobs. Although some ownership structures might have the potential to alter the strategies and objectives of a bank, these banks will also face many of the same risks associated with weak corporate governance. Consequently, the general principles of sound corporate governance should also be applied to all banks irrespective of their unique ownership structures.[4]

Compliance with International Accounting Standards

One of the prime international standards considered relevant for ensuring a safe and sound banking system is the 'Core Principles for Effective Banking Supervision' issued by the Basel Committee on Banking Supervision (BCBS). Accounting standards are now a part of the set of twelve standards that have been identified by the Financial Stability Forum as conducive to a robust financial infrastructure. Financial reporting and prudential supervision have slightly different perspectives. While the former is oriented towards capturing the historical position, the latter has a forward looking element particularly with reference to measurement of impairment and capital. An important challenge, therefore, is to ensure that accounting standards and prudential frameworks are mutually consistent. While working towards achieving this consistency between the two sets of standards, it is essential for the regulators to be in a position to address any implications that the changes in accounting standards may have for the safety and soundness of banks.[5]

Derivative activity in banks in India has been increasing at a brisk pace. While the risk management framework for derivative trading, which is a relatively new area for Indian banks (particularly more in respect of structured products), is an essential prerequisite, the absence of clear accounting guidelines in this area is a matter of significant concern. It is widely accepted that as the volume of transactions increases, which is happening in the Indian banking system, the need to upgrade the accounting framework needs no emphasis. The World Bank's ROSC on Accounting and Auditing in India has commented on the absence of an accounting standard which deals with recognition, measurement, presentation and disclosures pertaining to financial instruments. The Accounting Standards Board of the Institute of Chartered Accountants of India (ICAI) is considering issue of Accounting Standards on the above aspects pertaining to financial Instruments. These will be the Indian parallel to International Financial Reporting Standard 7, International Accounting Standards 32 and 39. The proposed Accounting Standards will be of considerable significance for financial entities and could therefore have implications for the financial sector. The formal introduction of these Accounting Standards by the ICAI is likely to take some time in view of the processes involved. In the meanwhile, the Reserve Bank is considering the need for banks and financial entities adopting the broad underlying principles of IAS 39. Since this is likely to give rise to some regulatory/prudential issues all relevant aspects are being comprehensively examined. The proposals in this regard would, as is normal, be discussed with the market participants before introduction. Adoption and implementation of these principles are likely to pose a great challenge to both the banks and the Reserve Bank.

Outsourcing Risks

Banks are increasingly using outsourcing for achieving strategic aims leading to either rationalisation of operational costs or tapping specialist expertise which is not available internally. 'Outsourcing' may be defined as *a bank's use of a third party, including an affiliated entity within a corporate group, to perform activities on a continuing basis that would normally be undertaken by the bank itself*. Typically outsourced financial services include applications processing (loan origination, credit card), document processing, investment management, marketing and research, supervision of loans, data processing and back office related activities, etc.

Outsourcing might give rise to several risks including, strategic risk, reputation risk, compliance risk, operational risk, exit strategy risk, counterparty risk, country risk, access risk, concentration risk and systemic risk. The failure of a service provider to provide a specified service, ensure security/ confidentiality, comply with legal and regulatory requirements can lead to financial losses/reputational risk for the bank and could also lead to systemic risks for the entire banking system in a country. It would therefore be imperative for the bank outsourcing its activities to ensure effective management of these risks.

It is in this background that RBI has issued draft guidelines on outsourcing, which is intended to provide direction and guidance to banks to effectively manage risks arising from such outsourcing activities. The underlying principles for any outsourcing arrangement by a bank are that such arrangements should neither diminish the bank's ability to fulfil its obligations to its customers and the RBI nor impede effective supervision by RBI. Outsourcing banks, therefore, should take steps to ensure that the service provider employs the same high standard of care in performing the services as would be employed by the banks if the activities were conducted within the banks and not outsourced. Accordingly, banks are not expected to outsource any activity that would result in their internal control, business conduct, or reputation being compromised or weakened.

Application of Advanced Technology

Technology is a key driver in the banking industry, which creates new business models and processes, and also revolutionises distribution channels. Banks which have made inadequate investment in technology have consequently faced an erosion of their market shares. The beneficiaries are those banks which have invested in technology. Adoption of technology also enhances the quality of risk management systems in banks. Recognising the benefits of modernising their technology infrastructure banks are taking the right initiatives. While doing so, banks have four options to choose from: they can build a new system themselves, or buy best of the modules, or buy a comprehensive solution, or outsource. In this context, banks need to clearly define their core competencies to be sure that they are investing in areas that will distinguish them from other market players, and give them a competitive advantage.[6] A further challenge which banks face in this regard is to ensure that they derive maximum advantage from their investments in technology and avoid wasteful expenditure which might arise on account of uncoordinated and piecemeal adoption of technology; adoption of inappropriate/inconsistent technology and adoption of obsolete technology.

Capacity Building

As dictated by the changing environment, banks need to focus on appropriate capacity building measures to equip their staff to handle advanced risk management systems and supervisors also need to equally equip themselves with appropriate skills to have effective supervision of banks adopting those systems. In the likelihood of a high level of attrition in the system, banks need to focus on motivating their skilled staff and retaining them.[7] Skill requirements would be significantly higher for banks planning to migrate to the advanced approaches under Basel II. Capacity building gains greater relevance in these banks, so as to equip themselves to take advantage of the incentives offered under the advanced approaches.

A relevant point in this regard is that capacity building should be across the institution and not confined to any particular level or any particular area. The demand for better skills can be met either from within or from outside. It would perhaps be worthwhile to first glean through the existing resources to identify misplaced or hidden or forgotten resources and re-position them to boost the bank's efforts to capitalise on available skills. This does not undermine the benefits that a bank may derive by meeting their requirements from the market, but is only intended to prioritise the process.

Conclusion

The global challenges which banks face are not confined only to the global banks. These aspects are also highly relevant for banks which are part of a globalised banking system. Further, overcoming these challenges by the other banks is expected to not only stand them in good stead during difficult times but also augurs well for the banking system to which they belong and will also equip them to launch themselves as a global bank.

NOTES

1. Dr. Y.V. Reddy on Banking Sector Reforms in India: An Overview at the Institute of Bankers of Pakistan, Karachi, Pakistan, May 18, 2005.
2. Dr. Alan Bollard, Corporate Governance in the Financial Sector, Christchurch, New Zealand, 7 April 2003.
3. Mark W. Olson, *Business Trends and Management Challenges for the Banking Industry,* Annual Economic Outlook Conference, Middle Tennessee State University, Murfreesboro, Tennessee, 16 September 2005.
4. Enhancing Corporate Governance for Banking Organisations, Consultative document issued by BCBS, July 2005.
5. Malcolm D. Knight, Banking and Insurance Regulation and Supervision: Greater Convergence, Common Challenges, Madrid, 22-23 September 2004.
6. UBS AG, *The Bank for Banks Industry Challenges*, August 2004.
7. Ms. K.J. Udeshi, Financial System Stability and Basel II—Way Forward, Sri Lanka, August 2005.

Analytics and Dynamics of Banking in Resurgent India

9

Manoranjan Sharma

Time present and time past
Are both present in time future?
And time future contained in time past
Footfalls echo in the memory,
Down the passage we did not take
Towards the door we never opened.
—T.S. Eliot

Macro-Economic Setting

The banking sector is a microcosm of the economy. Hence, the case for repositioning banks has to be situated in a proper historical and comparative perspective. The ongoing process of economic reforms transformed the Indian economy with significant changes in the policy frame of banks. The inexorable process of globalisation requires fine-tuning of the financial reforms package by synchronising the conflicting needs of allocative efficiency and equity within the overarching context of India's development efforts. The basic issues relating to the Indian economy in general and banking in particular need to be identified against this broad canvas of growth, modernisation and distributive equity. This emboldens us to say, *a la*, Confucius:

Our greatest glory is not in never failing;
But in rising each and every time we fall.

Current State of Economy

One of the fastest growing economies

The Indian economy is one of the fastest growing economies among the major emerging market economies. With the world economy growing at around 4 per cent, Indian economy, on an average, grew 5.8 per cent during the pre-reform period (1980-81 to 1989-90) and over 6.5 per cent during 1994-95 to 2006-07. In fact in the last few years, the Indian economy has been growing at an average rate of 8.5 per cent and is now moving into the double-digit mode with GDP rising by over 9 per cent in FY 07. Thus India has consistently achieved the second fastest growth rate in the world in the last few years. The emergence of India and China as the world's most dynamic region has caused a tectonic shift. Economies across Asia are being transformed from passengers to co-drivers of globalization. Nothing illustrates this better than the fact that Indian companies made 50 acquisitions with a total of US $957 million in 2000. But in 2006, Indian companies made 146 acquisitions aggregating US $20.2 billion in 2000 (*Times Higher Education Supplement*: 2004, 2005 and 2006). These are figures, which cannot be trifled with and the macro-economic landscape clearly shows that India has its own place in the sun-now and even more in the future.

Overview of Indian Economy

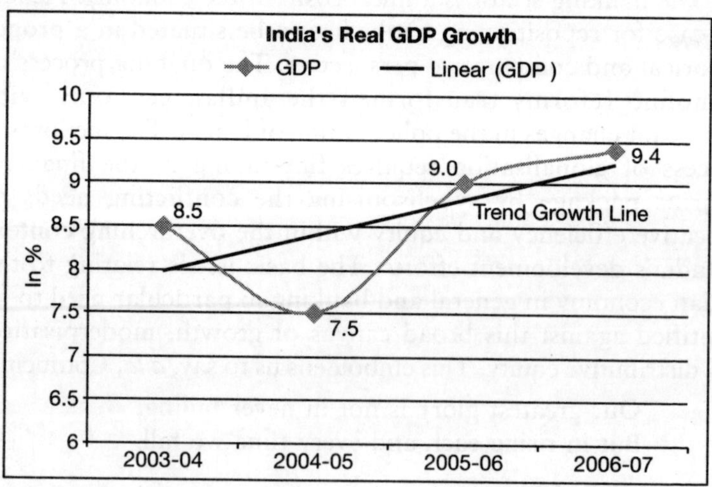

Comfortable Forex Reserves

Foreign exchange reserves of US $250 billion cover nearly one and half years of import requirements. Such exchange reserves provide stability to foreign exchange market and improve country's external rating.

Healthy Export Basket

The phased liberalisation of Export-Import policy over the years has resulted in diversification of export baskets and export of more value-added products and services. This has given rise to stability in export earnings. While world merchandise exports grew at 20 per cent, India achieved a remarkable growth of above 30 per cent growth in exports in the last 5 years.

Resurgent Industrial Sector/Enhanced Corporate Profitability

The liberalisation of industrial policy has improved efficiency and productivity of industrial sector in India. Greater capacity utilisation, diversification and value-addition have improved industrial production and enhanced corporate profitability in recent years. Industrial revival, in the post-reform period, has been broad-based, primarily driven by manufacturing sector with improved demand from rural population and rising exports. During the last 10 years, industrial production grew remarkably by about 7 per cent.

The acceleration in macroeconomic growth is manifested in robust economic indicators across the development spectrum, e.g., over 7 per cent GDP growth for four consecutive years, 20 per cent rise in exports for three years in a row, a record 30 per cent increase in corporate loans, 40 per cent increase in investment, 14 per cent rise in salaries in 2005, spending spree spearheaded by 50 per cent growth in home loans, 40 per cent rise in consumer credit. There are also aspects like wealth creation in stock markets, 50 per cent growth in mobile phones, booming airlines and auto industries, ascendancy of professional middle class, the emergence of new entrepreneurial class and the world's youngest workforce and a de-coupling of the Indian economy from the political processes and related uncertainties.

Buoyant Services Segments

1990s has been characterized by compositional change in GDP, where services sector has been led the expansion of GDP. With over 57 per cent share in the GDP, the services sector is the predominant segment, with communication services, financial services, business services (including IT) and community services being the main growth drivers. In the coming years, India will be the "International Hub" for Business Process Outsourcing, particularly in the areas of accounting, Data Mining, Financial consultancy, patent research, R&D in pharmaceuticals and biotechnology, legal services etc.

Controlled Inflationary Outlook

With an effective and responsive monetary policy, India is one of the lowest inflationary economies among the emerging market economies.

Explanatory Factors

Explanatory factors for the increase in per capita income stress "convergence" of appropriate policies, i.e. free flow of capital to the poorer countries, initiation of technological changes and positive cascading effects of information and communication technology (ICT). India's economy is thus in a growth mode at once high and broad-based transcending IT and other service sectors to encompass traditional industries like textiles, steel, ready-made garments, etc.

Future Growth Prospects

Boston Consulting Group's research indicates that India is better placed for future growth. India's capital markets operate with greater efficiency than China's. India's capital markets are also much more transparent. Companies can raise the money needed. India's legal system, which is certainly slow, is much more advanced and is able to settle sophisticated and complex cases. Its banking system has relatively few non-performing assets. India's democracy and media are vibrant. All these features provide a safety valve for the incoherent changes that modern day economic growth brings.

Goldman Sachs Report—BRIC

According to investment banker Goldman Sachs, over the next 50 years, the BRIC (Brazil, Russia, India and China) economies could become a much larger force in the world economy. BRIC encompasses over 40 per cent of the world's population and holds a combined GDP of $12.14 trillion. Brazil, India and China together with Russia (BRIC) will outstrip the current dominant members of the global economy within half a century. By 2050, the BRIC's economies together could be larger than the G6 (the US, Japan, England, France, Italy and Germany) in dollar terms. By 2025 they could account for over half the size of the G6. Currently they are worth less than 15 per cent. Of the current G6, only the US and Japan might be among the six largest economies in dollar terms in 2050. The list of the world's ten largest economies might look quite different in 2050.

According to Goldman Sachs India's economy could be larger than Japan's by 2032, and China's economy could be larger than the US by 2041. Among the BRIC members, India has the potential to record the fastest growth over the next 50 years. Growth could be higher than 5 per cent over the next 30 years and close to 5 per cent in the next 20 years. By 2030, China's per capita income could be around $30,000. In the US, income per capita by 2050 could reach roughly $80,000.

Deutsche Bank's Study on "India Rising"

The study persuasively argued that India could sustain a 6-8 per cent annual economic growth rate for the next 10-15 years. "Favorable demographics, increasing investment in education and infrastructure and further integration with the world economy" would push India's growth rate beyond China. "India will thus become the fastest growing economy out of 34 developed and emerging markets and the world's 3rd largest economy by 2020. Gross Domestic Product per capita will double from roughly $2,500 today at purchasing power parity to almost $5,000 in 2020."

Grey Areas

There are issues of concern, e.g., lack of real progress on reforms like attracting easier labour laws, PSU disinvestment, deregulation of education and agriculture, unbundling red-tape for businesses and moving towards single-window clearance, rise in inflation and interest rates damaging consumption and investment, lack of headway in critical infrastructure of power, transport, ports and water supply and FDI in retail, insurance, banking and infrastructure. There is also the danger of a sudden and prolonged fall in real estate and stock markets wiping out wealth and dampening sentiment and the threat of a global meltdown reducing foreign investment and slashing exports.

Box 1: OECD Survey: Salient Features

The first economic survey of India by the Organisation of Economic Cooperation and Development (OECD) identified and isolated the following constraining factors:

- 46 Central and over 200 state laws necessitating consolidation.
- Stringent labour laws are leading to decline in regular employment and rise in contractual jobs.
- Lack of flexibility accentuating labour market inequalities, leading to rising urban poverty rates.
- Manufacturing units in formal sector replacing labour with capital investment.
- Quiet reforms in some states providing more fluid labour markets.

The rapidly appreciating rupee may also adversely affect domestic producers, apart from exporters. It is disconcerting that despite a billion-strong population, a large proportion is of working age, there continues to be a skills shortage. All these factors require an accent on manufacturing resurgence, agricultural transformation, reduced regional disparities and a sharper focus on employment, health, education and gender equality to successfully meet the emerging onslaughts. Consequently, the banking system needs a reorientation of development strategies.

Enhancing Productivity

Attempts to increase productivity could conceivably be made in several ways. Such attempts range from legal solutions to new management styles to technology innovation. While continuing productivity-enhancing economic reforms, India must focus on reforming labour laws, financial systems, the legal environment, non-tariff barriers, and shifting to more market-friendly investment policies. Second, extending some of the benefits of growth in technology to a wider group of people is both a challenge and an opportunity. Third, the challenge of demographic transition requires creative thinking on various issues—domestic and international, economic and political, cultural and social.

Post-Reforms Banking—Watershed Development

Both economic theory and empirical evidence (Rajan and Zingales, 1998; Demirgúc-Kunt and Maksimovic, 1998) unmistakably bring out a strong correlation between finance and growth. While bank nationalization fostered growth with distributive justice, Indian banking sector emerged as a major growth driver, particularly since the onset of financial sector reforms as an integral part of Structural Adjustment Programme (SAP). Pre-reforms 'financial repression' was characterized by regulation of interest rates, statutory pre-emption of resources by government, cross-subsidization of interest rates, high and mounting level of non-performing assets (NPAs), etc. Post-reforms, the liberalization process attempted to transform the banking institutions into organizationally strong, financially viable and operationally efficient units by a process of well-sequenced and interconnected reforms in several segments.

Indian Banking—Salient Features

Dominant Segment of Financial System

Banking sector has predominant share in the Indian financial system and Indian financial system is primarily bank-based.

Robust Growth in Branch Network/Widespread Geographical Presence

Significant Growth in Business

SCBs recorded significant growth during 2006-07, with SCBs' non-food credit up by 28.4 per cent compared to an increase of 31.8 per cent in 2005-06. Non-food credit offtake during 2006-07 was fuelled by agriculture, industry, housing, small transport operators and retail loans. However, buoyancy in the capital market and increased postal savings led to lower growth in aggregate deposits. Aggregate deposits of SCBs registered a growth of 23.7 per cent during 2006-07 compared to 18.1 per cent in 2005-06, with advances recording 30.8 per cent growth in 2006-07 as against 27.6 per cent in 2005-06.

Active Contributor to Economic Growth

Banking sector has been playing a predominant role in asset creation with assets of SCBs constituting 72.5 per cent of GDP at factor cost at current price in 2005-06.

Key Element of Financial Sector Reforms

Interest rates are largely deregulated and Banks given the freedom to declare their own Prime Lending Rates (PLR). Call money, Certificate Deposits and Commercial Paper markets have been de-regulated. SLR and CRR have been gradually reduced to the present levels of 25 per cent and 7 per cent respectively. Prudential regulations have also been introduced in tune with global benchmarks. Public sector banks have been allowed to expand their capital base with equity participation. Dilution of equity has improved efficiency and increased competition in Banks.

Indian Banking in the Pre-Reform Phase

Pre-Reform Phase (1969—90)

The Indian financial system in the pre-reform period essentially catered to the needs of planned development in a mixed-economy framework, where the public sector occupied the 'commanding heights' of the Indian economy. Banks were directed to spread their branches in rural areas and allocate credit at concessional rates for agriculture, tiny and SSI sectors. Interest rates were controlled and it was structured to make bank credit available to favoured activities at concessional rates.

Indian Banking: First Generation Reforms

First Generation Reforms (1991—97)

A series of reform measures were initiated to establish an enabling environment for banks to overcome functional and financial constraints related to administered structure of interest rates, high levels of preemption in the form of reserve requirements, and credit allocation to certain sectors. Interest rates have been largely deregulated except for certain specific classes; these are: savings deposit accounts, non-resident Indian (NRI) deposits, small loans up to Rs. 2 lakh and export credit. Banks have been given the freedom to declare their own Prime Lending Rates (PLR). Call money, Certificate Deposits and Commercial Paper markets have been de-regulated. SLR and CRR have been gradually reduced to the present levels of 25 per cent and 7 per cent respectively. Prudential regulations for the banking system have also been introduced in tune with global benchmarks. Public sector banks have been allowed to expand their capital base with equity participation. Diversification of ownership has also led to greater market accountability and improved efficiency.

Indian Banking: Second Generation Reforms (Post-1997)

- Banks have progressively introduced information technology and initiated steps for business process re-engineering (BPR).
- Banks are directed to maintain a separate Investment Fluctuation Reserve (IFR) out of profits, towards interest rate risk. Focus has been provided on Risk Management and steps have been initiated for smooth migration to Basel-II.
- Board for Financial Supervision (BFS) constituted for supervision of financial system in general and banking sector in particular. An effective payment system has also been developed.
- In accordance with global practice, 90-days norms for asset classifications have been introduced.

Transforming Banking Landscape

Significant developments in the banking sector in the post-reforms phase transformed the face of Indian banking in a manner as never before. The entry of new players, including new private sector banks and foreign banks with the initial advantage of their lean structure, advanced technology and relatively lean asset portfolio jolted public sector banks (PSBs), particularly in metropolitan areas out of their historical 3-6-3-3 mode (borrow at 3 per cent, lend at 6 per cent, enjoy the surplus of 3 per cent and reach the golf course at 3 PM). Confronted with this challenge of staggering magnitude, PSBs responded effectively initiating tectonic measures. Such measures included upscaling their management capabilities, repositioning their competitive strategies, resorting to state-of-the-art IT architecture and increasing customer focus. Scheduled Commercial Banks' (SCBs') operating profit to assets ratio, which stood at 1.69 per cent in 1995-96, increased to more than 2 per cent in 2005-06. Concomitantly, net profit to assets ratio improved from 0.47 per cent to 1.13 per cent over the same period. Further, the spreads of SCBs came down to 2.78 per cent from 3.13 per cent. Such changes clearly indicate their efficiency and ability to function profitably within a narrower spread and their emergence as an important driver of economic growth and overall development.

Assets Break-up of Banking Sector

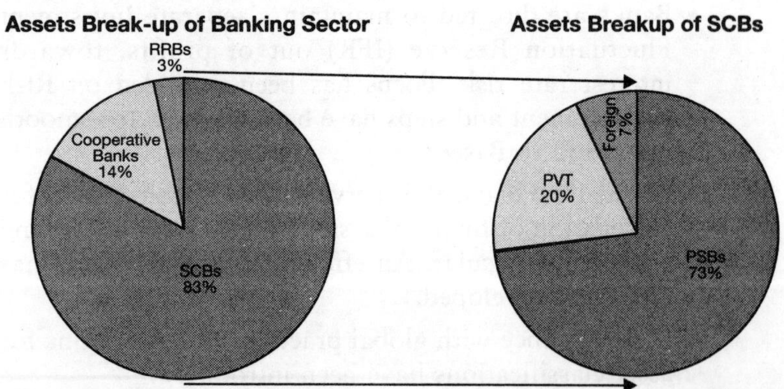

A synoptic view of the banking industry over the last 15 years reveals that banks have rapidly emerged as an important driver of economic growth and overall development (Table 1).

Table 1: Banking Industry in India: 1990-91 to 2005-06

Year/Bank Group	1990-91			1995-96			2005-06		
	PSB	Private	Foreign	PSB	Private	Foreign	PSB	Private	Foreign
1. No. of banks	28	25	23	27	35	29	28	27	29
(a) Listed	None	None	NA	2	9	NA	20	17	NA
(b) Non-listed				25	26	NA	8	10	NA
2. Share (in per cent) of									
(a) Assets	91.4	3.7	4.9	84.5	6.5	7.9	72.3	20.5	7.2
(b) Deposits	92.0	4.0	4.0	85.4	6.6	6.7	75.0	19.8	5.3
(c) Credit	93.0	4.0	3.0	82.4	6.8	8.9	72.9	20.6	6.4
(d) Income	89.4	3.3	7.3	82.5	8.2	9.4	72.4	19.7	7.8
(e) Expenses	90.0	3.3	6.8	84.1	7.5	8.4	73.1	19.7	7.3
(f) Profit	68.5	4.1	27.4	-33.3	55.6	77.8	67.2	20.3	12.5
Bank asset / GDP (per cent)		**56.3**			**50.4**			**78.2**	

PSB: public sector banks; NA: Not applicable; Listed: Banks listed on recognized stock exchanges.

Source: Reserve Bank of India.

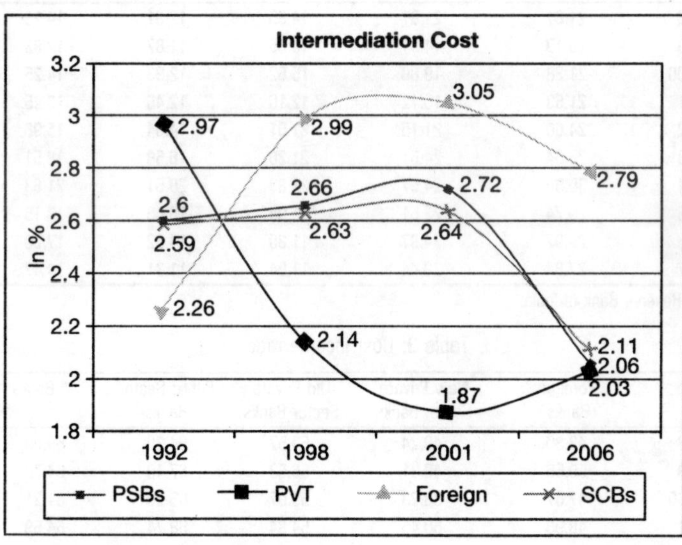

Source: Reserve Bank of India.

Banking Sector—Growth Indicators

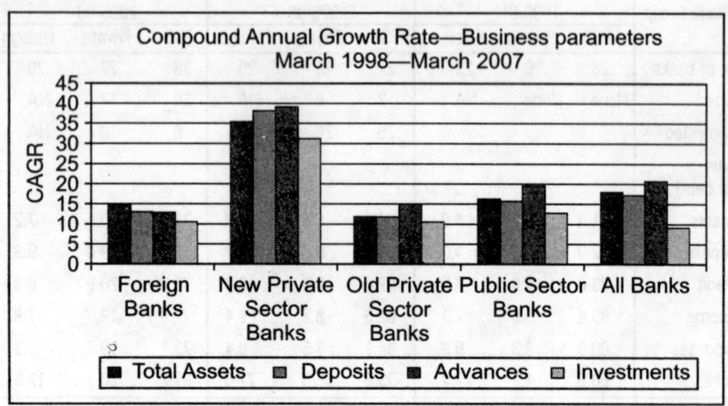

Table 2: Non-interest income as a percentage of Total income

Period	Foreign Banks	New Private Sector Banks	Old Private Sector Banks	Public Sector Banks	All Banks
Mar-98	21.61	21.37	14.85	12.91	14.28
Mar-99	19.19	14.91	13.05	11.87	12.83
Mar-2000	21.28	19.80	15.62	12.93	14.25
Mar-01	21.63	15.12	12.10	12.46	13.45
Mar-02	24.60	21.15	21.01	14.04	15.96
Mar-03	25.54	24.61	21.26	16.58	18.51
Mar-04	30.89	24.57	21.83	20.51	21.83
Mar-05	29.74	23.51	11.94	16.66	18.15
Mar-06	29.97	24.97	11.80	14.62	17.20
Mar-07	27.84	20.44	11.54	11.31	14.47

Source: Reserve Bank of India.

Table 3: Cost Income ratio

Period	Foreign Banks	New Private Sector Banks	Old Private Sector Banks	Public Sector Banks	All Banks
Mar-98	43.30	40.24	53.57	64.29	59.99
Mar-99	50.56	49.31	66.53	67.40	64.70
Mar-2000	47.67	38.23	55.07	65.29	61.21
Mar-01	48.96	50.45	54.84	68.74	64.59
Mar-02	49.12	47.73	44.28	55.08	53.16
Mar-03	46.64	46.12	43.19	49.29	48.33
Mar-04	46.21	50.16	42.80	45.09	45.60
Mar-05	49.41	52.56	53.79	48.53	49.35
Mar-06	46.10	50.66	57.38	52.03	51.45
Mar-07	45.14	55.14	48.84	51.54	51.18

Source: Reserve Bank of India.

Table 4: Return on Assets (RoA)

Period	Foreign Banks	New Private Sector Banks	Old Private Sector Banks	Public Sector Banks	All Banks
Mar-98	1.12	1.57	1.00	0.83	0.89
Mar-99	0.91	1.04	0.51	0.41	0.48
Mar-2000	1.23	0.97	0.84	0.56	0.66
Mar-01	0.96	0.81	0.60	0.40	0.49
Mar-02	1.32	0.44	1.04	0.72	0.75
Mar-03	1.55	0.89	1.18	0.96	1.01
Mar-04	1.64	0.83	1.19	1.14	1.14
Mar-05	1.30	1.07	0.32	0.87	0.89
Mar-06	1.53	0.96	0.60	0.81	0.88
Mar-07	1.65	0.84	0.89	0.82	0.90

Source: Reserve Bank of India.

Twin measures of profitability, i.e., return on assets and operating profit ratio and four efficiency measures of net interest margin, operating profit to staff expense, operating cost ratio and staff expense ratio (all ratios, except operating profit to staff expense with average total assets in the denominator) need to be improved. Hence, business volumes need to be increased by leveraging technology and massive downsizing and reskilling of staff to reduce still about 2.1 per cent intermediation cost in Indian banking (Table 5).

Table 5: Intermediation Cost* of Scheduled Commercial Banks: 1992—2006

(as percentage to total asset)

Year (end-March)	Public Sector Banks	Indian Private Banks	Foreign Banks	All Scheduled Commercial Banks
1992	2.60	2.97	2.26	2.59
1993	2.64	2.71	2.70	2.65
1994	2.65	2.49	2.65	2.64
1995	2.83	2.35	2.73	2.79
1996	2.99	2.47	2.78	2.94
1997	2.88	2.36	3.04	2.85
1998	2.66	2.14	2.99	2.63
1999	2.65	2.04	3.40	2.65
2000	2.53	1.83	3.22	2.48
2001	2.72	1.87	3.05	2.64
2002	2.29	1.44	3.00	2.19
2003	2.25	1.99	2.79	2.24
2004	2.21	2.02	2.77	2.20
2005	2.09	2.03	2.88	2.13
2006	2.06	2.03	2.79	2.11

* Intermediation cost = operating expenses.

Source: Computed from *Statistical Tables relating to Banks* in India, RBI, various years.

The fact that Indian banks have enhanced profits is commendable because of the decline in the Interest Spread (NIM) and clearly shows the strength and resilience of banks (Table 6).

Table 6: Interest Spread (NIM)

Period	Foreign Banks	New Private Sector Banks	Old Private Sector Banks	Public Sector Banks	All Banks
Mar-98	4.0	2.1	2.5	3.0	3.1
Mar-99	3.4	1.9	2.1	2.9	2.8
Mar-2000	3.8	1.7	2.2	2.7	2.7
Mar-01	3.7	2.0	2.4	2.9	2.9
Mar-02	3.3	1.1	2.3	2.8	2.6
Mar-03	3.4	1.6	2.5	3.0	2.8
Mar-04	3.5	1.9	2.5	3.0	2.9
Mar-05	3.3	2.2	2.7	3.0	2.9
Mar-06	3.5	2.2	2.8	2.9	2.8
Mar-07	3.7	2.4	2.8	2.7	2.7

Source: Reserve Bank of India.

Impact of Reforms on Banking Intermediation Cost

The asset quality of the SCBs improved significantly with the NPAs, which stood at 15.7 per cent of gross advances and 7 per cent of total assets in 1995-96, declining to 3.3 per cent of gross advances and 1.9 per cent of total assets in 2005-06. The improvement in terms of net NPAs has been even been more striking. This trend is expected to continue with gross NPAs and Net NPAs declining to 3.18 per cent and 1.53 per cent, respectively in 2006-07. The enabling architecture has been facilitated by initiatives like tighter provisioning and income recognition norms (assets with dues of over 90 days are treated as non-performing *vis-à-vis* 365 days a decade earlier), greater attention to recovery, stricter credit appraisal processes, the changing insolvency regime and enactment of the Securitisation and Reconstruction of Financial Assets and Enforcement of Security Interest (SARFAESI) Act. The empowerment of Asset Reconstruction Companies (ARCs), incorporation of the Credit Information Bureau (India) Limited (CIBIL) and Corporate Debt Restructuring (CDR) system have also helped to streamline the recovery mechanism and brought about a greater sense of credit discipline. Despite huge expansion in volume of advances, the

PSBs are better placed in terms of asset quality compared to the private banks.

Change beyond the Obvious

There has, however, been significant change in the relative market shares of Foreign Banks, New Private Sector Banks, Old Private Sector Banks and Public Sector Banks, Credit Deposit Ratio and Percentage Share of Advances (and Investments) in Total Assets (Tables 7-11) in the last decade.

Table 7: Market Share—Total Assets

Period	Foreign Banks	New Private Sector Banks	Old Private Sector Banks	Public Sector Banks
Mar-98	8.9	3.5	7.5	80.2
Mar-99	8.6	4.3	7.3	79.9
Mar-2000	7.8	5.6	7.3	79.3
Mar-01	8.2	6.3	6.8	78.7
Mar-02	7.6	11.9	6.4	74.1
Mar-03	7.1	12.0	6.1	74.8
Mar-04	7.1	12.8	6.3	73.7
Mar-05	6.8	13.3	5.8	74.0
Mar-06	7.5	14.9	5.6	72.1
Mar-07	8.4	16.4	4.9	70.3

Source: Reserve Bank of India.

Table 8: Market Share—Business (Deposits + Advances)

Period	Foreign Banks	New Private Sector Banks	Old Private Sector Banks	Public Sector Banks
Mar-98	7.9	3.5	7.7	80.9
Mar-99	7.1	4.1	7.6	81.1
Mar-2000	6.7	5.3	7.7	80.3
Mar-01	6.8	6.1	7.3	79.9
Mar-02	6.3	9.4	6.9	77.4
Mar-03	6.0	10.6	6.6	76.8
Mar-04	5.9	11.7	6.8	75.6
Mar-05	5.6	12.6	6.4	75.4
Mar-06	5.9	14.2	6.0	73.8
Mar-07	6.2	15.6	5.2	73.0

Source: Reserve Bank of India.

Table 9: Share of Deposits in Total Assets

Period	Foreign Banks	New Private Sector Banks	Old Private Sector Banks	Public Sector Banks	All Banks
Mar-98	66.5	84.5	86.8	85.7	84.0
Mar-99	62.5	80.3	85.9	85.3	83.2
Mar-2000	60.3	79.5	86.5	84.3	82.3
Mar-01	58.4	80.2	87.4	85.2	82.8
Mar-02	57.7	50.6	86.5	85.7	79.4
Mar-03	59.7	60.2	87.2	85.1	80.5
Mar-04	58.5	66.1	87.1	84.5	80.5
Mar-05	56.1	67.9	87.6	81.7	78.4
Mar-06	55.9	72.2	86.9	80.7	77.9
Mar-07	54.0	74.7	86.1	82.1	78.7

Source: Reserve Bank of India.

Table 10: Credit Deposit Ratio

Period	Foreign Banks	New Private Sector Banks	Old Private Sector Banks	Public Sector Banks	All Banks
Mar-98	71.4	50.9	53.5	51.4	52.9
Mar-99	65.5	49.0	52.3	48.5	49.9
Mar-2000	75.3	48.5	52.2	49.5	51.1
Mar-01	76.6	48.7	54.2	49.0	50.9
Mar-02	78.3	91.1	53.9	50.3	55.2
Mar-03	78.1	83.5	55.0	51.2	55.8
Mar-04	78.5	73.0	54.7	52.1	55.9
Mar-05	88.7	78.2	59.5	59.3	63.0
Mar-06	87.1	75.9	64.7	68.4	70.2
Mar-07	84.8	73.7	67.8	71.9	72.7

Source: Reserve Bank of India.

Table 11: Percentage Share of Advances (and Investments) in Total Assets

Period	Foreign Banks	New Private Sector Banks	Old Private Sector Banks	Public Sector Banks	All Banks
Mar-98	47.5 (28.0)	43.0 (34)	46.4 (32.4)	44.0 (37.7)	44.5 (36.3)
Mar-99	40.9 (34.5)	39.4 (37.2)	44.9 (34.0)	41.4 (38)	41.5 (37.3)
Mar-2000	45.4 (35.7)	38.5 (39.6)	45.1 (35.3)	41.7 (38.8)	42.0 (38.4)
Mar-01	44.7 (35.3)	39.0 (40.1)	47.3 (35.6)	41.7 (39.5)	42.2 (38.9)
Mar-02	45.2 (31.5)	46.0 (37.2)	46.7 (37.0)	43.1 (40.6)	43.8 (39.3)
Mar-03	46.6 (35.4)	50.3 (34.9)	48.0 (38.7)	43.6 (43.5)	44.9 (41.6)
Mar-04	45.9 (30.6)	48.3 (36.3)	47.7 (39.3)	44.1 (43.9)	45.0 (41.6)
Mar-05	49.8 (28.3)	53.0 (33.2)	52.2 (33.6)	48.5 (40.1)	49.4 (38.0)
Mar-06	48.7 (27.1)	54.8 (33.0)	56.2 (30.8)	55.2 (32.6)	54.7 (32.1)
Mar-07	45.8 (26.1)	55.0 (30.9)	58.4 (27.5)	59.0 (28.2)	57.2 (28.4)

Figures in parentheses indicate per cent share of investments in total assets

Source: Reserve Bank of India.

Banking in India: Driver of Economic Growth

Banking, as a sub-sector of the overall economic system, receives its impetus from the economic indicators. Reduced financial repression through statutory preemptions and enhanced prudential regulations together with progressive deregulation led to a heightened consciousness of ownership and capital structure, enhanced competition, increased autonomy, technological upgradation and performance change.

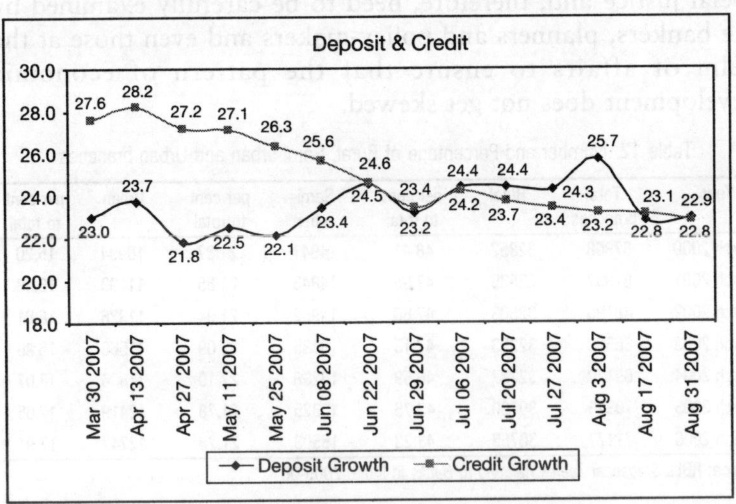

Indian Banking Sector: Recent Business Growth

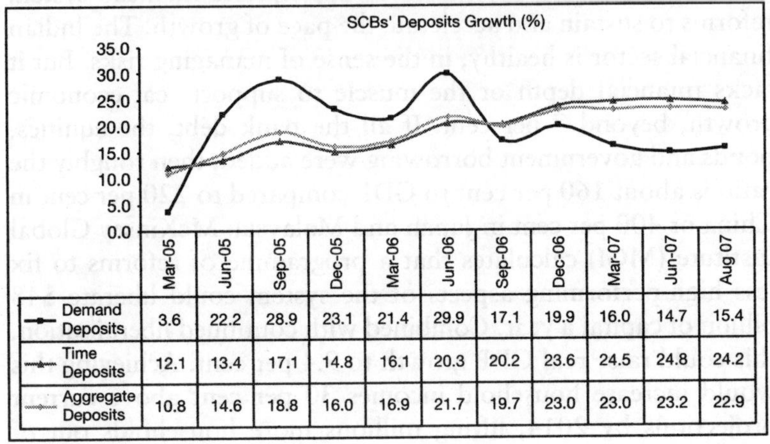

	Mar-05	Jun-05	Sep-05	Dec-05	Mar-06	Jun-06	Sep-06	Dec-06	Mar-07	Jun-07	Aug 07
Demand Deposits	3.6	22.2	28.9	23.1	21.4	29.9	17.1	19.9	16.0	14.7	15.4
Time Deposits	12.1	13.4	17.1	14.8	16.1	20.3	20.2	23.6	24.5	24.8	24.2
Aggregate Deposits	10.8	14.6	18.8	16.0	16.9	21.7	19.7	23.0	23.0	23.2	22.9

The overall position of bank branches masks disconcerting features with the proportion of rural branches reducing sharply from 48.4 to 43.2, and the proportion of urban branches increasing from 16.2 to 17.9 during the period March 2000 to March 2006. During the same period, the proportion of semi-urban branches declined marginally from 21.9 to 21.8. Such changes in the relative share of Rural, Semi-urban and Urban branches have important implications for economic growth, social justice and, therefore, need to be carefully examined by the bankers, planners and policy-makers and even those at the helm of affairs to ensure that the pattern of economic development does not get skewed.

Table 12: Number and Percentage of Rural, Semi-urban and Urban branches

Year	Total branches	Rural	per cent to total	Semi-urban	per cent to total	Urban	per cent to total
March 2000	67868	32852	48.41	14841	21.87	10994	16.20
March 2001	67937	32585	47.96	14843	21.85	11193	16.48
March 2002	68195	32503	47.66	14962	21.94	11328	16.61
March 2003	68500	32283	47.13	15135	22.09	11566	16.88
March 2004	69170	32227	46.59	15288	22.10	11806	17.07
March 2005	70373	30790	43.75	15325	21.78	12419	17.65
March 2006	71177	30769	43.23	15503	21.78	12747	17.91

Source: RBI's *Statistical Tables Relating to Banks* in India, 2005-06

Mckinsey Global Institute's (MGI's) Blueprint of Development

India's financial system needs appropriate financial system reforms to sustain and accelerate the pace of growth. The Indian financial sector is healthy, in the sense of managing risks. But it lacks financial depth or the muscle to support real economic growth, beyond 7 per cent. If all the bank debt, the equities, bonds and government borrowing were added, then roughly the ratio is about 160 per cent to GDP compared to 220 per cent in China or 400 per cent in Japan and Malaysia. McKinsey Global Institute (MGI) calculates that a programme of reforms to fix less high-performing aspects of the system could liberate $48 billion of capital a year. Combined with continued liberalisation, this could raise real GDP growth to 9.4 per cent. Achieving this would increase household incomes 30 per cent above current projections by 2014, lifting millions more households out of poverty. But this requires drawing more of the domestic savings into the formal financial system ($7 billion), improving capital allocation ($19 billion) and enhancing systemic efficiency ($22 billion).

MGI's study on global financial stock (debt+equity+deposits) worked out India's financial depth as a proportion of GDP to merely 137 per cent *vis-à-vis* China's 323 per cent. Hence, the financial sector must become wider and deeper in order to spread risk. Between 1999-2000 and 2005-06, the total assets of scheduled commercial banks (SCBs) in India increased from Rs. 11,05,464 crore to Rs. 27,87,891 crore. Current projections strongly suggest that the banking industry in India would continue to grow at a fast clip because of the country's strong and stable economic prospects and resurgence in the manufacturing sector.

Scheduled bank credit as a proportion of GDP progressively increased from 25.1 per cent in 1999-2000 to 38.4 per cent in 2004-05 and further to 45 per cent in 2005-06. But it is still much lower than in many other countries, e.g., Hong Kong (150 per cent), China (136 per cent), Taiwan (126 per cent), Singapore (109 per cent), Korea (107 per cent) etc. Despite 30 per cent increase in bank lending during the last three years, there is still potential for about 20 per cent credit growth because of low historical base and wide opportunities available, particularly in agriculture, micro credit (Sharma, 2004c; 2005c), SMEs, infrastructure and retail assets. Credit must, therefore, expand to bring about sustained high growth of income and employment. Credit growth of such a large magnitude has been broad-based encompassing corporate, agriculture and retail sectors. But it is important to ensure that the process of robust credit growth continues to be broad-based, inclusive and equitable.

Given the squeeze on spreads with about 75 per cent of banks' outstanding advances (as at June 2006) excluding export credit and small loans at rates below Benchmark Prime Lending Rates (BPLRs) of banks, pressure from corporate for finer rates and intensifying competition in the retail banking segment (Sharma, 2005a), banks now need to increasingly look at SMEs as a growth option (Sharma, 2004d; 2004e; 2005b). While banks have been given freedom to determine their lending rates, RBI has criticized the principles followed by them as 'opaque'. *RBI's Report on 'Currency and Finance' for 2005-06* justifiably maintains that BPLRs has ceased to be a reference rate, thereby hindering an assessment of the monetary mechanism.

Housing loans, which are inherently less risky, constitute one-half of retail banking assets and the consumer sector with relatively less NPAs than the corporate sector continues to be under-penetrated.

Banking development is not a one-off effort; it is a constant process of growth and transformation to meet the evolving requirements (Sharma, 2004b; 2004c). Meeting the challenge of change, in terms of people, products, delivery channels, processes, culture, structure and overall capabilities requires key structural changes, such as, introduction of real time gross settlement (RTGS), higher efficiency and productivity, adroit risk management, accent on non-interest income, etc.

Non-interest income as a proportion of total assets of PSBs remained constant at 1.2 per cent from 1993 to 2006. Intermediation cost, defined as the ratio of operating expense to total assets, reduced from 2.60 per cent in 1992 to 2.06 per cent in 2006 for PSBs *vis-à-vis* reduction of 2.97 per cent to 2.03 per cent for Indian Private Banks. The operating costs of banks, as a proportion of total average assets during 2003, in UK were 2.12 per cent, in Switzerland 2.03 per cent and less than 2 per cent in major European economies like Sweden, Austria, Germany and France.

Box 2: Indian Banking 2010: Towards a High Performing Sector
A Report by McKinsey & Company

India's transition into the 4th largest economy in the world by 2025 presupposes sustained high growth of the GDP at a rate of 8 per cent and above per annum. The Indian banking sector has to play an even more important role in this kind of economic transformation. The Report, while contemplating three different scenarios of the Indian banking landscape in 2010, maintained that the resultant change will be an outcome of the '*strong interplay between the decisions taken by policy-makers and actions by the bank managements*'.

The Report strongly commended the positive developments of the banking industry during the last decade. The Indian banking sector now is in a healthy position in the region on few key metrics, such as, growth, profitability and non-performing assets. Improved growth, innovation and value creation has, however, been limited to few players. The Report highlighted some of the major challenges like high intermediation cost and lower penetration, limited to few customers and geographies, compared to other countries. The structural weaknesses underlined in the Report related to fragmented industry structure, restrictions on capital availability and deployment, lack of institutional support infrastructure, restrictive labour laws and weak corporate governance. The future banking performance depends to a large extent in effectively addressing these issues.

The Report identified the following four challenges, which need to be addressed for robust future performance:

- Discontinuous growth in the market is driven by new products and services include opportunities in credit cards, consumer finance and wealth management on the retail banking side and in fee-based income and investment banking on the wholesale banking front. Addressing these issues require new skills in sales and marketing, credit and operations.
- Disappearance of windfall treasury gains as secular decline in interest rates, which is beginning to show a trend reversal, is exposing weak banks.
- With increase in interest rates, competition from foreign banks will intensify.
- Demographic shifts originating from changing age profile and household income, demand for enhanced institutional capabilities and service levels from consumers will further intensify.

Several forces will interplay in shaping the future growth of banking industry. Six key elements will form the part of regulatory stance through legislative action, such as, industry structure (3 to 4 global sized banks controlling 35-45 per cent of market, 6-8 national banks, controlling 20-25 per cent of market, 4-6 foreign banks with 15-20 per cent market share and the remainder being specialist players (geographical or product/ segment focused), freedom to deploy capital, creation of a unified regulator distinct from central bank, corporate governance, labour reforms and human capital deployment and support for creating industry utilities and service bureaus in the form of establishing world class payments, asset reconstruction companies, credit bureaus and back office utilities.

Key action emanating from bank managements will be on three major fronts, e.g., fundamentally upgrading organizational capability to stay in tune with the changing market, adopting value creating M&A as an avenue for growth and continually innovating to develop new business models to access untapped opportunities. PSBs in India needs to significantly strengthen their skill levels in sales and marketing, service operations, risk management and overall organizational performance ethic. PSBs are also likely to encounter the biggest challenge of strengthening human capital.

Facilitation of the coordinated action will help the banking industry to either scale up to a high performance growth trajectory (Scenario III) or to a stagnating growth phase. Moderate action by both policy-makers and bank managements will result in an evolution growth phase (Scenario II). It is only in the high performance or scenario III that the banking industry will emerge as the most comparable, competitive and efficient in world.

Relative Strength and Resilience of Indian Banks in Asia

Mr. Nandan Nilekani, former CEO of Infosys Technologies Ltd., justifiably stressed "the flat world created by the confluence of technology, globalization, demographics, rise of economic power of China and India is making companies fundamentally alter the business assumptions. What and When they produce, Whom they sell to, and at What price, and How they manage it all, the fundamental tenets of the business models are being continuously revisited..." Viewed against this backdrop, it is clear that globalization is here to stay.

Mr. N.R. Narayana Murthy, Chief Mentor of Infosys Technologies Ltd., has correctly pointed out "Globalization is about producing where it is most cost-effective, sourcing capital from where it is cheapest and selling it where it is most profitable." Viewed against this backdrop, it is clear that globalization is here to stay. Victor Hugo stressed long ago:

"The invasion of armies can be resisted but not an idea, whose time has come." Globalization "is certainly an idea, whose time has come." Globalization impacts the banking industry through intensified competition, accent on efficiency, productivity and cost reduction, streamlined risk management systems and practices and strengthened service quality and delivery and cross-selling of products/services. Other important elements of business complexities include product innovation, technological automation on a much larger canvas, competency building and investment in human capital, mergers and acquisitions (M&A), transparency, disclosure and market discipline.

Standard & Poor's analysis demonstrated that Indian banking is ahead of China, Indonesia, Philippines and Vietnam.

But the banking industries of Australia, New Zealand, Singapore, Hong Kong and Japan, and even Malaysia, South Korea, Taiwan and Thailand are ahead of India. Similarly, Moody's Investor Services data showed that Indian banking is better than its counterparts even in developed countries such as Japan, Singapore and Australia. Indian banks posted the highest Return on Equity (RoE) compared to their Asian peers in the last three years. According to Moody's, Indian lenders posted highest RoE of 20.38 per cent (system average of three years), closely followed by Indonesia at 20.19 per cent and New Zealand 18.83 per cent. Japan, the biggest economy in Asia posted negative returns of 6.42 per cent. Some of the international dimensions of Indian Banking are given in Annex I-VI.

Table 13: Performance of major banks across countries (as percentage of total average assets)

Country	Pre-tax profits		Net interest margin		Operating costs	
	2005	2006	2005	2006	2005	2006
US (10)	1.89	1.83	2.65	2.51	3.25	3.10
Canada (5)	1.01	1.32	1.79	1.64	3.00	2.56
Japan (13)	0.73	0.94	0.85	0.97	1.29	1.37
UK (9)	0.87	0.98	1.07	1.13	1.58	1.68
Germany (9)	0.37	0.47	0.63	0.66	1.15	1.19
France (6)	0.67	0.86	0.83	0.81	1.94	1.43
Netherlands (4)	0.59	0.55	1.10	1.14	1.30	1.45
Spain (5)	1.18	1.51	1.55	1.78	1.80	2.12
India (84)*	1.20	1.20	2.83	2.78	2.13	2.11

Values in parentheses indicate the number of banks included for 2006.
* As percentage of total assets.

A study of Return on Networth (RONW) of 28 PSBs and 17 private sector banks during 2006-07 and 2005-06 showed that Public Sector Banks' (PSBs) RONW was higher compared to that of private sector banks during 2006-07. Profit After Tax (PAT) as a percentage of networth, in the case of PSBs, rose from 15.02 per cent to 16.26 per cent between 2005-06 and 2006-07. A significant increase in the ratio was in the case of Bank of Maharashtra, where it increased from 3.29 per cent to 15.85 per cent. In Vijaya Bank's case, the increase was from 8.26 per cent to 20.45 per cent, UCO Bank's RONW rose from 9.90 per cent in 2005-06 to 14.30 per cent in 2006-07. In

2006-07 and 2005-06, PSBs had a higher RONW compared to private sector banks.

However, *FE Research Bureau's* study of 26 PSBs and 13 private sector banks revealed that private banks scored over PSBs in Net Interest Incomes (NII) during the year 2006-07. PSBs' NII during 2006-07 rose by 12 per cent to Rs. 58,613 crore from the previous year's Rs. 52,316 crore. The growth was higher for private banks at 38.8 per cent.

Post-reforms, Indian banking is relatively much stronger *vis-à-vis* other Asian counterparts in terms of product range, range of investment and financial options for depositors and financial health of primary and secondary capital markets. The relative strength and resilience of Indian Banks in Asia is incontrovertible as, for example, demonstrated by Standard & Poor's analysis. This analysis showed Indian banking to be ahead of China, Indonesia, Philippines and Vietnam. But the banking industries of Australia, New Zealand, Singapore, Hong Kong and Japan, and even Malaysia, South Korea, Taiwan and Thailand are ahead of India. Similarly, Moody's Investor Services data showed that the Indian banking sector has scored over its counterparts even in developed countries such as Japan, Singapore and Australia. Indian banks posted the highest Return on Equity (RoE) compared to their Asian peers in the last three years. According to Moody's, Indian lenders posted highest RoE of 20.38 per cent (system average of three years), closely followed by Indonesia at 20.19 per cent and New Zealand. But the banking sector now faces newer challenges, particularly in the context of Basel II norms, creating global brands, Anti Money Laundering, KYC Norms, changed role of Regulators and entry of new players. There is, however, no need to look at the future with trepidation. For, as G.B. Shaw said, *"In this world, there is always danger for those, who are afraid of it."* Similarly, Richard Baxter stressed *"dangers bring fears and fears more dangers bring."* Hence, the unfolding realities necessitate reoriented development strategies for growing business volumes, enhancing bottomline and even maintaining capital adequacy at present levels as a consequence of implementation of Basel II norms.

Performance Indicators Across Banks

It is customary to divide the Indian banking system into PSBs, private banks and specialized banking institutions. Most PSBs have acquired a reasonably high degree of compliance with the regulatory norms and enhanced capability to respond quickly to the challenges of the emerging economic environment. Despite marked improvement in terms of all performance indicators, such as, financial position, asset quality, return on assets (RoA), capital to risk weighted asset ratio (CRAR), productivity, profitability, there continue to be significant differences in the performance of various bank-groups over the last few years.

Table 14: Bank Group-wise Shares: Financial Performance

(Per cent)

Bank Groups	2002-03	2005-06
Public Sector Banks		
Income	74.5	72.4
Expenditure	74.8	73.1
Total assets	75.7	72.3
Net Profit	64.8	67.3
Private Sector Banks		
Income	18.5	19.7
Expenditure	18.6	19.7
Total assets	17.5	20.5
Net Profit	15.6	20.3
Foreign Banks		
Income	7.0	7.8
Expenditure	6.6	7.3
Total assets	6.9	7.2
Net Profit	19.6	12.5

Source: Reserve Bank of India. Cited in Inaugural Address by Smt. Shyamala Gopinath, Deputy Governor, RBI delivered at the 18th Annual National Conference of Forex Association of India on April 6, 2007 at Bangkok.

Intensified challenges and increased business complexities of the post-reforms era resulted, among others, in the decline in the share of public sector banks in the total income, expenditure and assets of the commercial banking system and an increase in the share of new private sector banks and foreign banks. The share in Income and Expenditure of Public Sector Banks declined from 74.5 and 74.8 per cent in 2002-03 to 72.4 and 72.3 per cent in 2005-06 respectively, whereas, Private and Foreign banks have witnessed growth in the same parameters. The trend is similar in case of the share in Total Assets.

Sweeping changes have transformed the market, increasing competition and stimulating the development of different models, products and methods of operating. Benchmarking product offering has rarely been so important and yet so difficult. This is why it is necessary to improve an understanding of the evolution of the market and, crucially, the response of the important players to these changes with a focus on competition, service and marketing. Banks must perform a SWOT analysis of emerging scenario to benefit from the changing state of affairs.

A SWOT analysis reveals that despite altered ground realities, PSBs continue to hold sway with three-fourths of assets and income. While the share in net profit grew for both Public and Private Sector Banks, the share of PSBs in the overall profit of the banking sector increased. This suggests that with operational flexibility, PSBs are competing relatively effectively with private sector and foreign banks.

Table 15: Bank Group-wise Market Share for Select Indicators

(In per cent)

Bank Group	Deposits		Advances	
	2002-03	2005-06	2002-03	2005-06
Public Sector Banks	79.6	75.0	74.2	72.9
Private Sector Banks	15.3	19.8	18.8	20.6
Foreign Banks	5.1	5.3	7.1	6.4

Source: Report on the Trends and Progress on Banking in India, RBI, various years.

The market share of PSBs declined consistently in case of both Deposits and Advances from 79.6 and 74.2 per cent in FY 2003 to 75.0 and 72.9 per cent in FY 2006, respectively. While the market share of both private sector banks and foreign banks increased, the increase has been more pronounced in case of private banks. Some of the basic reasons of faster growth of new private sector banks relate to diversification and perceptible shift of these banks from traditional banking. PSBs need to expand their market base by reaching out in a much greater measure to the under-penetrated but highly potential rural markets and tier II cities. Consumer growth is taking place at a fast pace in 17,113 villages with a population of more than 5,000. Of these, 9,989 villages are in 7 States, viz., Andhra Pradesh, Bihar, Kerala, Maharashtra, Tamil Nadu, Uttar Pradesh and West Bengal. Banks' approach to the rural lending will be guided mainly by commercial considerations in future. Rural financial institutions (RFIs) need to enlarge their role, functions and range of services offered so as to emerge as "one stop" destination for all types of credit requirements of people in rural/ semi-urban centres.

Table 16: Business and Profit per Employee

(Rs. in lakhs)

Bank Group	Business per Employee		Profit per Employee	
	2002-03	2005-06	2002-03	2005-06
Public Sector Banks	215.60	369.41	1.62	2.23
Private Sector Banks	399.69	475.38	2.48	16.24
Foreign Banks	861.97	1012.79	12.38	26.49

Source: Various Issues of *Performance Highlights*, Indian Banks' Association, Mumbai.

Among various productivity indicators, productivity indicators like business per employee and profit per employee are customarily used to analyse efficiency and productivity. While there has been a distinct improvement in post-reform productivity because of technological improvement and peer dynamics across all bank-groups, business per employee recorded an impressive rise of over Rs. 150 lakh in case of both PSBs and Foreign banks as against Rs. 76 lakh for Private Banks between FY 2003 and FY 2006. However, Profit per Employee surged in case of Private and Foreign Banks, whereas PSBs failed to record such a rise. This has important policy prescriptive implications for PSBs to effectively enhance their bottom line through streamlined systems and procedures, thrust on core competencies and exploration of new revenue streams.

The asset quality of banks improved significantly over the past decade with the NPAs of all Scheduled Commercial Banks (SCBs) declining sharply from 4 per cent of net advances in 2002-03 to 1.2 per cent in 2005-06. The other Bank-groups' asset quality is also in line with the industry trend, reflecting distinct improvement in recoveries by banks and better allocation of funds. Apart from concerted attempts by SCBs themselves, strong macro-economic performance and institutional measures initiated by RBI have helped to make the banking system stronger.

Table 17: Bank Group-wise Soundness Indicators

Bank Group	Net NPA/Net Advances Ratio		Capital Adequacy Ratio	
	2002-03	2005-06	2002-03	2005-06
Public Sector Banks	4.5	1.3	12.6	12.2
Old Private Sector Banks	5.2	1.6	12.8	11.7
New Private Sector Banks	1.5	0.8	11.3	12.6
Foreign Banks	1.7	0.8	15.2	13.0
All SCBs	4.0	1.2	12.7	12.4

Source: Report on the Trends and Progress on Banking in India, RBI, various years.

All bank-groups maintain CRAR significantly higher than the stipulated 9 per cent with the CRAR being 12 per cent for all Bank groups at the end of FY 2006. A number of innovative capital raising options initiated by RBI helped banks in shoring up their capital base by more than the required minimum.

Emerging Issues in the Indian Banking Sector

Banking Consolidation

With banking M&A in Europe doubling in 2006 to 96 billion Euros and Financial Services M&A growing 10 per cent on the previous year to 137 billion Euros, it is important to explore new opportunities for investment and value creation through an enhanced knowledge of banking M&A strategies. This necessitates identifying the challenges and solutions of creating and increasing value, getting the inside track on past, present and future deals and markets, analysing the real progress in removing barriers to banking consolidation and expanding the network Banks in emerging economies have been consolidating to exploit core competence, reduce operating cost and leverage large business volume. Financial sector liberalisation enhanced efficiency and competitiveness of Indian banks. Shrinking margin, intensified competition, stringent prudential norms, pressure on profits and limited options for organic growth have also made it necessary to explore ways for inorganic expansion.

Table 18: Top 10 Global Banks

World Ranking	Bank	Return on Assets (per cent)	Cost-Income Ratio (per cent)	BIS Capital Ratio (per cent)
1	Bank of America Corp	2.19	48.75	11.88
2	Citigroup	1.57	58.05	11.65
3	HSBC Holdings	1.19	51.33	13.54
4	Credit Agricole Group	0.77	61.10	10.00
5	JP Morgan Chase	1.47	62.31	12.32
6	Mitsubishi UFJ Financial Group	0.81	66.18	12.58
7	Industrial and Commercial Bank of China	0.96	36.30	14.05
8	Royal Bank of Scotland	1.05	53.01	11.73
9	Bank of China	1.28	46.32	13.59
10	Santander Central Hispano	1.05	49.57	12.49

The RBI has created an enabling environment by laying down guidelines on mergers and acquisitions. But the consolidation process within the banking system in recent years has primarily been confined to a few mergers in the private sector segment induced by precarious financial position of the banks. Narasimham Committee had advocated a four-tier structure for the banking system with 3 to 4 large banks, which could become international in character.

The size, structure and performance of banks have important implications for mergers and acquisitions (M&As) in the banking industry. Major drivers for attaining economies of size in India are leveraging the benefits of large size, expanding and diversifying bank loan portfolios to lessen the likelihood of failure and harnessing core competencies. But size must be seen as a facilitator rather than an all-inclusive mean to efficiency. In the ultimate analysis, mergers must be market-led and synergy-driven.

The fragmented organisational structure is reflected in that India has 11 banks within the top 500 banks of the world, of which only SBI is in the list of top 100 banks. Fragmentation is manifested even more starkly by the fact that nearly 80 banks have a market share of less than 2 per cent, with the number two player having a market share of just 6 per cent. Several old private sector banks with capital bases ranging from Rs. 75 crore to Rs. 150 crore make it difficult to prevent abuse of fiduciary responsibility. Hence, mergers for compliance with minimum net worth requirement or norms on diversified ownership cannot be ruled out in the future.

Table 19: Top Indian Banks

Ranking	Bank	Return on Assets (per cent)	Cost-Income Ratio (per cent)	BIS Capital Ratio (per cent)
70	State Bank of India	1.29	58.15	12.36
147	ICICI Bank	1.23	N.A.	13.35
255	Punjab National Bank	1.40	51.26	11.95
259	Bank of Baroda	1.21	51.00	12.47
281	Canara Bank	1.01	46.83	13.50
329	IDBI	0.64	53.20	14.80
335	HDFC Bank	1.80	46.30	13.08
378	Oriental Bank of Commerce	1.41	44.76	12.46
411	Bank of India	0.82	55.41	10.75
414	Indian Overseas Bank	1.26	47.07	13.27
495	Union Bank of India	1.00	46.76	11.41
507	Corporation Bank	1.66	41.61	14.66
533	Andhra Bank	1.65	50.05	11.33
548	Allahabad Bank	1.37	53.11	13.37
561	Central Bank of India	0.50	58.55	11.03
580	UTI Bank	1.47	49.60	11.08
601	Syndicate Bank	0.90	58.03	11.73
623	Indian Bank	1.06	56.23	N.A.
699	UCO Bank	0.34	58.01	11.12
708	United Bank of India	0.72	51.98	12.02
744	Jammu and Kashmir Bank	0.99	43.32	12.14
772	Vijaya Bank	0.57	46.47	11.94
805	Bank of Maharashtra	0.22	64.36	11.27
904	Federal Bank	1.36	44.64	13.76
916	Punjab and Sind Bank	0.57	61.80	N.A.
962	Karnataka Bank	1.80	38.38	11.78
988	Dena Bank	0.36	47.50	10.62

Post-April 2009, when restrictions on operations of foreign banks would be relaxed, the Indian Banks, especially PSBs and old private banks, would perforce have to consolidate and strengthen themselves for greater breadth of products, depth in delivery channels and efficiency in operations. With the overlapping functions in loans and advances, there is a need for convergence between banks and FIs, to usher in the concept of Universal Banking. There is also a need for further consolidation of other segments of financial sector, like insurance, commercial banking, merchant banking and long-term lending functions.

While PSBs have striking commonalities of policies and approaches, they and 'new generation' banks differ significantly in terms of operational issues, NPAs, organisational culture, mindset, attitude to work and HR issues—salary structure, role of trade unions, age-profile, promotions, transfers and postings. Mergers are now a matter of choice and no longer of compulsion. Size matters, but size alone does no matter. The optimal size of a bank is *inter alia*, a function of the size of the economy, its diversity in various segments, level of financial intermediation and, above all, degree of market mechanism and competition. Banks can ensure that they achieve the benefits envisaged an M&A transaction by planning properly, developing a clear and focused vision of integration goals, setting a realistic timetable and understanding the differences in corporate cultures, all while managing risks. Successful mergers and acquisitions require a holistic perspective, from screening and due diligence to all aspects of the integration process.

Corporate Governance

A series of corporate distress and accounting irregularities across countries damaged investor confidence and brought global financial markets under the scanner. The health of the economy is both a function and reflection of the financial and professional ethics of the corporate entities. This is applicable to the Indian banks necessitating implementation and maintenance of high standards of Corporate Governance norms.

A well-defined Corporate Governance Mechanism must be fair and civic-minded, fulfilling its duties to the entire spectrum of stakeholders and making integrity an article of faith across operations. The underlying principles of Corporate Governance are the values, ethics and commitment to follow best business practices. Thus, it rests upon the foundations of transparency, disclosures and fairness in dealing with the stakeholders' desires.

The corporate governance philosophy of banks has to be based on the pursuit of sound business ethics and strong professional acumen that aligns the interests of all segments of stakeholders as also the society at large. This is why corporate governance means much more than the conduct of business in accordance with shareholders' desires.

In line with the recommendations of the Consultative Group, banks were advised in June 2002 to adopt and implement appropriate governance practices to preserve shareholder trust while maximizing long-term shareholder value. As part of its efforts to promote sound corporate governance, the RBI has been focusing on ensuring 'fit and proper' owners and directors of the bank, diversified ownership and screening of the nominated and elected directors to satisfy the 'fit and proper' criteria. The 'Fit and proper' status of directors on the banks' board has often been expressed as a concern. However, measures are being taken up by Reserve Bank of India and the Central government to ensure greater transparency and better governance in banks. Changes in Sick Industries Companies Act (SICA) too have been made to address such concerns.

Good corporate governance encompasses appropriate checks and balances through external and internal audits and accounting, clear division of both horizontal and vertical responsibility, timely disclosures, transparency and a strong and independent Board. The basic objective is not just to safeguard the interests of shareholders but for all those who have a stake in the well-being of the corporate enterprise.

Banks are required to straddle mounting competition for higher efficiency and increasing expectations of shareholders. The bottom line is that corporate governance relates not merely to the individual firms or banks, but to the stability of the entire financial structure. Corporate governance in banks relating to approval of plans, policies, procedures and compliance with laws, regulations and the bank's own policies and procedures has improved substantially over the years. An international benchmark for corporate governance in banks requires establishment of policies and procedures for control and monitoring of credit risk, liquidity, capital and market risks. These risks should be reviewed periodically by the top management to check real and worrisome fault-lines.

The plans, policies and procedures for which the Board of Directors (BoD) is responsible can be grouped into the following four distinct classes:

1. The "basic building blocks" (strategy, decision processes, structure, distribution system, budgeting and planning systems);
2. The "back office" (operations strategy, information technology and management information systems);
3. "Safeguarding assets and liabilities" (credit, treasury and audit);
4. Human resources development (recruitment, retention, rotation, performance management, compensation and training).

'Doing everything better', as corporate governance is defined today, requires adopting a more scientifically designed corporate governance specific to the organization to take forward the best practices to enhance stakeholders' values. In the ultimate analysis, corporate governance practices must be institutionalized so that it transcends the regulatory framework in an attempt to align corporate structure, business and disclosure practices to implement Corporate Governance Philosophy.

Catalytic Role of Innovation

Innovation, which transcends invention, represents the point of convergence of invention and insight. The 21st century society witnesses the increasing importance of innovation in all fields, particularly technology and management. Constant innovation is a hallmark of successful growth companies; staying ahead of the competition requires inventiveness at the individual, group, and company levels. Organizational ethos needs to stress innovation as a key driver of growth that surprises and delights the customer with new, differentiated and relevant benefits. "Innovate or perish" has thus become central to banking efficiency.

Indian banks would be able to weather the competition and emerge as a key financial hub provided they are relevant to consumers in terms of technology, quality, reliability, pricing, performance and support. Convergence of the information and communication technologies (ICT), "technological evangelisation" and narrowing of "digital gap" require fostering an innovation culture to sustain competitive advantage by accelerating growth of both top and bottom lines. Growth, however, also creates a need for structure and control, which can make a culture of innovation difficult to sustain. Companies must institutionalize their innovation process by creating an environment in which creative thinking is central to their values, assumptions and action.

In view of the gross inadequacy of linear progression, banks need to continually slash costs and improve customer service with new products and competitive advantages by pioneering products and customised software solutions. Solutions have been developed in retail and corporate banking, credit cards, cash management, relationship banking, CRM, ATM, credit appraisal, trade finance, EAI, e-Commerce and m-Commerce. Some important innovations offering a range of value-added features tailored to the needs of customers include:

- A treasury solution covering forex, money market, securities and derivative transactions with powerful tools for the bank's treasury front desk, mid office and back office.
- A back office banking solution, which is completely parameter driven to facilitate user to change the parameters and generate reports in accordance with the RBI specifications.
- A unique customer service value added product targeted at corporate customers with large volume businesses.
- Retail banking software architectures to help retail banks streamline services while enhancing innovative and differentiated products.

- E Credit Card with a powerful set of e-enabled features, including automatic payment through a direct debit, access to card services and monthly statements on the net anywhere, anytime.

The rapid spread of micro credit and self-help groups (SHGs) exemplifies successful innovation at "the bottom of the pyramid" and has created a silent revolution in the countryside. Professor Mohd. Yunus and Grameen Bank were awarded the Nobel Peace Prize last year for their "efforts to create economic and social development." Such efforts need to be replicated on a larger macro canvas to create meaning and value in the lives of the poor and the vulnerable sections of society. With innovative technology, Indian banks are now altering the financial services scenario both in international markets and rural India. Some of the aggressive banking players have acquired technology at one-tenth the cost of global banks to bring a new value proposition to the customers. This is not a one-off effort but an evolutionary programme because requirements keep continuously evolving. This necessitates effective coordinated and concerted measures by various players.

Technological Transformation

The Banking industry in India has undergone a virtual metamorphosis with the mushroom growth of the new generation private sector banks. Technological advances have ushered in sweeping changes and altered the face of the Banking sector. The traditional brick and mortar banking is slowly yielding place to more modern concepts, where automation has served to conquer space, time and distance. Technology has worked as an enabler and force-multiplier in achieving business growth and excellence in banking by making financial dealings easier, faster and better. The Banking sector in India underwent massive transformation in the sequential stages of ALPMs (Automatic Ledger Posting Machines), stand alone PCs, branch automation, WAN (wide area network), core banking systems and mobile banking. There is no doubt that this process of branchless banking is certain to gather momentum in the future because of the following macro-economic drivers:

- estimated yearly saving of US $6 billion (Rs. 24,000 crore) India may have to fully shift to an e-payment system.
- 95 per cent potential cost reduction by shifting to non-branch banking.
- 5 times more transactions now occur via e-banking than inside a branch.
- 16 million Indians will be banking online by end-2007 as against 4.6 million in 2006.

Banks are internalising the need to step up IT initiatives. Besides viable benefits in payments and settlements and retail transactions, online data helps other business decisions. The implementation of modern technologies by various banks has helped these banks to effectively maximize the productivity and reduce costs by greater thrust on IT-enabled business. Raising the bar requires implementation of state-of-the-art technologies for both front and back-end operations to provide connectivity across countrywide branches and bringing about the conveniences of "anytime, anywhere" banking. Anticipating rapid growth and building suitable, scalable platforms requires increasing operational efficiency and exceeding customer expectations while bridging the gap and creating greater synergy between IT and business. The benefits are much more than savings in time, hassle, paperwork and money and help banks to cash in on new markets (both domestic and overseas) and reduce costs, gain visibility, control, and automate and streamline workflows to reduce human drudgery and possibilities of human error. Intelligent use of home banking (a combination of online, phone and mobile banking) would also keep customers happy through quality and efficient service banking technologies, such as, tracking and paying for credit cards, remitting money, repaying loan instalments, settling utility bills, etc. Despite the rapid growth of e-banking, there is immense latent potential because less than 10 per cent of 47 million bank customers subscribe to Net banking. This is because there are only 17.70 Net-enabled computers per 1,000 populations in the country. While phone banking is doing well at present, m-banking is poised to grow rapidly given the unprecedented growth of mobile banking technologies in India.

Box 3: Online Banking

Online Banking represents the point of convergence of the entire spectrum of financial dealings.

Basic Banking

- Check account balance.
- Check credit card transactions.
- Transfer funds.
- One screen view of complete banking relations with multiple service providers.

Mail Box

- Leave standing instructions.
- Contact the branch manager for redressal of grievances.
- Apply for new services like account opening.

Value Addition

- Cheque book or DD requests.
- Smart money orders.
- TDS enquiry.
- Demat services.
- Forex transactions.

Investments

- Transact in mutual funds.
- Buy insurance policies.
- Trade in stocks.
- Buy gold.

Loan Products

- Apply for a loan.
- Manage existing loans by tracking fluctuations in interest rates and EMIs.
- Compare products to get the best deal and service.

In conformity with the global trend of banks worldwide investing huge amounts in new technologies to effectively maximize the productivity and reduce costs by IT enabled-business, Indian Public Sector Banks incurred an expenditure of Rs. 10,676 crore on computerization and development of communication networks between September 1999 and March 2006. ATMs, internet banking, anywhere banking, Real Time

Gross Settlement (RTGS), cheque truncation, Customer Relationship Management (CRM), etc. have discernibly improved customer service and experience. The domino effect of technology has certainly better equipped banks to deal with risks. But the jury is still out on technological modernization and automation reducing cost of operations and cost-income ratios, improving cross-sell ratios, alignment of business strategy and IT strategy. There are also issues of effective security systems and IT safeguards in place to maintain the integrity, confidentiality and availability of data.

IT could help PSBs manage old generation legacy issues like managing large and voluminous documents through digitalisation of data, besides helping managing risks and treasury and cash management. Process improvements, technology innovations and overall support for business groups ensure that critical applications supporting business are optimized, interconnected and seamlessly integrated. Innovative business models and financial technologies, e.g., ATMs, Internet and Mobile Banking, 'Virtual' Banking, Home Banking, Electronic Funds Transfer at Point of Sale (EFTPOS), Image Processing, decision support systems (DSS) have been introduced for credit risk appraisal, forecasting loan delinquencies, investment decisions, etc. in the pursuit of optimised organisational design and company-wide process excellence. The next frontier would relate to micro-finance, global operations and high volume corporate business at minimal incremental cost.

With the RBI actively encouraging the banks to shift to internet banking and advocating real-time clearing systems, the IT adoption in the banking industry will increase. The large and prolific use of information systems in the banking and financial services sector is, however, fraught with the whole range of danger of security concerns, including misuse, data theft, forgery and fraud. This is particularly important because "*technology makes it possible for people to gain control over everything, except over technology.*" The progressive increase in the use of information technology for banking operations brings to the fore the need for effective IT safeguards and erection of firewalls. Security encompasses the user, the IT system, the environment and even the medium through which the transaction of processing and transmission takes place. The most important factor to be reckoned with is business continuity after security.

Studies have shown that while many frauds and other acts of financial commission are the work of insiders, disasters are the result of external factors. Given that disruptions are a way of life and that they may be triggered by unanticipated factors, it is essential that robust disaster recovery and management plans are in place and more importantly, regularly tested at periodic intervals. Put simply, security and reliability are no less important than the eased of use. To be sure, ICICI Bank's new grid-based debit card or Punjab National Bank's (PNB) virtual keyboard that can be used to key in log in credential, thus defeating logging software installed in the computer mark welcome advances, particularly against the widespread fears of hacking and tampering. But it is not always realized—much less felt—that the consumer is as much responsible for the security as the bank.

With about 700 to 800 million Indians being outside the formal financial services sector, technology companies, telecom companies, retailers and MFIs could provide better business models to reach out to this un-served population. The challenge and the opportunity to serve the under-banked but certainly not unbankable at lower cost through technology could distinguish the winners from the 'also-rans' in the increasingly turbulent world ahead.

Core Banking

SAP observed "Banks have grown-up for the most part with in-house developed IT and this has created a mess of legacy systems and most of the banks' IT budgets are wasted just running the show. Furthermore, many banks still view IT as a cost centre but good IT can improve service for customers. Banks must move away from product-centric silos and build umbrella architecture ...only then can cross-selling work effectively." This makes it necessary to identify latest means to optimize core banking activities and efficiencies, discover new opportunities to increase response and usability of systems while maintaining the quality and reducing cost of operations, benchmark core banking performance, enhance the management of core banking systems and analyze how technological solutions increase productivity, usability and effectiveness. Given this overarching scenario, it is no wonder that several banks are replacing their systems with more advanced and innovative systems. Yet while there are many systems available, the cost effectiveness of the implementation needs to be enhanced with best practices to positively impact profitability.

Profits and Profitability

A look at the position of the Net Profits of Public Sector Banks during the period 1969—2007 brings into sharp focus the sea change that has occurred since then. While there are considerable bank-wise variations in the post-reforms period marking an important reference point, the thesis of enhanced profit is incontrovertible. (Table 20)

Performance metric, risk-adjusted customer profitability requires an integrated, enterprise-wide profitability and performance management system. While the measure of bottomline strength varies from segment to segment, there is no doubt that profitability constitutes the fulcrum of banking business. Profit is no more the end product but it is in fact the starting block for all strategic decisions. Hence, there is a greater need to drive profitability because of inexorable pressures to maintain growth with dissipated treasury profits and constricted net interest margins. This paradigm shift from a departmental focus to an integrated, enterprise-wide framework must start with an incisive analysis of the past trends and performance of preceding years, identification of the grey areas and repositioning of strategies accordingly.

Attempts could also be made to identify possible and potential avenues for augmenting Net Interest Income either by maximising yield or by containing cost and reducing burden either by improving Other Income or curtailing Overheads. It is also important to vigorously pursue the concept of 'each branch as a profit center', change the transfer price mechanism from operating profit to net profit based TPM rates and create a

Table 20: Net Profits of Public Sector Banks

Net Profit (Rs. in crore)	1969	1975	1980	1985	1990	1994-95	1999-2000	2004-06	2005-06	2006-07
State Bank of India	2.80	6.53	12.00	32.00	85.00	85.00	715	4305	4407	4541
State Bank of Bikaner & Jaipur	0.10	0.20	0.27	0.45	4.78	4.78	8	206	145	306
State Bank of Hyderabad	0.13	0.08	0.12	0.30	5.80	5.80	44	251	427	506
State Bank of Indore	-0.02	0.09	0.09	0.13	2.05	2.05	9	133	139	190
State Bank of Mysore	0.15	0.17	0.21	0.30	2.85	2.85	3	206	217	249
State Bank of Patiala	0.04	0.07	0.13	0.32	9.98	9.98	33	287	303	367
State Bank of Saurashtra	0.02	0.11	0.07	0.20	2.90	2.90	14	41	60	87
State Bank of Travancore		0.20	0.25	0.40	3.90	3.90	21	247	259	326
Associates of SBI	0.42	0.92	1.14	2.10	32.26	32.26	132	1371	1550	2031
Total of State Bank Group	3.22	7.45	13.14	34.10	117.26	117.26	847	5656	5957	6572
Allahabad Bank	0.20	0.80	1.50	2.70	14.00	14.00	-76	542	706	750
Andhra Bank	0.10	0.30	1.10	3.80	7.80	7.80	-44	520	486	538
Bank of Baroda	0.60	2.90	5.90	9.90	25.00	25.00	176	677	827	1026
Bank of India	0.70	3.20	4.10	8.50	18.10	18.10	50	340	701	1123
Bank of Maharashtra	0.10	0.20	1.10	2.30	3.00	3.00	-41	177	51	272
Canara Bank	0.30	1.90	4.30	11.00	61.30	61.30	204	1110	1343	1421
Central Bank of India	1.10	1.30	3.60	6.80	10.20	10.20	-84	357	257	498

Net Profit (Rs.in crore)	1969	1975	1980	1985	1990	1994-95	1999-2000	2004-06	2005-06	2006-07
Corporation Bank	0.10	0.10	0.80	1.40	4.60	4.60	73	402	445	536
Dena Bank	0.20	0.60	0.80	1.80	1.50	1.50	30	61	73	202
Indian Bank	0.10	1.20	1.60	3.50	16.10	16.10	14	408	505	760
Indian Overseas Bank	0.10	1.60	4.50	5.00	7.00	7.00	10	651	783	1008
Oriental Bank of Commerce	0.00	0.00	0.50	1.50	12.90	12.90	114	761	557	582
Punjab & Sindh Bank	0.00	0.20	0.40	0.70	0.90	0.90	-7	-71	108	219
Punjab National Bank	0.80	3.20	4.00	12.00	28.70	28.70	86	1410	1439	1540
Syndicate Bank	0.30	1.60	1.50	6.00	8.20	8.20	-92	403	537	716
UCO Bank	0.50	2.10	2.30	0.50	-54.60	-54.60	-84	346	197	316
Union Bank of India	0.20	1.40	2.30	5.10	22.00	22.00	106	719	675	845
United Bank of India	0.50	1.30	1.20	0.20	1.20	1.20	-197	300	205	267
Vijaya Bank	0.10	0.60	0.40	0.30	7.29	7.20	32	381	127	331
Total of Nationalised Banks	6.00	24.50	41.90	83.00	195.10	195.10	270	9494	10022	12950
Other Public Sector banks										
IDBI Ltd.								307	561	630
Total of Public Sector Banks	9.22	24.50	41.90	117.10	312.36	312.36	1117	15477	16540	20152

Source: Reserve Bank of India.

dedicated 'Profit Planning' outfit to exclusively budget and monitor profits and profitability of operational units. Such goal setting with a definite action plan would reflect the true health of each branch, facilitate weeding out of unremunerative branches and enhance profit pool. There has to be a sharper focus on effective MIS to constantly track Cost & Yield drivers and provisions, monitoring, mid-term evaluation and corrective action in the light of the rapidly evolving situation.

There has been considerable improvement in restricting NPAs, which constitute the singlemost unplanned expenditure. Hence, there is an imperative need for continued vigil on this count and prudence in asset mix. Concerted attempts at enhancing income and reducing expenditure are needed simultaneously with each unit working as a profit centre. Strengthening of core competencies and exploring new businesses to achieve long-term sustainable growth requires enhanced growth, particularly in income, profits, networth and quality of assets and a paradigm shift in the business mix with an accent on rebalancing existing portfolio by eliminating unremunerative business, repricing, leveraging additional business from existing clients and new business with higher yield, e.g., SMEs, retail lending with due diligence and housing (<20 lakh).

Holistic profitability and performance management requires implementation of an enterprise-wide profitability system and integration of important elements of profitability, e.g., micro management, risk management, factoring ABC data into the decision-making matrix and thrust on 5Cs, 6M and 7Ps (Table 21).

Table 21: Growth Triggers

5Cs	6Ms	7Ps
Character	Man	Product
Capital	Money	Project
Capacity	Machine	Purpose
Conditions	Material	Place
Collateral	Market	People
	Men	Policies
		Profit

Appropriate Risk Management Architecture

Advances in technology and telecommunications, innovation in banking products and services and increasing globalisation of financial markets enhanced the significance of risk management. The traditional face of banks as mere financial intermediaries has altered because of the paradigm shift from balance sheet to off-balance sheet intermediation, move from capital adequacy to capital efficiency and transition from banking to financial services. Appropriate risk management architecture is a function of the size, complexity of business, risk philosophy, market perception and the level of capital of banks. Irrespective of the method used, the key to risk management lies in timely delivery of risk information to the decision-makers, with the time, tools and incentives to act upon it. As Francis Bacon pointed out:

> If a man will begin with certainties, he shall end in doubts; but if he will be content to begin with doubts, he shall end in certainties.

Capital base of PSBs needs to be enhanced to meet growth of off-balance sheet activities, sensitivity of banks balance sheet to changes in interest rates, and the implications of increasing globalization and Basel II compliance. Basel II would impact capital requirement, profitability, risk management, borrowers, rating agencies, technology, asset quality in different ways. While most banks are on track to meet the Basel II norms, they have to go a long way in terms of streamlined risk management—identification, control and mitigation of risk, prudent asset liability mix, adequate capital provision, transparency and disclosure norms, etc.

What is important is not simply to avoid all dangers but to navigate all risks with intelligence and foresight. Competition needs to foster convergence towards best practice in risk management because of growing role of market forces, need for internationally consistent prudential norms, a high-quality financial infrastructure and interdependence of prudential standards. Hence, risks must be mitigated by improved integrated risk management mechanisms, revitalized IT systems and adopting a service oriented architecture (SOA) to minimise risk exposure, streamlined systems and procedures and honing the skill set for client selection, industry analysis, concentration, risk ratings, use of benchmarks, etc. Measuring and managing risk across a range of diverse business activities through Integrated Risk Management requires a comprehensive framework, enhanced understanding and communication of risk issues internally by establishing Integrated Risk Management and use of advanced modelling techniques to manage inherent risks in e-business.

Dr. Y.V. Reddy, the RBI Governor justifiably stressed, "Basel II is considered to be highly complex, making its understanding and implementation a challenge to both the regulator and the regulated community." This makes it necessary to simultaneously tackle several issues, such as, technology, banking and risk management systems, identify process gaps, system gaps, data gaps, manpower skill sets, cost of implementation etc. and take appropriate steps to meet the emerging requirements. Competition, consolidation and convergence could help in surmounting capital constraint, streamlining risk management, maximising return on capital, greater use of technology for efficiency gains, more robust risk-based pricing and closer alignment with international best practices. Most Indian Banks have to build comprehensive risk managements systems with strengthened technological capability and specialized manpower for undertaking risk modeling and also suggesting effective risk management strategies. A risk return culture also needs to be built into the banking operations to ward off unforeseen contingencies due to operational risks.

While Risk Management *per se* is not alien to banks, Basel II makes a differentiation by making the RM initiatives/concepts/organization an integral part of the business strategy. Basel II compliance indeed presents a huge business opportunity provided Banks think beyond compliance to transform themselves as vibrant and globally competitive entities. Risk Management is emerging as an important business differentiator in the face of rapid economic growth being witnessed by the domestic/global economy.

Basel II affords an opportunity for banks to undertake a thorough review of risk management processes and consolidate, as Banks now understand the relationship between cost and return. Regulator has the most crucial role. The Regulator desires proper recording and reasoning of every aspect of RM systems in terms of risks inherent to the business. The whole process needs to be documented by way of ICAAP. Pillar II has a deeper significance as it gives scope to the Regulator to determine the required level of capital and empowers them to stipulate buffer capital above the regulatory capital level.

RBI has already helped the banks by broadening the definition of Tier I and Tier II for the purpose of capital adequacy. New forms of capital have already strengthened the capital base.

Pillar III is a key challenge to accurately measure and assess the risks in an increasingly uncertain business environment. It is a process, where internal risks of systems/initiatives are translated to external disclosures. Market analysts/rating agencies are likely to place increasing emphasis on bank's response to Pillar III requirements. Compliance of the same is likely to be rewarded with strong confidence and improved ratings. This requires putting in place an Integrated Enterprise-wide Risk Management Policy (IRM Policy) to establish and implement effective risk management by identifying, assessing, prioritising, monitoring and managing risks in a planned and integrated manner.

The rollover to Basel II Framework is constrained by inadequately skilled human resources for risk management, significant increase in the capital charge for banks, low level of MIS, complex minimum standards set even for the Internal Rating Based (IRB) foundation approach necessitating deft maneuverability on the part of Indian banks. Hence, Basel II implementation with effect from March 31, 2007 is likely to accelerate the emerging trend of consolidation to overcome capital constraint, streamlining risk management, maximizing return of capital, greater use of technology for efficiency gains. A winning strategy therefore involves implementing and monitoring best risk management initiatives, capabilities to extend geographical boundaries, expand market/products, going for mergers/acquisitions.

An objective overall analysis needs to be tempered by the special circumstances of financial systems in emerging market countries and opportunities given for "graduation" with rising levels of sophistication. Implementation of Basel II guidelines requires vastly improved IT architecture for business decisions and to cope appropriately with the Pillar 3 disclosure requirements, bank-wise loan policy, streamlining credit delegation, prudential limits for single/group borrowers/industries and sensitive sectors/regions, sharing of information on bad debts and defaulters among banks, advanced risk measures linked to variation, duration and better gap analysis and developing systems to measure and control operational risks, managing market and interest rate derivatives risk and evaluate off balance-sheet exposure risk. Introducing a comprehensive credit rating system covering all exposures and stress testing it for efficiency will be a major real time challenge for the banks. Capacity building both in banks and the regulatory bodies requires streamlined MIS, reskilling staff and enhanced supervisory capabilities, development of domestic rating agencies and increased rating penetration, use of national discretion and improved governance standards and oversight.

While Basel II better aligns regulatory capital with actual risk, it transcends regulatory compliance to provide an opportunity to achieve distinctive competitive advantage by adroit risk management. Such risk sensitive measures would impact capital requirement, profitability, risk management, borrowers, rating agencies, technology, and asset quality in different ways. Datar and Banerjee's (2004) conclusion that public sector banks would need additional 14 per cent of Tier 1 capital to cover operational risk while private banks would need an additional 12 per cent may mot find universal acceptability, capital infusion is certainly imperative. The current shortfall in banking capital (estimated at between US $6 billion and 8 billion) is likely to rise with bank lending rising fast. Banking capital could be shored up by public equity offers, venture capital, selling stakes to large foreign banks to meet fluctuations in capital requirements stemming from fluctuating quality of risk exposures and fully meet all elements of expected losses by provisioning and availability of exclusive capital to support unexpected losses.

The prescribed framework by BIS under Basel II stresses policy framework for risk management (board-driven), organization structure (top management driven), definition of roles and responsibilities (field level), skill sets of people (field driven), IT backbone/infrastructure for data management, roadmap for moving to higher levels of approaches in consultation with RBI; credit risk management—credit policy, credit risk organization (credit groups) and credit risk rating framework (3 models)—at borrower and facility levels.

Studies on the impact of capital adequacy on bank behaviour in India (Nachane *et al.* 2000, Ghosh *et al.* 2003) together with cross-country experiences suggest an accent on competition, consolidation and convergence to surmount capital constraint, streamline risk management, maximize return on capital, greater use of technology for efficiency gains and more robust risk-based pricing. With banks gaining in size and diversifying into new areas, there is, however, the danger of emergence of greater systemic risk. The challenges are many but the pay-off could be huge in terms of the Indian banking system being in sync with international best practices and enhanced strength and resilience.

Cross-Selling

Cross-selling implies the offer of additional banking products to the existing bank customers with a view to expanding banking business, reducing the per customer cost of operations and providing more satisfaction and value to the customer. The crossing selling may take place on the liability side (i.e., different kinds of deposit accounts) or on the asset side (i.e., loans for different requirements) or between the two. It could be either at the initiative of the customers or a bank can implement it as a coherent strategy.

Cross-selling is rapidly emerging as an important growth tool with transaction accounts having the best cross-sell base and reduced significance of geographic expansion into new markets. Fee based 3rd Party products provide an opportunity to provide sophisticated/customised product offerings. Bundled or wrapped around banking products, payroll accounts and relationship across life stages help to acquire clients across asset classes and achieve higher share of the wallet. Increased customer loyalty with higher product holding strengthens long-term relationships through insurance, transaction behaviour provides strong insights into customer need and volatility of interest income reduced. But cross-selling involves not just more products but provides value addition through transactional convenience, research, statements, asset allocation, etc. and eliminates the hassle of multiple relationships. It is essential for a product offering to be matched with 'Single view' of entire relationship of the customer, ability to communicate and educate the customer on asset classes and asset allocations, timely statements and advice and meeting life stage needs through Credit, Savings, Mutual Funds, Overdraft, Structured Products.

Effective cross-selling requires collection of data and preparation of data base of the customers, identification of customers and suitability of products and charting the strategy to market products, imparting proper training to the staff to create team spirit and sharing with them the strategy for undertaking cross-selling, selecting target customers and narrowing down the product range, or even development of new products if necessary, to meet the specific needs of the group and effective delivery. Cross-selling is not a transaction based activity, it is primarily, a relationship building exercise through activities, such as, bancassurance, syndication/derivative products/futures market, on-line trading/bullion trading, merchant banking, wealth management and private equity opportunities, which are more profitable for banks than plain vanilla lending and borrowing. It is necessary to bring about a harmonious synthesis between banks and insurance companies with an accent on fee-income, wealth management, bancassurance, mutual funds, capital markets, structured products, credit/debit cards.

Banks and FIs in India are increasingly vying for a substantial share of new business in various markets. Cross-selling is widely considered to be necessary to surmount the challenges of slashing costs, increasing efficiencies and developing synergies in banking and insurance industries. While the average "cross-sell ratio" for an FI is 2, Wells Fargo has a cross-sell ratio of 5.2 products per Community Banking household, 6 for Wholesale Banking customers and 7 for average middle-market commercial banking. It has thus "zigged where others zagged." Clearly, this convention defying performance has important policy prescriptive implications for Banks and FIs across the development spectrum.

International Standards and Codes

International standards and codes have evoked greater interest because of increasing cross-border flows, upscaling of technology and availability of large institutional funds, such as, pension funds and mutual funds. As the significance of these mutually reinforcing forces rapidly increase, the stake rise higher, particularly in the wake of highly publicized accounts of misleading financial reporting and other improprieties within corporations across countries. Such events have generally surprised executives and board members, who either had no advance warning that they would occur or were not even aware of the risks facing their companies. Today, this knowledge gap is no longer acceptable. This makes it imperative for Boards of Directors, CEOs and CFOs to not only design and implement appropriate corporate governance processes, but also to assess the risks their businesses face today and can reasonably expect to face in the future and; to manage those risks in an appropriate manner. It, therefore, becomes necessary to minimize systemic risks by transparent operations and uniform definitions benchmarked against international norms for credible financial statements and other disclosures that are key means for communicating a firm's operating results and its overall health, as well as for making various operating activities more transparent.

Risks can fester and spread anywhere inside an organization. This makes it necessary to identify, prioritise and manage risks to enhance performance and ultimately, business value with thrust on the following areas: **Business Process Risk Management**—risk profiling; risk polarization; analysis and management of threat; systems assessment; process and control evaluation; risk assurance (including internal audit services); business continuity planning (including disaster recovery) and corporate governance. **Decision Support**—ensuring integrity of information; developing decision rules; structuring management information flows and instituting systems that provide decision-makers with early warning signals. **Performance Management**—improving delivery and vendor management; optimising supply chain management; rationalising inventory management; achieving cost reductions. **Activity based and unit based costing**—enabling a comprehensive and systematic basis to price for products and services.

Organizations today find themselves struggling to maintain the minimum required controls expected of them in a new, increasingly regulated, business environment. The traditional audit process is intended to provide assurance that control systems are adequately designed, and within a specific timeframe, operating effectively. However, the audit process typically occurs significantly after the transactions are completed, and is rarely able to test all transactions in a comprehensive way for controls compliance. Therefore, there is a significant risk to many organizations that errors and fraud occur and remain undetected, negatively impacting their bottom line. To assist in the efficient capture and evaluation of data, sophisticated software tools need to be used for evaluation of disclosure controls and procedures and internal controls over financial reporting.

Disclosure of reliable information facilitates market discipline, strengthens confidence and reduces the chance for rumors and misleading information that could cause market instability. The sequencing of the structure of reporting is a function not only of constitutional, legal and institutional mechanisms but also the safety and soundness of institutions and systemic soundness and stability. Indian accounting standards lag behind global practices in Consolidation of Accounts, Segment Reporting, Deferred Tax Accounting, International Transactions and Combinations, Joint Ventures and Related Party Transactions. These aspects make it difficult for the Central Bank to effectively discharge its responsibilities of ensuring financial market stability.

Despite the categorical recommendations of Malegam and Bhave Committees, India is yet to adopt global benchmarks in respect of derivatives accounting, lease accounting, interest Capitalisation and Accounting, Extraordinary and Non Operating Income and Expenses, Results from Discontinued Operations and Formatting and Presentation of Accounts. While there are several issues involved here, some of the important issues relate to the valid approach, adequate coverage of issues, symmetrical treatment between participants, linkage between international standards and codes and financial stability and issues of coverage of standards in IMF surveillance.

Consequent to the introduction of the financial sector reforms, Indian Banks have been partially practicing the international standards. However, in many areas like segment reporting, fair values of financial instruments, related party transactions, strategic investments and marketable securities etc., Indian Banks are not entirely in tune with international standards of accounting. What is basically required is setting of standards domestically with an international character, consultative and participative processes of setting, prioritising, and incentivising, monitoring and reorienting and effective implementation.

Without in any way reducing the significance of standards and codes in the emerging landscape, the calibrated Indian approach is predicated on heightened awareness on the part of the official agencies, self-regulating bodies and market participants rather than making it a statutory requirement.

Broadening Inclusive Growth—The Question of all Questions

The principal goal of development is not just to create sustainable improvements in terms of per capita income, but also to enhance the overall quality of life of the 'teeming millions' of India. The inherent limitations of the dynamics of capitalism as a mode of production have highlighted the resonant theme of inclusive growth to improve things for the vast and hapless human resource. There are still persisting concerns that the banks have been unable to include vast sections of the society, especially the underprivileged ones, into their fold. Vast swathes of the rural hinterland are still underdeveloped, with very little safety nets for both employment generation and poverty alleviation. Agriculture is still sensitive to the vagaries of nature. Government directed approach may not always optimise returns. But empirical studies show that such approaches contribute to employment generation and poverty alleviation substantially, especially in those areas, where sections of the populace have very poor skills or knowledge base. Hence ethically grounded issues of "inclusive" growth, distributive equity, "banking at the bottom of the pyramid", development of agriculture and rural non-farm sector (RNFS) driven by a process of policy deliberation have increasingly come to the fore.

70 per cent of India resides in villages and lives off a meager 20 per cent of GDP. Given the manifest need to ensure financial independence through financial inclusion, the strategy must transcend corporate calculus and promote a virtuous economic cycle. Dr. C. Rangarajan has persuasively argued, "The objective of financial inclusion is to extend the scope of activities of the organized financial system to include within its ambit people with low incomes. The attempts here must be to lift the poor so that they come out of poverty." While 41 per cent of the population continues to be unbanked at the macro level, the proportion is higher in the North Eastern and Eastern regions. The total number of saving accounts, as per cent of number of households, was 137 in rural areas and 244 in the urban areas on the eve of reforms in 1991. Despite wide-ranging economic reforms, the differential continued to be similar even by 2005. In case of credit accounts, the situation has deteriorated for rural households while showing significant improvement in the urban areas, underscoring the stark urban-rural divide.

The revolution of 'rising expectations' has acquired contextual immediacy as almost 60 to 80 per cent of enterprises and individuals within the country lack access even to basic financial services, such as, savings and credit. Small, marginal and sub-marginal farmers constitute nearly 80 per cent of the total cultivators cultivating fragmented landholdings averaging around 1.41 hectares. Financial security is available to only 12-15 per cent of the 40 crore labourers, i.e., 5-6 crore labourers. The NSSO 2003 survey underscored that of the 89.35 million cultivator households, 43.42 million (48.6 per cent) are indebted. Households with 1 hectare or less land accounted for 66 per cent of all cultivator households. About 45 per cent of these marginal farmers were indebted to either formal sources or non-formal sources or to both. While institutional sources accounted for 57 per cent of loans, non-institutional sources accounted for the remaining 43 per cent. Nearly 55 per cent of cultivator households are not indebted at all making it necessary for the banking system to reach out to them to improve both volumes and outreach at the branch levels.

The Rural Financial Access Survey conducted by the World Bank and NCAER in the states of Andhra Pradesh and Uttar Pradesh in 2003 also reached same conclusion. This survey showed that in the states covered only 21 per cent rural households had access to formal credit; small and marginal farmers were at a relative disadvantage and only 11.8 per cent of marginal farmers in Andhra Pradesh and 13.5 per cent in Uttar Pradesh obtained loans from banks; the time taken for final clearance of a loan proposal ranged from 24 to 33 weeks and was generally collateralized and only 42 per cent rural households had access to savings deposits. Evidently, fulfilment of financial needs in terms of accessibility, affordability and timeliness of loans to the vulnerable sections in the transforming socio-economic milieu has emerged as a key policy variable. Clearly this situation necessitates a renewed thrust on increasing the ground level credit disbursement for agriculture and non-farm sector, percolating consumer banking to grass-roots, issue of 'softer' credit cards to masses, bring 90 per cent of their branches to the 'anywhere banking' platform, launch no-frills accounts with miniscule balance and install a wider ATM network with low-cost machines.

The SHG-Bank Linkage Programme, introduction of Kisan Credit Card, the Government of India's accent on doubling of agriculture credit over a period of three years (2004-05 to 2006-07) and ITC's e-choupal concept attempted to transform the process and pattern of rural credit in India. But bankers continue to be recalcitrant to promote the flow of credit to this sector, in any case to the desired extent, as borne out by RBI's successive reports on *Trends and Progress of Banking*. While this recalcitrance stems from the confluence of several forces and factors, mention may here be made of "information asymmetry", absence of requisite documentation of income, insistence on collateral security, an inadequate understanding of the rural scenario, the credit delivery system and the variety of activities subsumed under the broader agricultural category with variable cash flows based on the seasonality of the produce and the harvesting period. In propelling the growth of agriculture to a higher and more sustainable growth trajectory and usher in a 'second Green revolution', various innovative options, including sanctioning a flexible 'credit line' to the farmers instead of the conventional term loan and working capital could justifiably be explored. This credit line could be a function of size of land-holdings, the nature of the financing activity and the collateral security available.

The rural economy has to be vibrant and resilient to achieve the avowed goal of growth with distributive equity. The reform of the national financial architecture must lead to early and sustained results to deal more effectively with future challenges and to raise general living standards. There cannot be any, what F.R. Leavis termed in a different context, "blunting of edge, blurring of focus and muddled misdirection of attention" (Leavis, 1972). With cutting edge products/services at competitive prices, Banks can enhance access to affordable financial services, such as, savings, loan, remittance and insurance services to the 'teeming millions' of India. Banks can thus reach the underprivileged sections of society and simultaneously exploit the immense business potential at the "bottom of the pyramid" (Sharma, 2007 b). Towards this end, implementation of various priority lending schemes, fostering of organic relationship between the rural masses and the Banks, extending banking to the doorsteps of villagers, forming and linking SHGs and promoting micro finance in a big way (Sharma, 2007 a) would further the cause of total financial inclusion. In view of the criticality of agriculture, improved growth in agriculture will have a multiplier effect on the national economy. In some of the developed countries, statutory back-up is provided for financial inclusion of those excluded. India also can follow similar strategies and also revisit the branch expansion drive to stride faster and longer in the pursuit of creating meaning and value in the lives of the poor, the marginalized and the vulnerable sections of society. We can here do no better than to refer to the moving words of Adam Smith, who said more than two centuries ago: "No society can surely be flourishing and happy, of which the far greater part of members are poor and miserable. It is but equity, besides, that they who feed, clothe and lodge the whole body of people should have such a share of the produce of their own labour as to be themselves tolerably well fed, clothe and lodged" (The Wealth of Nations, Book I, Chapter VIII, "Of the Wages of Labour"). These are powerful and inspiring thoughts and need to be acted upon in all earnestness.

Creating Meaning and Value in the Lives of Vulnerable Sections Through Micro Finance

Cross-country experience clearly shows that micro credit is the key to socio-economic transformation. Organizations like SHARE, BASIX, SEWA, MARYADA, PRADAN, etc. in India have made a commendable difference to the multitude of the rural poor. Microfinance involves the provision of a broad range of financial services, such as loans, deposits, payment services, money transfer and insurance to poor and low income households. A study published by Sa-Dhan on the growth potential of the Microfinance, specifically MFIs, forecasts ~10 times increase in loan portfolio of MFIs by 2010.

The various delivery models include Self Help Groups, Grameen Model, and Joint Liability Groups etc. The common theme across all models is that of solidarity groups, use of social/peer pressure to induce good performance, achieving low delivery cost through aggregation. Target group includes both poor and 'vulnerable poor' but not destitute. The vision and the Biblical grit to preserve with this experiment stresses the need for soft money and even equity/long-term capital when it comes to certain financing needs of the end customer. Microfinance begins with credit and then evolves into other products. Micro credit does not only deliver macro benefits but has also brought about a silent revolution in rural areas. Micro credit generates huge volumes for the Banks on account of handling large volume of transactions with ease through technology and dwindling margins in other segments of banking

SHGs constitute a key element in the development strategy because of their socio-economic multiplier effects. What sharply distinguishes SHGs from earlier approaches is its focus on the credit needs of the poor, whose capacity to save is extremely limited and thus induces economic development in an area where it is needed most. The formation of SHGs as a catalyst for change was encouraged by mounting overdues of the rural banking system, high intermediation cost, burden of subsidised interest rates, write-offs and implementation problems of centrally controlled structures and mechanisms. A significant instrument of promotion of micro credit in India in a sustainable manner has been the SHG programme and its linkage with banks.

With a modest beginning, this project steadily progressed in terms of number of SHGs financed, bank loans disbursed, number of SHGs refinanced and refinance disbursed. The success of SHG Bank Linkage emanates from its alignment with Indian history and circumstances and capitalization on the country's vast network of rural bank branches. Despite credit linkage of more than 1 million SHGs and mobilization of about Rs. 6000 crore as credit from the formal financial institutions, there are real geographical, sectoral and product asymmetries with MF still forming a small proportion of the total bank credit in India. There are still serious demand-supply imbalances, limited involvement of commercial banks, small size of microfinance institutions (MFIs), minuscule outreach of MFIs in terms of the proportion of poor households served, covering less than 5 per cent of India's rural poor (as compared to 65 per cent in Bangladesh), almost entire focus on rural areas, mono product and extremely skewed distribution across states with a few states, mostly in South India, accounting for over three-fifth of the credit linkage. Even among the southern states, a skewed pattern is discernible. Further, the scope of Indian MFIs continues to be extremely narrow with only India's three top MFIs offering composite services. These and other issues need to be addressed to move to a much higher plane, particularly because as per various estimates, 15-20 million households of the target population were microfinance clients as of 2005. Assuming a total size of 70 million households, this implies a penetration level of 20 per cent–30 per cent.

In this context, microfinance is synonymous with credit for low income individuals with savings and remittances are still absent from the standard offering. But micro-insurance is fast gaining a significant share of the market. Banks have emerged as strong allies in providing on-lending funds; MFIs are not growing fast enough to absorb available funds. There are organizations of various legal forms practice microfinance—NGOs, non-banking finance companies, cooperatives, banks etc. But there is conspicuous absence of a legal charter that recognizes the uniqueness of microfinance operations. Building sound MFIs requires attention on both financial (adequate capitalisation of >15 per cent, financial flexibility relating to availability of long-term and short-term debt for on-lending, building infrastructure and systems and start up capital for new MFIs) and governance (appropriate policies and practices to manage risk) issues.

Accent on SMEs

Diverse and dynamic needs of SMEs in the Indian economy require, apart from the conceptual change in SMEs, a variety of innovative and fast track methods of SME financing. Given the squeeze on spreads with about 70 per cent of banks' total outstanding advances at rates below Benchmark Prime Lending Rates (BPLRs) of banks, pressure from corporates for finer rates, intensifying competition in the retail banking segment, banks now need to increasingly look at SMEs as a growth option, particularly with an accent on key sunrise growth sectors like Food and Agribusiness, Life-sciences, Engineering, Telecommunications, Media and Information Technology, Infrastructure, Retailing and Textiles. In view of the overarching significance of the service sector in the rapidly emerging Indian economy, there is a manifest need to focus on a suite of specialized products with a high quality service proposition customized for heavy cash-flow business operations, such as, travel agents, airlines, educational institutions, clubs and societies, etc.

The development of entrepreneurship requires not just direct inputs but more importantly a broader framework characterised by stable economic conditions, relatively easy access to capital and an efficient physical infrastructure. This is necessary for the accentuation of a paradigm shift from the ethos of dependency and vulnerability to self-reliance and globally competitive capability. The spectrum of these promotional measures would influence the determinants of growth by removing bottlenecks to business development for all firms. While e-commerce can take the forms of Business to Business (B2B), Business to Consumer (B2C) and Consumer to Consumer (C2C), banks can play an increasingly greater role in B2B and B2C transactions.

Streamlining Rural Financial Institutions (RFIs)

In view of the estimated demand for food grains during 2011-12 at 298.38 million tonnes and the need for equity and distributive justice, the central government directed banks to double their agriculture and other priority sector lending in the coming three years. While this annual growth of 30 per cent is contextually significant, streamlining the credit delivery system is much more important, given the decrepit state of RFIs in India. RFIs, particularly cooperatives, continue to suffer from systemic weaknesses, such as, high transaction cost, high risk costs, low margins, high NPAs and low capitalisation. In view of the severity of the crisis the RFIs are afflicted with, attempts to improve credit delivery systems need to be well supported by multi-dimensional strategies comprising general strategies, thrust on recovery performance and institution and area specific measures. What is fundamentally needed today is a paradigm shift and a frontal attack on the basic problems afflicting RFIs because the viability of RFIs is inexorably linked to business-related factors, viz. low level of deposits with a large proportion of high cost deposits, low level of advances with an unprofitable mix and injudicious funds management.

An efficient and vibrant rural credit delivery mechanism requires maintaining a higher capital adequacy ratio, facilitating restructuring of the system through an exit and privatisation policy, implementing stricter and more transparent accounting and disclosure norms, enhancing rule-based supervision and reduced reliance upon public sector funding because of its unsustainability, highly volatile and socially/economically undesirable nature. Any strategy to streamline banking must necessarily address these basic concerns with the support of all players in the system. While financial recapitalisation is expected to cleanse the balance sheets of cooperative banks, its success is contingent on organisational, structural, operational and systemic reforms (Sharma, 2001; 2004a; 2004c).

Full Capital Account Convertibility (CAC)

Issues relating to full capital account convertibility (CAC) and the preparedness of banks require removal of operational and regulatory constraints in the repo market against the backdrop of a decision for a gradual movement towards a pure inter-bank call money market. Further developments are needed in terms of eligible collaterals, membership, etc. to integrate different segments of the money market so that the money market as a whole is enabled to cope better with market fluctuations in the run-up to fuller CAC. Given the increased technical complexity of most business activities including banking and the rapid pace of change in financial markets and practices, PSBs need to devise imaginative ways of responding to the evolving challenges within the context of their diversified ownership.

With the adoption of fuller CAC, issues relating to competency strengths of small national banks, redressal of inter-country regulatory conflicts in management of foreign banks, market structure, competition and regulatory conflicts of global financial conglomerates may arise. Competitiveness of Indian conglomerates requires their acquiring a semblance of international size and clarity in regulatory approach.

Critical Success Factors

The transforming socio-economic milieu and the need to align with the fast changing world necessitate a paradigm shift from product society banking to knowledge society banking.

The introduction of innovative business models and financial technologies the world over has received an impetus through slashing operating cost through higher labour productivity, technology, innovation (Sharma, 2003; 2004b; 2005d) and business process reengineering (BPR), further reduction in NPAs, micro-planning, predominantly branch-centric profit planning and monitoring, CBS and market-centric HRD/HRM policies and manpower planning. Ageing staff, new skill sets, working in a computerised environment, foray into emerging areas necessitate recruitment of new and specialised staff, extensive training and mindset changes, etc. Basel recommendations have also stressed the need to bring about tectonic changes for higher profits and profitability.

Measures relating, *inter alia*, to market focus, effective Corporate strategy, greater use of multiple channels like ATMs, Internet and Mobile Banking, etc., efficient credit dispensation and monitoring, besides building up sound financials, can help banks to meet the financial needs of emerging growth sectors and determining solutions transcending the traditional realm of banking.

Customer focused orientation necessitates renewed emphasis, because as Mahatma Gandhi stressed "a customer is not dependent on us, we are dependent on customers." Banks are now moving from transaction to customer-centric solutions as the challenge for the bank is to retain customer loyalty. This is why enterprise-wise quality improvement programmes need to be assiduously pursued with an accent on Customer Service to create new, clearly differentiated value. Customer management requires product management, product delivery management, convenience management and customer delight management based on financial expertise and cutting-edge technology. Several banks have designed innovative integrated delivery channel architectures together with initiating an effective Customer Relationship Management (CRM).

Some of the critical success factors also relate to enhanced organisational effectiveness of banks by management of deregulated interest, judicious asset-liability management (ALM), realistic market segmentation, product differentiation, technology upgradation and corporate governance. Reducing the transaction and overall intermediation cost, improving yield of assets and slashing both gross and net NPAs would be helpful in bringing about a structural transformation in sync with best practices.

Addressing the challenges of KYC/AML, international standards and codes, accounting transparency and various supervisory issues require adequate IT-enablement and effective re-skilling of manpower. Enhancing income, curbing interest expended and operating expenses, managing varied credit, marketing and operational risks, diversification in banking activities, portfolio investment, payments and settlements systems, etc. need to be resolved on the basis of resource-mix, investment opportunities, demanding standards of customers and patterns of shifting value to streamline the banking system as an integral part of the blueprint of development. The changed financial architecture has significant implications for corporate strategy, organisation and performance necessitating a move for banks to become 'one-stop financial shops' and to integrate Lean with Six Sigma to deliver Six Sigma quality with Lean speed and maximum value (Sharma, 2004f).

Banking success requires imaginative strategic planning, organisational restructuring, streamlining of human resources and significant changes in the legal, regulatory and supervisory framework. The process of competition, convergence, consolidation, compliance and cost efficiency needs to be carefully pursued by banks through changes in products, technology, structure, processes, detection and elimination of "cost drivers" and introduction of advanced management concepts and practices to successfully introduce new financial instruments and strategies.

There has been thrust on volume-led growth to competitive balance sheet size, migration from interest income to non-interest income and capital adequacy to capital efficiency because of increased competition in financial market in general and banking sector in particular. Progressively reducing net interest margin, stiff competition for good corporate loans with development of capital market and increased market capitalization and relentless pursuit of the strategy of balance sheet growth to maintain reasonable profit growth have also been receiving added emphasis.

Accent on Human Resources Development

While recruitment has always been an integral element of the growth of banks, it is being increasingly realised that the human capital is the key to the success of any organization and even more so of the banks. It is necessary to develop a proper recruitment strategy and ensure that it dovetails with the identified objectives of banks, identify, attract and retain talent through flexible compensation packages and an institutional mechanism of recognition and reward. Hence, suitable training, assessment of the recruitment strategies that help create future leaders and exploration of the benefits of organic growth are also necessary in managing flow and flux, reacting to market dynamics and changing needs of the industry. Since banks need to transform to remain competitive and be ahead of the game, banks must constantly reassess and adapt the business strategy to better reflect the changing workforce dynamics and the increasingly competitive banking environment. Such reassessment and adaptation of the business strategy must objectively examine habits and processes developed painstakingly over the years as an integral part of Strategic Human Resource Management (SHRM).

Banks reward their staff. The reward to staff is, however, not comparable to those given by private or foreign banks. Things are constantly improving in this area with the liberal financial autonomy package to all PSBs announced by the GoI last year and the realisation by PSBs to effectively face the challenges posed by other players. But the banks need to make use of this opportunity in a greater measure.

In the changed post-reforms scenario, the role of HR transformed from its traditional base as a support function to becoming an integral part of functions and working of banks. Given the utter inadequacy of generalizations and one-size-fits-all approaches, HR persons need to constantly interact with persons in other Departments to find out their concerns and challenges to enhance the organizational efficiency of each Department. What is required is working smarter, not just harder. Questions, such as, 'What is my purpose in this organization?' and 'What is the best use of my time right now in delivering my own purpose and the organisation's purpose?' require an innovative and out-of-box view of business practices, suitable training, assessment of the recruitment strategies that help create future leaders and exploration of the benefits of organic growth are also necessary in reassessing and adapting the HR strategy to better reflect the changing workforce dynamics and the increasingly competitive banking environment. The technological and academic training of employees must be dovetailed with the requirements of organizational growth and profitability.

Talent management requires differentiating the company by building business capability through excellent programs to attract, engage and retain the top valued employees, underlining the importance of talent differentiation, aligning the talent management strategy to the overall business plan and implementing an individual approach towards the top employees. Human capital development must be effectively linked to financial performance to drive superior financial performance. The increasing market scarcity of talents with the right technical and behavioural competencies combined with a 'values-fit' to the organization is made much more difficult by the high attrition rate. Retention of the talent through monetary and non-monetary strategies is needed to ensure business growth and continuity. Johann Wolfgang von Goethe said, "Treat people as if they were what they ought to be, and you help them become what they are capable of being." This is precisely banks' need to do by the use of the three-dimensional HR strategy of resourcing talent, HR development and institution of a reward mechanism. This is a tall order and requires consistently placing employees/ customers on a high pedestal and constantly working towards their betterment and satisfaction; evolving a constantly re-conceptualized and innovated HR policy to suit the changing trends; conducting interfaces and using HR tools like staff meeting, brainstorming sessions, quality circle etc. to instill a sense of teamwork and exploit the latent talents of the employees. Formulation of succession planning, thrust on transfer, job rotation and Development Programmes must also be important elements of the growth theoretic of banks.

Tracking Growth Stimulants

Thrust on volume-led growth to competitive balance sheet size, migration from interest income to non-interest income and capital adequacy to capital efficiency is needed to maintain benchmarks of return on assets (>1 per cent), return on owned funds (>18 per cent), net non-performing loans (<1 per cent), capital adequacy (9 per cent), cost to income ratio (<40 per cent), net interest margin (>3.5 per cent) and intermediation cost (<1 per cent).

In bracing for tomorrow, a paradigm shift in bank financing through innovative mechanisms, such as, templates for assessing customer risk and pricing product offerings, credit scoring, availability and use of information is manifestly needed. Retail banking requires product development and differentiation, innovation and business process re-engineering, micro planning, marketing, prudent pricing, customisation, technological upgradation, home/electronic/mobile banking, cost reduction and cross-selling.

Banks are implementing strategies to immune their balance sheets from interest rate fluctuation by greater attention on non-interest income segments. Growing services sector and financial market have created new avenues for fee-based income. For instance, the share of off-balance sheet exposure of SCBs in their total assets increased sharply from 58 per cent in March 2002 to about 236 per cent in March 2007, reflecting banks' strategy to use a cushion against interest rate risks.

Merchant banking, international trade, funds transfer, payments and settlements, consultancy services, financial derivatives, utility services etc., opened up new income sources for banks. But there has to be a transition from branch banking to virtual banking, market segmentation to customer segmentation and product planning to customer profitability.

Table 22: Off-Balance Sheet Exposures (OBS)—per cent to Total Assets and Share

Period	Foreign Banks	New Private Sector Banks	Old Private Sector Banks	Public Sector Banks	All Banks
Mar-98	374.3 (55.1)	76.5 (4.4)	32.0 (4)	27.5 (36.5)	60.3
Mar-99	280.1 (50.5)	79.0 (7.2)	24.0 (3.7)	23.0 (38.7)	47.5
Mar-2000	334.1 (53.2)	71.7 (8.1)	28.8 (4.3)	21.4 (34.4)	49.2
Mar-01	359.3 (51.3)	72.8 (8.1)	28.4 (3.4)	27.2 (37.3)	57.3
Mar-02	405.1 (53.8)	49.4 (10.3)	25.6 (2.9)	25.4 (33)	57.1
Mar-03	522.8 (51.1)	87.8 (14.6)	38.0 (3.2)	30.0 (31.1)	72.2
Mar-04	728.1 (53.8)	150.0 (19.9)	46.4 (3)	30.6 (23.3)	96.8
Mar-05	1128.7 (58.9)	171.0 (17.5)	43.0 (1.9)	37.9 (21.6)	130.0
Mar-06	1352.1 (62.3)	190.2 (17.3)	42.0 (1.4)	42.9 (18.9)	163.3
Mar-07	1943.3 (69.5)	218.1 (15.1)	44.3 (1)	48.4 (14.4)	235.7

Figures in parentheses indicate individual bank group's share in total OBS exposures of all banks.
Source: Reserve Bank of India.

Where Do We Go From Here?

Liberalisation of markets, privatisation of ownership and globalisation of economy provided an impetus to the process of competition, consolidation (Sharma, 2004h) and convergence. But in strengthening the continuous cycle of competency and development, fostering a virtuous cycle of regenerative broad-based and higher growth, the focus has to be on technology, infrastructure (Sharma 2000; 2002) and human resources, which provide the cutting edge of development.

The Great Indian Vision

Post-reforms, the Indian economy underwent wide ranging changes necessitating a change in the mindset of banks with thrust on identified areas and mechanisms. However, this paradigm shift in the role of banks and financial institutions needs also to be accompanied by an attitudinal change. While we cannot change the direction of the wind, we can certainly trim our sails to succeed in the stormy days ahead. There is a fair measure of consensus that development strategies require overcoming mass deprivation and building an inclusive society. Towards this end, enabling frameworks to help increase access and opportunity towards financial inclusion and a conscious coverage of sections, which have been either not covered or under-covered by the banking sector, particularly through low cost ATMs, products, facilities and arrangements are sorely needed. This is why the realization of the Great Indian Vision of achievement of the status of a developed nation by 2020 depends on balanced and equitable development—a process of economic growth that is inclusive, equitable and all encompassing.

The challenges ahead of the PSBs relates to networking and providing core banking solutions, implementation of Basel II and improvement of risk management systems. It is also necessary for them to restructure branches, redeploy manpower, reduce operational risk and transaction cost by progressively greater use of the convergence of information and communication technology (ICT), containing accretions under NPAs, enhancing customer service, thrust on other income and optimizing efficiency, implementation of new accounting standards; enhancement of transparency and disclosures; and compliance with KYC aspects.

The long-term vision for India's banking system must stress transition from domestic arena to the global field with a combination of new technologies, strengthening of prudential norms, adoption of international benchmarks, consolidation within the financial system and management of organisational change. Banks must attempt adroit management of risk by mitigating concentration risk, uniform spread of risks over the entire spectrum of assets, reduce capital requirement by increasing low risk assets and improved profitability. There are also important issues of innovation and product diversification and business process reengineering, streamlined internal control, upgradation of technological infrastructure of the financial system and human resources development and exploitation of latent "glocalisation" (think global, act local) potential as the catalyst of transformation.

In this overarching scenario, it is manifestly clear that the rural economy (Sharma, 2004g) has to be vibrant and resilient to achieve the avowed goal of growth with distributive equity. It needs no clairvoyance to perceive that in this huge task of national resurgence, banks have an increasingly important role to play. In view of the transformation of the socio-economic milieu, we need to align ourselves with the fast changing world and must move from product society banking to knowledge society banking. We must adopt effective strategies for acquiring, analyzing and assimilating information on an ongoing basis and effect midcourse correction, wherever necessary. This is why the institutions need to respond to developments around them, react to them suitably and tailor their policy, procedures and operations accordingly in conformity with the needs of the present and the expectations of the future.

REFERENCES

Bank for International Settlements (2001): *Annual Report 2001.*

—— (2002): *Annual Report, 2002.*

Basel Committee on Banking Supervision (2004): International Convergence of Capital Measurement and Capital Standards: A Revised Framework, BIS, Switzerland, June.

Bank for International Settlements (1996): *Amendment to the Capital Accord to Incorporate Market Risks*, Basel, Switzerland, January.

Caprio, G. and Summers, L. (1993): "Financial Reform: Beyond Laissez-Faire", (ed.), D. Papadimitriou, *Financing Prosperity into the 21st Century,* New York: Macmillan.

Cotavarria, Dziobek, L.C., Kanaya, A. and Song, I. (2000): "Loan review, Provisioning and Macroeconomic Linkages", *IMF Working Paper No. 195 (222.imf.org)*

Dale, R. (1992): *International Banking Deregulation: The Great Banking Experiment*, Blackwell Publishers, Oxford.

Datar, M.K. and Banerjee, S.S. (2004): *Basel II: Implications for Indian Banks*, Research Study for Indian Institute of Banking and Finance (mimeo), Mumbai.

Demirgúc-Kunt, A., & Maksimovic, V. (1998): "Law, Finance and Firm Growth", *Journal of Finance*, 53.

Eichengreen, B., Rose, A. and Wyplosz, C. (1995): "Exchange Rate Mayhem: The Antecedents and Aftermath of Speculative Attacks", *Economic Policy,* 21.

Ghosh, S., Nachane, D.M., Narain, A. and Sahoo, S. (2003): "Capital Requirements and Bank Behaviour: An Empirical Analysis of Indian Public Sector Banks", *Journal of International Development*, 15(2).

Goodhart, C. (1995): "Should the functions of Monetary Policy and Banking Supervision Be Separated?" *Oxford Economic Papers.*

Greenspan, Alan (2000): "Technology and Financial Services", Remarks before the Journal of Financial Services Research and American Enterprise Institute Conference in honor of Anne Schwartz, Washington on April 14, BIS Review 34/2000.

Leavis, F.R. (1972): *The Common Pursuit*, Harmondsworth: Penguin.

Hellmann, T., Murdoch, K. and Stiglitz, J.E. (2000): "Liberalisation, Moral Hazard in Banking and Prudential Regulations: Are Capital requirements Enough?" *American Economic Review*, 90(1).

Levine, R. (1997): "Financial Development and Growth: Views and Agenda", *Journal of Economic Literature*, 35.

Nachane, D.M., Narain, A., Ghosh, S. and Sahoo, S. (2000): "Capital Adequacy Requirements and the Behaviour of Commercial Banks in India: An Analytical and Empirical Study", *DRG Study No* 22, Reserve Bank of India, Mumbai.

Rajan, R.G., and Zingales, L. (1998): "Financial Dependence and Growth", *American Economic Review*, 88.

Reserve Bank of India (1991): *Report of the Committee on Financial System,* (Chairman: M. Narasimham), Bombay.

—— (1998): *Report of the Committee on Banking Sector Reforms*, Narasimham Committee Report-II, Bombay.

—— *Report on Trend and Progress of Banking in India*, various years, Bombay.

Sharma, Manoranjan (2000): "Infrastructure Development—Shifting Paradigms", *International Symposium in honour of Professor Kirit Parikh*, IGIDR, Mumbai, July.

—— (2001): "Rural Financial Institutions in Early Third Millennium: Present Position, Expedient Issues and Emerging Challenges", *Emerging Institutions for Decentralised Rural Development* (ed.) S.P.Jain, NIRD, Hyderabad.

—— (2002): "Infrastructure Development—Roadmap for the Future", *Liberalisation and Globalisation of Indian Economy* (ed.) K.R. Gupta, Atlantic Publishers, New Delhi.

—— (2003): "Innovate or Perish—The Success Mantra", *BECON.*

—— (2004a): "Rural Financial Institutions in India: Challenge of Change", *Rural Development in India*, Volume II (ed.) K.R. Gupta, Atlantic Publishers, New Delhi.

—— (2004b): "Banks have much to do if winning streak is to continue", *Business Line*, Feb. 24.

—— (2004c): "Resuscitating Rural Financial Institutions in India: Catalytic Role of Micro Finance", *Sixth Conference on Money and Finance*, IGIDR, Mumbai.

—— (2004d): "Big Transition Travails for Small Units", *Business Line*, April 9.

—— (2004e): "Financing of SMEs in a Globalising World—Expedient Issues and Paradigm Shifts", *FICCI Conference on Global Banking: Paradigm Shift*, September.

—— (2004f): "Quality Management—Retrospect and Prospect", *Global Conference on Emerging Issues in Business and Technology*, South Carolina Campus, Western Illinois University, USA, October.

—— (2004g): "Changing Dynamics of Rural Markets—Stray Thoughts", *Rural Marketing Summit*, 2004, October.

—— (2004h): "Banking Consolidation Must Be Synergy-driven", *Business Line*, Dec. 30.

—— (2005a): "Steady Growth of Retail Banking in India: Issues, Policy and Strategies", *Studies in Money, Finance and Banking*, Atlantic Publishers, New Delhi.

—— (2005b): "Rural Non-Farm Sector in India: Issues and Evidence", *Leading Issues in Indian Economy*, (ed.) Manoranjan Sharma, Atlantic Publishers, New Delhi.

—— (2005c): "Emerging Contours of Micro Finance: Where Do We Go From Here?" *The Business Review*, Volume 4, No.1, Summer.

—— (2005d): "Innovation in Banks: Need to Push Full Throttle Ahead", *Professional Banker*, September.

—— (2007a): "Micro Finance in India: Impressive Achievements but Miles to Go", *India's Transforming Financial Sector*, (ed.) Manoranjan Sharma, Atlantic Publishers, New Delhi.

—— (2007b): "Financial Inclusion, Microfinance and SMEs—Business Opportunities", *India's Transforming Financial Sector Money,* (ed.) Manoranjan Sharma, Atlantic Publishers, New Delhi.

World Bank (2002): "Bank Loan Classification and Provisioning Practices in Selected Developing and Emerging Countries", *Finance Forum*, June.

Annex I: Ownership of Banks Share in Total Credit (in per cent)

	1994			1999			2004		
	State Owned	Pvt.	Frn.	State Owned	Pvt.	Frn.	State Owned	Pvt.	Frn.
Latin America	15	79	6	11	55	34	11	47	42
China and India				78	17	5	71	24	5
Other Asia	16	73	11	30	57	13	31	56	14
Other EMEs	33	67	1	18	80	1	15	83	2
Central Europe	45	34	21	20	33	48	10	13	77

Annex II: Real Bank Credit to the Private Sector: Emerging Markets

	1990—94	1995—99	2000—04	2005
Brazil	24.3	0.9	1.4	19.7
Mexico	27.6	-11.7	-0.5	12.0
India	3.4	6.9	13.5	30.0
China	10.6	16.0	12.5	9.4
Indonesia	9.7	12.3	9.0	1.5
Korea	9.0	-12.9	9.1	24.5
Philippines	12.2	12.3	-0.4	-1.3
Malaysia	-	12.6	7.9	12.2
Thailand	19.2	3.5	-1.7	0.6
Russia	-	-6.6	25.0	31.3
South Africa	4.5	7.6	9.7	11.7

Annex III: Sources of Financing in Emerging Markets

	Domestic Bank Credit		Domestic Debt Securities Outstanding		Stock Market Capitalization		International Financing	
	As a per cent of Gross Domestic Product							
	1999	2005	1999	2005	1999	2005	1999	2005
China	130	169	22	33	33	39	3	3
India	51	65	23	41	42	68	4	5
Korea	81	97	60	91	69	82	14	12
South Africa	69	77	51	49	197	223	11	10
Brazil	56	62	55	74	42	61	22	16
Mexico	35	28	12	30	32	34	28	16
Malaysia	161	135	84	90	184	139	23	31
Thailand	133	94	26	48	48	67	19	11
Russia	31	22	5	4			16	12

Annex IV: Key Performance Indicators: Emerging Banking Systems Averages

	State Owned Banks		Private Domestic Banks		Foreign Owned Banks		All commercial Banks	
	1999	2004	1999	2004	1999	2004	1999	2004
Non-Performing Loans as per cent of Total Loans	18.3	10.7	8.4	4.7	7.0	2.9	10.2	4.9
Capital Adequacy (Risk Weighted Capital Adequacy Ratio (in per cent)	13.3	13.7	14.7	13.5	15.7	14.4	13.0	13.8
Return on Assets	-1.3	1.5	0.7	1.7	1.0	0.9	-0.1	1.9
Return on Equity	-14.7	21.2	12.2	19.1	10.5	11.6	3.7	20.4

Annex V: Ratio of Household Credit to Personal Disposal Income (per cent)

	2000	2001	2002	2003	2004	2005
Emerging Markets						
Czech Republic	8.5	10.1	12.9	16.4	21.3	27.21
Hungary	11.2	14.4	20.9	29.5	33.9	39.3
Poland	10.1	10.3	10.9	12.6	14.5	18.2
India	4.7	5.4	6.4	7.4	9.7	..
Korea	33	43.9	57.3	62.6	64.5	68.9
Philippines	1.7	4.6	5.5	5.5	5.6	..
Taiwan Province of China	75.1	72.7	76	83	95.5	..
Thailand	26	25.6	28.6	34.3	36.4	..
Mature Markets						
Australia	83.3	86.7	95.6	109	119	124.6
France	57.8	57.5	58.2	59.8	64.2	69.2
Germany	70.4	70.1	69.1	70.3	7.5	70
Italy	25	25.8	27	28.7	31.8	34.8
Japan	73.6	75.7	77.6	77.3	77.9	77.8
Spain	65.2	70.4	76.9	86.4	98.8	112.7
United States	104	105.1	110.8	118.2	126	132.7

Annex VI: Key Performance Indicators: Emerging Banking Markets Bank Capital to Assets

	2001	2002	2003	2004	2005	2006
Brazil	8.9	8.6	69.2	9.7	9.2	9.3
Mexico	9.4	11.1	11.4	11.2	12.0	11.8
Russia	..	14.4	14.8	14.0	13.2	12.5
China	..	..	4.9	4.9	5.5	6.1
India	5.3	5.5	5.7	5.9	6.4	6.6
Korea	4.8	4.7	4.6	5.6	6.8	6.6
Malaysia	8.3	8.7	8.5	8.2	7.7	7.6
Thailand	5.9	6.1	7.4	8.0	9.6	9.2
South Africa	9.0	9.3	8.0	8.2	7.9	7.8
Bank Non-Performing Loans to Total Loans						
Brazil	5.6	4.8	4.8	3.8	4.4	..
Mexico	5.1	4.6	3.2	2.5	1.8	2.0
Russia	6.2	5.6	5.0	3.8	3.2	2.7
China	29.8	26.0	20.4	12.8	9.8	7.5
India	11.4	10.4	8.8	7.2	5.2	3.3
Korea	3.4	2.4	2.6	1.9	1.2	0.9
Malaysia	17.8	15.9	13.9	11.7	9.6	8.7
Thailand	11.5	16.5	13.5	11.9	9.1	8.9
South Africa	3.1	2.8	2.4	1.8	1.5	1.2
Bank Provisions to Non-Performing Loans						
Brazil	126.6	143.6	144.6	162.1	145.4	..
Mexico	23.8	138.1	167.1	201.8	232.1	213.0
Russia	108.1	112.5	118.0	139.5	156.3	159.3
China	..	..	..	..	..	..
India	..	..	46.4	56.6	60.3	58.9
Korea	..	..	..	..	..	..
Malaysia	37.6	38.1	38.9	41.0	45.4	50.1
Thailand	47.1	62.9	72.8	79.8	83.7	79.4
South Africa	46.0	46.0	54.2	61.3	64.3	..
Bank Return on Assets						
Brazil	-0.1	1.9	1.5	1.8	2.1	2..3
Mexico	0.8	-1.1	1.7	1.5	2.4	3.1
Russia	2.4	2.6	2.6	2.9	3.2	2.5
China	..	..	..	0.8	0.8	..
India	0.5	0.5	1.0	1.1	0.9	0.9
Korea	0.7	0.6	0.2	0.9	1.3	1.3
Malaysia	1.0	1.3	1.3	1.4	1.4	1.3
Thailand	..	..	..	1.7	1.9	2.3
South Africa	0.8	0.4	0.8	1.3	1.2	1.2

(*Contd.*)

	2001	2002	2003	2004	2005	2006
			Bank Return on Equity			
Brazil	-1.2	21.8	17.0	18.8	22.8	24.5
Mexico	8.6	-10.4	14.2	13.0	19.5	25.0
Russia	19.4	18.0	17.8	20.3	24.2	20.1
China	..	..	..	13.7	15.1	..
India	10.4	15.3	18.8	20.8	13.3	12.7
Korea	12.8	10.9	3.4	15.2	22.5	21.0
Malaysia	13.3	16.7	17.1	16.6	14.1	..
Thailand	32.8	4.2	10.5	16.8	14.2	15.1
South Africa	8.9	5.2	11.6	16.2	15.2	16.0

M&A in Indian Banking Industry: Performance Evaluation

10

Prakash Singh

ABSTRACT

Mergers and Acquisitions has been a buzzword in Indian banking industry. There is a talk of need of consolidation in the industry everywhere. The oft-cited reason is that, with the increased competition from foreign banks from the year 2009 and the enforcement of Basel 2 norms, there is a need for proactive consolidation in the banking industry rather than a late reaction to distress signals from sick banks. This research work on "Mergers and Acquisitions in Indian Banks: Reasons, Conditions for success and Post-merger performance" seeks to study whether there is really a need of consolidation? If yes, what could be the justifiable reasons for M&A? Is there really a positive impact of M&A on the post-merger performance of merged entities?

Introduction

> Consolidation alone will give banks the muscle, size and scale to act like world-class banks. We have to think global and act local and seek new markets, new classes of borrowers. It is heartening to note that the Indian Banks' Association is working out a strategy for consolidation among banks.
>
> —P. Chidambaram

Consolidation in the banking industry is crucial from various aspects. The factors inducing consolidation include technological progress, excess retention capacity, emerging opportunities and deregulation of various functional and product restrictions. A strong banking system is critical for sound economic growth so it is natural to improve the comprehensiveness and quality of the banking system to bring efficiency in the performance of the real sectors. I have carried out my research with respect to two recent mergers in the Indian Banking Industry that we have taken as case-studies: Global Trust Bank with Oriental Bank of Commerce and Centurion Bank with Bank of Punjab. Finally, I have also analyzed two prospective mergers that might materialize in the near future: Centurion Bank of Punjab with Lord Krishna Bank and Canara Bank with Dena Bank. My approach to this research work is structured as follows:

1. Capturing the reasons/need for consolidation in the Current Indian Banking scenario
2. Analyzing the bank performance pre-merger and post-merger to identify key areas of improvement post-merger
3. Determining conditions for a successful merger
4. Identifying possible mergers that can occur or make sense given the factors identified in the Public and Private Banks space
5. Conclusion

Overview of Indian Banking

India has a long history of both public and private banking. Modern banking in India began in the 18th century, with the founding of the English Agency House in Calcutta and Bombay. In the first half of the 19th century, three Presidency banks were founded. In 1935, the presidency banks were merged together to form the Imperial Bank of India, which was subsequently renamed the State Bank of India. Also that year, India's central bank, the Reserve Bank of India (RBI), began operation. Following independence, the RBI was given broad regulatory authority over commercial banks in India. In July 1969, the government nationalized all banks whose nationwide deposits were greater than Rs. 500 million, resulting in the nationalization of 54 per cent more of the branches in India, and bringing the total number of branches under government control to 84 per cent

Between 1969 and 1980, the number of private branches grew more quickly than public banks, and on April 1, 1980, they accounted for approximately 17.5 per cent of bank branches in India. In April of 1980, the government undertook a second round of nationalization, placing under government control the six private banks whose nationwide deposits were above Rs. 2 billion, or a further 8 per cent of bank branches, leaving approximately 10 per cent of bank branches in private hands. The share of private bank branches stayed fairly constant between 1980 to 2000. In the early 1990s, the government embarked on a policy of liberalisation and gave licences to a small number of private banks, which came to be known as New Generation tech-savvy banks, which included banks such as UTI, ICICI Bank and HDFC Bank. This, along with the rapid growth in the economy of India, kick-started the banking sector in India. It has seen rapid growth with strong contribution from all the three sectors of banks, namely, government banks, private banks and foreign banks.

The next stage for the Indian banking has been set-up with the proposed relaxation in the norms for Foreign Direct Investment, where all Foreign Investors in banks may be given voting rights which could exceed the present cap of 10% (49% with some restrictions) and the coming in of Basel 2 norms in 2009.

Consolidation in the Indian Banking Industry

Possible Benefits of Consolidation in Indian Banking

- As competition heats up, many banks having bigger size, will command more in the market. A bigger bank would have more staff strength, greater geographical reach, more financial resources, more delegated power and less operational and transactional costs due to economies of scale. A bigger financial conglomeration can easily withstand external assaults more effectively.
- Mergers and acquisitions can help banks with complimentary expertise to boost up their combined talents as well as on presenting a vastly improved performance. For instance, a foreign bank with proven

merit in treasury operations when merged with a bank with investible surpluses could generate substantial profits.

- The geographical and regional spread would get widened when banks with different strongholds merge. Based on the principles of synergy, the business volume and geographical reach of consolidated entity automatically increases by many folds.
- Similarly, the market image and brand name of the consolidated entity will always likely to get a boost in comparison to the individual banks. This will lead to a better market image, which in turn translates to better performance expectations by the investors and the analysts, thus finally leading to better valuations in the market. We know, that better market valuations mean better shareholder returns leading to an even better market image. Thus, a reinforcing vicious cycle would set in.
- The larger size, greater geographical penetration and enhanced market image and other synergic factors would inevitably increase the bargaining power of the new bank. In a competitive world where the battle is fierce, a better bargaining power position is always an invaluable asset.
- The business in near future is unlikely to remain localized but bound to go global. In view of the saturating environment at domestic front, banks will have to venture overseas without any hesitation. Initial foray into overseas markets are always made through strategic alliances and joint ventures. A merged entity with bigger market size, greater geographical spread, sound financial position, good image, greater resistance etc. would necessarily be successful in the overseas. All these virtues also help in acquiring tenders and bids.
- The consolidated entity can serve the end user, i.e. the customer in a better way through providing single window service by offering a variety of services like

conventional banking, merchant banking, mutual funds, insurance etc. under one umbrella leading to innovation and origin of new hybrid products and services like bancassurance.

Risk Associated with Consolidation

- When two banks merge into one then there is an inevitable increase in the size of the organization. Big size may not always be better. The size may get too widely and go beyond the control of the management. The increased size may become a drug rather than an asset.
- Consolidation does not lead to instant results and there is an incubation period before the results arrive. Mergers and acquisitions are sometimes followed by losses and tough intervening periods before the eventual profits pour in. Patience, forbearance and resilience are required in ample measure to make any merger a success story. All may not be up to the plan, which explains why there are high rate of failures in mergers.
- Consolidation mainly comes due to the decision taken at the top. It is a top-heavy decision and willingness of the rank and file of both entities may not be forthcoming. This leads to problems of industrial relations, deprivation, depression and demotivation among the employees. Such a workforce can never churn out good results. Therefore, personal management at the highest order with humane touch alone can pave the way.
- The structure, systems and the procedures followed in two banks may be vastly different, for example, a PSU bank or an old generation bank and that of a technologically superior foreign bank. The erstwhile structures, systems and procedures may not be conducive in the new milieu. A thorough overhauling and systems analysis has to be done to assimilate both the organizations. This is a time consuming process and requires lot of cautious approaches to reduce the frictions.

- There is a problem of valuation associated with all mergers. The shareholder of existing entities has to be given new shares. Till now a foolproof valuation system for transfer and compensation is yet to emerge.
- Further, there is also a problem of brand projection. This becomes more complicated when existing brands themselves have a good appeal. Question arises whether the earlier brands should continue to be projected or should they be submerged in favor of a new comprehensive identity. Goodwill is often towards a brand and its sub-merger is usually not taken kindly.

Current Scenario

Between 1969, when the first set of 14 private banks was nationalized and now, the banking landscape changed dramatically. There has been no further nationalization, and indeed the trend appears to be reversing itself, as nationalized banks are issuing shares to the public, in what amounts to a step towards privatization. The Indian banking sector has witnessed the introduction of several "new private banks", either newly founded, or created by previously extant financial institutions. The new private banks have grown quickly in the past few years, and one has grown to be the second largest bank in India. India has also seen the entry of over two dozen foreign banks since the commencement of financial reforms.

In 1969, India had 89 commercial banks. By March 2004, this number had climbed to 290. In 1969, there were 73 scheduled commercial banks (SCBs). Now, there are 90 of them, excluding the 196 regional rural banks (RRBs). The total number of branches during the three-and-a-half decades jumped over eight-fold, from 8,262 to 69,071. The growth has been phenomenal in rural India where the number of branches zoomed from 1,833 to 32,227. In contrast, the number of branches in the metropolitan cities grew at a slower pace, from 1,503 to 9,750. The total deposits of all scheduled commercial banks shot up by almost 332 times and their advances soared 240.50 times. However, The Banker's list of the top 1000 banks of the world has only 20 Indian banks. Only six of them come in the top 500 group. The State Bank is positioned 82nd, ICICI Bank 268th, Punjab National Bank 313th, Canara Bank 405th, Bank of Baroda 425th and Bank of India 474th. Even in the Asian context, only one Indian bank—State Bank of India—figures in the top 25 banks based on Tier I capital, even though Indian banks offer the highest average return on capital among Asian peers.

The trend towards consolidation has been driven by the need to attain meaningful balance sheet size and market share in the face of intensified competition, whereas the trend towards convergence is driven across the industry to provide most of the financial services such as banking, insurance, investment, cash management etc. to the customers under one roof. In this scenario, if banks are to be made more effective, efficient and comparable with their counterparts functioning abroad, they would need to be more capitalized, automated and technology oriented, even while strengthening their internal operations and systems. Similarly, in order to make them comparable with their competitors from abroad with regard to the size of their capital and asset base, consolidation would be necessary. Broadly, there is a consensus that consolidation is inevitable and that the government must create an enabling situation where the leaders are encouraged to take the lead. Eight to ten big banks will dominate the industry over the next five years or so.

RECENT MERGERS

GTB and OBC

GTB

Global Trust Bank was one of best service oriented and modern banks of the new private banks. It was promoted by Mr. Ramesh Gelli and in six years of its operations it created many records and achieved many landmarks. It had a presence in all the major cities and focussed its lending to the SMEs and to the export sector. It was bullish on the use of technology and was a pioneer in computerization of the banking industry in the country.

The gains from the merger

The new entity had access to huge customer base in western and southern parts of India as these were the regions where GTB had a very prominent presence. The new entity also inherited the technological progress in which GTB was a pioneer. GTB was a technologically advanced bank and hence the merger with OBC helped OBC to vastly scale up its technology usage and no additional expense had to be incurred to improve the technological expertise as both the banks used common platforms. The new entity also enjoyed 'Economies of scale' as there were major opportunities for cross-selling and fund raising. Several activities of the merged entities now benefited from economies of scale.

Terms of the deal

The GTB accounts were to be transferred to OBC, this was a major headache for the new entity as it was a distress merger and it had to be done in such a manner so that there is no loss transferred to the shareholders of the bank in distress. This resulted in loss of value for the shareholders of the OBC. OBC had to treat the reserves of GTB as provisions for bad debt, as GTB had lend to sectors with very high probability of default. The Assets/Liabilities of GTB were obtained by OBC at market value but this did not include Government securities. All the employees of GTB were transferred to OBC.

Issues

NPA levels of OBC increased post merger and it had to take in huge losses incurred by GTB, as a result its growth dipped significantly after the merger. It had to bear the brunt of the default risk of the sectors to which GTB provided loans. There were many culture issues as the entire workforce of GTB, a private entity, was to be transferred to OBC which was a public sector bank. The working environment of both the banks was entirely different and there was a gap in the salaries given.

If we look at the RoE of both the banks prior to the merger, by 2002 RoE for GTB has almost gone to zero. The phenomenon was set since 2000, as the other expense, provisions and

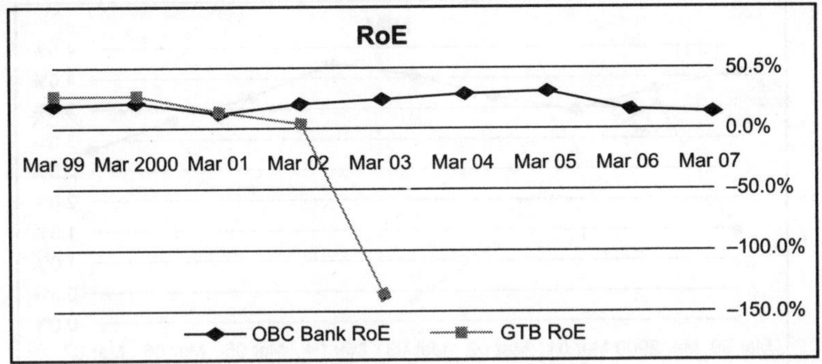

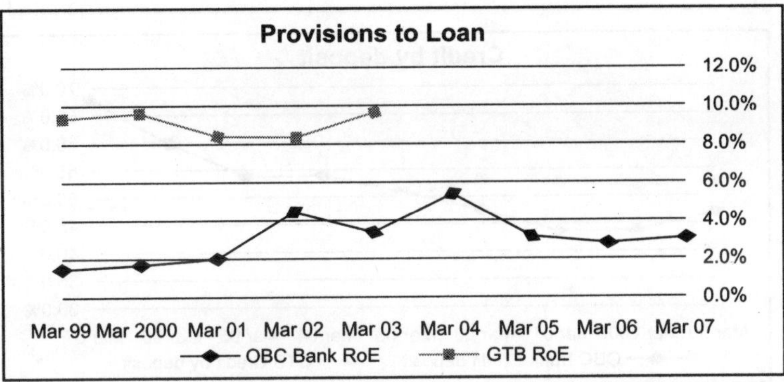

contingencies column of the P&L statement kept on growing. This occurred as GTB being a new bank has to rely on risky loans as its cost of deposit were high. Further it has a huge stock market exposure as GTB's big loan accounts included brokers like Ketan Parekh. After the market crashed in 2001 these loans turned bad. Other expense and provisions increased from 35 crores in 1999 to 336 crores in 2003, which is one of the main reasons for the company going in red. The riskiness of GTB's assets can be seen through their higher provisions to loan ratio as compared to OBC. After merger OBC's provision ratio has also increased, though it has been able to reduce it significantly, but still the current position is higher than its 2000-01 value of around 2%.

The NIM for GTB was also low despite of it having risky assets. This has caused a decrease in NIM of OBC post merger. Since 2004 NIM for OBC has been monotonically decreasing.

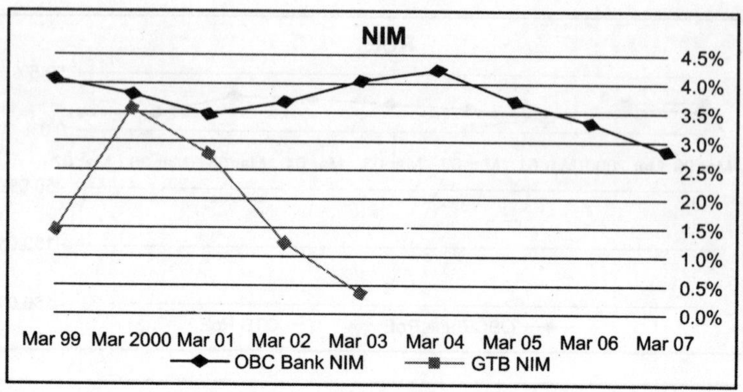

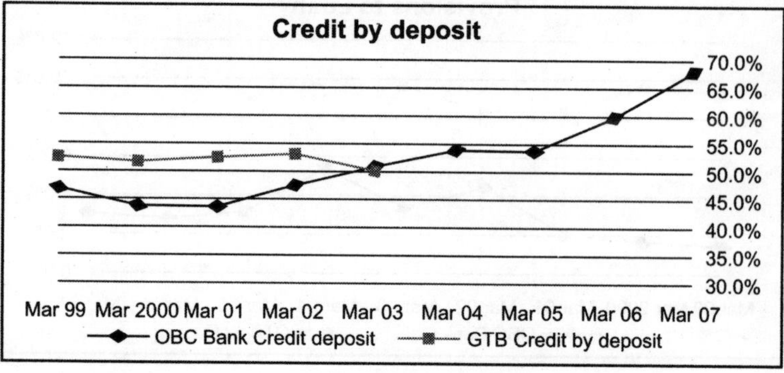

Post merger the C/D ratio has improved, this shows that OBC now has a larger pool of customers to lend because of geographic diversity.

Centurion Bank and Bank of Punjab

Highlights of the merger—Centurion Bank and Bank of Punjab

New entity to be named 'Centurion Bank of Punjab' and will be of book value of more than Rs. 300 crores.

- Management decisions
  - o Centurion Bank's chairman Rana Talwar to take over as the chairman of the merged entity.
  - o Centurion Bank's MD Shailendra Bhandari to be the MD of the merged entity.

- o KPMG India Pvt. Ltd. and NM Raiji & Co. are the independent valuers and Ambit Corporate Finance was the sole investment banker to the transaction.
- o Swap ratio has been fixed at 4:9, that is, for every four shares of Rs. 10 of Bank of Punjab, its shareholders would receive nine shares of Re. 1 of Centurion Bank.
- o There has been no cash transaction in the course of the merger; it has been settled through the swap of shares.
- o There will no downsizing via the voluntary retirement scheme.

Gains from the merger (Centurion and BOP)

Some of the major points which brought out the synergy were:

- Combined entity the Punjab-Centurion bank to be the among the top 10 private sector banks in the country.
- Merged entity to benefit from the fact that Centurion Bank had recently written of its bad loans against equity.
- Branch network of the two banks to complement each other. The combined entity to have a nationwide reach due to extensive reach of both the banks in different geographical areas.
- Centurion Bank was strong in South India, Maharashtra and Goa whereas Bank of Punjab was strong in Punjab, Haryana and Delhi. While Centurion Bank had 82 per cent of its business coming from retail, Bank of Punjab was strong in the Small and Medium Enterprises (SMEs) segment and agricultural sector, this resulted in a geographical synergy as it helped both the banks in reaching areas they were not present in and if grown organically, would have taken a lot of time.
- The book value of the bank to go up to around Rs. 300 crore. The higher book value would have helped the combine entity to mobilize funds at lower rate; the

combined strength of the two banks would have resulted in higher operational efficiency in handling of money.

- The combined bank to be a full-service commercial bank with a strong presence in the Retail, SME and Agricultural segments, but this also resulted in lending to sectors with high risk associated with them.

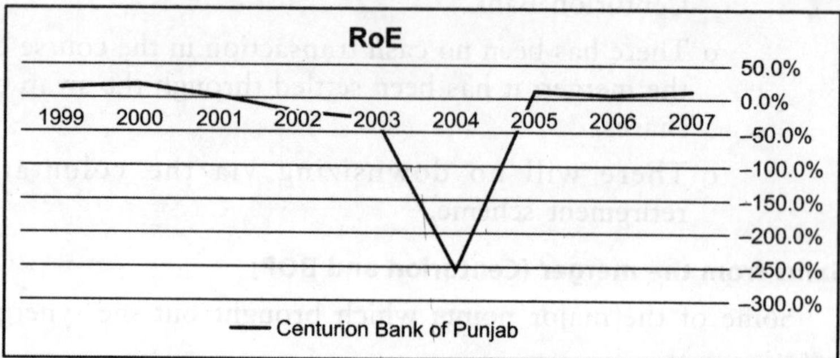

The RoE for Centurion Bank in 2004 is negative as it has written off its bad loans in this year. This was a positive thing for the merger, as none of the partner has huge amount of bad loan in their book. Post merger RoE though has improved but has still not reached the levels prevalent in year 1999-2000.

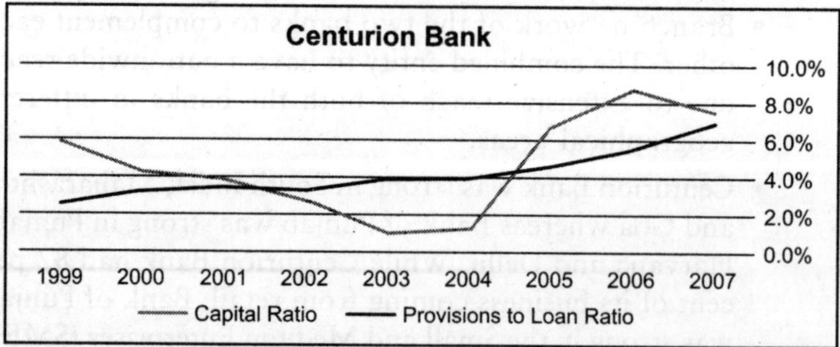

The benefit of this deal to Centurion is that POB had a very high capital ratio. As a result the capital ratio of the merged entity is much higher than Centurion Bank's capital ratio. But the provision to loan ratio has kept on increasing for the bank. This shows that they have continued issuing riskier loan to grow faster than the industry. Centurion Bank's management has the vision to make the bank one of the top three players in India, and to fulfill that they are willing to take a riskier path. This can also be confirmed by the fact that the C/D ratio of the combined entity has also grown since merger because of aggressive lending. It has grown from 57% in 2005 to 73% in 2007.

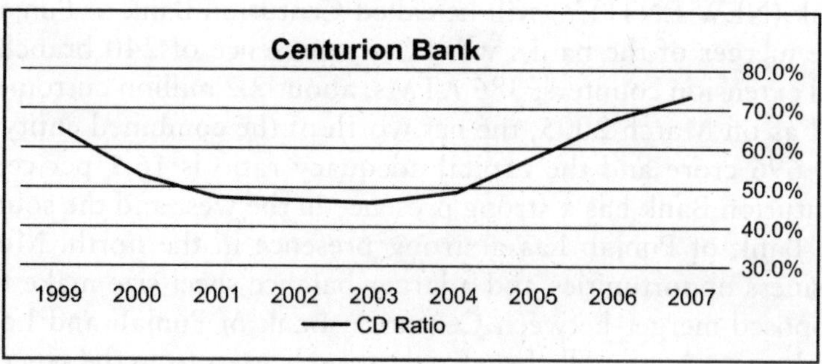

Prospective mergers

Lord Krishna Bank and Centurion Bank of Punjab

One of the latest mergers, which is currently in progress, is that of Lord Krishna Bank and Centurion Bank of Punjab. The current status is that the merger has been approved by the Board of Directors and it is due for approval from shareholders.

Lord Krishna Bank

The bank has 112 branches, 44 ATMs, mostly in Kerala and south India and its business stood at Rs. 3,699.8 crore till March 31, 2006. The bank has made a recovery from the red during the previous fiscal.

Centurion Bank of Punjab

CBP has 249 branches, 402 ATMs, 5,000 employees and is listed on major Indian bourses and Luxembourg Stock Exchange, CBP has already applied for licenses to an additional 30 branches. CBP's business (deposits and advances) stood at Rs. 17,824.5 crore till June 30, 2006. It has a strong presence in the west and the south. The merger will add about Rs. 2,500 crore to CBP's existing balance sheet size of Rs. 12,500 crore.

About the Merger

It has been approved by the Board of the Directors. The share-swap ratio has been fixed at 5:7, i.e. Lord Krishna Bank shareholders will receive seven shares of Centurion Bank of Punjab for every five LKB shares held by them. The combined bank (NEW ENTITY) will be called Centurion Bank of Punjab. The merger of the banks will have a presence of 240 branches and extension counters, 386 ATMs, about 2.2 million customers and as on March 2005, the net worth of the combined entity is Rs. 696 crore and the capital adequacy ratio is 16.1 per cent. Centurion Bank has a strong presence in the west and the south, the Bank of Punjab has a strong presence in the north. More business opportunities and a larger balance sheet size make the proposed merger between Centurion Bank of Punjab and Lord Krishna Bank mutually beneficial for both apart from the synergy from different geographical reach. While LKB, which is not a listed bank, gets some presence in North India, CBP, which is primarily based up north, gets to expand its network southwards. The combined entity is looking at a business figure in excess of Rs. 20,000 crore which will help its standing among private sector banks. The new entity is also hoping to grow at 35 per cent year-on-year.

Moreover, with Basel-II norms due for implementation by March 2007, many small banks will find it unviable to run the business as they will need more capital to provide for market and operational risks and implement modern technology. A merger of two profitable banks will help them both tide over these problems because the capital adequacy ratio of CBP is presently 12 per cent and likely to increase to over 14 per cent, keeping in view the capital requirements post merger and there is little overlap in the businesses of the two banks. CBP needs the additional business to compensate for its relatively higher cost structures. It can cross-sell its banking products through the LKB network, including traditional banking products and fee-based services like wealth management products, to affluent NRI customers. The merger will be valuable to Centurion Bank of Punjab (CBoP) as Lord Krishna Bank (LKB) has a very safe loan assets, i.e. their provision to loan ratio is very low. So this will result in improving the asset quality of CBoP. For LKB share holders the benefit is that CBoP has a better capital ratio as compared to LKB, which will give them better chance to grow, as the combined entity will have a higher CAR then the 9% required.

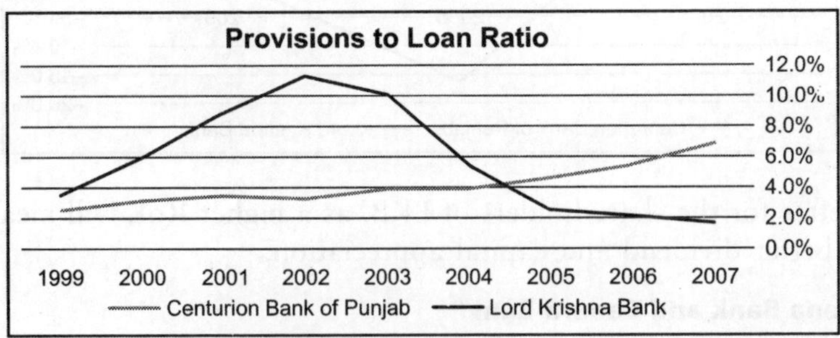

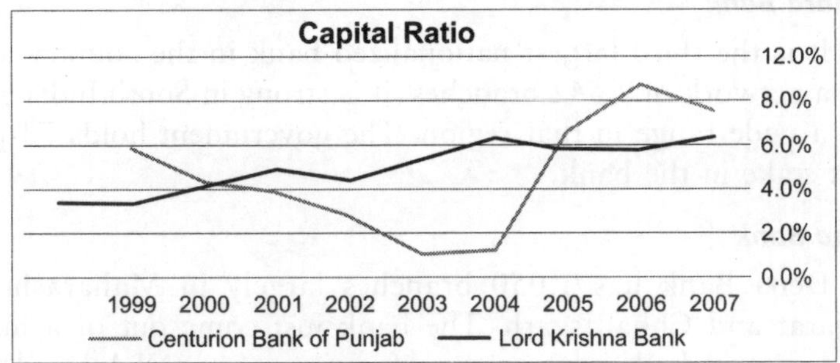

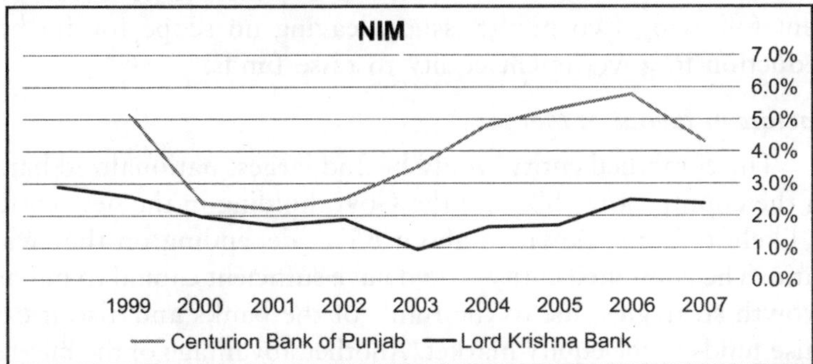

Further NIM and RoE of Centurion Bank is also better than Lord Krishna Bank, which will make the merged entity

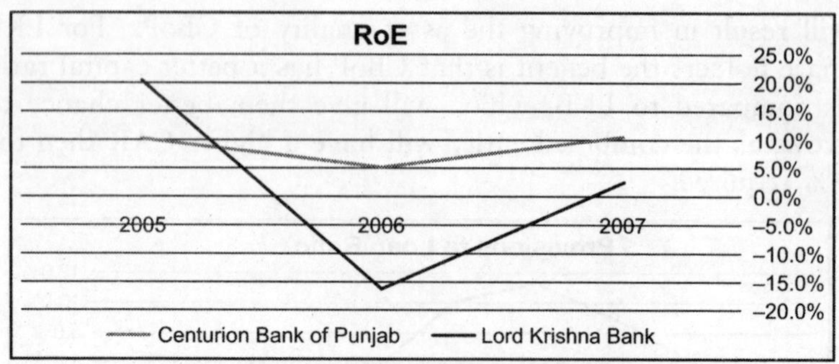

better for the share holders of LKB, as a higher RoE will mean a better dividend and capital appreciation.

Dena Bank and Canara Bank

Canara Bank

It is the third largest nationalized bank in the country and has a network of 2,542 branches. It is strong in South India and has a wide range in that region. The government holds 73 per cent stake in the bank.

Dena Bank

Dena Bank has 1,050 branches largely in Maharashtra, Gujarat and Chhattisgarh. The bank just come out of a huge burden of sticky loans or non-performing assets (NPAs) and the government holding in the bank has come down to 51.19 per cent following two public issues, leaving no scope for further reduction in government equity to raise funds.

Factors in favour of Merger

The combined entity would be 2nd largest nationalized bank in the country after SBI and the Govt. holding in the new entity is likely to come down to about 65%, depending on the swap ratio. The combined entity would have sufficient capital to pursue growth strategies due to the funds of the banks and also it can raise funds in the equity market. Another advantage of the merger is of a Pan-India geographical presence which will be due to the different geographical presence of both the banks in the country.

Factors against the Merger

Political opposition especially from Maharashtra can spell trouble for the merger as it may derail the current process.

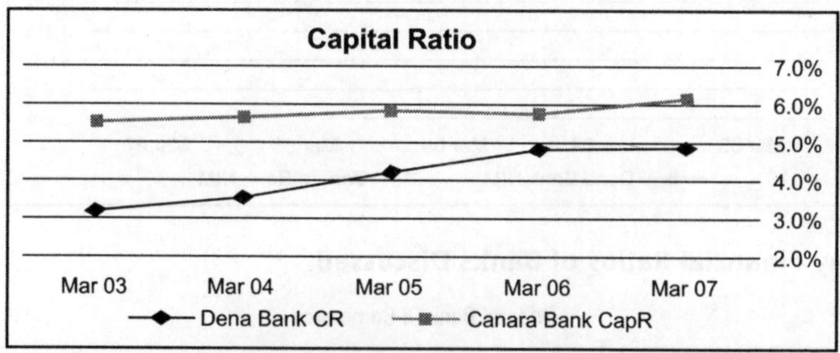

Dena Bank has reached a stage where the government's stake in the bank is 51.19%, as a result the government is now not willing to allow the bank to issue new equity offers, as it will dilute its stake in the company. As a result the growth of the bank seems to have hit a wall. This merger will help it to expand further as currently the government's stake in Canara Bank is 72-73%.

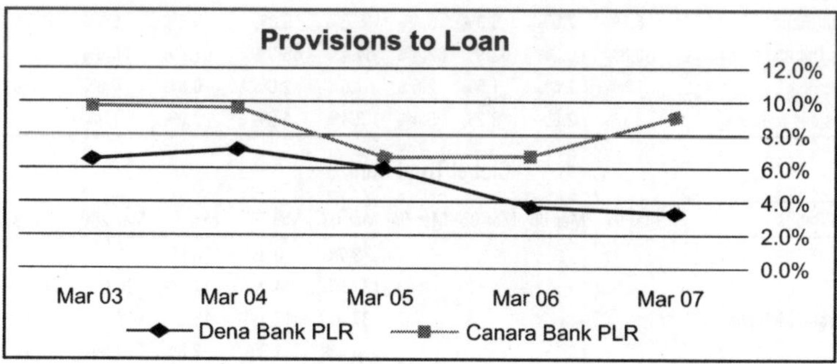

The benefit to Canara Bank is that, Dena Bank has better quality assets. As a result the merged entity will have relatively less risky asset. This can be seen from the provisions to loan ratio for both the banks. Further even having less risky assets, NIM for Dena bank is higher than Canara Bank. That is also an area where Canara Bank can learn from Dena Bank.

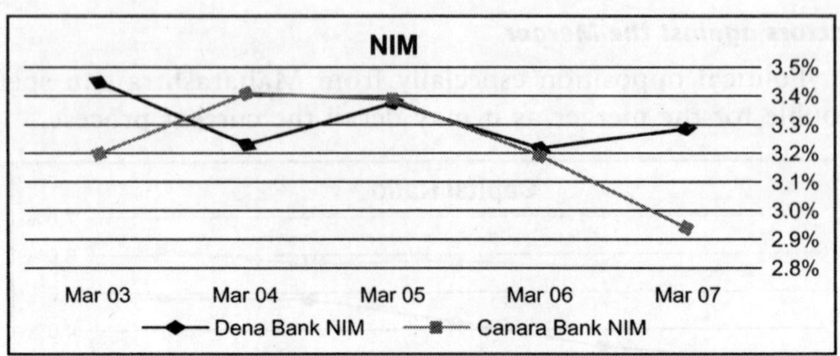

Key Financial Ratios of Banks Discussed

Oriental Bank Of Commerce

Main Ratios	Mar 07	Mar 06	Mar 05	Mar 04	Mar 03	Mar 02	Mar 01	Mar 2000	Mar 99
ROA	1.1%	1.3%	2.0%	1.8%	1.4%	1.1%	0.8%	1.3%	1.4%
ROE	13.5%	16.8%	31.4%	28.7%	24.5%	20.2%	13.6%	21.0%	19.9%
Levergae Multiplier	12.4	13.3	15.8	15.7	17.8	18.7	17.3	16.3	14.5
NIM	2.9%	3.3%	3.7%	4.2%	4.1%	3.7%	3.5%	3.8%	4.1%
Yield on earning assets	8.8%	8.5%	8.7%	9.6%	11.0%	11.5%	12.2%	13.2%	13.1%
Cost of Funds	6.7%	5.6%	5.3%	6.0%	7.7%	8.3%	9.0%	9.7%	9.5%
Spread	2.1%	3.0%	3.4%	3.6%	3.4%	3.2%	3.2%	3.6%	3.6%
Burden Ratio	1.3%	1.6%	2.0%	0.8%	1.4%	1.4%	2.0%	1.7%	1.8%
Credit/Deposit	68.1%	60.0%	53.9%	54.0%	51.2%	47.5%	43.6%	43.8%	47.0%
Capital Ratio	8.1%	7.5%	6.3%	6.4%	5.6%	5.3%	5.8%	6.1%	6.9%
Term Deposit to Assets	58.8%	60.2%	62.9%	62.4%	64.4%	66.9%	67.6%	66.6%	64.2%
Credit Risk	1.8%	1.6%	1.5%	2.6%	1.6%	2.0%	0.8%	0.6%	0.6%
Provisions to loans	3.1%	2.8%	3.2%	5.4%	3.4%	4.5%	2.0%	1.7%	1.5%

Global Trust Bank

Main Ratios	Mar 07	Mar 06	Mar 05	Mar 04	Mar 03	Mar 02	Mar 01	Mar 2000	Mar 99
ROA					-3.7%	0.2%	0.9%	1.7%	1.6%
ROE					-137.3%	4.2%	14.4%	26.6%	26.7%
Levergae Multiplier					37.3	17.1	15.2	15.6	16.9
NIM					0.4%	1.3%	2.8%	3.6%	1.5%
Yield on earning assets					9.0%	10.2%	12.5%	13.2%	13.6%
Cost of Funds					8.7%	9.9%	11.2%	11.2%	12.9%
Spread					0.4%	0.4%	1.3%	2.0%	0.6%
Burden Ratio					4.0%	1.5%	1.3%	0.6%	-0.7%
Credit/Deposit					50.2%	53.1%	52.5%	51.8%	52.5%
Capital Ratio					2.7%	5.8%	6.6%	6.4%	5.9%
Term Deposit to Assets					73.9%	71.4%	69.1%	67.9%	73.7%
Credit Risk					4.4%	3.8%	3.6%	4.0%	4.0%
Provisions to loans					9.6%	8.4%	8.4%	9.6%	9.4%

Centurion Bank of Punjab

Main Ratios	Mar 07	Mar 06	Mar 05	Mar 04	Mar 03	Mar 02	Mar 01	Mar 2000	Mar 99
ROA	0.8%	0.5%	0.7%	-3.1%	-0.3%	-0.5%	0.1%	0.8%	0.9%
ROE	10.5%	5.3%	10.1%	-256.5%	-30.5%	-19.2%	3.3%	19.1%	15.7%
Levergae Multiplier	13.2	11.5	15.0	81.6	96.3	36.4	26.0	23.1	17.1
NIM	4.3%	5.8%	5.4%	4.8%	3.5%	2.5%	2.2%	2.4%	5.1%
Yield on earning assets	9.7%	11.7%	10.5%	12.4%	12.9%	11.8%	11.9%	13.2%	20.5%
Cost of Funds	6.4%	7.3%	5.9%	7.7%	9.1%	9.4%	9.7%	10.4%	15.5%
Spread	3.3%	4.4%	4.6%	4.6%	3.7%	2.5%	2.2%	2.7%	5.0%
Burden Ratio	2.6%	3.9%	3.8%	6.1%	3.8%	4.0%	1.6%	0.9%	3.2%
Credit/Deposit	73.2%	67.5%	57.2%	48.9%	46.3%	47.0%	47.6%	53.1%	64.8%
Capital Ratio	7.6%	8.7%	6.7%	1.2%	1.0%	2.7%	3.8%	4.3%	5.9%
Term Deposit to Assets	53.3%	52.1%	59.2%	66.5%	71.1%	65.1%	62.5%	63.6%	63.8%
Credit Risk	4.1%	3.0%	2.2%	1.7%	1.6%	1.2%	1.2%	1.2%	1.2%
Provisions to loans	6.9%	5.5%	4.6%	4.0%	3.9%	3.3%	3.4%	3.2%	2.6%

Dena Bank

Main Ratios	Mar 07	Mar 06	Mar 05	Mar 04	Mar 03	Mar 02	Mar 01	Mar 2000	Mar 99
ROA	0.7%	0.3%	0.3%	1.1%	0.6%	0.1%	-1.5%	0.4%	0.8%
ROE	14.2%	6.0%	6.3%	31.1%	18.8%	2.0%	-38.8%	8.3%	17.7%
Levergae Multiplier	20.5	20.7	23.7	28.1	31.5	32.5	25.2	20.8	21.8
NIM	3.3%	3.2%	3.4%	3.2%	3.4%	2.9%	3.1%	3.1%	3.9%
Yield on earning assets	8.1%	7.8%	8.5%	9.5%	10.8%	11.2%	11.8%	11.8%	13.1%
Cost of Funds	5.5%	5.1%	5.8%	7.2%	8.3%	9.3%	9.8%	9.9%	10.3%
Spread	2.7%	2.7%	2.7%	2.3%	2.4%	1.9%	1.9%	1.9%	2.8%
Burden Ratio	2.1%	2.7%	3.0%	1.1%	2.0%	2.5%	4.1%	2.1%	2.4%
Credit/Deposit	63.4%	57.4%	52.8%	51.2%	50.1%	48.5%	50.7%	53.9%	52.7%
Capital Ratio	4.9%	4.8%	4.2%	3.6%	3.2%	3.1%	4.0%	4.8%	4.6%
Term Deposit to Assets	49.4%	50.3%	49.7%	49.5%	50.3%	50.7%	50.2%	50.5%	52.4%
Credit Risk	1.9%	1.9%	2.7%	3.1%	2.7%	2.4%	3.4%	4.7%	4.8%
Provisions to loans	3.3%	3.7%	6.0%	7.2%	6.6%	5.9%	8.3%	11.1%	11.2%

Canara Bank

Main Ratios	Mar 07	Mar 06	Mar 05	Mar 04	Mar 03
ROA	1.0%	1.1%	1.3%	1.5%	1.3%
ROE	16.6%	19.6%	22.1%	27.0%	23.0%
Levergae Multiplier	16.3	17.4	17.2	17.6	18.0
NIM	2.9%	3.2%	3.4%	3.4%	3.2%
Yield on earning assets	8.3%	7.8%	8.0%	8.8%	9.3%
Cost of Funds	6.2%	5.3%	5.3%	6.0%	6.9%
Spread	2.2%	2.5%	2.7%	2.7%	2.4%
Burden Ratio	1.5%	1.6%	1.8%	1.5%	1.6%
Credit/Deposit	69.0%	66.0%	60.0%	56.5%	56.5%
Capital Ratio	6.2%	5.8%	5.8%	5.7%	5.5%
Term Deposit to Assets	58.4%	57.9%	57.1%	56.5%	56.4%
Credit Risk	5.4%	3.9%	3.4%	4.6%	4.7%
Provisions to loans	9.1%	6.8%	6.7%	9.6%	9.7%

Lord Krishna Bank

Main Ratios	Mar 07	Mar 06	Mar 05	Mar 04	Mar 03	Mar 02	Mar 01	Mar 2000	Mar 99
ROA	0.1%	-1.0%	1.2%	1.3%	1.3%	0.0040	0.7%	0.2%	0.5%
ROE	2.3%	-16.2%	20.3%	20.2%	23.6%	0.0911	14.1%	3.8%	15.7%
Levergae Multiplier	15.7	17.0	17.3	15.7	18.8	22.523	20.3	23.9	29.5
NIM	2.4%	2.5%	1.7%	1.6%	0.9%	0.0186	1.7%	1.9%	2.6%
Yield on earning assets	8.0%	8.5%	8.4%	9.7%	10.3%	0.1133	12.4%	14.5%	15.3%
Cost of Funds	6.3%	6.6%	7.0%	8.6%	10.0%	0.1015	11.2%	12.8%	13.0%
Spread	1.7%	2.0%	1.4%	1.1%	0.3%	0.0119	1.2%	1.7%	2.3%
Burden Ratio	2.8%	4.5%	0.2%	-0.1%	-0.6%	0.0125	0.7%	1.4%	1.4%
Credit/Deposit	63.0%	55.8%	51.1%	55.0%	51.7%	0.5078	55.1%	56.8%	61.6%
Capital Ratio	6.4%	5.9%	5.8%	6.4%	5.3%	0.0444	4.9%	4.2%	3.4%
Term Deposit to Assets	72.9%	76.2%	78.7%	77.8%	76.4%	0.742	71.3%	71.3%	71.2%
Credit Risk	1.0%	1.1%	1.2%	2.7%	4.5%	0.0499	4.2%	2.9%	1.8%
Provisions to loans	1.7%	2.1%	2.6%	5.6%	10.1%	0.1141	9.0%	6.0%	3.6%

REFERENCES

Agénor, Pierre-Richard (2001): "Benefits and Costs of International Integration: Theory and Facts", *World Bank Policy Research Working Paper No 2699*, World Bank, Washington, DC.

Akhavein, J.D., Berger, A.N., Humphrey, D.B. (1997): "The Effects of Megamergers on Efficiency and Prices: Evidence from a Bank Profit Function", *Review of Industrial Organisation*, 12, 95-139.

Berger, A.N., Hanweck, G.A., Humphrey, D.B. (1987): "Competitive Viability in Banking: Scale, Scope and Product Mix Economies", *Journal of Monetary Economics*, 20, 501-20.

Berger, A.N. and Mester, L.J. (1997): "Inside the Black Box: What Explains Differences in the Efficiencies of Financial Institutions?" *Journal of Banking and Finance*, 21, 895-947.

Berger, A.N., Rebecca S. Demsetz, Philip E. Strahan (1999): "The Consolidation of the Financial Services Industry: Causes, Consequences, and Implications for the Future", *Journal of Banking and Finance*, 23, 135-94.

Clarke, G.R., Cull, M.S. "Martinez Peria and Sánchez S.M. (2002): 'Bank Lending to Small Businesses in Latin America: Does Bank Origin Matter?" *World Bank Policy Research Working Paper No 2760*, World Bank, Washington, DC.

De Long, G.L. (2001): "Stockholder Gains from Focusing versus Diversifying Bank Mergers", *Journal of Financial Economics*, 59 (2), 221-52.

Dean Amel, Colleen Barnesb, Fabio Panetta and Carmelo Salleo (2004): "Consolidation and Efficiency in the Financial Sector: A Review of the International Evidence", *Journal of Banking and Finance*, 28, 2493-2519.

Demsetz, R.S. and Strahan, P.E. (1997): "Diversification, Size, and Risk at Bank Holding Companies", *Journal of Money, Credit, and Banking*, 29, 300-13.

Dymski, Gary (1999): *The Bank Merger Wave*, M.E. Sharpe, Armonk, NY (2002): "The Global Bank Merger Wave: Implications for Developing Countries", (mimeo), University of California, Riverside, CA, April 8.

Houston, J.F. and Ryngaert, M.D. (1994): "The Overall Gains from Large Bank Mergers", *Journal of Banking and Finance*, 18, 1155-76.

Hughes, J.P., Lang, W., Mester, L.J. and Moon, C.G. (1996): "Efficient Banking Under Interstate Branching", *Journal of Money, Credit, and Banking*, 28, 1043-71.

Kaminsky, Graciela L., Carmen M. Reinhart and Vegh, C.A. (2003): *Journal of Economic Perspectives*, 17(4), 51-74.

Ramachandran, V.K. and Madhura Swaminathan (eds) (2005): *Financial Liberalisation and Rural Credit in India*, Tulika, New Delhi.

Ram Mohan, T.T. (2004): "Consolidation of Banks: A Case of Misplaced Priorities", *EPW*, 39,50, 5283-87.

Rhoades, S.A. (1994): "A Summary of Merger Performance Studies in Banking, 1980—93, and an Assessment of the Operating Performance and Event Study Methodologies", Federal Reserve Board Sta Study No. 167.

Ray, Mamata (2003): *Regional Financial Institutions: Lending Behaviour and Path-Dependence, Madras 1921—1969*, PhD thesis, University of Calcutta.

Shetty, S.L. (2005): "Regional, Sectoral and Functional Distribution of Bank Credit" in Ramachandran and Swaminathan (ed), 50-119.

Woo, Jung-en (1991): *Race to the Swift: State and Finance in Korean Industrialisation*, Columbia University Press, New York.

Universal Banking in India: Progress and Assessment

11

A. Karunagaran

INTRODUCTION

Ever since the Indian financial sector embarked upon sweeping financial reforms in early 1990s, the financial sector has undergone tremendous change in all dimensions. The banking system, being the major constituent of the financial sector, received a greater impact. The reform process aimed at enhancing competition thereby increasing efficiency in the system through entry of new players. The reforms virtually changed the entire landscape of the financial system. In the process, the distinction between banks and non-banking financial intermediaries (NBFIs) was greatly blurred. Until then DFIs being part of NBFIs were the single most important conduit between sources and deployment of funds for the projects requiring long-term finance. Such long-term finance was deployed as per the plan priorities for assured return. The market-oriented approach, coupled with the new prudential norms, seems to have adversely impacted these institutions, which operated in a protective environment both on liabilities and assets sides. The Second Narasimham Committee on banking reforms came out with explicit recommendations that the DFIs be converted into either bank or non-bank financial companies (NBFCs). Subsequently, a Working Group (Chairman: S.H. Khan), viz. "Harmonizing the Role and Operations of Development Financial Institutions and Banks" (1998), also advocated 'progressive movement towards universal banking' for DFIs. The RBI as regulator came out with a 'Discussion Paper', which spelt out '...the question of transformation of a DFI into a bank should ideally be considered after a period, say of five years from now...'.

It's more than 7 years since the Reserve Bank of India made the above announcement, which spurred a widespread debate and discussion on 'universal banking' in India. It is against this backdrop that an attempt is made here to examine the progress of universal banking in India and related issues. This paper attempts to trace the rationale for establishment of DFIs in the present context, looks at the recent trends of DFIs in the international context *vis-à-vis* the Indian perspective and the concept of universal banking. It highlights some broader issues based on select country experience, including those related to regulatory and supervisory arena that may arise in the Indian context on resorting to universal banking framework. Attempt is made to provide particular focus on the progress made so far in the direction of 'universal banking'. Although it is too short a period to make feasible impact study of universal banking in India, an attempt is made here to trace if there is directional changes in the style of functioning by the commercial banks, which are akin to universal banking phenomenon.

Purely from the point of pedagogic convenience, this paper is structured in 6 Sections. Section I introduces the problem in perspective. Section II traces the rationale of establishing the DFIs in the international perspective and the recent trend of DFIs migrating to universal banking in select Asian countries. On the basis of a review of empirical studies, Section III deals with the concept and select issues relating to universal banking. Section IV besides providing the background of establishing DFIs, outlines a brief assessment of DFIs in India and the necessity for their transformation into universal banking framework. Section V deals with the move towards universal banking in India. Towards this end, it traces the origin of issues relating to universal banking, initiatives, progress so far, legal and regulatory provisions, regulatory and supervisory concerns, if any, etc. Section VI concludes with some suggestive remarks.

SECTION II

1. Rationale of Establishment of DFIs and the Recent Trend: An International Outline

In the aftermath of Second World War, both the developed countries and newly independent countries emerging out of the colonial exploitation, were desperate in rebuilding their economy and attempted to promote rapid industrial development, which required long-term investment finance. Consequently, DFIs were set up in a number of countries both among the developed and developing ones. However, the development finance institutions existed much earlier too. Literature reveals that the earliest modern type of development banking institutions came into existence with the establishment of the Credit Mobiliser in France as early as in 1848 for financing of Continental European railway expansion. In Asia too, such institutions were established in the early part of 20th century. An important example of such an institution is the Industrial Bank of Japan (IBJ) founded in 1900. Historically, DFIs played a key role in the speedy industrial development of Europe and Japan as richly revealed by the literature. DFIs were set up with the objective of augmenting the absorptive capacity of firms for commercial exploitation of innovative technology over a long gestation period. Over a period, the role and responsibilities of DFIs greatly got multiplied, viz. apart from providing long-term loans and project finance, DFIs were expected to promote new and innovative projects, enhance managerial skills, develop entrepreneurship and help develop technological capabilities and so on. Significantly, DFIs were the only source of venture capital in many of the developing countries till as late as later twentieth century. Even in India, venture capital finance was initiated by a DFI. Cross country experience reveals that by and large, DFIs were either in public sector and quasi public sector, though there were also DFIs in private sector. DFIs considerably achieved their objectives of providing medium- to long-term finance, high risk and long gestation infrastructural projects, technical and project consultancy and expertise to new projects during 50s to 70s. DFIs laid strong foundation in many of the Asian countries to be known later as industrialised countries to the world. It is also revealing that all DFIs functioned broadly on similar lines. Such DFIs were characterised by low emphasis on profitability, thrust on developmental objectives, access to concessional source of funds, either directly or indirectly from the government. This was also the case with DFIs in India. In Japan, the Japan Development Bank (JDB) has been extending project finance, long-term finance at reduced interest rate and JDB had the direct access to funds from government. Similarly, Korean Development Bank has also been extending the term finance, infrastructure and other developmental projects, and the source of funds were allocated by the government in the annual Budget, as also from government guaranteed sources of funds. In Thailand, the Industrial Finance Corporation of Thailand functioned as a typical development finance institution with direct access to the concesional funds from their Central bank as also other fiscal concessions to funds raised by the DFI, which extended concessional term loans, etc. Over a period of time, however, as there were large scale structural changes in the economies across the world at a fast pace, these institutions could no longer function in their original objectives and style as well. DFIs suffered in-built structural weaknesses, coupled with this, the increased globalisation and access to newer and multiple sources of funds for the borrowers also had a strong impact on their functioning in their original form and intent. As the financial reforms were aimed at fostering efficiency, transparency and stability in the financial system in a globalised framework, the role of DFIs and the support provided by the government and its corresponding impact on the fiscal sustainability, came to be widely debated. It may be pointed out that these and other factors made DFI to disappear in many countries, or to reincarnate a different species of institutions. DFIs for their own survival in the changing framework had to resort to large scale innovations and diversification to newer products/services and were constrained to move in the direction of universal banking as a strategic response to rapidly changing environment.

2. Trend of Migrating to Universal Banking

In most of the developing countries, which resorted to a calibrated process of financial reforms to foster efficiency, profitability, competition based financial system, and the move towards globalisation on the one side, and DFIs' continued reliance on the governmental budgetary support for their functioning on the other side, could not be sustained. In order to cope with the fast changing economic and financial environment, DFIs, across countries, transformed into commercial banks or universal banks. For instance, Development Bank of Singapore (DBS), which had been one of Singapore's main sources of medium- and long-term financing, became universal bank. It has been actively engaged in providing short-term banking facilities, including trade financing and working capital financing, to consumer credit and so on though it was originally established as purely a DFI. It also provides investment banking services, portfolio management services and custodian services. Similarly, the Industrial Finance Corporation of Thailand has been converted into a universal bank and provides a wide range of products and services ranging from working capital to term finance, project consultancy, risk management tools and so on. The Development Bank of Philippines, the earliest DFI in the country, transformed as early as 1989 into somewhat like a universal bank and by 1995 it became a full-fledged universal bank with multifarious style of functioning. The Korea Long-Term Credit Bank, a private sector DFI, gradually transformed into a universal bank and has been providing integrated services. Even the Korea Development Bank undertakes a wide range of investment banking, securities trading, term and working capital financing activities not only within Korea but also in the entire Asia-Pacific region. Thus going by the international experience based on the select countries experiences, it is clear that universal banking has been the strategic response of DFIs. Even in Indonesia, a similar trend of converting the DFI into banks that carry out integrated services was observed. In Japan, the Development Bank of Japan was formed in 1999 by taking over the erstwhile Japan Development Bank Hokkaido-Tohoku Development Finance Public Corporation. Since then it has been providing a wide range of integrated services to clients' needs in line with the universal banking by greatly diversifying into a number of activities that are akin to commercial banking, investment banking, etc., apart from continued provision of term finance. It has been pointed out that with increased deregulation pressure from the globalisation process, coupled with increasing financial disintermediation, even banks in both developed and developing countries are strategically responding in order to safeguard their profitability performance and to improve their competitive position. A survey of literature reveals that both DFIs and banks have been responding differently due to the process of globalisation. Such strategies of DFIs stressed their transformation into universal banks, the achievement of a larger scale, mainly through internal growth or synergic mergers and takeovers, even diversification towards non-bank or non-financial activities, spreading across the borders of activities, and the use of new orgnisational set-ups to better suit the fast economic changes. Thus transformation to universal banking is not necessarily restricted to the DFIs but is also observed in respect of the traditional commercial banks, in the sense that a typical conservative commercial banking is losing its spirit to broaden into more diversified activities to become 'one stop shop'.

SECTION III

1. Universal Banking: the Concept

Universal banking simply means the 'one-stop shop', where banks provide all financial services along with the commercial banking, i.e. investment banking including selling of insurance products, etc. In other words, in addition, to the traditional conservative banking, it provides a wide range of financial and banking services and products under one roof. Universal banking does not differentiate between pure banking and non-banking financial activities. The term 'universal bank' refers to blending of commercial banking and investment banking, i.e. issuing, underwriting, investing and trading in securities. In a slightly broader sense, universal bank refers to banks that offer a wider menu of financial services, beyond the typical conservative commercial banking. However, universal banking need not mean that every institution conducts all types of business activities. In the spectrum of banking, specialised banking is on the one end and the universal banking on the other end.

Universal banking can also take variety of forms. For instance, though both Swiss and Germany have the universal banking, in practice, there are substantial differences between these two countries' systems (Rich and Walter, 1993). The Great Depression seriously affected the banking systems in both the Continental Europe and United States. The United States chose to discard the system of universal banking through the enactment of Glass-Steagall Act in 1933. However, the German and Swiss banking systems, even after the turmoil of the World War II, continued with the universal banking system by strengthening their respective supervisory and regulatory system (Rich and Walter, 1993). In fact, universal banks spurred industrial growth in Germany. The debate on universal banking in the United States continued almost throughout the twentieth century (Krosner, 1996) until as recently as the enactment of Gramm-Leach-Bliley Act in 1999.

2. Country Experience with Universal Banking

In this paper, the analysis of country experience deliberately focuses on German and Swiss systems, mainly because these countries have universal banking system for a fairly long period, even compared with the rest of the continental Europe.

Universal banking has played a great role in the continental Europe in general and specifically in countries, such as, Germany and Switzerland. To be sure, universal banking has been prevalent in other countries, such as Spain, etc., since the end of World War II. The experience of universal banking across countries, including Germany and Swiss or other European countries, revealed almost no conclusive evidence either in favour of or against it anywhere. There is substantial debate in the literature both for and against the system of universal banks. Those favouring universal banking argued that as universal banks were, by and large, bigger in size, there was a clear link between size and scope deriving scale economies. Such banks spread their overhead costs over many clients and assets. An empirical study by Forestieri (1993) had established prevalence of 'economies of scope' in a number of countries in Europe with universal banking. Such banks have the advantage of expanding into the full and wide range of products and services, while minimizing their risk of failures and therefore adding to stability. White (1986) also reached at a similar conclusion that universal banks, though involved in securities trading, had lesser chances of failure. Benston (1990) explored that banking crises during the pre-Glass-Steagall era were mainly due to the then prevailing system of universal banking. He concluded that these crises were mainly due to the flaw in the internal control system and inadequate supervision in general and had nothing to do with the universal banking framework *per se*. In fact, it has been prominently pointed out that universal banks played a crucial role in rebuilding the German economy from the devastation of World War II. Universal banks could be very useful, especially in countries, where capital markets play limited role while the economy demands large scale investment. Furthermore, as universal banks were better placed to understand and appreciate the activities and fund requirements of the borrowing units and accordingly offer 'tailor-made' products and services, the banks could not only develop strong relationship with the borrowing firms, but also ensure proper end use of funds. Raghuram (1996) added one more dimension by highlighting that the universal banks could use the reputation gained in one product/service to sell the others easily. There was also a view that though the 'too big to fail' theory did not always hold good, the relative chances of failures for smaller institutions were greater than the universal banks and thereby systemic stability could be secured.

3. Merits of Universal Banking

Literature reveals that the universal banking results in greater scale economies in the form of lower cost, higher output and better products due to optimum use of their resources. In particular, the following advantages are often cited in favour of universal banking. Economies of scope arise as universal banks offer multi-product and services. This is based on the logic that costs of offering various activities by different units are greater than the costs of offering them together. A universal bank is expected to be a large institution capable of offering a wide range of products and services. Hence, it would entail better utilisation of resources/inputs with high possibilities of both scale and scope economies. This is more so in the case of extensive use of information technologies. Borio and Filosa (1994) pointed out that large scale could also avoid the wasteful duplication of marketing, research and development and information-gathering efforts. Customers have the advantage of obtaining all possible financial and banking services/products at a single point and it relieves them from the hassle of searching different service providers for different services.

Universal banks are also better placed *vis-à-vis* specialised banks to handle situations arising out of swings in business cycles by better allocation of resources within the organisation. Proponents of universal banking thus argue that specialised banking system can present considerable risks and costs to the economy. By offering a broader set of financial products than what a specialised bank provides, universal bank is able to establish long-term relationship with the customers and provides them a package of financial services through a single window. It is important to note that this benefit stems from the very nature/purpose of universal banking.

4. Select Issues

As universal banking combines both the commercial banking and investment banking and other non-banking financial activities under one roof, certain issues arise in their operations.

Larger the banks, the greater are the devastation on the system. In the event of any failure, a systemic crisis could be triggered. The inertia of 'too big to fail' itself might succumb to the excessive risk taking as general tendency is that the government would step in to rescue the bank.

Furthermore, it is argued that universal banks are particularly vulnerable because of their role in underwriting and distributing securities and active participation in the derivative trading. Historically, an important apprehension has been that by virtue of their sheer size, universal banks would gain monopoly with undesirable consequences (Borio and Filosa, 1994). Universal banks have been blamed for fostering cartels and enhancing the power of large non-banking firms. Saunders (1984) came out with a number of shortcomings arising from its multiple roles, which, *inter alia,* can be broadly grouped as (a) conflict of interests and (b) impact on systems stability.

A. Conflict of Interests

One of the most commonly pointed out lacuna of universal banking is the 'conflict of interests' that arises mainly because of multiple roles performed by the universal banks. Being both lender and underwriter of equity of the same company, banks have a privileged access to the inside information of the company. Hence, it is feared to be misused by the banks for their own advantage at the expense of depositors or the investors. In fact, this was one of the key premise on which the Glass-Steagall Act was enacted way back in 1933. This resulted in separation of investment banking from the traditional banking business and continued as the hallmark of banking practice in United States for almost seven decades till the enactment of Gramm-Leach-Bliley Act, 1999.

The literature dwells on the conflict of interests, comprehensively. Here, however, it is consciously restricted to the following forms which nevertheless are not entirely mutually exclusive, viz. (1) banks will promote the equity issue underwritten in spite of being aware of the company's actual weakness; (2) as a fund manager, the bank would sell all the unsold securities to the account holders/third parties merely to shift the risks from its own basket; (3) transfer the 'risk of default by its borrower firm' to outside investors by issuing securities to repay its own loans thereby distributing the risk of default by its borrower across the investors; (4) access to inside information of the borrowing unit for bank's own use. These are not only theoretical possibilities but were also occasionally established in individual cases. Santos (1998) had, however, observed that the vital issue regarding any potential conflict of interests as outlined above rests not merely on their existence, but whether there are sufficient incentives and opportunities for the banks to exploit them to their favour and at the cost of the customers. Somewhat supporting the above, Kroszner and Rajan

(1994) in their empirical study concluded that universal banks even during the pre-Glass-Steagall time did not systematically exploit the conflict of interests. Rich and Walter (1993) maintained that many of the characteristics attributed to universal banking were misconceptions, which failed to justify the reality of universal banking. However, the view that 'possibility of potential conflict of interests', irrespective of whether banks have incentive or otherwise to exploit them, in the case of universal banking, could not be brushed aside.

B. *Stability of the System*

Soundness and stability always remain the uppermost concern of the banking and financial system. For, banks are more 'fragile' than the non-banking organisations for several reasons; of which, the most important being that failure of an individual bank would be detrimental to the entire banking system. This, in turn, has not only serious macroeconomic implications but also involves very expensive corrective measures. Above all, it has a long-term impact on the economy. Banks are highly leveraged institutions as their entire business is based on the borrowed funds which are disproportionately higher *vis-à-vis* their owned funds or capital. Further, the very structure of assets and liabilities inherently make them highly vulnerable to the liquidity crises due to duration or maturity mismatches. Moreover, any failure of an individual bank will have cascading effect over the entire system, because of the inter institutional exposures as part of the payment system. This was precisely the reason why financial system in general and banking system, in particular, world over has been highly regulated, even in the case of a highly open economy. Therefore, banking system's stability has become the overwhelming reason for the regulation and supervision of their assets and liability structure. The stability of the banking system sometimes even becomes the deciding factor in choosing between universal banking and traditional commercial banking. Universal banks' exposure to equity market and other sensitive sectors has been the single most frequently pointed out reason against its own stability as well as its implications for systemic stability. Moreover, such risks arise in relatively a very short span of time compared with the risks arising out of the traditional lending business, leaving little time to repair the system. Besides, as universal banks in general are larger in size, any failure of one bank could have a 'knock on' effect on the entire system through 'contagion'.

5. Empirical Evidence

Empirical evidence towards universal banking is mixed. There is no conclusive evidence in the literature to prove that the universal banking is universally accepted as the best. The empirical studies, especially directed at the "existence of economies of scale" in universal banks, do not provide conclusive evidence. Significantly, a number of studies show that the economies of scale in commercial banking were exhausted at very low deposit levels (Benston *et al.* 1983; Clark, 1988). On the contrary, some studies even showed diseconomies (Mester, 1992 and Saunders and Walter, 1994). However, Santos (1998), who conducted a comprehensive review of the subject, came to the conclusion that a number of empirical studies surveyed gave mixed results disproving that banks conducting securities trading were always highly risky. Thus the experience world over did not yield conclusive evidence on adverse impact of universal banking on the systemic stability. Interestingly, empirically even the "economies of scope" is not clear, though studies by Gilligen, Smirlock and Marshall (1984) pointed out the existence of economies of scope with the joint use of information technologies, to an extent. Benston (1990) added one more dimension to the scope economies stating that as banks offer almost the same kinds and proportion of services, it is difficult, if not impossible, to conduct meaningful empirical studies of economies of scope on the question of monopolistic positions of bank. It has been often stated that instead of saying that German banks control German industry, it would be more appropriate to say that the three largest German banks possess significant holdings in some of the largest German companies. Significantly, the study also found out that only on very rare occasions did German banks intervene in the restructuring of companies. A study by Canals Jordi (1997) however, concluded that the legal and practical acceptance of universal banks have been the most flexible model

SECTION IV

1. DFIs in India: A Brief Assessment

India has a long and chequered history of financial intermediation. The system comprised both institutions and markets. The markets were, however, characterised by scarcity of instruments, shortage of players and therefore lacked depth. Consequently, the Indian financial system, by and large, remained institution-centric. DFIs in India were set up not merely on theoretical arguments of development economics but also on strong empirical reasoning. Private sector was not developed notwithstanding the fact that India had a fairly diversified industrial base for a developing country, with a number of well-established industrial houses at the time of Independence. As capital market was in infancy, industries had to depend on own profits and banks for financing new investments and inventories. The menu of options for policy-makers to choose at that point of time was limited. The vision of the first Prime Minister of India was firmly in favour of planning in a manner that the State would occupy the 'commanding heights' of the economy while the private sector would play a role supplemental to that of the State. The resultant mixed economy model was unique among the contemporary economies. This model entailed that the State undertakes large investments out of the resources it mobilizes through non-inflationary, and, if necessary, inflationary sources of financing. Given the fact that productivity of investment would not change significantly in the short-to-medium term, economic growth can be maximized only by raising, *a la* Harrod-Domer, the level of investment. But banks cannot provide investible funds on long-term basis without obtaining funds on long-term and continuous basis. These factors led to establishment of the first DFI, viz. IFCI in 1948. Over the years, a number of DFIs were established both at the national and State levels (SFCs and SIDCs) to provide long-term finance for developmental pursuits. ICICI was set up in 1955, IDBI and UTI in 1964. Some of the specialised FIs, viz. Exim Bank (1981),

TFCI (1989), IIBI[1] (1956) and IDFC (1997) were also established to meet the greatly diversified requirements of the different sectors in the economy, viz. export and import, agriculture, sick industries, tourism, infrastructure, etc. Similarly, on the refinance front, NABARD (1982), NHB (1985) and SIDBI (1990) were also established at different points of time. Most of these institutions were recognised under Section IV-A of the Companies Act, 1956. This made it possible for these institutions to access easy and captive market for raising of resources through issue of bonds, which qualified for the SLR purposes of the investing banks. Besides, DFIs had access to the concessional funds through the National Industrial Credit (Long-Term Operation) Fund from the Reserve Bank. DFIs also had the access to safe forex sources of funds, wherein even the exchange rate risks were borne by either the government or RBI. On the deployment front too, DFIs had marked areas of deployment as per plan priorities with assured return. Significantly, though these institutions constituted a significant part of the financial system they were outside the purview of regulation and supervision of the RBI till 1992. Moreover, DFIs constituted heterogenous financial institutions governed by different statutes. Even after coming into the fold of RBI and till the establishment of Board for Financial Supervision (BFS) in 1994, DFIs were not regulated and supervised by the RBI on par with the banking system. With the reforms in financial sector in full swing transiting from commercial banks, DFIs and NBFCs and market orientation of the economy, DFIs is one segment of the financial sector, which seem to have bore the maximum brunt of economic reforms. The key reason is that DFIs remained unregulated or underregulated for a fairly long duration coupled with their operation within a captive environment.

As pointed out earlier, our own experience in India revealed that the structure of the system was mainly concerned with

1. Originally it was established as Industrial Reconstruction Corporation of India (IRCI) then it was converted into Industrial Refinance Corporation of India and then converted as IIBI under Companies Act, 1956.

expansion of credit in line with the developmental plan pursuits, with little orientation towards commercial viability. With more than six decades of their existence in India, DFIs played an important role in promoting investment in the Indian industry. For instance, it could be cited from the first Narasimham Committee, which strongly commended the role of DFI's stating '...a commendable record of providing much needed finance for the term requirements of industry at a time when the capital markets were not sufficiently developed and have contributed significantly to industrial development...'. It is also worth pointing out that the DFIs, besides allocating their resources in line with planned type of industries, also attempted to channelise their flow towards the backward states (RBI, 1991). DFIs thus played a catalytic role in converting knowledge creation to knowledge commercialisation for sustained technological progress, especially when the stock market in India was in a nascent stage. DFIs were the major and only source of long-term finance for several segments of the industry. They played a sustained role in providing impetus to interaction between firms and technology institutes by developing programmes and providing facilities to encourage such interaction (RBI, 2003). Financial institutions have historically played a very significant role in financing the long-term requirements of funds of the economy as the alternative sources of long-term funds, i.e. capital market, particularly debt segment, had not developed (RBI, 1999).

The importance of DFIs could be seen in their size of financial assets in the system. For instance, the percentage of financial assets of term lending institutions (TLIs) increased from 9.65% at the end-March 1981 to as high as 16.23% at end-March 2000. This proportion, however, sharply came down to 5.16% at end-March 2005 (Table 1).

As DFIs functioned on the assured source of funds, with the economic and financial reforms, the RBI reduced the level of Statutory Liquidity Ratio (SLR) to the statutory minimum of 25%. This relieved the entire banking sector from the obligation of locking up their huge resources in the bonds issued by the DFIs. Coupled with this, the National Industrial Credit (Long-

Table 1: Relative Position in terms of Financial Assets (% to the Total of the system)

end-March	1981	1991	1996	1997	1998	1999	2000	2001	2002	2003	2004	2005
All Banks	73.84	64.53	64.55	63.27	63.00	63.11	62.98	64.04	69.03	71.52	70.78	75.84
All-FIs	26.16	35.47	35.45	36.73	37.00	36.89	37.02	35.96	30.97	28.48	29.22	24.16
TLIs	9.65	15.90	13.47	14.74	15.43	15.78	16.23	14.76	9.31	8.91	8.15	5.16
Inv Is	13.41	16.23	19.13	18.98	18.88	18.82	18.68	18.76	19.07	16.49	18.07	16.28
SLIs	2.72	2.79	2.27	2.35	2.03	1.78	1.61	1.95	2.12	2.61	2.54	2.26
Others	0.38	0.55	0.58	0.66	0.66	0.52	0.49	0.48	0.47	0.47	0.46	0.46

Worked out based on the Published data from RTP various volumes, RBI.
TLIs: Term Lending Institutions; Inv Is: Investment Institutions; SLIs: State Level Institutions.

Term Fund) [NIC (LTO)], which was a major window of concessional funds from the Reserve Bank of India for the DFIs, was also shut with the Government of India's decision announced in the Budget 1992-93. Thus on the resources side, all major sources of long-term concessional funds were sealed. Consequently, DFIs were constrained to raise resources from the market at market rate of interest to lend at 'developmental rate of interest' (expectedly lower rate of interest) that did not augur well for their long-term sustainability. Similarly, on the lending side too, they encountered problems relating to the commercial viability of the projects, particularly in situations of economic downturn, e.g. textiles, etc. Simultaneously, banks were also given freedom to extend term finance, which led to competition with banks, which were better placed in terms of cost of raising resources. Under these circumstances, when DFIs were required to progressively adhere to the international prudential norms, their intrinsic strength got exposed with huge NPA levels and accumulated negative profits leading to erosion of capital in some cases. Under these circumstances, Committees formed to examine the functioning of DFIs recommended their conversion into universal banks (for detailed discussion see Karunagaran, 2005).

SECTION V

1. Move towards Universal Banking in India

In line with the emerging trend of strategic response to the fast switching economic and financial environment around the world, as outlined in the previous sections, in India also there have been references relating to 'universal banks' as early as in 1991 itself. For instance, the First Narasimham Committee Report has spelt out for '...8 to 10 national banks with a network of branches throughout the country engaged in universal banking...'. The Second Narasimham Committee strongly recommended that, over a period of time, DFIs should convert themselves into banks and eventually, there would only be two forms of intermediaries, viz. banking companies and non-banking finance companies (NBFCs). It stressed mergers between strong banks/FIs as that would make for greater economic and commercial sense. To make way, it even recommended that one of the largest DFI, viz. IDBI should be corporatised and converted into a joint stock company under the Companies Act. This was followed by Khan Working Group, though it was more sympathetic towards DFIs, it also suggested that DFIs be issued a full-fledged banking license over a period of time. Incidentally, developments all over the world also suggested that continuance of the differentiation between banks and DFIs would reduce the efficacy of both kinds of institutions and will reduce the efficiency with which the financial system could perform by the pooling function (RBI, 1998). Thus during the later 1990s, the entire thought process towards the DFIs in general was towards their migrating to universal banking. This was strongly supported by their precarious financial position. Hence there emerged the need for a financial reforms package, which in the words Reddy (2006) aimed at '... a dynamic mix of private and public ownership and transition of DFIs ... into new incarnations...'.

2. Legal Provisions Relating to Universal Banking in India

As far as banking business in India is concerned, the Banking Regulation Act, 1949 is the key governing Act, though banking activities also need to take into account many other related legislations, viz. RBI Act, 1934, Negotiable Instruments Act, SBI Act, Bank Nationalisation Act, etc. There is no legislative distinction between commercial banking and investment banking or any explicit legislative restriction for the banks to conduct investment banking activities. But banks have traditionally been maintaining the 'arms length' distance from investment banking. A plausible reason could be the pursuit of the British style of banking with strict separation between commercial banking activity and investment banking activity. Some countries, such as, United States, had till recently legislative restrictions in the form of Glass-Steagall Act, 1933. This prohibited combining of commercial banking and investment banking. However, with the enactment of Gramm-Leach-Bliley Act, 1999, these restrictions were removed. In India the separation of commercial banking and investment banking and other non-banking financial activities though were customary in style, later they received regulatory accent.

3. Policy Initiatives

A. *Major Policy Initiatives by the Regulator*

A series of deliberate policy initiatives have been undertaken by both the Government of India and the Reserve Bank of India to enable the banking system to migrate to universal banking framework without coercing any institution. Banks were permitted to invest in capital market instruments including the underwriting of shares in the early 1990s. With the financial sector reforms, banks were given abundant freedom to go much beyond their traditional conservative commercial banking related to working capital finance. Since 1992-93, projects including infrastructural projects, were promoted by banks, wherever financially feasible. This led to direct competition between banks and DFIs. But the more tangible momentum for the universal banking in India seems to have set in with the acceptance of recommendations of the Second Narasimham Committee's Report (1998) set up by the government and the consequent initiation of series of initiatives by the Reserve Bank for the eventual move towards universal banking. Reserve Bank, as a regulator, came out with a 'Discussion Paper', which outlined various issues in resorting to universal banking while preferring the system of universal bank in the long run for obvious reasons. It favored a '....time gap of 5 years or so till such time the capital market could also simultaneously grow to a dependable level...'. Reserve Bank as a regulator and supervisor of the banking system, laid the formal road map, especially for the DFIs, by way of giving a set of detailed guidelines. In respect of commercial banks, RBI asserted that banks in India are 'no more traditional and pure commercial banks'. However, the regulatory authority laid 'the foundation' as an active facilitator for the system to move towards universal banking without explicitly spelling out so, in India, even as early as 1980s. For instance, even in the later part of 1980s, a number of large banks were permitted to open their subsidiaries to deal with merchant banking activities, mutual funds activities, housing finance subsidiaries and so on. In effect most of the larger and mid-sized banks cutting across public and private sector were moving in the direction of universal banking even before the formal announcement came through, from the Regulator or a debate was initiated in the later 1990s. Thus the commercial banks and DFIs in India have already set the direction to move away from their traditional watertight compartmentalised activity and consequently becoming universal banking. Simultaneously, either voluntarily or due to compulsion, there has also been a number of bank mergers. All these developments would lead not only to universal banking milieu but even beyond that and ultimately to the emergence of 'financial conglomerates'.

In recent years banks have been permitted to take part in wide array of activities in-house, which till recently were strictly barred for banks, for instance, insurance business either with or without risk participation or as sub-agents, i.e. referral models. Practically all major banks in both public and private sector have already commenced exploiting the vast business potential of bancassurance in one form or the other. All these developments are pointer to the fact that universal banking system has become real in India both in letter and spirit.

As far as DFIs were concerned both RBI as well as government were more forceful for their moving to become banks. Consequently, RBI even advised FIs to work out the transition paths for their evolution towards universal banks.

As the principle of "Universal Banking" has become the desirable goal, considerable progress has already been made by permitting banks to diversify into investments and long-term financing and DFIs to lend working capital, etc. For this purpose DFIs were also permitted to raise short-term resources in the form of issue of Term Deposits, Inter Corporate Deposits, Commercial Papers, Term Money Borrowings *albeit* with a prescribed limit equivalent to one time Net Owned Fund as early as late 1980s.

B. *Key Policy Initiatives by the Government*

Given the built-in structural weaknesses of DFIs, the Government of India undertook several periodic initiatives to protect and reinvigorate DFIs. For instance, with the concerted initiatives by the Government of India, the financial liabilities of two major FIs, viz. IDBI and IFCI Ltd., were restructured with the help of major investors, such as, banks, insurance companies and other FIs. This restructuring helped to bring down the cost of funds of these FIs to improve their financial health.

The repeated attempt to revitalise DFIs through a variety of restructuring measures did not significantly improve the financial health of major DFIs. It was only then that the IDBI had to approach the Government of India to corporatise by repealing the IDBI Act so as to pave the way for its ultimate conversion into a universal bank. Accordingly, the Central Government announced the proposal for corporatising IDBI by introducing the necessary legislative changes. In order to strengthen its capital, the International Bank for Reconstruction and Development (IBRD) loan outstanding in respect of IDBI was transferred to the Central Government and replaced with a long-term bond, which qualified as Tier I capital. Further, all the loans outstanding in respect of NIC (LTO) Fund of RBI was also transferred to Government of India and the same were in turn treated as government's contribution towards strengthening of capital of IDBI.

One of the key initiatives was the introduction IDBI Repeal Bill. Some of the important features of the Repeal Bill when it was introduced are:

- On the date decided by GoI the Industrial Development Bank of India Act was repealed and the undertaking of the IDBI shall vest in the company to be called 'Industrial Development Bank of India Limited'.

- The new company shall be deemed to be a banking company under Section 5(C) of the Banking Regulation Act, 1949 and carry on the banking business as per the provisions of the Act and is not required to obtain license from the Reserve Bank.
- Further, the new company would be given exemption from maintaining the SLR under Section 24 of the Banking Regulation Act, 1949 for a period of five years from the appointed day.

When the Bill was further referred to the Standing Committee on Finance, the Committee had in turn recommended for more regulatory forbearances, *inter alia,* exemptions from maintenance of CRR for five years and certain tax exemptions for the newly converted banking company. The Cabinet approved the amendments to the Bill on August 11, 2003 to incorporate provision in the Bill so as to ensure that the new banking company also continues to be a development bank, which will provide term lending to large, medium and small industries.

4. Progress Towards Universal Banking

A. *Select DFIs Conversion to Universal Banks*

Taking advantage of the propitious environment created as a result of wide range policy initiatives by the RBI and the GoI favourable to universal banking coupled with their own disadvantageous position in terms of both raising of resources and profitable deployment of funds, some FIs took proactive initiatives in this direction. For instance, ICICI Ltd. had approached the RBI with its proposal for conversion to a bank by means of reverse merger with its subsidiary ICICI Bank Ltd. The RBI gave clearance after the merger case was cleared by the High Court of Mumbai and the clearance was subject to certain terms and conditions relating, *inter alia*, to reserve requirements, prudential norms, etc. ICICI became the country's first DFI to become universal bank by merging itself with its own subsidiary ICICI Bank Ltd. in 2002.

IDBI Act, 1964 was repealed on December 30, 2003 and corporatised under the Companies Act, 1956 and IDBI became a universal bank by merging itself with its own subsidiary, viz. IDBI Bank Ltd. IDBI even after its conversion, not only continues to provide term loans as per the mandate of the new statute, it ventured into personal banking on a large scale, provides demat services, capital market, home finance, trade finance, investment banking and so on. Stock broking, clearing banking activities are also provided by the bank. It is worth pointing out that IDBI Bank also provides rehabilitation finance, which is aimed at extending both financial as well as non-financial skill support to rehabilitate the potentially viable weak and sick industrial units by way of merger, takeover, etc. Such activities are typical of a DFI. Besides the above, IDBI Bank continues with the Bills financing, Bills rediscounting and participates in money market related activities like CPs, CDs, etc.

B. *Changing Pattern of Bank Credit*

Against the above backdrop, an attempt is made to analyse if any pattern is emerging in the operations of banking institutions during the post-reforms period. Towards this aim, select variables have been analysed in the following paragraphs.

With the major DFIs converting into universal banks and some of the key DFIs turning sick, it becomes extremely important to see if banking sector is coming forward to fill the vacuum created by the DFIs. It is interesting to note that in the Indian context, the larger banks seem to be taking the lead in deploying their larger proportion of non-food credit towards industry. In fact this is an important development from the point of development of industry, especially during the post-DFIs' conversion into banks. This indicates an encouraging scenario of meeting the credit needs of industry (both term loans and working capital). It would be even more appropriate for a different reason that this trend also indicates that the larger sized banks are in the direction of becoming universal banks. This would enable the small and medium sized banks to continue to meet the working capital requirements and concentrate on the rest of the sectors of economy. This is further strengthened by the growth in bank credit to industry by the banks as per their size as presented in Table 2 and (Chart 1). It clearly reflects that in the case of large banks the credit to industry is growing at a healthy trend whereas the growth rate shown is negative in the case of small and medium sized banks.

Table 2: Bank Credit to Industry—According to Size of the Banks (percentage growth)

	1994	1995	1996	1997	1998	1999	2000	2001	2002	2003
SBs	19.1	43.1	42.6	15.3	16.8	7.7	21.5	9.7	-3.2	-13.9
MBs	9.7	34.2	39.6	21.8	14.8	20.7	17.3	6.5	-3.6	12.9
LBs	6.8	7.9	23.9	11.9	14.7	16.4	13.2	11.4	18.0	14.5

SBs= Smaller banks (up to Rs. 5000 cr), MB= Medium sized banks between Rs. 5000 cr to 20000 cr and LBs = Large banks (above Rs. 20,000 cr of assets).
Source: BSR, RBI.

Chart 1: Bank Credit to Industry (% of Non-Food Credit)

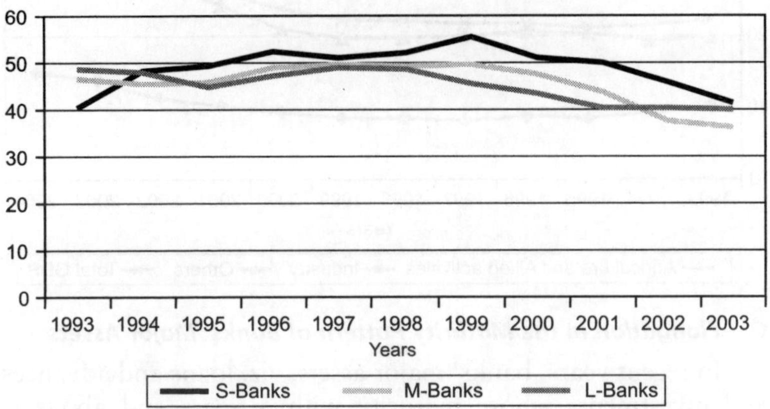

Interestingly, one of the RBI studies also pointed out '...it has been found that the share of DFIs declined in the 1990s, while the share of banks rose from a low level during 1985—90 by more than double during 1995—2001 thereby overtaking the position of FIs in project finance...' (RBI, 2003). This is significant from the point of moving towards universal banking scenario as banks in general and larger banks in particular could be in a position to step into the shoes of DFIs in so far as meeting the requirements of project financing which requires not only large size financing but also involves longer gestation period.

Further, the total bank credit as a ratio to GDP for industry (Chart 2) steadily picked up from the mid-1990s. This also supports our conclusion that the move of major DFIs towards universal banking did not hamper the industrial sector with dearth of credit.

Chart 2: Bank Credit to GDP Ratio—By Sector

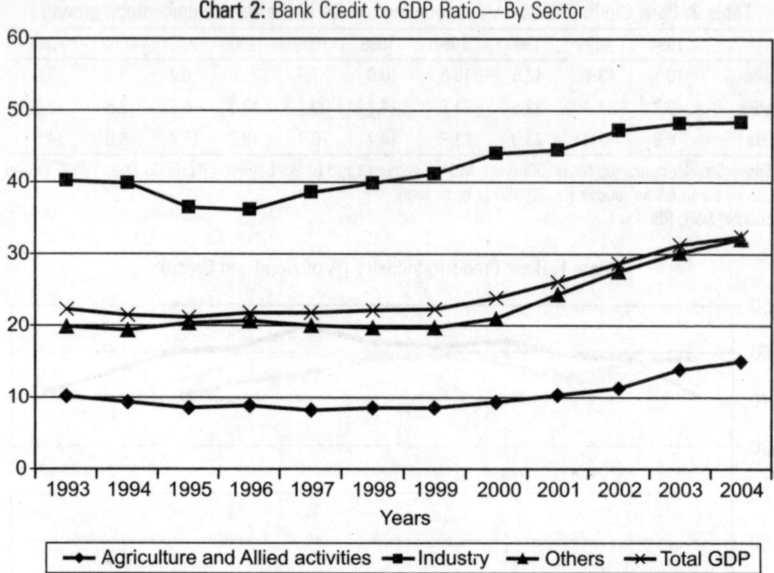

C. *Elongation in the Maturity Pattern of Banks' Major Assets*

In recent years, banks' major assets, viz. loans and advances and investments whose maturity with 5 years and above is increasing. Consequently, the proportion of their Assets in this category is on the increase as can be seen in Table 3.

Table 3: Pattern of Loans and Investments of Banks (percentage share in 5 years and above maturity)

	Public Sector Banks		Old Pvt Banks		New Pvt Banks	
	Loans	Investments	Loans	Investments	Loans	Investments
2002	13.8	56.9	10.8	59.9	21.8	25.4
2003	13.8	58.2	11.6	56.9	21.4	19.8
2004	14.9	63.3	13.1	61.4	21.1	21.1
2005	15.5	57.1	15.0	54.4	18.9	18.6

Source: RTP various issues, RBI.

D. *Banks in Investment Activities*

Banks' investments in equities of corporates have been restricted to 5% of their incremental deposits of the previous year by the RBI as a prudential measure in order to have their restricted exposures to the capital market. However, in majority of the cases banks were unable to utilise even this 5% limit towards the equity investments. Instead they continued to have higher exposure in the GoI securities despite great deal of relaxation in the SLR requirements for obvious reasons. This trend continued for a fairly long period during the post-reforms period. Banks' role in the investment activities in general seems to have picked up only during the later part of the post-reform period. The proportion of their investment activities, however, does not seem to be funding the equities (Table 4). This attitude by the banks, irrespective of their ingenious reasons, would only have a 'crowding-out' effect.

Table 4: Scheduled Commercial Banks' Investments

(end Mrach) (in per cent)

		2000	2001	2002	2003	2004
1.	Govt. Securities	70.6	71.4	71.9	74.8	74.8
2.	Other domestic securities	27.6	26.4	25.7	22.9	23.1
	of which: shares and debentures of companies only	16.2	16.6	17.3	15.4	13.5
3.	Foreign securities	1.8	2.2	2.4	2.2	1.7

Source: Worked out from RBI publications.

E. *Diversification in Banks' Activities*

Practically all banks, irrespective of size in India both in public and private sector have over the years greatly diversified into multitude of banking as well as non-banking activities, and more so since the reforms. Diversification of activities by banks was partly the strategic response to the pressure thrown up by the financial and economic reforms coupled with the process of globalisation. Incidentally, the banking related statutes were also amended from time to time to accommodate the banking companies to legally undertake a wide array of activities, which were the result of constant innovations to meet the requirements of competition. Here for the purpose of analysis, we have deliberately chosen larger banks based on the size of assets size, viz. State Bank of India, Punjab National Bank, Canara Bank and IDBI Bank Ltd. from public sector and ICICI Bank from the private sector. It is significant to point out that there is ample evidence to conclude that these banks had already been functioning on the lines of universal banking, and their size has been an important contributing factor for these institutions to exploit both scope and scale economies. A quick survey on the types of products and services by these banks revealed that these institutions provide practically a wide range of financial services and products devoid of their traditional and conventional commercial banking. Though practically all the public sector banks have one or more wholly owned subsidiaries to carry out the non-banking financial activities, major banks, viz. SBI, PNB, ICICI Bank, IDBI Bank, Canara Bank have more number of subsidiaries. Interestingly, even some of the mid-sized PSBs, viz. Bank of Baroda, Bank of India and Indian Bank have more wholly owned subsidiaries in the areas of non-banking and insurance activities. State Bank of India enjoys the largest banking franchise in India and along with its 7 Associate Banks, SBI Group has the unrivalled strength of over 14,000 branches, the largest in the world. SBI is one of the widely diversified public sector banks in India. For instance, SBI Life Insurance is a joint venture between the State Bank of India and Cardif SA of France. SBI owns 74% of the total capital and Cardif the remaining 26%. In 2004, SBI Life Insurance became the first company amongst private insurance players to cover 30 lakh lives. It extensively utilises the SBI Group as a platform for cross-selling insurance products along with its numerous banking product packages such as housing loans, personal loans and credit cards. SBI's access to over 100 million accounts provides a vibrant base to build insurance selling across every region and economic strata in the country. SBI's foray in lease financing, corporate finance, investment activities, capital market related activities, merchant banking, trade finance in the areas of both import and export finance, housing finance, etc., makes it the country's largest universal bank.

Punjab National Bank, the largest nationalised bank, also renders a wide range of commercial banking and investment banking activities, including capital market related and selling of insurance products, mutual fund, merchant banking, lease finance, credit card business, housing finance, etc. PNB was undertaking all capital market related services through its wholly owned subsidiary until it was merged with the parent bank recently. Presently, the bank itself undertakes all the capital market activities in-house. It has a separate subsidiary for housing finance and for the PNB Gilt, a wholly owned subsidiary, undertakes the services related to GoI securities, Treasury Bills, merchant banking related activities.

Similarly, Canara Bank is also rated as a potential financial conglomerate among public sector banks, with its wide range of subsidiaries and sponsored institutions, providing a host of services to the diverse clientele groups. It functions as a financial supermarket. The roots of Canara Bank's diverse activities go back to 1980s, when it undertook a major diversification drive. Canara Bank has as many as eight subsidiaries, sponsored institutions and joint ventures. The Bank has explored emerging areas, challenging fields with the aid of these subsidiaries. It has subsidiaries in the areas of housing finance, mutual funds, merchant banking and capital market related areas. It provides wide range of products and services in-house, viz. corporate finance, project finance, advisory services in the areas of industry and agriculture. Besides, it provides debenture trustee services, etc. Of late, it is also into bancassurance in collaboration with M/s Aviva Life Insurance Company Pvt. Ltd. It is particularly worth being pointed out that one of its subsidiary, viz. Canbank Computer Services Limited, is engaged in Information Technology and software development services, training and consultancy in IT related matters, besides Registrar and Share Transfer Agency Services. The Company is a member of NASSCOM and registered as a Software Solution Provider for World Bank Projects.

Among the private sector banks, ICICI bank stands out not only as the biggest domestic bank, but also the largest financial conglomerate in the country. ICICI bank together with its subsidiaries has been providing the widest possible range of banking and non-banking financial and insurance services. To make a mention of few of the areas, it has the largest credit card business in the shortest time, provides customized corporate products because of its long standing experience as a DFI, merchant banking, financing the IPOs of corporates, issues bonds/debentures, besides providing the property solutions, etc. It also has mutual fund subsidiary, export credit insurance with ties up with ECGC.

As pointed out earlier, the banking laws in India do not define what is a universal bank, going by their operational diversity and scale of operations, all these major banks could be conveniently classified as universal bank but from legal point of view they are banks. In fact the Banking Regulation Act, 1949 only defines 'banking,' and 'banking company' and 'banking policy'. Over a period of time, with Banking Regulation Act having undergone several rounds of amendments, the definition of banking has been widened to include a host of activities, which were originally not part of it. Thus the term 'commercial banking' and 'universal banking' are left to the convenience of the operational and academic classification.

A study on scope for universal banking in India in early 1990s by Ray (1994), while analysing cost-efficiency found that the banks in India have been gradually taking the responsibility of term financing (developmental finance). Banks found such term financing to be highly cost-efficient. The study clearly revealed that the banks have been found to realise overall scale economies if output is defined in terms of term loans, other loans and deposits. Furthermore, the study also indicated that the presence of substantial economies of scale with respect to the developmental banking activities and confirm the presence of scope economies for development financing among banks.

F. *Banks Raising Funds in the Capital Market*

Access to long-term resources is a necessity for universal banks as they will have to do diverse lending stretching beyond the traditional boundaries of working capital requirements of the corporate sector. It, therefore, becomes a necessity for universal banks to access long-term resources. In the Indian context, the corporate bond market is yet to pick up to a greater extent. As not many corporates come out with bonds/debentures which meet the requirements of the investors, banks have greater scope for issuing bonds. The investors seem, however, to be more interested in investing in these bonds more from tax saving point of view rather than for pure investments. Such bonds, therefore, need to carry some tax sops for some more time. The newly turned universal banks, viz. ICICI and IDBI continued to raise resources through the capital market both by way of equity and debenture issues. It is a good trend that these universal banks continue to raise resources by way of issuing bonds as that would not only help them meet repayment obligations in respect of their erstwhile long-term bond borrowings as well as to continue lending long-term to corporate sector. These two banks alone raised resources significantly as can be seen in Table 5. However, more banks, at least the larger ones, should get into raising of resources by way of bonds/debentures. This, besides increasing the long-term resources for onward long-term lending, will also deepen the debt market.

Table 5: Banks in the Capital Market

(Rs. Cr)

	Public Sector Banks			Pvt Sector Banks			
	Public Issues	Pvt Placement		Public Issues		Pvt Placement	
2003-04	1,104	16	3,728	0	1,352#	63	2,895
2004-05	3,336	21	4,948	4,108	1,478#	34	5,604

Refers to Debt Issues by the IDBI and ICICI.
Source: RTP, RBI.

5. Some Issues

As emphasized in a neo-classical framework, the Indian economy has become increasingly outward oriented giving the market greater role in achieving the allocative efficiency. In tandem with this development, during the last one decade or more, the banking scene has undergone tremendous change. The Reserve Bank of India as a Regulatory and Supervisory Authority consciously introduced a wide array of measures and initiatives to strengthen the banking system and put it on par with global standards in terms of compliance of internationally recognised prudential norms, *inter alia,* relating to assets classification, capital standards, accounting and auditing standards, exposure norms, disclosure norms, risk management techniques, etc. The upshot of the overall financial reforms seem to be a consensus in moving towards universal banking set up. However, universal banking has its own set of problems.

The global experience on universal banking, as outlined earlier, had thrown out two most prominent issues, viz. conflicts of interests and systemic stability. However, these were problems associated/experienced in the case of universal banking system, which were already well-established and had been functioning over several decades. In a country like ours, where the universal banking is just emerging on the banking horizon, it has to encounter many more important issues:

- Universal banking need not result in economies of scope and scale especially if the banks were not of appropriate size. On the contrary, it might even lead to be more expensive, if the sufficient number of transactions in each of the specialised financial activity were not up to 'breakeven' level. Therefore, there is danger that even the smaller banks might venture into universal banking, out of expediency without realizing the potential of particular type of business activity. Such an adventure might even lead to failures, which will have an impact on the system. Though there need not be a legislation to prevent any bank opting for the universal banking in general, there could be sufficient regulatory disincentives for the smaller banks jumping into the bandwagon of universal banking.
- Internationally, studies on universal banking have established that the size of the banks plays a key role. As a natural corollary of this, there would be a number of attempts for mergers and acquisitions among banks/DFIs/NBFCs leading to emergence of financial conglomerates in India. Such developments need encouragement, provided they are healthy, genuine, transparent and do not hamper competition and stability.

- India, being a vast country, it requires various types of institutions to cater to varied needs of different sets of people. Even universal banks would hardly be in a position to meet varied needs, such as functions of rural cooperatives, urban cooperative banks, RRBs, etc. Therefore, this needs due consideration, while moving towards the universal banking framework.
- The financial conglomerates, generally manage their risks on a consolidated basis on business lines even cutting across legal entities. However, the supervisory and regulatory authorities have a special obligation to protect the depositors and the banking system. Unless the supervisor is in a position to distinguish between risks arising out of banking and non-banking activities, their own task would be in jeopardy.
- Investment banking, especially that relating to derivatives, forms a very important part of the universal banking. Investment banking conducted either in the form of 'agency type' or 'principal type' would be more riskier than the traditional banking. Moreover, as these are new areas in India, it would be all the more complex for domestic banks. Therefore, such banks require high professional standards supported by sophisticated risk management techniques at the bank level. Besides, banks should be encouraged to develop voluntarily, sufficient 'fire wall' between the activities of high risk activities and the normal commercial banking activities, in a universal banking framework.
- As banking system in India had been tradition bound and functioned in a closed environment for several decades, exposure to universal banking scenario might give banks a tendency to behave recklessly and indulge in irresponsible speculation in investment activities due to 'demonstration effect'. That will lay on the line not only a particular bank but also erode the confidence of the depositors and throw the entire system in abyss, by way of bank run. Moreover, the loss in the trading/

investment related activities occurs at relatively greater pace than the losses arising out of the normal lending business, i.e. NPAs due to default, etc. Consequently, banks, which were not exposed to such an environment, would almost collapse instantly. Given such a situation, if the supervisory/regulatory authority is found to be not well prepared with suitable policy response, it will have all the more serious implications on the system. Therefore, there is strong justification to tighten both regulation and supervision of banking in the emerging scenario in India.

- Universal banking is portrayed not only with wide range of functions/products/services innovated as an outcome of financial reforms and globalisation process, but has also become highly complex. In the process, it might even impede transparency in many intra-institutional transactions. The direct corollary of these developments is that the job of regulators and supervisors has become much more complex and demanding. This would be more so, in India where we have the system of multiple regulators for different activities.
- The upshot of all the above developments point to the requirement of thorough understanding of such innovative hybrid products/services as also their implications principally on the systems safety and stability with appropriate policy guidelines, by the regulator/supervisor. Above all, the critical issue boils down to how well the multiple regulators/supervisors are prepared to prevent the possible 'regulatory arbitrage' in an universal banking framework.
- The problem of 'moral hazard' seems to be very high among the public in India. This implies that if anything goes wrong in the financial sector for whatever reason, there is strong expectation that Central Government or Reserve Bank would always come to the rescue of depositors. Such general inertia would only encourage banks, especially universal banks, to indulge in high risk activities. Therefore, regulators and supervisors

have additional responsibility to be highly transparent on the misdeeds of the particular bank in trouble. It is also necessary to highlight to the general public their role/responsibility to safeguard their own interest as also the system. It is necessary for the supervisory authority, in such circumstances, to make it clear to the market as also to the general public that the 'safety valve' from the Central Bank is available only against the risks arising out of the normal commercial banking activity and not for all kinds of misdeeds in market related activities. For this financial literacy needs to be encouraged and implemented at various levels.

- As universal banks undertake a wide range of activities from core banking to highly complex derivative operations, there would be problem for the regulators to exactly pinpoint the cause of failure of an institution especially if the regulatory authorities happened to be more than one. There is possibility of passing the buck to save one's own skin from public embarrassment.
- It is not impossible to contemplate that in the emerging banking scenario, at least in the short to medium term, there would be a few large 'universal banks' surrounded by a large network of smaller to medium sized commercial banks besides, cooperative banks and of course, regional rural banks due to their respective locational and other advantages. The pertinent point that needs to be emphasised is that, as the appetite for risk taking and actual amount of risk taken by these different sets of institutions would widely vary, the policy prescriptions also accordingly need to be discrete, including that of the ratio of capital to risk weighted assets and the risk based supervisory attention.
- It is because of the above reasons that the financial system the world over, has been most stringently regulated, even in the case of an open economy, where market takes a leading role. The rationale behind such requirement was that regulation and supervision was required to correct 'market failure' as banks tend to

take more risks than the prudent limit. This will, in turn, have an adverse impact on the system and India is no exception to this problem.

SECTION VI

Concluding Remarks

Experiences across countries were clearly in the direction of DFIs moving away from the traditional development banking towards universal banking. Major DFIs in India are, therefore, on the right track. The regulatory and supervisory authorities, however, need to be well prepared with appropriate tools/norms, to meet the challenges thrown out of the complex situation arising out of universal banking and financial conglomerates.

The possibility of regulatory arbitrage could be minimized if the system was regulated by a unified regulatory authority, as against the present system of multiple regulators. To begin with, it seems to be the right time to seriously explore Reddy's formula, i.e., Apex Regulatory Authority (for more details see Reddy, 1999). In the meantime, it is essential to have systemised coordination among all the existing supervisory and regulatory authorities, viz. SEBI, RBI and IRDA including regulatory wings in the Central Government supported by necessary legislations. Consolidated supervision would become more relevant in the emerging scenario. It may be pointed out here that, in United States, while the Gramm-Leach-Bliley Act opened up the banking system for universal banking set-up, at the same time, it had also proposed for an integrated supervisory model called as 'Umbrella Supervisor', especially aimed at supervising the financial system as conglomerates.

The appetite for risk taking and actual amount of risk taken by universal bank and commercial and cooperative banks differ drastically. Accordingly the regulatory/supervisory norms/ prescriptions need to be different.

Sufficient proactive policy environment needs to be created for the banks to opt for healthy and transparent mergers and consolidation based on the economies of scale/scope to reap the benefits of synergies. However, larger banks should be mandated to put in place sophisticated risk management techniques.

Recognising the possible emergence of financial conglomerates, the Reserve Bank of India has already issued a set of guidelines for consolidated accounting as a first step in the direction of consolidated supervision, which is a step in the right direction.

DFIs reincarnation into universal banks does not seem to affect resource requirement of industry and services. However, the equity and corporate debt market needs to be developed to step into the shoes of DFIs, while universal banks continue to play active role both in working capital requirement as well as term finance based on the commercial viability of the projects.

A vast country like India which has been institution-centric for a fairly long period with less dependence on the capital market by the corporate sector for corporate finance, larger commercial banks moving towards universal banks seems to be in the right direction, especially when it has been concluded that the DFIs in their original façade could sustain no more in the changed environment. There needs to be encouragement in this direction rather than stifling regulation and control but positive regulation is a must.

Furthermore, a vast country like India continues to require services and specialised skills acquired by different sets of banking and financial institutions to serve the requirements of widely varied and scattered sections of the country at large. Therefore, there is full justification for the existence and functioning of the existing set-up of financial system alongside emergence of universal banking in India. For that matter, in no country, universal banks seem to have been able to eliminate specialised institutions from business (RBI, 1999).

REFERENCES

Benston, G.J. (1990): *The Separation of Commercial and Investment Banking: The Glass-Steagall Act Revisited and Reconsidered*, New York: Oxford University Press.

Benston, G., Berger, A., Hanweck, G. and Humphrey, D. (1983):

"Economies of Scope and Scale", *Conference Proceedings*, USA: Federal Reserve Bank of Chicago.

Borio, Claudio E.V and Filosa, Renato (1994): "The Changing Borders of Banking: Trends and Implications", *BIS Economic Papers*, No. 43, December.

Canals, Jordi (1997): *Universal Banking–International Comparisons and Theoretical Perspectives*, New York: Oxford University Press.

Clark, Jeffrey A. (1988): "Economies of Scale and Scope at Depository Financial Institutions: A Review of Literature", Federal Reserve Bank of Kansas City, September/October.

Forestieri, G. (1993): *Economies of Scale and Scope in the Financial Services Industry: A Review of Recent Literature*, Financial Conglomerates, Paris, OECD, 63-124.

Government of India (1998): *Report of the Committee on Banking Sector Reforms* (Chairman: Shri. M. Narasimham), New Delhi.

IDBI (1998): *Report of the Working Group on Harmonising the Role and Operations of Development Financial Institutions and Banks*, Mumbai.

Karunagaran, A. (2005): "Should DFIs be Revived?" *Economic and Political Weekly*, Money Banking and Finance Special Number, March.

Kroszner, Randall (1996): "The Evolution of Universal Banking and its Regulation in Twentieth-Century America", *Universal Banking: Financial System Design Reconsidered*, Anthony Saunders and Ingo Walter (Ed.), New York: Irwin Professional Publishers, 70-99.

Kroszner, Randall and Raghuram, Rajan (1994): "Is the Glass-Steagall Act Justified? A Study of the US Experience with Universal Banking before 1933", *American Economic Review*, September, Vol. 84.

Mathur, K.B.L. (2003A): "Development Financial Institutions at the Crossroads", *Economic and Political Weekly*, February 22.

Mester, L. (1992): "Traditional and Non-traditional Banking: An Information-Theoretic Approach", *Journal of Banking and Finance*, Vol. 16.

Rajan, Raghuram (1996): "The Entry of Commercial Banks into the Securities Business: A Selective Survey of Theories and Evidence", *Universal Banking: Financial System Design Reconsidered*, I. Walter and A. Saunders (Eds), Chicago: Irwin, 282-302.

Ray, Indrajit (1994): "Cost-Efficiency of Universal Banking in India: An Analysis of Scale and Scope Economies", *Prajnan*, Vol. XXII, No. 2.

Reddy, Y.V. (1999): Key Note Address at the Seminar on "Harmonising the Role and Operations of Development Financial Institutions and Banks", June 28, *RBI Bulletin* , Mumbai.

Reserve Bank of India (1991): *Report of the Committee on the Financial System* (Chairman: Shri M. Narasimham), November, Mumbai.

—— (1999): "Harmonising the Role and Operations of Development Financial Institutions and Banks", *A Discussion Paper*, January, Mumbai.

—— (2004): *Report of the Working Group* (Chairperson: Smt Shyamala Gopinath) on *Monitoring of Systemically Important Financial Intermediaries* (Financial Conglomerates), Mumbai.

—— (2003): *Report on Trend and Progress of Banking in India*, 2002-03.

Rich, Georg and Christian, Walter (fall 1993): "The Future of Universal Banking", The *Cato Journal*, Cato Institute, Vol. 13, No. 2, Washington DC USA: Massachusetts Avenue, N.W.

Santos, A.C. Joao (1998): "Banks in the Securities Business: A Review", *Working Paper No. 56*, BIS, Basle.

Saunders, A. (1984): "Conflicts of Interest: An Economic View", *Deregulating Wall Street*, Ingo Walter (Ed.), New York: John Wiley and Sons.

Saunders, A. and Walter, Ingo (1994): *Universal Banking in the United States: What Could We Gain? What Could We Lose?* New York: Oxford University Press.

Regional Rural Banks in India: Past, Present and Future

12

Biswa Swarup Misra
P.K. Raut

Inception of Regional Rural Banks (RRBs) in the mid-1970s was an innovative experiment in streamlining the rural credit delivery mechanism in India. With joint shareholding by Central Government, the concerned State Government and the sponsoring bank, an effort was made to integrate commercial banking within the broad policy thrust towards social banking without being oblivious to the distinctive local peculiarities. RRBs were intended to evolve as specialized rural financial institutions for developing the rural economy by providing credit to small and marginal farmers, agricultural labourers, artisans and small entrepreneurs. Over the years, the RRBs, which are often viewed as the small man's bank, have taken deep roots and have become an inseparable part of the rural credit structure.[1] RRBs have played a key role in rural institutional financing in terms of geographical coverage, clientele outreach, and business volume as also contribution to development of the rural economy.[2] However, just after five years of their existence, their financial viability emerged as an area of concern. This is why several committees have been formed from time to time to look at the seemingly intractable problems afflicting RRBs. The Committee to Review Arrangements for Institutional Credit for Agriculture and Rural Development (CRAFICARD) was the first to investigate the problems of RRBs way back in 1981. In view of the vastly altered ground realities, the Sardesai Committee Report on RRBs (2005) revisited a whole range of issues of considerable contemporary significance to the RRBs. During this span of 25 years, 15 other committees were formed to address the viability concerns of RRBs. Considered in a proper historical and comparative perspective, the issue of merger of small and uneconomic RRBs is not new having been highlighted in 1984 by the Working Group on RRBs (Kelkar Committee). Twenty-one years down the line, there have been a spate of activities leading to consolidation of RRBs. Twenty-eight RRBs of 9 sponsor banks in 6 states were merged to form 9 new entities with effect from September 2005.

The restructuring and amalgamation of RRBs is at once both complex and delicate affair. It is complex as the multitude of the exercise is spread over different states, involving different sponsor banks with differences in performance of the merged entities. It is equally delicate as it attempts to reposition the new entity as a stronger entity, which should be able to successfully overcome the transitional (different work culture subject to a new framework) problems associated with merger and ultimately the synergy from the merged entities should enable the new entity to face the business challenges more effectively. In view of the amalgamation exercise pursued since September 2005, it becomes instructive to enquire whether any discernible pattern emerges from the amalgamation, the desirability of the sort of restructuring pursued and some thoughts on the possible course of restructuring in the future. With this broad objective, the rest of the chapter is schematized as follows: Section I briefly traverses the genesis and performance of the RRBs and brings into sharp focus the need for restructuring. Some thoughts voiced on possible restructuring by the different Committees that were appointed to study the problems of RRBs in the past are analysed in Section II. Possible pattern in the spatial performance of RRBs, which would guide the process of restructuring, has been explored in Section III. The content and character of restructuring and amalgamation pursued till date with the flagging of some issues on the possible course of restructuring form the subject of discussion in Section IV. Section V sums up the main issues emerging from the discussion and attempts to place matters in perspective.

Section I
Genesis and Performance

Genesis

The genesis of the RRBs can be traced to the philosophy of what was then termed as 'social banking' and is currently known as 'inclusive banking'. Nationalisation of 14 major banks in India in 1969 constitutes a milestone in India's attempt towards inclusive banking. Notwithstanding the nationlisation of banks, the need for a stronger institutional arrangement for providing rural credit was considered imperative to give a thrust to inclusive banking. This quest for inclusive banking was concretised by the Narasimham Committee in recommending the creation of RRBs in 1975 as a new set of regionally oriented rural banks, which would combine the local feel and familiarity of rural problems characteristic of cooperatives and the professionalism and large resource base of commercial banks. Subsequently, the Regional Rural Banks (RRBs) were set-up through the promulgation of RRBs Act[3] of 1976. Their equity is held by the Central Government, concerned State Government and the Sponsor Bank in the proportion of 50:15:35.

Performance

A remarkable feature of their performance over the past three decades has been the massive expansion of their retail network in rural areas. From a modest beginning of 6 RRBs with 17 branches covering 12 districts in December 1975, the number swelled to 196 RRBs with 14,446 branches working in 518 districts across the country in March 2004. RRBs with a large branch network in the rural area form around 43 per cent of the total rural branches of commercial banks. The rural orientation of RRBs is formidable with rural and semi-urban branches constituting over 97 per cent of their branch network. The growth in the branch network has enabled the RRBs to expand banking activities in the unbanked areas and mobilise rural savings.

Given the modest beginning, it could justifiably be maintained that RRBs, over the years, made impressive strides in terms of various performance and development indicators. This thesis can be substantiated by the fact that deposits of RRBs grew by 18 times and advances by 13 times between 1980 and 1990. Between 1990 and 2004, deposits and advances grew by 14 times and 7 times respectively (Table 1). Between the year 2000 and 2004, loans disbursed by RRBs more than doubled reflecting the efforts taken by the banks[4] to improve credit flow to the rural sector. The average per branch advances also increased from Rs. 25 lakh in March 1990 to Rs. 154 lakh in March 2003. The deployment of credit relative to the mobilsation of resources shows that the credit-deposit ratio of RRBs was more than 100 per cent during the first decade of their operations up to 1987. Though the CD ratio subsequently came down, of late, it has shown an improvement and went up from around 39 per cent in March 2000 to 44.5 per cent in March 2004.[5]

The mandate of promoting banking with a rural focus, however, would be an enduring phenomenon only when the financial health of the RRBs is sound. With built-in restrictions[6] on their operations, it is not unreasonable to expect that the financial health of the RRBs itself would be a matter of concern. As regards their financial status, during the year 2003-04,

Table 1: Evolution of RRBs: Select Indicators

(Rs. crores)

Parameter	1980	1985	1990	1995	1996	1997	1998	1999	2000	2001	2002	2003	2004
No. of RRBs	85	188	196	196	196	196	196	196	196	196	196	196	196
Capital	21	46	91	166	358	705	1118	1380	1959	2049	2143	2141	2221
Deposits	222	1315	4023	11141	14171	17976	22191	27059	32226	38294	44539	49582	56295
Investments	20	164	60	1348	2879	3891	5280	6680	7760	8800	9471	17138	21286
Advances	262	1405	3384	5987	7057	7908	9021	10559	12427	15050	17710	20934	25038
Total assets	426	2320	6081	14886	18969	24376	29468	35820	42236	49596	56802	62500	70195
Interest earned	NA	NA	480	1158	1421	2033	2624	3281	3938	4619	5191	5391	5535
Other income	NA	NA	113	72	89	103	136	151	207	240	370	430	697
Total income	NA	NA	593	1230	1511	2136	2760	3432	4145	4859	5561	5821	6231
Interest expended	NA	NA	326	851	1065	1462	1773	2131	2565	2966	3329	3440	3363
Operating expenses	NA	NA	254	657	726	804	845	982	1056	1165	1459	1667	1825
Provisions and contingencies	NA	NA	NA	120	171	673	72	99	96	128	163	132	289
Total expenses	NA	NA	581	1509	1791	2265	2617	3113	3621	4130	4787	5107	5187
Operating profit	NA	NA	12	-279	-280	-129	143	319	524	729	774	714	1044

Note: Total expenses are excluding provisions and contingencies.

163 RRBs earned profits amounting to Rs. 953 crore whereas 33 RRBs incurred losses to the tune of Rs. 184 crore. 90 RRBs had accumulated losses as on March 31, 2004. Aggregate accumulated loss of RRBs amounted to Rs. 2,725 crore during the year 2003-04. Of the 90 RRBs with accumulated loss, 53 RRBs had eroded their entire owned funds as also a part of their deposits. Further, NPAs of the RRBs in absolute terms stood at Rs. 3, 299 crore as on March 31, 2004. The percentage of gross NPAs was 12.6 during the year ending March 31, 2004. While 103 RRBs had gross NPAs less than the national average, 93 had NPAs more than it. The present restructuring exercise of the RRBs is being driven by the poor financial performance of the RRBs. Before we delve into the restructuring strategy pursued, it would be worthwhile to revisit the various suggestions at restructuring of the RRBs. This has been attempted in the next section, i.e. Section II.

Section II
Restructuring Strategies

The financial viability of RRBs, has engaged the attention of the policy-makers from time to time. In fact, as early as 1981, the CRAFICARD addressed the issue of financial viability of the RRBs. The CRAFICARD recommended that 'the loss incurred by a RRB should be made good annually by the shareholders in the same proportion of their shareholdings'. This recommendation was not accepted. But under a scheme of recapitalisation, financial support was provided by the shareholders in the proportion of their shareholdings. Subsequently, a number of committees have come out with different suggestions to address the financial non-viability of RRBs. For instance, the Working Group on RRBs (Kelkar Committee) in 1984 recommended that small and uneconomic RRBs should be merged in the interest of economic viability. In a similar vein, the Agricultural Credit Review Committee (ACRC, i.e. Khusro Committee), 1989 pointed out that 'the weaknesses of RRBs are endemic to the system and non-viability is built into it, and the only option was to merge the RRBs with the sponsor banks. The objective of serving the weaker sections effectively could be achieved only by self-sustaining credit institutions'. The Committee on Restructuring of RRBs, 1994 (Bhandari Committee) identified 49 RRBs for comprehensive restructuring. It recommended greater devolution of decision-making powers to the Boards of RRBs in the matters of business development and staff matters. The Committee on Revamping of RRBs (1996) (Basu Committee) once again mooted the option of liquidation.

The Expert Group on RRBs in 1997 (Thingalaya Committee) held that very weak RRBs should be viewed separately and possibility of their liquidation be recognized. Such RRBs might be merged with neighboring RRBs. The Expert Committee on Rural Credit, 2001 (Vyas Committee I) was of the view that the sponsor bank should ensure necessary autonomy for RRBs in their credit and other portfolio management system. Subsequently, another committee under the chairmanship of Chalapathy Rao in 2003 (Chalapathy Rao Committee) recommended that the entire system of RRBs might be consolidated while retaining the advantages of regional character of these institutions. As part of the process, some sponsor banks may be eased out. The sponsoring institutions may include other approved financial institutions as well, in addition to commercial banks. The Group of CMDs of Select Public Sector Banks, 2004 (Purwar Committee) recommended the amalgamation of RRBs on regional basis into six commercial banks—one each for the Northern, Southern, Eastern, Western, Central and North-Eastern Regions. Thus, there is a diversity of options suggested by different committees, which examined the issue of financial viability and restructuring strategies for the RRBs ranging from vertical merger(with sponsor banks) to horizontal merger (among RRBs operating in a particular region).

More recently, a committee under the chairmanship of A.V Sardesai revisited the issue of restructuring the RRBs (Sardesai Committee, 2005). The Sardesai Committee held that 'to improve the operational viability of RRBs and take advantage of the economies of scale, the route of merger/amalgamation of RRBs may be considered taking into account the views of the various stakeholders'. Merger of RRBs with the sponsor bank is not provided in the RRBs Act, 1976. Mergers, even if allowed, would not be a desirable way of restructuring. The Committee was of the view that merging a RRB with its sponsor bank would militate against the spirit of setting up of RRBs as local entities and for providing credit primarily to weaker sections. In the light of various options for restructuring, the Committee was of the view that 'a change in sponsor banks may, *in some cases* help in improving the performance of RRBs. A change in sponsorship may, *inter alia*, improve the competitiveness, work culture, management and efficiency of the concerned RRBs'. Against this backdrop, a number of issues need further probing. The prime issue is whether any pattern is noticed for the poor performers among the RRBs, i.e. are they confined to any particular region of operation or to some specific sponsor banks. In case there is a systematic pattern, the approach to restructuring would take a shape, which is different from one in the absence of any identifiable pattern. Such an attempt to search for a specific pattern in the performance of the RRBs is attempted in the next section.

Section III
Presence and Performance of RRBs in the Spatial Dimension

Notwithstanding their expansion, the presence and performance of RRBs show wide variation both across States and sponsor banks. Although RRBs are spread over 26 States, they have most of their presence in 7 States, i.e. Andhra Pradesh, Bihar, Karnataka, Madhya Pradesh, Maharashtra, Rajasthan and Uttar Pradesh. Uttar Pradesh has the highest number of RRBs, i.e. thirty-six, and Kerala has only two amongst the major States of the country. The north-eastern States like Manipur, Meghalaya, Mizoram and Nagaland have only one RRB. Likewise, 7 sponsor banks amongst 28, *viz.* Bank of Baroda, Bank of India, Central Bank of India, Punjab National Bank, State Bank of India, United Bank of India and UCO Bank account for more than three-fifths of the RRBs. More than 160 RRBs earned profit in March 2004 while 150 RRBs were found to be earning profits for three consecutive years beginning with the year 2000-01. More than half of these loss-making RRBs are found to be operating in four States, i.e. Bihar, Madhya Pradesh, Maharashtra and Orissa. Seen at the level of sponsor banks, three banks, *i.e.* Bank of India, Central Bank of India and State Bank of India accounted for more than half of the loss-making RRBs.

As a number of sponsor banks have promoted RRBs in more than one States, it is logical to ask whether the presence of RRBs sponsored by a few banks, whose area of operation is

Table 2: States and Sponsor Bank-wise Distribution of RRBs

Sr. No.	State	RRBs		Sr. No.	Sponsor bank	RRBs	
		No.	Profit-making			No.	Profit-making
1	Andhra Pradesh	16	15	1	Allahabad Bank	7	7
2	Arunachal Pradesh	1	0	2	Andhra Bank	3	3
3	Assam	5	4	3	Bank of Baroda	19	15
4	Bihar	16	8	4	Bank of India	16	10
5	Chhattisgarh	5	3	5	Bank of Maharashtra	3	1
6	Gujarat	9	8	6	Bank of Rajasthan	1	0
7	Haryana	4	4	7	Central Bank of India	23	15
8	Himachal Pradesh	2	2	8	Canara Bank	8	8
9	Jammu & Kashmir	3	1	9	Corporation Bank	1	0
10	Jharkhand	6	3	10	Dena Bank	4	4
11	Karnataka	13	12	11	Indian Overseas Bank	3	2
12	Kerala	2	2	12	Indian Bank	4	4
13	Madhya Pradesh	19	14	13	J & K Bank	2	1
14	Maharashtra	10	5	14	Punjab & Sind Bank	1	1
15	Manipur	1	0	15	Punjab & National Bank	19	17
16	Meghalaya	1	1	16	State Bank of Bikaner and Jaipur	3	2
17	Mizoram	1	1	17	State Bank of Hyderabad	4	4
18	Nagaland	1	0	18	State Bank of India	30	18
19	Orissa	9	3	19	State Bank of Indore	1	1
20	Punjab	5	5	20	State Bank of Mysore	2	2
21	Rajasthan	14	10	21	State Bank of Patiala	1	1
22	Tamil Nadu	3	3	22	State Bank of Saurashtra	3	3
23	Tripura	1	0	23	Syndicate Bank	10	10
24	Uttar Pradesh	36	34	24	United Bank of India	11	9
25	Uttaranchal	4	4	25	UCO Bank	11	7
26	West Bengal	9	8	26	Uttar Pradesh State Co-operative (U.P.S.C.) Bank	1	0
				27	Union Bank of India	4	4
				28	Vijaya Bank	1	1
	Total	**196**	**150**		**Total**	**196**	**150**

Note: Based on three consecutive years performance beginning with the year 2000-01.
Source: Statistical Tables relating to banks in India (various issues).

confined to some specific States, is camouflaging the performance of better run RRBs. There can be three possibilities in such a situation. One, irrespective of the State, the RRBs sponsored by some banks are incurring losses; second, irrespective of sponsor banks, certain States are simply not conducive to better performance for RRBs and third, there is nothing inherent either with a sponsor bank or a particular State in which the RRBs operate to contribute to the performance of RRBs and it is a combination of some other factors. To explore these possibilities, an attempt needs to be made to assess the presence of RRBs sponsored by different banks across States and their performance. Such an attempt is made in Table 3 where performance of sponsor banks across regions is depicted.

Seen from the perspective of the State in which they are operating, 6 out of the 9 loss-making RRBs in Bihar are sponsored by the Central Bank of India, two by UCO Bank and one by SBI. Of the 4 loss-making RRBs found in Madhya Pradesh, one each is sponsored by the State Bank of India, Central Bank of India and UCO Bank. Likewise, of the four-loss making RRBs found in Orissa, three are sponsored by State Bank of India and one by UCO Bank. It emerges from the sponsor bank's perspective that the RRBs in which they have a stake and which are not earning profits go beyond a single State. It is spread across the States in which they have a presence. For instance, the 9 loss-making RRBs sponsored by Central Bank of India are spread across Bihar, Madhya Pradesh, Maharashtra and West Bengal. Similarly, the 12 loss-making RRBs sponsored by SBI are spread across Andhra Pradesh, Arunachal Pradesh, Bihar, Jammu & Kashmir, Jharkhand, Madhya Pradesh, Nagaland, Orissa and Uttaranchal. The same is the case with the RRBs sponsored by Bank of Baroda and UCO bank. Hence, there does not emerge a strong systematic pattern so as to infer whether the peculiarities of any particular sponsor bank or a specific State in which they operate, drives the performance of RRBs.

In the absence of a systematic pattern for poorly performing RRBs, a one-size-fits-all approach to restructuring will undermine the complexities involved in the entire process. Given the state of affairs, let us now consider the experience gained from the

Table 3: Performance of RRBs across Sponsor Banks and Regions

Sponsor bank	No of RRBs	State	Loss-Making
Allahabad Bank	7	Uttar Pradesh (6), Madhya Pradesh (1)	
Andhra Bank	3	Andhra Pradesh (2), Orissa (1)	
Bank of Baroda	19	Uttar Pradesh (9), Rajasthan (5), Gujarat (3), Madhya Pradesh (1), Uttaranchal (1)	Madhya Pradesh (1), Rajasthan (1), Uttar Pradesh (1)
Bank of India	16	Uttar Pradesh (3), Madhya Pradesh (4), Maharashtra (4), Jharkhand (4), Orissa (1)	Jharkhand (1)
Bank of Maharashtra	3	Maharashtra (3)	
Bank of Rajasthan	1	Rajasthan (1)	
Central Bank of India	23	Bihar (8), Chhattisgarh (1), Madhya Pradesh (7), Maharashtra (3), Rajasthan (1), Uttar Pradesh (2), West Bengal (1)	Bihar (6), Madhya Pradesh (1), Maharashtra (1), West Bengal (1)
Canara Bank	8	Uttar Pradesh (3), Karnataka (4), Kerala (1)	
Corporation Bank	1	Karnataka (1)	
Dena Bank	4	Gujarat (3), Chhattisgarh (1)	
Indian Overseas Bank	3	Orissa (2), Tamil Nadu (1)	
Indian Bank	4	Andhra Pradesh (2), Tamil Nadu (2)	
J & K Bank	2	Jammu & Kashmir (1)	Jammu & Kashmir (1)
Punjab & Sind Bank	1	Punjab (1)	
Punjab National Bank	19	Uttar Pradesh (6), Punjab (3), Rajasthan (2), Bihar (4), Himachal Pradesh (1), Haryana (3)	
State Bank of Bikaner and Jaipur	3	Rajasthan (3)	Rajasthan (1)
State Bank of Hyderabad	4	Andhra Pradesh (4)	
State Bank of India	30	Andhra Pradesh (5), Arunachal Pradesh (1), Assam (1), Bihar (1), Chhattisgarh (3), Himachal Pradesh (1), Jammu & Kashmir (1), Jharkhand (2), Karnataka (1), Madhya Pradesh (3), Meghalaya (1), Mizoram (1), Nagaland (1), Orissa (3), Uttar Pradesh (2), Uttaranchal (3)	Andhra Pradesh (1), Arunachal Pradesh (1), Bihar (1), Jammu & Kashmir (1), Jharkhand (2), Madhya Pradesh (1), Nagaland (1), Orissa (3), Uttaranchal (1)
State Bank of Indore	1	Madhya Pradesh	
State Bank of Mysore	2	Karnataka (2)	
State Bank of Patiala	1	Punjab (1)	
State Bank of Saurashtra	3	Gujarat (3)	
Syndicate Bank	10	Andhra Pradesh (3), Haryana (1), Karnataka (4), Kerala (1), Uttar Pradesh (1)	
United Bank of India	11	West Bengal (5), Assam (4), Manipur (1), Tripura (1)	Manipur (1)
UCO Bank	11	West Bengal (3), Bihar (3), Orissa (2), Rajasthan (2), Madhya Pradesh (1)	Bihar (2) Madhya Pradesh (1), Orissa (1)
Uttar Pradesh State Co-operative (U.P.S.C.)	1	Uttar Pradesh (1)	Uttar Pradesh (1)
Bank Union Bank of India	4	Uttar Pradesh (3), Madhya Pradesh (1)	
Vijaya Bank	1	Karnataka (1)	

Note: The brackets indicate the number of RRBs by the sponsor banks. The position was as on March 31st 2004.
Source: Report on RRBs (Sardesai Committee, 2005), Reserve Bank of India.

attempts at restructuring pursued till date to be able to draw a road map for the future.

Section IV
Restructuring in Practice

To begin with, the sponsor banks submit amalgamation proposal to the NABARD (National Bank for Agricultural and Rural Development), an apex body for the RRBs. On a scrutiny of the proposals, NABARD apprises the Government of India (GoI) of its observations on the amalgamation proposal. The final decision with regard to amalgamation is taken by the Central Government. As on 31st March 2006, 27 cases of amalgamation were effected in 12 states. Another 13 proposals ratified by NABARD are awaiting GoI's assent. Besides, 3 more proposals for amalgamation submitted by State Bank of India in Madhya Pradesh, Jharkhand and Uttaranchal are under the scrutiny by NABARD. If the proposals for amalgamation under different stages of ratification are also considered, in all there have been 43 cases of restructuring attempted till date. The Sardesai Committee had recommended two options for the merger of the RRBs, *viz.*:

- Merger between RRBs of the same sponsor bank in the same State.
- Merger of RRBs sponsored by different banks in the same State.

The restructuring of RRBs pursued till date has been designed along the first of the two options suggested by the Sardesai Committee. Amalgamation of RRBs can be conceptualised amongst three categories of RRBs. Theoretically, it can be merger of two or more profit-making entities, profit-and-loss-making entities or loss-making entities. While merger of only profit making RRBs make one end of the spectrum, that of only loss-making RRBs, the other end with the merger of the profit-and-loss-making RRBs falling in between the two. Seen in terms of this categorisation, we find, in majority of the cases (19 out of 27), it has been the merger of the profit-making RRBs of a particular sponsor bank in a particular State, which has been effected. However, there have been instances of amalgamation

Table 4

Sl.No.	Sponsor Bank	Names of the RRBs amalgamated	New name	State	With effect from
1.	State Bank of India	Gorakhpur KGB Basti GB	Purvanchal Gramin Bank	Uttar Pradesh	12.09.2005
2.	Bank of Baroda	Valsad Dangs GB Surat Bharuch GB Panchmahal Vadodara GB	Baroda Gujarat Gramin Bank	Gujarat	12.09.2005
3.	Central Bank of India	Akola Kshetriya GB, Buldhana GB, Yavatmat Kashetriya GB	Vidharbha Kshetriya Gramin Bank	Maharashtra	12.09.2005
4.	Union Bank of India	Samyut KGB , Kashi GB, Gomti GB	Kashi Gomti Smyut GB	Uttar Pradesh	12.09.2005
5.	Punjab National Bank	Kapurthala Firozepur KGB, Gurudaspur Amritsar KGB	Punjab GaminBank	Punjab	12.09.2005
6.	Canara Bank	Tungabhadra GB, Chitradurga GB, Kolar GB, Sahyadri GB	Pragathi Gramin Bank	Karnataka	12.09.2005
7.	Syndicate Bank	Malaprabha GB, Bijapur GB, Netravati GB, Varada GB	Karnataka Vikas Gramin Bank	Karnataka	12.09.2005
8.	Dena Bank	Kutch GB, Banaskantha Mehsana GB, Sabarkantha Gandhinagar GB	Dena Gujarat Gramin Bank	Gujarat	12.09.2005
9.	UCO Bank	Begusarai KGB, Bhagalpur Banka KGB, Munger KGB	Bihar KGB	Bihar	12.09.2005
10.	Punjab National Bank	Vidur GB, Muzaffarnagar Kshetriya GB, Hindon GB	Uttar Pradesh GB	Uttar Padesh	12.09.2005
11.	Punjab National Bank	Haryana KGB, Hissar Sirsa GB, Ambala Kurushetra GB	Haryana GB	Haryana	12.09.2005
12.	UCO Bank	Cuttack Gramya Bank, Balasore Gramya Bank	Kalinga GB	Orissa	12.09.2005
13.	State Bank of Saurashtra	Jamnagar Rajkot Gramin Bank, Surendranagar Bhavnagar GB, Junagadh Amreli GB	Saurashtra GB	Gujarat	02.01.2006
14.	United Bank of India	Cachar Gramin Bank, Lakhimi Gaonlia Gramin Bank, Pragiyotish Gaonlia Bank, Subansiri Gaonlia GB	Assam Gramin Vikash GB	Assam	02.01.2006
15.	Bank of Baroda	Marudhar KGB, Aravali KGB, Bundi Chittorgarh KGB, Bhilwara Ajmer KGB, Dungarpur Banswara KGB	Baroda Rajasthan Gramin Bank	Rajasthan	12.01.2006
16.	Punjab National Bank	Shekhawati GB, Alwar Bharatpur Anchalik GB	Rajasthan Gramin Bank	Rajasthan	24.01.2006

(Contd....)

Sl.No.	Sponsor Bank	Names of the RRBs amalgamated	New name	State	With effect from
17.	UCO Bank	Jaipur Nagaur Anchalik GB, Thar Anchlik GB	Jaipur Thar Gramin Bank	Rajasthan	27.01.2006
18.	Punjab National Bank	Bhojpur Rohtas GB, Magadh GB, Nalanda GB, Patliputra GB	Madhya Bihar Gramin Bank	Bihar	10.02.2006
19.	Bank of Baroda	Raebareli KGB, Sultanpur KGB, Kanpur KGB, Allahabad KGB, Pratapgarh KGB, Fatehpur KGB, Faizabad KGB	Baroda Easter Uttar Pradesh Gramin Bank	Uttar Pradesh	23.02.2006
20.	Central Bank of India	Champaran KGB, Vaishali KGB, Madhubani KGB, Mithila KGB, Gopalganj KGB, Saran KGB, Siwan KGB	Uttar Bihar Kshetriya Gramin Bank	Bihar	01.03.2006
21.	Allahabad Bank	Bhagirath GB, Shravasti GB, Sarayn GB	Lucknow Kshetriya Gramin Bank	Uttar Pradesh	01.03.2006
22.	Allahabad Bank	Chattarasal GB, Tulsi GB, Vindhyavasini GB	Triveni Kshetriya Gramin Bank	Uttar Pradesh	01.03.2006
23.	Andhra Bank	Chaitanya GB, Godavari GB	Chaitanya Godavari Gramin Bank	Andhra Pradesh	01.03.2006
24.	State Bank of Hyderabad	Sri Saraswathi GB, Sri Sathavahana GB, Sri Rama GB, Golconda GB	Deccan Gramin Bank	Andhra Pradesh	24.03.2006
25.	Bank of Baroda	Bareilly KGB, Shahjahanpur KGB	Baroda Western Uttar Pradesh Gramin Bank	Uttar Pradesh	31.03.2006
26.	Bank of India	Dewas Shajapur KGB, Rajgarh Sehore KGB, Nimar KGB, Indore Ujjain KGB	Narmada Malwa Gramin Bank	Madhya Pradesh	03.04.2006
27.	State Bank of India	Kakathiya GB, Manjira GB, Nagarjuna GB, Sangameshwara GB, Sri Vishakha GB	Andhra Pradesh Gramin Vikas Bank	Andhra Pradesh	31.03.2006

Source: NABARD.

of profit-and-loss-making RRBs also. For example, UCO Bank sponsored Begusarai KGB, Bhagalpur Banka KGB, Munger KGB have been amalgamated to form the new Bihar Kshetriya Gramin Bank. While Begusarai KGB made profits in 2004, the other two were incurring losses. Similarly, in Rajasthan, the loss-making Marudhar KGB has been merged with the profit-making

Aravali KGB, Bundi Chittorgarh KGB, Bhilwara Ajmer KGB and Dungarpur Banswara KGB to form the Baroda Rajasthan Gramin Bank. Again in Maharashtra, Vidharbha Kshetriya Gramin Bank has been formed by merging the loss-making Akola Kshetriya GB with the profit-making Buldhana GB and Yavatmat Kashetriya GB of the Central Bank of India. In Bihar, under Central Bank of India's sponsorship, Champaran KGB, Vaishali KGB, Madhubani KGB, Mithila KGB, Gopalganj KGB, Saran KGB, Siwan KGB were merged to form Uttar Bihar Kshetriya Gramin Bank. Of the merged entities, only Gopalganj KGB and Siwan KGB earned profits in the year 2004 and the rest all incurred losses. Again 10 out of the 13 proposed amalgamations awaiting Central Government's ratification are among profit-making RRBs and in only three cases between profit-and-loss-making RRBs. Neither there has been any instance of merging of purely loss-making RRBs nor any contemplated till date.[7]

In the present amalgamation exercise, though broadly banking service earlier provided by the merged entites would be made available to the customers, there would be some rationlisation of branch network of the merged entities under the new dispensation. The success of the merged entity to a great extent would depend on their ability to expand business on a sustainable basis by providing better banking services. Enabling technology has greatly facilitated the scope for business growth, which the amalgamated units can adopt by taking advantage of the economies of scale, better administration and governance practices. A merger of RRBs is not only of their balance sheets but also more importantly it is the synthesis of different work culture, management practices and business strategies of the merged entities. In the limited sense of balance sheet strengthening, the merger of the RRBs that are making profits can be appreciated. The merger of profit-and-loss-making RRBs even in this limited sense raises certain apprehensions. Merger of profit-and-loss-making RRBs operating in a contiguous area has the possibility of bringing some rewards in terms of housekeeping, better administrative control, etc. But there is an equal possibility that the new entity becomes financially unviable, the inefficiencies are compounded and the merged entity falls under its own dead weight. The transition phase would be relatively more difficult to tide over in such cases. Further in the present milieu of restructuring and amalgamation the broader question still remains unanswered as to what would be the role of sponsor banks *vis-à-vis* the merged entities.

Studies on the role of sponsor banks indicate that the umbilical cord hypothesis holds for the RRBs (Misra, 2006; Malhotra, 2002). Misra (2006) demonstrates that the profit-making RRBs are able to reap the synergy from their association with the sponsor bank. The sponsor bank, however, is found to act, as a drag on the financial health of the loss-making RRBs. The literature (Malhotra, 2002 etc.) recognises a host of reasons for the drag. It could be due to competition for business rather than co-operation between the RRB and the sponsor bank, which are co-present in a particular geographical area. Else, it could simply be, because of the apathetic attitude of the sponsor bank towards the RRBs when it requires a supporting hand. Support could be in the form of advice on financial decisions, or meeting skill requirements of the RRBs or management of the affairs of the RRB. The loss-making RRBs need focused attention of all the stakeholders, in general, and of the sponsor bank, in particular, so as to transform them into profitable ventures. In view of the differential impact the sponsor banks have on the profit-and-loss-making RRBs, the merger of profit-and-loss-making RRBs can at best be seen as an experiment in reaping economies of scale, scope and size.

Based on the recommendations of the Narasimham Committee Report (1992), reforms were initiated in 1993 to turn around the failing RRBs. To enhance financial viability, a new set of prudential accounting norms of income recognition, asset classification, provisioning, and capital adequacy were implemented. RRBs were also required to make full provisioning for bulk of their non-performing assets. Furthermore, they were permitted to lend to non-target group borrowers up to 60 per cent of new loans beginning in 1993-94. Permission was also granted to introduce new services, such as loans for consumer durables. All these have led to a situation, where the RRBs are placed on an equal footing with the commercial banks with an additional restriction on their area of operation. The restriction in their area of operation can be seen as a challenge, which the RRBs are to tackle by developing an appropriate business model. In the pursuit of developing an appropriate business model, the merger of RRBs with the sponsor bank perhaps would not go against the 'spirit of setting up of RRBs as local entities and for providing credit primarily to weaker sections'. In that case, the ongoing merger of individual RRBs can be seen as an intermediate step to the subsequent merger of the new entites with their sponsor bank. The present-day RRBs might be treated as the rural finance branches of the concerned sponsored banks. In the ultimate analysis, if the present-day RRBs are integrated with their mainstream sponsorer commercial bank and identified as their 'rural finance' branches, this will involve a greater stake of the sponsor bank in reaching to the poor in the rural areas. The case for a vertical merger is stronger in cases where both profit-and-loss-making RRBs have been merged as the sponsor bank would be in a better position to absorb the financial burden of the loss-making RRBs.

The other option is to institutionalize certain changes in matters relating to the governance of the RRBs. First is the issue of the selection and tenure of chairman of the RRB. At present, the sponsor bank nominates the chairman of the RRB. Two directors in the board of the RRBs are also from the sponsor bank. In case the chairman and the directors do not belong to the same level of hierarchy in the sponsor bank, the independence of the institution of the chairman is severely constrained. Recognising this aspect, the Sardesai Committee notes, 'The Chairmen of most of the RRBs are from sponsor banks, which limits the freedom and decision making capacity of the RRBs'. Often the nomination as chairman of the RRB is perceived as an unwanted assignment and is a case of mismatch between the kind of person needed and the person who actually gets nominated. As the chairman of a RRB has a pivotal role to play in its functioning, the issue of nominating the chairman needs due attention. Seen in a broader perspective, there is a need to revisit the notion that the chairman of a RRB be nominated by the sponsor bank. Is it really the case that the majority shareholder appoints the chairman in a banking concern? If we see in practice, the Government of India holds majority shares of the nationalized banks, but the Chairman-cum-Managing Director (CMD) of the nationalised banks are selected from the banking sector through a due process of selection and the Central Government has allowed operational freedom to commercial banks. Selection through a due process rather than nomination perhaps will be a better approach to choose the chairman of a RRB. The Sardesai Committee's observations in this context are pertinent, 'As the Chairmen of RRBs are from the sponsor banks, there could be several potential areas of conflicts of interest. In this context, the process of appointment may be reexamined to explore the possibility of appointing a Chairman from the open market through a transparent process'.

The institution of RRBs has been in existence for nearly thirty years since their inception. Hence, there would be a pool of talent available in the RRB system itself. This pool of talent could be given an opportunity in the selection of the chairman. Further, as has been suggested by the Sardesai Committee, the composition of the Board of the RRBs may be Board broad-based through inducting professionals such as agricultural experts, bankers, management experts, etc., for strengthening the Boards of RRBs. Fixed tenure of the chairman and other key professionals posted in RRBs, say of 3-5 years, to ensure continuity in planning and execution of various policies was also suggested by the Sardesai Committee. As issues like selection of the chairman, induction of professionals in the Boards of the RRBs are of crucial importance in determining the performance of the RRBs, there is a need to statutorily incorporate them in the RRB Act.

Section V

Conclusion

Transformation in any structure is effected when it is subject to a sequel of transitions over time. Transitions in turn could be foresight-led or circumstances/crises-driven. The RRBs, which are in existence for around three decades in the Indian financial scene, have undergone a series of transitions over the last decade. The elements of transition were more an outcome of the forces of change that the banking system was subjected to since the onset of financial sector reforms in the early 1990s. Prudential norms for RRBs around mid-1990s is a case in point. Among other things, the single-most important concern of the RRBs from the early days of their inception was their financial viability. With RRBs progressively acquiring a measure of strength and resilience, the time is now apposite to move from 'crises-driven' reforms to 'consensus-driven' reforms to refashion RRBs as an integral element of the blueprint of banking development.

Merger of RRBs of a particular sponsor bank within a state has been initiated to improve the financial viability of RRBs. This merger is found both among profit-making RRBs and also between profit-and-loss-making RRBs. At the present juncture, it is difficult to hazard a guess on the impact of merger of profit-and-loss-making RRBs on financial viability and profitability. As RRBs over time have graduated to shoulder the role and responsibility of their sponsor banks, the option of merging the RRBs with their sponsor bank may be considered. Working as the 'rural finance' arm of the mainstream sponsor bank, the RRBs would have additional leverage to do better in expanding the reach of banking services to the poor. Pending vertical merger, there is an urgent need to address certain key governance issues like selection of its chairman and professionalism of the Board of RRBs. Resolution of these and other issues are necessary for the amalgamated RRB to meet the test of time and emerge as financially viable entities. To be sure, the issues involved may appear tricky and there may not seem to be any easy answer. But the full gamut of issues involved in resuscitation and resurgence of RRBs need to be carefully considered and coordinated and concerted measures taken with a sense of urgency to realize the goals of planning and economic development.

NOTES

1. Debate in the XV Lok Sabha on Regional Rural Bank (Amendment Bill, 2004).
2. RRBs alone have organised roughly 12 lakh self-help groups, 45 per cent of the total self-help groups in the country. RRBs have also issued over 40 lakh Kisan Credit Cards to the farmers and organised over 5,000, out of 11,000, farmers' clubs under NABARD scheme.
3. RRBs were established "with a view to developing the rural economy by providing, for the purpose of development of agriculture, trade, commerce, industry and other productive activities in the rural areas, credit and other facilities, particularly to small and marginal farmers, agricultural labourers, artisans and small entrepreneurs, and for matters connected therewith and incidental thereto" (RRBs Act, 1976).
4. Though the growth in credit when seen in isolation gives an impression of the impressive strides made by RRBs in disbursing credit, they account for a very small proportion (around 3 per cent) of the total assets of the Indian banking sector, despite their significant branch network.
5. While CD ratio for 50 RRBs was more than 60 per cent that for 87 banks was less than 40 per cent in March 2004.
6. Following the recommendations of the Narasimham Committee (1991), there have been gradual relaxations in their choice of clientele and area of operations.
7. Till date refers to 31st March 2006, unless specified otherwise.

REFERENCES

Akhavein, J.D., Berger, A.N., Humphrey, D.B. (1997): "The Effects of Megamergers on Efficiency and Prices: Evidence from a Bank Profit Function", *Finance and Economic Discussion Series 9*, Board of Governors of the Federal Reserve System.

Barth, J.R., Caprio, G., Levine, R. (2004): "Bank Supervision and Regulation: What Works Best?" *Journal of Financial Intermediation*, 13(2): 205-248.

Benston, George J., Hanweck, Gerald A. and Humphrey, David B. (1982): "Scale Economies in Banking", *Journal of Money, Credit, and Banking*, Vol. XIV, No. 4, Part 1, Nov.

Bhatt, Nitin and Y.S.P., Thorat (2004): "India's Regional Rural Banks: The Institutional Dimension of Reforms", *National Bank News Review, NABARD*, April-September.

Bose, Sukanya (2005): "Regional Rural Banks: The Past and the Present Debate", *Macro Scan*, URL: http://www.macroscan.com/fet/jul05/ fet200705RRB_Debate.htm.

Consideration of the Regional Rural Banks (Amendment) Bill, 2004, *Proceedings Other Than Questions and Answers (XIV Lok Sabha).*

Das, Prasant (2000): "Sustainability through Outreach: The Maiabar Lighthouse Shows the Way", *National Seminar on Best Practices in RRBs*, February 2000, Lucknow: BIRD.

Joshi, V.C. and Joshi, V.V. (2002): "Managing Indian Banks", *Response Books*, New Delhi.

Kannan, R. (2004): "Regional Rural Banks", Available from http:// www.geocities.com/kstability/learning/banking2/rrb.html

Malhotra, Rakesh (2002): "Performance of India's Regional Rural Banks (RRBs): Effect of the Umbilical Cord". Website: http://www.alternative-finance.org.uk/rtf/rrbsmalhotra.rtf.

Misra, Biswa Swarup (2006): "Performance of RRBs in India: Has Past Anything to Suggest for Future?", Compendium of Papers, Bankers' Conference.

Mohan Jagan (Mar 19, 2004): "Regional Rural Banks Need a Shot in the Arm", *Financial Daily* from The Hindu Group of Publications.

Reddy, Y.V. (2000): "Future of Rural Banking" Address at Prof. G. Rama Reddy's Third Endowment Lecture, Hyderabad, *Reserve Bank of India Bulletin*, January.

Reddy, Y.V. (2000): "Rural Credit: Status and Agenda", *Reserve Bank of India Bulletin*, November.

Report on Trends and Progress of Banking in India (Various Issues), *Reserve Bank of India*, Mumbai. Website www.rbi.org.in

Reserve Bank of India (June 2004): *Report of the Advisory Committee on Flow of Credit to Agriculture and Related Activities From the Banking System.*

Reserve Bank of India (2005): *Report of the Internal Working Group on RRBs*, Chairman: A.V. Sardesai, Mumbai. Website *www.rbi.org.in*

Reserve Bank of India (2002), *Annual Accounts of Scheduled Commercial Banks in India (1989—2001)*, Mumbai. Website www.rbi.org.in

Revell, J. (1979): "Inflation and Financial Institutions", *Financial Times*, London.

Sharma, K.C., Josh, P., Mishra, J.C., Kumar, Sanjay, Amalorpavanathan, R. and Bhaskran, R. (2001): "Recovery Management in Rural Credit", *Occasional Paper No. 21*, *NABARD*, Mumbai.

Statistical Tables Relating to Banks in India (various issues), Reserve Bank of India, Mumbai. Web Site www.rbi.org.in

Thingalaya, N.K. (2000): "The Other Side of the Rural Banking", *BIRD*, Lucknow.

Velayudham, T.K. and Sankaranarayanan, V. (1990): "Regional Rural Banks and Rural Credit: Some Issues", *Economic and Political Weekly* (September 22), 2157-64.

Marketing in Banks

M. Santhana Gopalan

1. Introduction

In recent years, there has been a greater awareness in the Indian Banking industry of the need for marketing of products. This process of a sharper thrust on marketing has gained momentum with the increasing adaptation by banks to information technology related products. Every bank, big or small, public sector or private sector or foreign, is marketing its services to customers by evolving new financial products and adopting new strategies. But, were the banks in India so market savvy before the 1990s? Or, for that matter, was marketing such a prominent topic for discussion among bankers on such a mass scale then, as it is now?

The reasons are very much there to be seen. The period between the year 1969 and the 1990 was predominantly a period of development banking. Spurred by the well-known socio-economic objectives of nationalization, the public sector banks went in for phenomenal branch expansion during the seventies to cover practically all parts of the country. Regulated interest rate and directed lending ruled the roost. Thus, the banker of this period never thought or found it necessary to ascertain the needs and requirements of the customer. Since there was a level playing field and the competitors functioned in similar environment, the banker, at his best adopted a "selling" stance. He pushed his range of banking products hard enough among the customers in order to achieve the predetermined levels of deposits and advances fixed. This being the environment, the scope for marketing was limited to conventional marketing tools like market segmentation, advertisements in the print media, etc.

With the advent of economic liberalization since the mid-1991, the financial sector in general and the banking sector in particular underwent a remarkable transformation. New private sector banks with greater technology orientation have emerged. Automation of banking operations gained in importance. Competition in the market has increased. The public sector banks also embarked on computerization of branches, networking of branch operations, introduction of new services such as Automated Teller Machines (ATMs), Telebanking Services, Internet Banking, Internet and SMS Purchases, Real Time Payment and Settlement Systems, Online Trading in Shares/ Securities and so on. Customer retention and more so, attracting and retaining high networth customer has come to occupy the center stage of banking environment.

During the same period, the software industry in India also began to grow culminating in the increase in purchasing power of the *bourgeoisie* class. The banks, which were largely averse to retail lending, started retail lending in a big way in view of the demonstrated latent potential of retail banking in India. This prompted banks to veer to segmentation banking from mass banking and further to customer specific business. Further, Banks started focusing not only on retaining High Networth Customers but also began concentrating on acquiring the neo-rich High Networth Individual Customers.

With its emphasis on **Customer Centricity** to entire banking operations, the bank marketing concept has provided a way out in the form of a host of new banking services and instruments. Such instruments have emerged during the last decade. The query a banker used to ask himself was: If the bank customer does not want our usual banking services, what does he want? The evolution of reply to this question has resulted in the emergence of marketing of financial products/services in banks as the principal survival strategy for banks has been confronted with an accelerating pace of disintermediation. In other words, in order to attract valuable customers, the banks began to give more emphasis on marketing of financial services. For instance, the new generation Private Sector Banks like ICICI Bank and HDFC Bank introduced the model of Direct Selling Agents (DSAs) as a market penetration strategy

The following flow chart provides the evolution of marketing in banks in India:

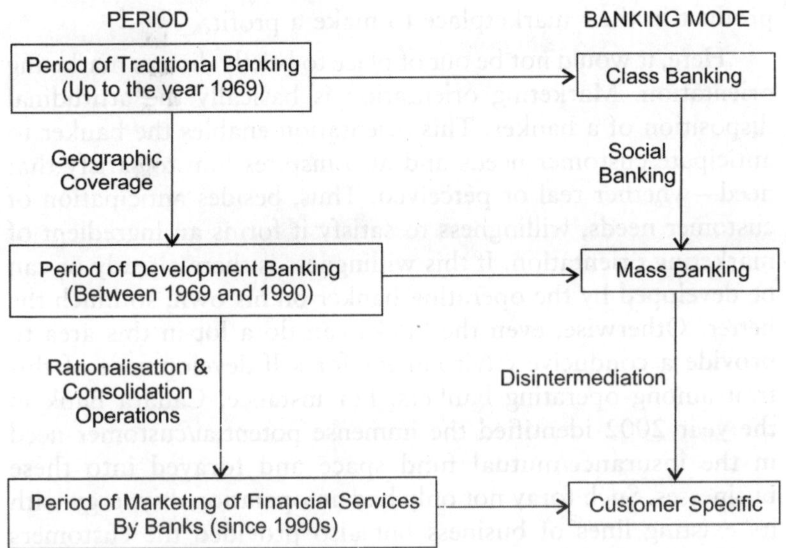

2. Marketing—The Concept

Marketing is an overused, but often misused term. To be sure, promotion or selling, is an integral part of marketing. But marketing is much more than mere promotion and selling of goods/services and brings into focus the orientation of the organization—and therefore of all the people in it—to its internal and external relationships. While the basic components of marketing concept are (a) identifying customer needs, (b) managing delivery to customer, and (c) achieving customer satisfaction, the basic components of selling are (a) designing the product (b) managing delivery to customer, and (c) maximizing the profit from product. Thus, the differences between marketing and selling concepts are quite fundamental in nature.

The balance of power has shifted to the market with alarming pace. The nature of demand, the multiplicity of choice, the rise of affluence and the availability of information have all contributed to this paradigm shift. To be in the market, marketing is the *sine qua non*. Marketing is more so an attitude; it is the ability to stand back and take an objective look, enhanced by both experience and vision at what has to be done to the product in their marketplace to make a profit.

Here, it would not be out of place to briefly discuss marketing orientation. Marketing orientation is basically the attitudinal disposition of a banker. This orientation enables the banker to anticipate customer needs and also inspires him to satisfy that need—whether real or perceived. Thus, besides anticipation of customer needs, willingness to satisfy it forms an ingredient of marketing orientation. If this willingness is there already or can be developed by the operating banker on his own, so much the better. Otherwise, even the banks can do a lot in this area to provide a conducive environment for self-development of this trait among operating bankers. For instance, Canara Bank in the year 2002 identified the immense potential/customer need in the insurance/mutual fund space and forayed into these businesses. Such foray not only had an operational synergy with its existing lines of business but also provided the customers with wider array of choice of financial services under a single roof.

3. Features of Financial Products/Services

The marketing concept is applicable to both marketing of products and services. Since banks are part of service industry and carry out marketing of financial services, there are certain special features such as:

Intangibility: Services are intangible, it is impossible for customers to sample—taste, feel, see, hear or smell—a service before they buy it. Consequently, a company's promotional programme must portray the *benefits* to be derived from the service, rather than emphasizing the service itself. Four promotional strategies that may be used to suggest service benefits are:

- **Visualization:** For example, apart from usual features of a term deposit like the amount of deposit, rate of interest, period of deposit, the term deposit receipt should also portray the annual yield from the deposit. This would facilitate the customer to know the actual income that he is entitled to.
- **Association:** Connect the service with a tangible good, person, object, or place. For instance, Bank of Baroda has linked its services to Rahul Dravid who is the Brand Ambassador to the Bank.
- **Physical representation:** ICICI Bank uses color—gold, platinum or silver—for its credit card services to symbolize wealth and prestige.
- **Documentation:** Canara Bank cite facts and figures in their business advertisements to substantiate claims of dependability, performance and growth.

Inseparability: Services typically cannot be separated from the creator-seller of the service. For example, service quality at the counter of a Banks' branch/ATMs/marketing staff is all pervading and entails the entire range of products/services since it attracts more of Word of Mouth (WoM) Marketing.

From a marketing standpoint, inseparability frequently means that direct sale is the only possible channel of distribution, and an individual seller's services cannot be sold in diverse markets. This feature limits the scale of operation in a services firm. One person can put through only limited clearing transactions in a day or pay cash (Quantum-wise and number of payment) only to so many customers.

As an exception to the inseparability feature, services may be sold by a person, who represents the creator-seller, for instance, the use of Direct Selling Agents by ICICI Bank in selling the products of that bank.

Heterogeneity: It is impossible for a service industry, or even an individual seller of services, to standardize output. Each "unit" of the service is somewhat different from other "units" of the same service. Service Quality in a bank is incumbent upon the nature of products/services, the location where the service is rendered, the people rendering the service and the people to whom the service is rendered.

Banks should therefore pay special attention to the product-planning stage of their marketing programs. Management must do all it can to ensure consistency of service quality from the beginning and to consistently maintain high levels of service quality.

Perishability and Fluctuating Demand: Services are highly perishable, and they cannot be stored. For instance, cash held above the standard cash limit only increases the cost and would reduce the profitability of banking business.

There are exceptions to this generalization regarding the perishability and storage of services. For instance, if the cash held over and above the standard cash limit could be used for a far higher remunerative business purpose in a short period of time then the excess cash holding would mean storage of services.

Marketing Strategies for Different Service Features

Characteristic	Marketing Response
Intangibility	Provide tangibility through Physical appearance of the facility Furnishings Employee uniforms Logo Websites Packaging Advertising
Perishability	Adjust pricing to influence demand Capacity management: adjusting services to match demand
Variability	Gap analysis for identifying gaps in quality employee empowerment Improving service delivery processes Service guarantees
Inseparability	Employee training Disintermediation

4. Management of Service Quality

Quality is about exceeding Expectation: Quality service ensures that customers are satisfied with what they have paid for. However, satisfaction is a relative term since the service recipient compares the current experience to some prior set of expectations. Further, what may seem like excellent service to one customer may be mediocre to another customer. Thus, a bank has to identify customer expectations and work hard to exceed them. Aspects like 'Customer Delight' and exceeding of customer expectations require painstaking efforts on the part of the bank. The employees, who have the highest impact on the service perceptions, are those working at the counters of the branch of a bank. This makes it more important for management to engage in **internal marketing** in which efforts are made to sell the firm's own employees on the idea that they work for a superior company of which they can be proud of. For instance, the **family concept adopted by Canara Bank propelled the pride of the employees** to perform at a higher plane.

Address Service Quality Dimensions: The inseparability feature of services means that a service is not produced until the time it is consumed. Thus, it is difficult to make a pre-purchase evaluation of quality of service. Thus, marketing of service requires creative ways to illustrate the benefits of the specific service. These include:

- **Search qualities:** Those features of a product that the customer can examine prior to purchase. For instance, the premium Current Account introduced by some banks facilitates a customer to search for value added facilities the product provides *vis-à-vis* the regular current account.
- **Experience qualities:** These are product/service features that customers can determine during or after consumption. For instance, the remittance of funds using the RTGS system in banks, enables the customer to assess the service quality through his experience of the services under RTGS system.
- **Credence qualities:** These are attributes that are difficult to be evaluated even after experiencing them. For instance, the ATM services by different banks are difficult to be evaluated unless and until the value added services are factored into the evaluation.

In all, the attitude of a banker becomes a major component in marketing of financial services. Thus, the banker would have to work from ***within*** the market. This may sound simplistic. But this strategy has strong theoretical underpinnings in the writings of influential management gurus like Peter Drucker, Micheal Porter, Tom Peters and Kotler himself. It has been persuasively argued that companies have to work from the market *in,* rather from the company *out,* in devising strategies.

Evaluation of Service Quality: Researchers Parsuraman, Zeithamal and Berry have developed the SERVQUAL instrument, which defines five generic dimensions along which customers evaluate service quality. These are:

- **Reliability:** The ability to perform the promised service accurately and dependably. For instance, carrying out of the standing instructions promptly by banks.
- **Responsiveness:** Willingness to help the customers and provide prompt service. For instance, the "May I Help You" counter at bank branches provides not only assistance to the customers in respect of business but also guides them with certain financial advices.
- **Assurance:** Knowledge and courtesy of employees and their ability to inspire trust and confidence.
- **Empathy:** Caring and individualized attention that a bank provides to its customers. For instance, the personal banking branch of a bank provides individualized attention.
- **Tangibility:** The appearance of the physical facilities, equipment, personal and communication materials.

5. Measuring Service Quality

Customer experience of a service is crucial to determining future patronage. Hence, measuring the positive and negative service experience of a customer is essential to the service industry including banking services. For this purpose, it is essential that customer responses are collected through following research methodologies:

- General survey of customers.
- Specific product/service oriented survey.

- Segment-wise customer survey.
- Assessment through "mystery shopper" method (where from agency/research units acts as shopper).
- Locating the "lost customer" and obtaining their responses.
- Adopting the Critical Incident Technique (the bank collects and closely analyzes specific customer complaints).

Then, the product/service gap is identified and a gap analysis is carried out.

Gap Analysis: It is a measurement tool used to gauge the difference between the customer's expectation of service quality and what actually occurred. A flow chart depicting the various gaps is provided below:

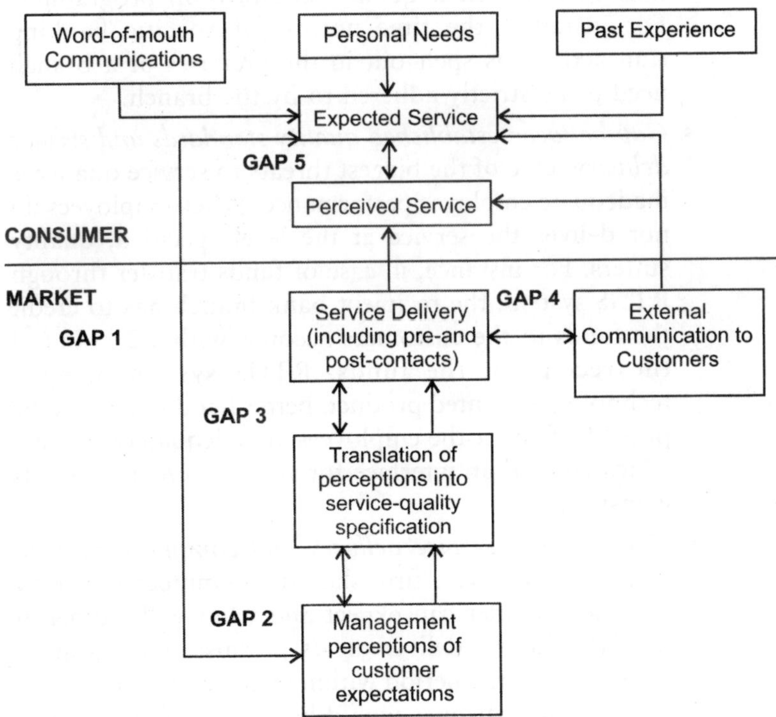

A bank can improve upon its services by identifying the specific places in the service system where there is a wide gap between what is expected and what is provided. Some major gaps include:

- *Gap between consumer expectations and management perceptions.* A major quality gap occurs when a firm's management does not understand what its customer's expectations are owing to the operations orientation of the firm rather than customer orientation. For example, closure of business by a bank by 2.00 PM to carry out the closure of books for the day even though it is not convenient for customers who want to carry out their banking transactions during their lunch hour.
- *Gap between management perception and quality standards set by the bank.* Quality suffers when a bank fails to establish a quality specification programme. For instance, the time norms for specific banking transactions as spelt out in the premises of a branch need to be strictly adhered to by the branch.
- *Gap between established quality standards and service delivery.* One of the biggest threats to service quality is inadequate employee performance. When employees do not deliver the service at the level specified, quality suffers. For instance, in case of funds transfer through RTGS system, the recipient bank branch has to credit the funds to the customers account within 2 hours of the receipt of the funds. RTGS system being a technology-oriented product, better handling would be possible if either the employees are adequately trained/ educated or if an interface for systemic credit of funds is installed.
- *Gap between service delivery and communication to customer.* A service firm should communicate exactly what a customer can expect and what will happen if the firm doesn't deliver on its promise. For instance, banks specify the period within which credit of amount of outstation cheques would be made and if the same

does not take place within the specified time, interest on the amount of the cheque for the days of delay is paid to the customer.

- *Gap between expected service and perceived service.* Sometimes customers perceive the quality of the service differently from that expected. Thus, even when communications accurately describe what service quality is provided and can be expected, customers are less than satisfied. For instance, high yielding deposit scheme of a bank with a lock-in-period is perceived differently by the customer on account of the lock-in-period.

6. The Importance of Relationship Marketing in Services

It will not be out of place to bring into focus the relevance of **Relationship Marketing** in services. The reality of many services being rendered on an ongoing or periodic basis coupled with the reality of customers forming relationship with people rather than goods paves the way for relationship marketing. Repeated contact between customers and service providers facilitates relationship marketing. Moreover, products intangibility often requires reselling efforts. As Levitt (1981) has noted:

> The most important thing to know about intangible products is that the customers usually don't know what they're getting until they don't get it. Only then do they become aware of what they have bargained for; only on dissatisfaction do they dwell ... in keeping customers for intangibles, it becomes important regularly to remind and show them what they're getting so that occasional failures fade in relative importance.

The core subject as the services marketing field has developed—service quality—also has stimulated interest in relationship marketing. The object of improving service quality, after all, is to engender customer loyalty. A natural extension of the strong interest in service quality is growing interest in relationship marketing. Effective relationship marketing should help a company capitalize on its investment in service improvement thereby bringing down the defection rate.

Reichheld and Sasser (1990) have demonstrated across a variety of service industries that profits climb steeply when a company successfully lowers its customer defection rate. Based on the analysis of more than 100 companies in two dozen industries, these researchers found that the firms could improve profits from 25 per cent to 85 per cent by reducing customer defections by just 5 per cent. Not only do loyal customers generate more revenue for more years, the costs to maintain existing customers frequently are lower than the costs to acquire new customers. An analysis of a credit card company showed that lowering the defection rate from 20 per cent to 10 per cent doubled the longevity of the average customer's relationship from 5 years to 10 and more than doubled the net preset value of the cumulative profit streams for this customer from $135 to $300.

The relationship between a bank and a customer occurs over a time interval that may encompass one or more exchanges. However, even if the interval includes a single transaction, the exchange relationship often extends beyond the time of actual transaction. Because the exchange involves psychological/social resources as well as economic resources, the duration of the relationship includes the various stages of the selling process—prior to a particular transaction (e.g., payment of cash for purchase of Demand Draft), during the transaction (e.g., purchase of the Demand Draft) or afterwards (e.g., up to payment of the Demand Draft). In exchanges, the relationship can include regular or intermittent transactions (e.g., standing instructions for periodical funds transfer) or continuous transactions (e.g., transactions in current account of a firm/company). The figure below provides a hypothetical illustration of the sequential stages of a relationship-building process that happens over time between the customer and the bank.

Typical Stages in the Relationship Marketing Process

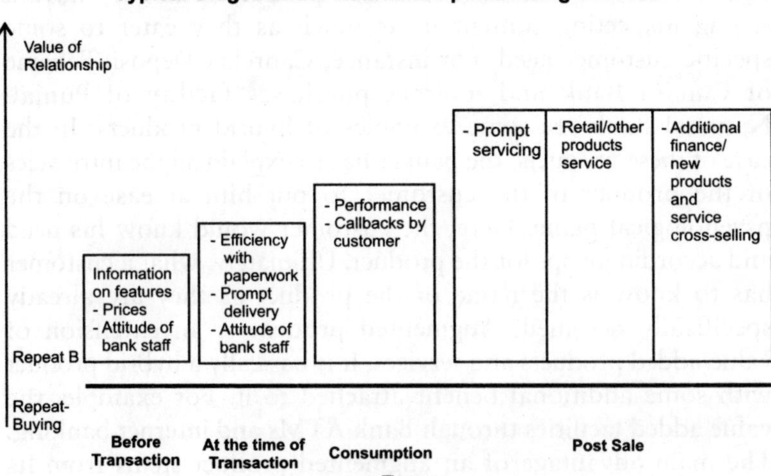

7. Components of Marketing: The Hinge

The traditional marketing approach hinges upon 4Ps, i.e., Product, Promotion, Price and Place. Considering the unique characteristics of services, Booms and Bitner suggested 3 additional Ps, i.e., People, Physical Evidence and Processes. The prevalent practices of the banks in India in marketing of financial services are also touched upon.

(A) Product

Financial products of banks can be segregated into basic products, hybrid products, augmented products. **Basic products** are essentially those products which define what kind of business we are in. For instance, some basic products of a bank are current account, savings bank, term deposit, recurring deposit, cash credit, term loan, overdraft, draft and funds transfer. These products define the business of commercial banking and they do not necessarily have a strong marketing content. Strong marketing content would mean that the product must be specifically designed keeping in view the needs of the customer in a well-defined market segment. Since basic products are the main tools of commercial banking, their marketing content cannot be rated very high. **Hybrid products** are usually a combination of two or more basic products and they have a strong marketing content in as much as they cater to some specific customer need. For instance, Canrelax Deposit Scheme of Canara Bank and internet purchases facility of Punjab National Bank are some examples of hybrid products. In the case of these products, the banker has to explain all the intricacies of the product to the customer to put him at ease on the psychological plane. Here, the customer would know his need and accordingly opt for the product. Ultimately, what a customer has to know is the name of the product as they are already specifically designed. **Augmented product** is an extension of value-added products and services. It is basically a hybrid product with some additional benefit attached to it. For example, the value added facilities through Bank ATMs and internet banking. The main advantage of an augmented product stems from its strong marketing content. The augmented product is made out of the hybrid product which itself has a strong marketing content.

In order to cater to vast customer base and also to face the increased competition, the banks in India have since the mid-1990s introduced new products/services such as Automated Teller Machines (ATMs), Anywhere Banking, Internet Banking, Telebanking, Debit Cards, online trading and so on. While enabling the banks to serve its huge client base they have also been used as talking points in the market place. Further, the new products have the following advantages:

- The technical requirements of each market can be built into the product from the outset.
- The market positioning can be planned in advance, therefore avoiding many harmonization problems over distribution channels.
- Organizational attitudes do not have a chance to harden around products.

Financial products fall along various points in the tangibility spectrum. Tangibles like physical facilities and electronic gadgets can be used to deliver perceptions of value of the intangibles, i.e. branch environment and credit card "store" credit. The tangibles provide the perception to the customer about the quality of service rendered. Service quality can be defined as the perception of the actual service quality (P) less the expectation of customer (E).

SERVICE QUALITY = P—E

The key for service quality is to exceed expectations. This obviously means that a bank needs to be able to measure the expectations of the customer.

The customer judges the service quality through the following aspects:

- **Competence:** Possession of requisite skills and knowledge by the banker about the product and the market.
- **Courtesy:** The qualities of politeness, respect, consideration and friendliness of the banker.
- Credibility: The trustworthiness and integrity of the banker.
- **Security:** Freedom and risk or doubt in the banker.

(B) Promotion

Marketing Communication is the instrument by which firms attempt to inform, persuade and remind its target market, using both direct and indirect means, of the products/services they sell as well as about the company as a whole. Although communications directed to target markets are the mainstay of the communications program, firms need to communicate with all its stakeholders (customers, shareholders, regulators, suppliers, channel partners, employees and government agencies). Firms develop specific communication plans directed towards the stakeholders.

Integrated Marketing Communications (IMC) is the careful coordination of all communications for a product/service to ensure consistency of messages at every contact point. The strategies behind marketing communication programs have changed dramatically over the years. Firms have learnt that emphasizing IMC, rather than treating each element in isolation amplifies the message intended for the target market. IMC therefore is a "force multiplier."

Thus, the key pillars of a firm's communication plans are:

- The target market for whom the message is intended.
- The communication objectives of the campaign.

The advent of technology has today opened up multifarious communication channels, which are capable of customization and are also cost effective considering the ever escalating airtime charges of television/radio. The flow chart below provides the numerous advertisement medium available.

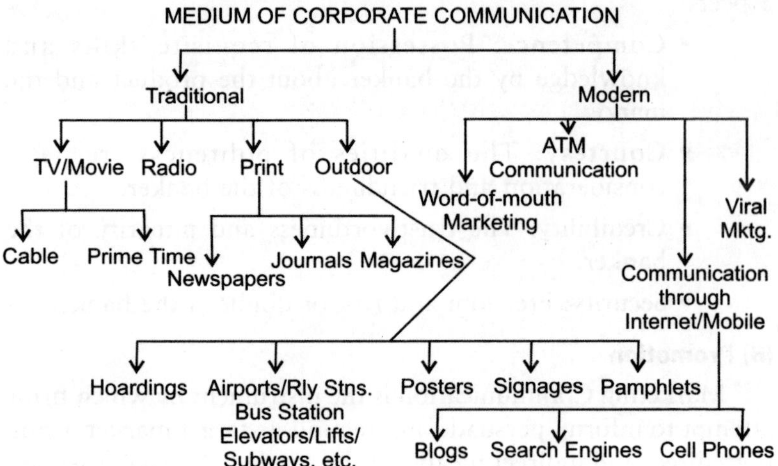

(C) Pricing

With the deregulation of the financial sector, the banking industry in particular has been freed from the shackles of administered price structure. Now pricing is fast becoming a strategic tool for bankers as never before. With the database on price sensitivity and cost-benefit orientation, banks have to adjust themselves to market realities. Asset-Liability management as a tool of strategic planning is being used in a big way. The revision in interest rates on deposits and the reduction in the Prime Lending Rate by various banks are an eye-opener to this phenomenon. Banks are now consciously considering the generation of income from fee based services. At the time of introducing new products generally various banks adopt various pricing models. Revenue generation through product is worked out as a product of total market, the market share and the yield.

Revenue generation = Total market × market share × market yield.

In order to face competition and overcome it, the pricing is done taking into account the volume aspects.

(D) Place

With the branch licensing policy being annulled after the recommendations of the Narasimham Committee Report on the Financial System (1991), banks are now been given greater freedom to open branches. Banks have for quite sometime gone in for extension counters, satellite branches, mobile branches, specialized branches besides the normal branches.

With the advent of information technology in the banking arena, banks have forayed into new areas such as installation of ATMs, Online Trading and the concept of Home banking, customer terminals and so on. Information Kiosks, Internet banking are also gaining grounds. The emphasis and the adoption of Core Banking Solution, Structured Financial Messaging System (SFMS), the National Electronic Funds Transfer (NEFT) system and Real Time Gross Settlement (RTGS) system would usher in metamorphic change in the operations of the banks in general and PSBs in particular. While the introduction of Core Banking Solution, RTGS and SFMS would make the Indian Banking System, particularly the PSBs, more techno-savvy along with associated operational risks, there would be substantial human capital. Such human capital could be effectively redeployed into marketing the financial products for achieving market niche structure. Further, the adoption of Outsourcing Policy and the Doorstep Banking Scheme could possibly change the banking business model in the days ahead.

(E) People

In a service industry, people both within (stakeholders and the stockholders) and without (customers and public at large) matter the most. For a bank, the perception of the public in general and the satisfaction of the customers, in particular, through service quality rendered by the employees of the Bank is the crux. In other words, brand image gets created based on this perception of service quality.

(F) Physical Evidence

Financial firms should tangibilise the intangible aspects of the financial service by providing physical evidence of the service quality outcome. The elements of the physical evidence are:

- The physical location of the service.
- Office layout and ambience.
- Employee uniforms and nametags for key service employees.
- A formal and routine way of greeting the customers.
- Signages within the service locations, so that customers know which counter to approach.
- Comfortable waiting areas which alleviates the distress of customers in case of delay
- External signages that identify the service location should be well maintained.

(G) Processes

The process of marketing of financial services can be assessed through the following critical concepts:

- Developing the strategic framework.
- Carrying out a market audit.
- Competitive analysis.

Developing a strategic framework: Banks have for long adhered to a formal approach to long-term planning. However, it is now felt that translating the corporate mission into a coherent strategic framework is more important. In other words, the long range plan (Five-Year Plans) made up of figures/numbers are carefully being replaced by more "goal-oriented" plans like "We have to be the highest profit making bank in India". This is mainly due to the visible change in the market place.

Here it would not be inappropriate to refer to the assertion of Tom Peters (Drucker *et al.*, 1990):

> Over the years we have developed a style of doing business that is detached, calculating, dispassionate, analytical, methodological, dull and hard. My own hypothesis about tomorrow's survivors is that they will be fast, intuitive, opportunistic, hustling, caring, trusting, empathizing, cheer leading, emotional, mistake making and action taking.

The major objective to frame marketing strategies is to increase profit. Several main principles must be followed to reach the objective:

- Select the markets that are growing and select the market for growing, look at demographics, customer attitudes and lifestyles.
- Aim for market share, not just through prices and products but through people also.
- Increase market.
- Recruit people with the right values, train them and motivate them.
- Get the cost base down, through an intelligent and integrated use of information technology.

Carrying out a marketing audit: A marketing audit should be carried out within the context of the overall strategic investigation. According to Kotler, marketing audit is a comprehensive, systematic, independent and periodic examination of a company's marketing environment, objectives, strategies and activities with a view to determining problem areas and opportunities and recommending a plan of action to improve a company's marketing performance.

While the significance of marketing audit is universally acknowledged, marketing audit is hampered by the following problems:

- Insufficient knowledge of customer's behavior and attitudes.
- Failure to segment the market in the most advantageous way. Lack of marketing planning process.
- Lack of a marketing planning process.

- Price-cutting rather than improvements in value.
- Misunderstanding the bank's marketing strengths and how they relate to the market.
- Organizational structure incompatible with the marketing strategy.
- Failure to invest for future development, particularly in the area of human resources.

These problems if addressed to would render a bank more healthy.

Competitive analysis: Competitive analysis should be at the heart of strategic planning, since acquiring and retaining competitive advantage over rivals is what ensures survival. But the concept of competitive advantage is not straightforward and banks have to assess carefully both the actual and potential forces surrounding them. For instance, the new generation private banks, which are techno-savvy, are able to grab more high networth customers from the public sector banks based on the speed of delivery. However, this situation might not persist for long as the public sector banks have started reducing their workforce through voluntary retirement scheme and are also equipping themselves with technology. This is reflected by the fact that State Bank of India is now increasingly capturing the credit card market, which was earlier led by foreign banks and new private sector banks.

Further, the Indian banks are also going in a big way for ISO certification, which could be effectively used as a talking point by them in the market place.

8. Marketing Strategies for the Future

The future strategies in respect of marketing of financial services by banks will concentrate on what is uncommon and unique to each bank. Banks will have to create a strong brand equity for themselves. Creation of such brand equity would enable the services of banks to be marketed with greater ease. Towards this end, the basic characteristics of intangibility, inseparability, heterogeneity and variability of financial services have to be focused upon. To sum up, the marketing strategies are to be conceived by addressing the following:

Understanding the Market	Understanding the Customer
1. Size by turnover and by profits	1. Define the existing customer
2. Competitors by turnover and by profits	2. Define the potential customer
3. Customer type by category and size	3. Service/product type buying criteria
4. Geography by units and potential	4. Sales and lost sales opportunity analysis
5. Segmentation by turnover and by profits	
6. Influence of technology and innovation	

Understanding the Competitor	Understanding the Products
1. Define characteristics & sales procedure	1. Our Services/product categories
2. Service/products offered	2. Competing Services/Products
3. Product strategies and who their customers are	3. Product life cycle
4. Promotional tactics and marketing strength	4. Product promotion to enhance its life/ improve business
5. Technological strengths	5. Costs involved
6. Sales strength and financial strengths	

A comprehensive marketing strategy based on an interplay of these four basic elements would help banks to consolidate their entire existing product/service spectrum as also to enter the market for new products.

REFERENCES

Bhattacharya C.B. and Ruth N. Bolton. Relationship Marketing in Mass Markets in Sheth Jagdish N. and Atul Parvtiyar, *Handbook of Relationship Management* (2002), Response Books, Sage Publication, 331-332.

Lewitt. T. (1981). *Marketing Intangible Products and Product Intangibles.* Harvard Business Review, 59(5), 94-102 in Sheth Jagdish N. and Atul Parvtiyar, *Handbook of Relationship Management* (2002), Response Books, Sage Publication, 151.

Parasuraman, A., Berry L.L., and Zeithamal, V.A., (1991). *Understanding the Customer Expectations of Service.* Sloan Management Review, 32(3), 39-48 in Nandita Dalal, Marketing Management (2006), A publication of Symbiosis Centre of Distance Lerning, Pune.

Reichheld, F.F. (1993) and Sasser, W.E., Jr. (1990). *Zero Defections: Quality Comes to Services.* Harvard Business Review, 69(1), 105-111 in Sheth Jagdish N. and Atul Parvtiyar, *Handbook of Relationship Management* (2002), Response Books, Sage Publication, 152.

Solomon Michael R. and Elnora W. Stuart. *Marketing—Real People, Real Choices* (2003), Pearson Education (Singapore) Pte. Ltd., 351-64.

Stanton William J., Michael J. Etzel and Bruce J. Walker. *Fundamentals of Marketing* (1994), McGraw-Hill Book Co. Singapore, 537-41.

Housing Finance in India: Issues and Priorities

14

Atanu K. Das

Housing policy fails under all types of governments and economic systems, in general, for the same reason: a tendency to treat the housing sector as a social welfare issue rather than a viable economic sector... The important role public investment in residential infrastructure plays in stimulating private investment has been largely ignored, and property rights have remained fuzzy in a financial climate that does little to foster the much needed long-term housing investment.

Stephen K. Mayo made this assertion almost one and half decades back in one of his articles in 'Finance and Development'. Probably this assertion requires a revisit today, especially, in the Indian context, with 'housing' having emerged as one of potential growth drivers in the economy. A slew of initiatives at the government, regulatory and institutional levels make housing as one of the most promising segments. This paper examines the varied dimensions of the vibrant housing market in India and measures to mitigate possible downside risks.

Housing Finance in the Development Paradigm

Housing constitutes an integral component of the socio-economic development of a country because of its criticality in terms of developmental policy initiatives and interventions. This is reflected in the sustained efforts of the Government to improve housing and habitat conditions through appropriate financial allocations in the successive Five Year Plans and a spate of fiscal measures from time to time.

Institutional financial market in serving the housing sector has deepened and widened considerably, spreading to different segments of the population. Financial institutions themselves have recognized the good value proposition in funding the housing sector in an increasing manner. The housing sector has been progressively becoming market driven, thanks to the growing number of players, increased competition and the huge demand supply lag. Affordability of the housing has also increased manifold over the years, with rising income levels and the emergence of a strong and vibrant middle class segment. The McKinsey Global Institute has recently estimated that if India continues to maintain the current growth trajectory, its income levels are slated to triple and its consumer market expected to be the fifth largest by 2025. The study reveals that the big urban middle class will comprise "seekers" (annual income of Rs. 2,00,000 to Rs. 5,00,000—lower middle class) and "strivers" (annual income of Rs. 5,00,000 to Rs. 10,00,000—upper middle class). It also indicates that the middle class will control 58% of total income and will account for about 41% of the population by 2025. Such a scenario holds a lot of promise for the housing finance sector to contribute increasingly to the economic growth process through various linkage effects.

Investment in Housing and construction triggers a series of investments in various other sectors. From Heavy Industries like Steel, Cement to industries like Paint, Furniture and even to Small Scale Industries, Housing affects as many as 269 industries directly and indirectly. Housing also ranks third amongst 14 major industries in terms of total linkage effects in the Economy. In terms of contribution to the GDP, as per research findings, for every rupee invested in Housing and construction, 78 paisa gets added to the GDP. Housing ranks fourth in terms of the multiplier effect on the economy, ahead of sectors like transport and agriculture.

Profile of Indian Housing Sector

Housing ranks next only to food and clothing amongst basic human needs. Integrated housing development not only satisfies the basic human needs but also facilitates holistic development within the parameters of a planned welfare economy. Safe, secure and affordable housing by any means increases employment and educational opportunities for individuals and enriches communities leading to a better civil society and better quality of life. Besides, the direct contribution which housing makes to GDP, it increases social capital. Social capital is intelligible wealth that comes with good social network with clean environment, hygienic living and quality housing.

Table 1: Population, Housing and Households Situation *(in million)*

	Population		Census Houses		No. of Households	
	1991	2001	1991	2001	1991	2001
Rural	628.7	742 (18.0%)	142.98	177.54 (24.2%)	111.54	138.27 (20.7%)
Urban	217.6	285 (31.0%)	52.04	71.56 (37.5%)	39.49	53.69 (36.0%)
Total	846.3	1027 (21.4%)	195.02	249.10 (27.7%)	151.03	191.96 (27.1%)

The figures in bracket indicate decadal growth (Source: Census of India, 2001).

India, with its billion plus population, still witnesses an acute shortage of dwelling units. Despite sharp increase in the Usable Housing Stock from 70 million units in 1961 to 178 million units in 2001, the shortfall in 2001 was estimated at 40 million dwelling units (Table 1). The shortfall in dwelling units occurred due to the high population growth, especially in urban areas. Studies reveal that the population in the five most populous cities of India, namely Mumbai, Kolkata, New Delhi, Chennai and Hyderabad are set to increase at a scorching pace of more than 50% between 1995 and 2010 and by 2025 the number is slated to more than double. The 2001 Census reveals that the decadal population growth in the urban areas is one and a half times higher than the national average. All these statistics point to a high level of migration of population from rural and semi-urban areas to a more urbanized form of settlement. The percentage of population staying in urban areas has progressively risen from 23.34% in 1981 to almost 28% in 2001.

For the first time, Census 2001 revealed a figure of 13 million 'houseless households' in the country. This involves a total houseless population at a staggering 6.5 crore in the country, placing onerous responsibility on the developmental planning process in the country.

Housing Finance in India: A Profile

Housing finance market in India has been consistently exhibiting rapid growth in the past few years with an estimated CARG of 38%. However, the growth has been largely in urban areas and is largely confined to the middle/high income groups. Housing finance in India has the following institutional structure.

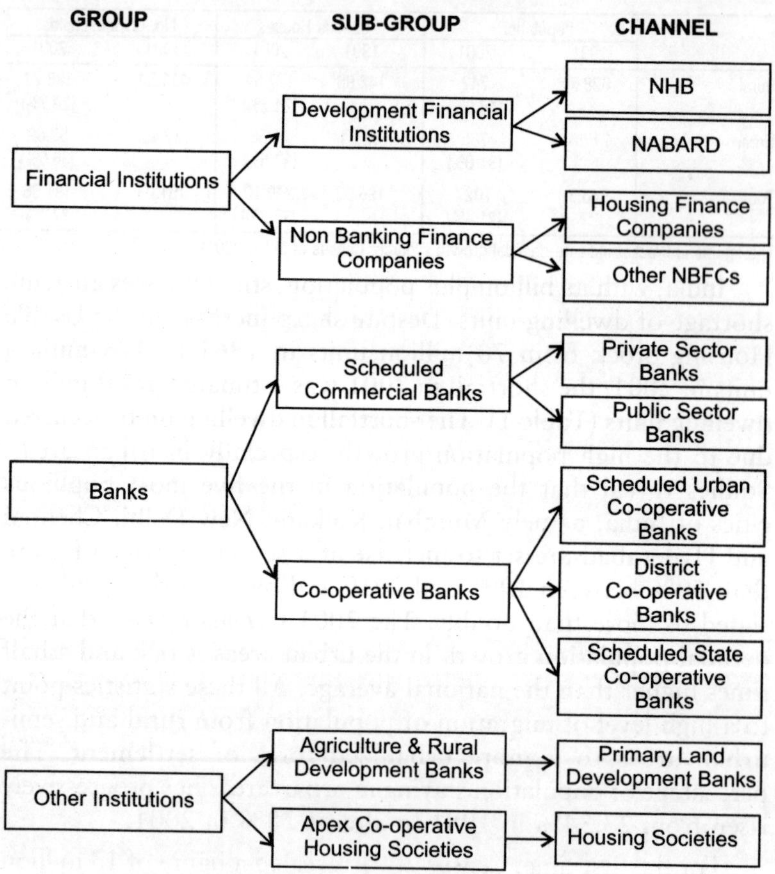

Among the various institutional entities, scheduled commercial banks (SCBs) account for a major share of the housing portfolio. A robust network and access to low cost retail resources have enabled SCBs to offer home loan products at competitive rates. More than 65% of the housing disbursements are accounted for by SCBs, followed by the HFCs, with little over 30% share in loan disbursals.

Table 2: Housing in Retail Portfolio of Banks

Amt in Rs. Crore

Variables	Outst. At March 05	Outst. At March 06	% Variation
Housing Loans	1,34,276	1,79,116	33.4
Consumer Durables	3810	4469	17.3
Credit Card Receivables	8405	12434	47.9
Auto Loans	35043	61369	75.1
Other Personal Loans	85077	1,18,351	39.1
Total Retail Loans	2,66,610 (23.7)	3,75,739 (25.5)	40.9
Total SCB Advances	11,25,056	14,73,723	31.0

Note: Figures in parentheses represent percentage share in total loans & advances.

Source: Report on Trends and Progress of Banking in India, 2005-06, Reserve Bank of India.

RBI's *Report on Trend and Progress of Banking in India* brings out the sustained rise in retail banking. During 2005-06, while SCBs' total advances grew by 31%, growth in outstanding retail portfolio worked out to about 41% (Table 2). About half of the banking system's outstanding retail portfolio at March 2006 was accounted for by housing loans alone, with increase in retail share in the total advances of the banking system to 25.5%, from 23.7% a year ago. Among loans to sensitive segments, finance to real estate was about 60%, increasing progressively since 2004. The active role of the SCBs in housing finance can also be gauged from the volume of refinance availed by them. Refinance availed by SCBs from the National Housing Bank (NHB) as also the share of SCBs in total refinance extended by NHB also exhibited progressive rise year after year. During the period 2000-01 to 2005-06, direct housing finance disbursements by Primary Lending Institutions (PLIs) rose sharply from Rs. 19059 crore to Rs. 86034 crore. While the share of Commercial Banks in total direct housing finance disbursements rose from 29.1% in 2000-01 to 68.1% in 2005-06, the share of Housing Finance Companies fell from 66.3% to 31.9% and that of cooperative institutions fell even more strikingly from 4.55% to Nil during this period (Table 3).

Table 3: Direct Housing Finance Disbursals

(Rs. in Crore)

Primary Lending Institutions (PLIs)	2000-01	2001-02	2002-03	2003-04	2004-05	2005-06
1. Commercial Banks	5,553	8,566	23,553	32,816	50,398	58,623
2. Housing Finance Cos.	12,638	14,614	17,832	20,862	26,042	27,411
3. Co-op Institutions	868	678	642	623	421	-
4. TOTAL	19,059	23,858	42,027	54,301	76,861	86,034
5. Annual Growth (in %)	35.07	25.18	76.15	29.21	41.54	11.93

It is certainly welcome that outstanding bank credit to housing rose from Rs. 16143 crore in 2001 to Rs. 1,86,429 crore in 2006. But what is particularly welcome is that housing loan as a proportion of gross bank credit (GBC) rose almost four fold 3.4% in 2001 to 12.9% in 2006 (Table 4).

Table 4: Housing and Outstanding Gross Bank Credit

(Rs. in crore)

Particulars	23-Mar-01	22-Mar-02	21-Mar-03	19-Mar-04	18-Mar-05	31-Mar-06
1. Gross Bank Credit (GBC)	4,69,153	5,36,727	6,69,534	74,64,383	10,40,909	14,45,837
2. Housing	16,143	22,346	36,587	51,981	1,28,728	1,86,429
3. Hsg. as % of GBC	3.44	4.16	5.46	6.80	12.37	12.89

Source: RBI.

Table 5 shows the position of outstanding credit by Housing Finance Companies over the period 2000-01 to 2005-06.

Table 5: Outstanding Credit by Housing Finance Companies

(Rs. in crore)

Particulars	2000-01	2001-02	2002-03	2003-04	2004-05	2005-06
Housing Loans	33,250	41,844	49,238	59,111	70,534	86,129
Other Loans	8,163	9,666	13,358	15,847	15,692	17,576

Source: NHB.

It may be observed that outstanding housing loans by HFCs has grown by a compounded annual average growth rate (CAGR) of 21% between 2001 and 2006. HFCs' other loans, however, have grown at a CAGR of 17% over the same period.

The housing industry's high profile has had a lot to do with active support and initiatives from the Government as well as RBI in the recent past.

Government Initiatives

The National Housing and Habitat Policy was adopted by the Government of India during 1998 primarily to prop up the housing investment environment. The policy was revised in 2005 and subsequently, the Task Force set up by the Ministry of Urban Affairs and Employment suggested, *inter alia*, setting up of a National Shelter Fund and Risk Fund with initial corpus from the Government, for serving the underserved segments.

Other initiatives by the Government included fine tuning of fiscal concessions in acquisition of housing properties under the IT Act, effective monitoring of the Two Million Housing Programme, enactment and applicability of SARFAESI Act to HFCs, efforts to develop a RMBS market for liquidity, launching of the Jawaharlal Nehru National Urban Renewal Mission and construction of rural houses under the "Bharat Nirman" programme. Besides, FDI has been allowed up to 100% under the automatic route in townships, housing, built-up infrastructure and construction development projects. The SEZ policy is also likely to bring in world class residential premises as positive spillover for the housing sector.

RBI Initiatives

Major initiatives taken by the Reserve Bank of India include classification of housing loans up to Rs. 15 lakhs as priority sector lending and stipulation of housing loans linked to incremental deposit mobilization. To provide impetus to the rural housing credit, RBI has also formulated guidelines for synchronization of loan repayment schedules with the crop cycles. Further, RBI has also adopted a flexible approach in stipulating risk weights on housing loans that clearly discern housing finance as a national priority from commercial estate/realty funding for speculative purpose, a major conduit for overheating in the economy.

In addition to the above initiatives, the earlier dependence on public agencies alone is now slowly giving way to create a strong public-private partnership for addressing the housing and habitat issues. Recently, the National Housing Bank made a move to acquire stakes in housing finance companies engaged primarily in rural housing finance. Housing shortage in rural India is likely to be over 47 million by 2012. Other initiatives by NHB include refinancing options to RRBs, a composite loan scheme in partnership with banks/microfinance institutions/ SHGs. It is also making moves to set up a mortgage credit guarantee institution with the aid of international funding organizations (ADB, IFC). NHB's proposed creation of a new breed of certified independent mortgage counselors will also be a major move in spreading the financial literacy further and for enabling the (potential) borrowers to take informed decisions, in preference to their dependence on direct selling agents.

The Big Picture

When one looks at the future, the 'big picture' appears to be indeed bright. A comparison of the Mortgage Finance to GDP ratio places India at the bottom with a penetration rate of less than 2%, lower than 9% for Thailand, 36% for Singapore and 51% for USA. There is, thus, enough latent growth potential in the housing finance sector, especially in view of the low housing penetration and lack of depth in the mortgage market.

The much talked about 'Demographic Dividend' also augurs well for the housing finance industry in India. India's demographic structure now features about 60% of the population in the working group, i.e., in the 15-64 age bracket. Such a structural shift, coupled with progressive nuclearization of the family structure adds to the demand for higher number of dwelling units and concomitantly, has a significant bearing on the role of the housing finance entities. The demographic dividend is likely to continue up to the mid-twenties and to that extent, the buoyancy in the housing sector is likely to sustain over the medium haul.

Rapid strides in Infrastructure development like the Golden Quadrilateral Project and the National Highways Development Programme, which have progressed at an impressive speed is bound to trigger off a fresh round of Housing and habitation through further development of semi-urban and rural areas as well as setting up of new Satellite Townships. Initiatives relating to SEZs have been at the centre stage of India's export competitiveness strategies and housing sector is expected to receive a major impetus concomitant to the implementation of over 250 planned SEZs.

As per a Goldman Sachs Report on the Development of the "BRIC Economies", India is projected to have the fourth largest Economy in less than 30 years time from now. In order to achieve that level of growth, it is imperative, among others, for the housing industry to continue its contribution to the economy at an increased pace in the future as well.

Elsewhere across the world, housing finance, of late, has had interesting and equally intriguing developments that countries like India can look up to for influencing the policy environment. If the immediate past is anything to go by, the housing slump in USA and its reported ramifications are strong rejoinders to countries like India wherein bank credit has grown at an unprecedented pace, driven by the housing sector, among others. This makes it necessary to identify the factors that triggered the US housing problem and to draw critical lessons from the same.

US Housing Slump: Imperatives for India

Residential mortgage marked in USA is huge. It has some $10 billion worth of liens, 75% of which are repackaged into securities, mostly by the government sponsored mortgage majors—Fannie Mae and Freddie Mac. Risk perceived for most of this market is low. Two-thirds of the mortgage borrowers enjoy good credit and a fixed interest rate and can depend on the value of their houses remaining much higher than the credit/ borrowings. All these were just until recently, when the sub-prime issue raised its head, with ominous prospects looming large at present. Today, a growing minority of loan books look very different, featuring weak borrowers with dubious records, adjustable rates and little or no cushion on home equity.

The result is found, among others, in new distress websites such as "iamfacingforeclosure.com", sending panic waves among those whose mortgages are in trouble. Quite a number of persons are saddled with mortgages they cannot afford on houses fast losing in value. This is of concern to those who sought high yielding mortgage backed securities when a booming realty market made mortgages look absolutely safe. It also impacts investment which packaged the securities. The trigger may have far reaching implications for the US economy, with possible geopolitical ramifications.

Housing Slump in USA: The Triggers

Mortgage markets in USA have hit the bottom in just about one decade. Sub-prime borrowers—long shut out of house ownership—now account for one in five new mortgages and 10% of all mortgage debt. In the early part of the decade, low short-term interest rates led to a bonanza in adjustable—rate (floating) mortgages. Even more exotic products featured in the shelf, including the infamous 'teaser loans' with introductory period of interest at less than 1%.

A recent report by Credit Suisse analysts estimates that 80% of sub-prime loans made in 2006 included low 'teaser rates'—almost eight out of ten Alt-A loans were 'liar loans', based on scanty or even no documentation. Loan to value ratios were often over 90%, with a second piggy-bank loan (the case of ever greening in India) routinely thrown in.

As the mortgages were reset to higher rates and borrowers who had lied about their income failed to pay up, the trap was triggered. Another study by Christopher Cogan of First American Core Logic estimates that 60% of all adjustable rate loans made since 2004 are due for resetting in payments that will be more by 25% or above, one-fifth being the monthly repayment rate that could soar by 50% or more. The study also reveals that 7% of all American house owners had 'negative equity', houses being of lesser worth than their mortgage. Among the buyers in 2006, the percentage is much higher at 18%.

The lethal combination of higher payments and negative equity makes 1.1 million mortgages (or 13% of all adjustable mortgages originated between 2004 and 2006) worth $326 billion heading for repossession in the next few years. The harshest year is projected to be 2008, when many mortgages will be reset and few borrowers left with much equity. The study also demonstrates that every percentage point drop in house prices would bring 70,000 additional repossessions.

US Bankers' Reaction

The chopping up and selling on of risk is likely to have an impact on banks. However, banks may even get an opportunity to buy the assets of imploding sub-prime lenders at a much higher discount. But, in the process, they would probably have to take a heavy toll in their provisioning requirements.

Bankers confront a dilemma. Investors have started shunning sub-prime and other risky mortgages, with spreads widening dramatically. And any reluctance on bankers' part and tightening of loan standards may lead to a classic credit crunch. Already '*countrywide*', USA's largest mortgage lender, has stopped no-money-down mortgages. HSBC has cut back on second lien loans. Freddie Mac recently announced not to buy sub-prime loans.

Just as borrowing becomes harder, there could be a glut in the housing market. Falling demand and soaring supply spell ill for construction and house prices, thereby affecting the broader economy. The repercussions could be traced to job losses in construction and related industries, lesser consumer spending by way of the 'Wealth Effect', triggering thereby, recessionary trends. Usually, it is reckoned that in US market a $100 drop in wealth reduces spending by $3-5 a year. It could even be more.

Regulator's Recipe

Four federal regulators in USA have meanwhile tightened their regulatory mechanisms for pre-empting any severe eventuality. They have already proposed stricter lending guidelines on adjustable sub-prime loans.

However, many of the riskiest mortgages have been made by independent, non-bank lenders viz., New Century, Ownit and Fremont (now tending to collapse) which are overseen by state regulators, and are outside the Federal ambit. It is the state regulations (few have laws against predatory lending) which would need to be tightened up in the right earnest.

Many put the blame on loose monetary policy, with disastrous consequence for home buyers and lenders. When the

Federal Reserve cut interest rates after the tech bubble burst, it inflated another bubble in housing. A similar story is visible in Euro Area with housing investment and prices shooting up at a fast clip.

The Fed's main worry is inflation, if it were to unwind monetary policy the traditional way. The music of the mess is far too loud and clear, thanks to the sub-prime menace or what Alan Greenspan termed as "***Democratization of credit***'.

ISSUES IN THE INDIAN CONTEXT

Much of the spurt in housing finance owes as much to the growing potential in the housing sector as to the recessionary trends a few years back and the slow growth in the non-food credit of SCBs. Having stabilized at relatively low levels, credit growth in 2006-07 featured serious rebalancing efforts on the part of banks, due as much to the regulator's stress on moral suasion as to their own 'due diligence' initiatives for preempting possible impairment in their loan books and the attendant effects on earnings and their bottom line. Part of the rebalancing can also be attributed to the northward movement in interest rates in response to frequent firming up of key policy rates.

Going by the developments within the country and elsewhere in the world, there are a few issues that need to engage the attention of the policy-makers and the housing finance institutions. Some such issues are briefly discussed below.

Imperatives for Inclusive Housing

Housing finance as a financial service is relatively young in India, with the earliest mortgages dating back only to 1978. Notwithstanding the unprecedented spurt in the volumes recently, housing finance accounts for only about 4% of India's GDP, much lower than other countries like Korea, China, Thailand, Malayasia. Moreover, coverage of housing has been largely confined to the middle and high income group, bypassing the all important low income group, in the urban as well as the rural locations. Further, out of the 1.1 billion population, a whopping 70% is below 36 years of age and an estimated one-third below 18. 'Demographic Dividend', as such a shift is more commonly referred to, makes greater outreach for housing finance as one of the most prerequisites for inclusive growth to be a reality.

National Housing Bank, one of the pioneers in the realm of providing and regulating housing finance, has identified for inclusive housing finance to emerge as a vital component of the financial inclusion movement. These include:

- Mapping and segmentation of the market.
- Identification of segment-wise financial needs.
- Development of new, innovative loan products.
- Strengthening institutional credit delivery mechanism.
- Upgrading market infrastructure.
- Changes in legal and regulatory systems.

Effective Loan Administration

The emergence of housing on the national map as a vital growth driver continues to engage policy attention, regulators and various institutional entities, including banks. Although the Government keeps on catalyzing growth prospects in housing through various fiscal and developmental schemes, the Reserve Bank of India, rightly so, has been cautioning about the potential problems out of possible overheating in the realty market. Enhanced risk weights on banks' exposure to sensitive segments like real estate and stringent provisioning norms are some of the regulatory initiatives that would do a world of good to the loan portfolio of the banks. Many of the major banking players have already been emphasizing a host of 'due diligence' aspects in the pre- and post-sanction stage of housing loans.

Quite justifiably, the focus on stepping up retail housing loans has continued relentlessly, as retail component (up to Rs. 15 lakhs) does not entail much speculation as in the commercial estate/realty sector. The East Asian crisis had stemmed, among others, from unprecedented speculative activity in the real estate and sudden crash in asset prices concomitant to massive capital flight.

Nonetheless, even within the retail component, unbridled loan expansion has implications for possible delinquency and the tendency of adverse selection. The increasing incidence of frauds in housing loan is duly recognized by the regulators and the policy-makers alike, which is a healthy sign of the importance attached to systemic stability. The importance of effective systems and procedures in the realm of housing finance, with a 'prevention better than the cure' approach, can hardly be overemphasized in this regard. There is a need for taking comprehensive checks on such important issues as strict compliance with the KYC norms, foolproof enquiry into the client profile, effective documentation and monitoring mechanism and above all, a commitment for hand holding as the overarching objective of housing finance.

Product Innovation

Mushrooming of housing finance players, unprecedented market expansion, the burgeoning demand supply gap and the entry of new classes of borrowers necessitates product innovation in housing finance as one of the essentials for sustained growth. Imperatives on innovation are applicable as much to tailor-made niche based products as to the processes and delivery channels, for capitalizing the huge opportunities available in the housing market. Product innovation, particularly for commercial banks, not only offers greater market access, but also higher margins in the competitive space. Commercial banks these days are striving hard to provide solution, not merely service, to the customers, taking advantage of the process of convergence in products, processes and delivery modes. For example, cross-selling has emerged as a major conduit for banks to extend comprehensive solutions as per client expectations and housing finance deserves to be an integral part of the product package, complemented with solutions in wealth management, bancassurance, online remittance facility and so on.

From packaged solution, there is a need as well to develop viable variants of conventional housing loan products for specific clientele segments, taking recourse, wherever necessary, to strategic alliance with specialized entities. Reverse mortgage is one such variant that promises to be lucrative, though the initial response, given the typical social fabric in the country, is not as encouraging as it should have been. But it is indeed suitable for the kind of demographic shift that the country is witnessing now. Consequently, and sooner than later, reverse mortgage may become one of the most preferred options of housing clients.

Institutional Developments

In contrast to advanced countries, Indian housing finance market has quite some distance to cover, in terms of the required market infrastructure to support the huge potential and rising demand in the housing sector. In developed countries, housing stocks and mortgages are leading indicators of economic activity and are, thus, tracked intensely. However, in India, lack of comprehensive MIS on housing is a major constraint that constrains the requisite analytical work and affects appropriate policy formulation. A comprehensive data base is one of the major prerequisites to formulate strategic policy shifts. The data base could include such important parameters as housing stocks, sale transactions, delinquency, segment-wise profile of home owners and price movements, to name a few. India severely lacks such important data profiles. National Housing Bank, however, has made certain moves recently that could at least partially obviate such constraints.

The National Housing Bank (NHB), the government's apex housing refinance institution, has launched India's first housing price index to track fluctuations in the property market and collect data on the parallel black economy. The data is expected to form the basis for policy decisions like rationalizing stamp duty, capital gains tax, municipal tax and determining mortgage rates.

The housing price index, which is called the NHB RESIDEX index, was launched by Finance Minister Shri P. Chidambaram on July 11, 2007. As maintained by Shri R.V. Verma, Executive Director and Chief Vigilance Officer, NHB, launching of Housing Price Index would help to know the gap between the documented price and the actual transacted price. While NHB has so far created just an aggregate index, it would refine this model to create indices for low-, middle- and high-income houses. A pilot index has already been developed for five cities—Delhi,

Bangalore, Bhopal, Kolkata and Mumbai—for five years from 2001 to 2005. Initially, NHB would bring out the index for these cities every six months. In the next phase, NHB proposes to compile the indices for 35 cities with a population of over a million and will subsequently cover 63 cities under the Jawaharlal Nehru National Urban Renewal Mission. This is indeed a novel and innovative move for tracking the price movement in housing assets and take mid-course measures whenever necessary.

There is also a need to set up an electronic registrar on housing transactions as also a comprehensive mortgage information system, linked to the property registration system in various States. It is welcome that NHB is actively pursuing these goals. Perhaps, the most striking constraint in the housing sector is the absence of an active secondary mortgage market which impinges on the depth and liquidity in the housing finance market.

Risk Management Architecture

An effective risk management mechanism, as we inch closer to the Basel II timeline, is of utmost significance if housing finance is to conform to the tenets of systemic stability and healthy loan books. Securitization has proved to be an effective conduit worldwide for risk mitigation in housing loans. It is one of the most useful risk sharing concepts, which can help lower the cost of credit, broad base the pool of investors and lessen the volatility in availability of capital. However, success of securitization market depends on the ability to understand the behaviour of mortgage assets under varying economic conditions and for various client segments. Risk perception, with regard to liquidity, interest rate, maturity profile, credit and prepayment, helps in effective pricing of housing assets. Measures, such as, implementation of regulations for mortgage guarantee as a follow up to the Finance Minister's Union Budget announcement on February 28, 2007, offering insurance to protect borrowers and lenders against defective titles, loans for housing to economically weaker sections could be important elements of the risk mitigation strategy

Recently, the National Housing Bank (NHB) undertook a study, in collaboration with Administrative Staff College of India, to analyze the nature of credit and repayment risk in the Indian housing market. The study was based, among others, on borrower characteristics, loan profile and property features, using the Cox Proportional Hazard (CPH) model. The study findings appear to be of considerable significance as far as formulating strategic and operational strategies by the lending institutions. Some of the findings are as follows:

- Longer term loans usually carry relatively lower risk, except for loans under the 10-15 years tenure.
- Presence of a co-obligant helps in mitigating risk under most circumstances.
- Loans disbursed for up-gradation of property have a higher risk.
- Self-employed borrowers carry a higher risk than employed borrowers, but employed borrowers with small loans carry the maximum risk.
- Smaller loans have a higher risk of default during the later years of loan age.
- Loans with term between 5-15 years carry a higher risk as compared to below 5 years and above.
- The share of default in the category of self-employed borrowers is higher than the overall default rate.
- Loans for new dwelling units are found to have higher risk compared to loans for old dwellings.
- Smaller loans have a lower initial prepayment risk compared to larger loans.

The study indicates that as the housing finance industry matures further, there will be a need to consider the risk adjusted returns from different housing loan portfolios in various demographic/geographic/income segments and accordingly earmark the required capital allocation. Notwithstanding the apparent slowdown in the housing finance at present, considering the potential in the housing market, primary lending institutions will surely need to inculcate a risk return culture not only as a regulatory requirement, but for strength and stability of their bottom line.

Concluding Observations

It is well-recognized that housing and realty constitute one of the key triggers for overheating in the economy. A booming housing market can aid as well as hamper growth prospects in the other segments of the economy. From the systemic point of view, housing finance needs to re-engage the attention of financial players for containing delinquency levels to the bare minimum. The answer to the varied risk dimensions should in no case lead to credit aversion, as the same will be inimical with much wider implications. Greater self-regulation and informed lending procedures will indeed be decisive in making the housing finance market more inclusive and growth oriented. As competitive forces gather further steam and the potential home buyers multiply, housing finance providers will need to keep an eye on maintaining the quality of housing assets, in preference to mere size of such assets.

Total shortage of dwelling units during the Eleventh plan period is estimated at about 74 million, necessitating additional investment level of Rs. 1,20,000 crore (conservatively based on expenses of Rs. 1.2 lakh per house). Such a level will require banks and HFCs to step up their outstanding housing portfolio from Rs. 2,40,000 crore at present to over Rs. 4,00,000 crore by 2012. This is indeed a tall order, but it could be converted into reality, if new modes and methods of housing finance are scouted on an ongoing basis. For instance, the recently introduced Reverse Mortgage concept, with a lead time, has the potential to redefine the nuances of housing finance in a big way. It could, of course find resistance in the countryside, with very few likely to be as forthcoming and as receptive as their urban counterparts to go for such a product. Promotion of such new schemes/services can also be facilitated by reinvigorating the 'Financial Literacy' drive, which is aimed at eliminating information asymmetry between the financially excluded segments and those forming part of the formal financial system. Capital market, through the debt securitization mode, could be another rewarding option if a secondary mortgage market develops soon with broad based participants. The hand holding aspect, earlier referred to, brings in the concept of an 'appropriate technology' that is so very essential in fructifying the housing dreams of the un/under-privileged. Low cost building technology is a crucial factor, besides finance, that enhances the affordability of house construction for the poorest of the poor.

REFERENCES

Mayo, Stephen K. (1994): "Housing Policy: Changing the Structure", *Finance & Development*, March 1994.

National Housing Bank (2006): Trend and Progress of Housing in India: 2005-06.

Reserve Bank of India (2006): Trend and Progress of Banking in India.

Sharma Manoranjan (2005): "Steady Growth of Retail Banking in India—Issues, Policies and Strategy" in *Studies in Money, Finance and Banking* (ed.) Manoranjan Sharma, Atlantic Publishers and Distributors, New Delhi.

"The Economist" (2007): March 24-30 Issue, Vol. 382, No. 8521, 73-75, published by The Economist Newspaper Ltd, London.

Interest Rate Risk: Issue of Considerable Contextual Significance for the Indian Banking System

15

A.K. Misra

INTRODUCTION

Financial markets around the world are rapidly integrating into a single global marketplace with advances in communications and information technology, deregulation of financial markets and the rising importance of institutional investors. However, deregulation of financial markets and rapid pace of financial innovations have increased volatility in the financial markets and thus, financial assets are now under increasing threat. Volatility in financial prices leads to changes in the value of financial assets and liabilities. Consequently, the earnings of financial institutions are vulnerable to such changes.

Prior to 1990s, the Indian financial system was inefficient and financially unsound. The profitability of Indian banks was extremely low despite the rapid growth of deposits. The government virtually stipulated all interest rates offered and charged by banks. A staggering 63.5 per cent of bank deposits statutorily pre-empted by the RBI and the government in the forms CRR, SLR and other directed credit. Credit rationing was inevitable to achieve the objectives of monetary policy. Allocative efficiency was grossly undermined due to financial repression including directed credit and investment. The banking system had serious survival problem due to accumulated losses and consequent erosion of capital.

Against this overreaching context, the Committee on the Financial System, under the chairmanship of Narasimham, appointed in 1991, advocated removal of constraints on balance sheet and a gradual deregulation of interest rate prescriptions.

Pursuant to the recommendations of the Narasimham Committee, prudential regulations, such as income recognition, asset classifications, provisioning and capital adequacy have been implemented for the banks, financial institutions as well as for non-bank financial companies in a phased manner. Both deposit and lending rates have been progressively deregulated/ rationalised. Directed investment by way of SLR has been reduced.

As a step towards deregulation of interest rates, call money rate was freed in 1989. Structure of administered interest rate has been almost totally dismantled. Prescriptions of rates in term deposits, including conditions of premature withdrawal and offering of uniform rate irrespective of size of deposits have been dispensed with. Providing more operational autonomy to banks, the concept of Prime Lending Rate (PLR) was introduced in April 1997. Since then, the norms relating to the operation of PLR by banks has been substantially rationalised and liberalised. Banks have been given freedom to declare their own PLR along with a maximum spread. Banks also have now freedom to offer lending rates on a fixed rate or a variable rate basis. At present, PLR serves the ceiling rate for credit limit of up to Rs. 2 lakh and a floor for loans or credit limits above Rs. 2 lakh.

Thus, banking environment in India in the post-reform period underwent a significant transformation during the last decade. The package of reforms proposed by the Narasimham Committee in 1991 became the starting point of decontrol in the Indian banking system. Increased competition has resulted in the banks becoming more conscious of their business and intrinsic health and profitability of both the individual constituents and of the system as a whole.

Volatility of financial prices and consolidation of manufacturing and service sectors has posed another set of challenges for the banking system. Consequently, banks are experiencing an increase in credit, interest rate as well as exchange rate risks.

Of late, management of risks has received increasing attention in the Indian banking system. While introduction of capital adequacy norms brought credit risk into focus, the issue of guidelines on asset-liability management and risk management systems in banks has placed management of interest rate risk on top of the agenda in the Indian banking system. This paper discusses sources and measurement of interest rate risk in the Indian Banking System. Various techniques of measurement of interest rate risk have been discussed and applied to estimate the interest rate risk faced by Indian banks. It is found that public sector banks, as a group, are more vulnerable to interest rate risk as compared to private sector banks and foreign banks.

SOURCES OF INTEREST RATE RISK

As financial intermediaries, banks are confronted with various types of financial and non-financial risks. These relate to credit, interest rate, forex, liquidity, equity price, legal, regulatory, reputational and operational risks. These risks are highly interdependent. Events that affect one area of risk can have ramifications on a range of other risk categories. This is why banks are progressively becoming circumspect to improve their ability to identify measure, monitor and control the overall risk.

Interest rate risk management forms one of the most critical components of market risk management in banks. As opposed to a completely regulated regime earlier, almost complete deregulation of interest rates has exposed banks to adverse impact of volatility in interest rates. Generally, the net interest margin (NIM) of banks is a direct function of interest rate movements. Consequently, movements in interest rate have a bearing on the earning ability of assets and the cost of liabilities. The overarching objective of interest rate risk management is to ensure a cash flow mechanism that is devoid of major mismatches in both assets and liabilities segments. As financial intermediaries, banks encounter interest rate risk in several ways as briefly discussed below:

Re-pricing Risk

The primary form of interest rate risk arises from timing differences in the maturity (for fixed rate) and re-pricing (for floating rate) of assets, liabilities and off-balance-sheet (OBS) positions. While such re-pricing mismatches are fundamental to the business of banking, they can expose a banks' income and assets underlying economic value to unanticipated fluctuations as interest rates variations tend to be too frequent and volatile.

Yield Curve Risk

Re-pricing mismatches can also expose a bank to changes in the slope and shape of the yield curve. Yield curve risk arises when unanticipated shifts of the yield curve have adverse effects on banks' income or economic value of their asset portfolio.

Basis Risk

The risk that the interest rate for different assets and liabilities may change in different magnitudes is called basis risk. Such risk arises due to imperfect correlation in the adjustment of the rates earned and paid on different instruments with otherwise similar re-pricing characteristics. When interest rates change, these differences can give rise to unexpected changes in the cash flows and earnings spread between assets, liabilities and Off-balance Sheet (OBS) instruments of similar maturities or re-pricing frequencies.

Embedded Option Risk

An additional and increasingly important source of interest rate risk arises from the options embedded in many bank assets, liabilities and OBS portfolios. Formally, an option provides the holder the right, but not the obligation, to buy, sell, or in some manner, alter the cash flow of an instrument or financial contract. Options may be stand-alone instruments, such as, exchange-traded options and over-the-counter (OTC) contracts, or they may be embedded within otherwise standard instruments. While banks use exchange-traded and OTC-options in both trading and non-trading accounts, instruments with embedded options are generally most important in non-trading activities. They include various types of bonds and notes with call or put provisions, loans giving borrowers the right to prepay balances and various types of non-maturity deposit instruments, which give depositors the right to withdraw funds at any time, often without any penalties. If not adequately managed, the asymmetrical pay-off characteristics of instruments with optionality features can pose significant risk.

Re-investment Risk

Uncertainty about future interest rate gives rise to re-investment risk as future cash flows will be re-invested at a rate unknown at present. Ordinary yield curve, without bootstrapping, does not take into account the re-investment risk.

REVIEW OF LITERATURE

The concept of risk has acquired centrality in the management of financial institutions. With the de-regulation of financial market and explosive volatility of interest rates, management of interest rate risk has become the focal point of balance sheet management. Financial intermediation often exposes banks to interest rate risk by creating mismatches in the maturity structure and re-pricing terms of their assets and/ or liabilities.

In developed countries, interest rates were de-regulated in 1970s. Several studies have been undertaken in these countries to examine the impact of interest rates fluctuations on commercial banks and other financial institutions. Flannery (1981) examined interest rate volatility on commercial banks profitability in USA. He found that interest rates fluctuations affect more on liabilities portion of balance sheets. However, since 1980s, active use of interest rate derivatives has reduced the impact of interest rate change on profitability. Similarly, Yourougou (1990) examined interest rate risks on various components of assets and liabilities of balance sheets of depository and other financial intermediaries. He found that these institutions also affected, in a limited manner, the upward movement of interest rates. Recent studies offer convincing evidence that commercial banks and other financial institutions in USA are exposed to interest rate risk. According to Desmukh, Greenbaum and Kanates (1983), commercial banks can serve as a financial intermediary in transferring surplus funds to deficit units and it in this process exposed itself to interest rate risks.

Across the world, commercial banks and other financial institutions expose themselves to interest rate risks and lose their global competitiveness as cost of capital is linked to interest rate sensitiveness (Zimmmer & McCaulay, 1991). Madura and Zarruk (1995) examined interest rate risk on commercial banks in Canada, Germany, Japan and UK. These countries have significant external exposures. They found that commercial banks of these countries were quite sensitive to short-term interest rate fluctuations and relatively stable with respect to longer-term interest rate volatilities. They also found that commercial banks with relatively diversified portfolios and also geographic diversification had lower interest rate risks.

Another line of empirical research has focused on the impact of interest rate risks on banks' equity returns. Bae (1991), Booth and Officer (1985) and Flannery and James (1984) reported negative relationship as banks generally fund longer-term with shorter-term liabilities. Shella and Chen (1990) found that bank equity returns were sensitive to change in long-term risk free yields, though not to those of short-term yields. Neuberger (1991) found that interest rate sensitivity on banks' equity had declined since 1977 through 1990, because of large-scale use of interest rate risk derivative products.

After the financial sector deregulation in India, interest rates gradually came down from an average of 18 per cent in 1993-94 to 10 per cent in 2003-04. With the declining interest rates in recent years, banks earned substantial profit through sales of investments. Trading income constituted more than half of their non-interest income and it was the primary driver of banks' profit and profitability during the financial years 2002-03 to 2004-05. Holding of large government securities was considered a significant risk for banks as interest rates bottomed out. Interest rates have reversed their direction and rising yields have forced many banks to make provisions for depreciation on investment portfolio.

In the Indian context, not many studies have so far been undertaken on interest rate risk on financial institutions' earnings. Large holdings of government securities by banks have been considered as significant risk to banking sector in India. Interest rates, after bottoming out, have reversed their cycle and managing interest risk needs to be re-designed and new techniques have to be used to monitor interest rate risk on an ongoing basis. Resource raising and deployments, both for advances and investments, need to be dovetailed with interest rate risk management. In his working paper titled 'Managing Interest Rate Risk on Government Securities', Amadou (2005) assessed and measured the interest rate risk on government securities and demonstrated that the current Investment Fluctuation Reserves (IFR) would not be sufficient to cover interest rate risk on Indian banking sector.

Sarkar (2005) while analysing interest rate risk on investment portfolio of the Indian banking system found that huge investment of Indian banks, particularly public sector banks in government securities, pose serious risk once interest rate cycle reverse. With a high duration of G-sec portfolio than other banks' group, public sector banks in India were more prone to interest rate risk. As a part of periodic interest rate sensitivity analysis, RBI in 2003, found that interest rate risk of Indian banks was manageable with an increase in interest rate of 200 basis prints (bps). However, after 2003, interest rate has increased further and risk perception has also enhanced. Amadou (2005) found that interest rate risk sensitivity in Indian banking system has increased considerably since the onset of de-regulation of interest rate in 1993. Amadous' scenario analysis revealed that an increase in one percentage interest rate would result in a loss of 133 per cent of net profit of Indian banking sector. For PSBs, it would be 153 per cent, and 123 per cent and 39 per cent for Private and Foreign banks respectively.

Credit risk has been the traditional focus of banking supervision (Patnaik & Shah, 2003). According to these authors, interest rate risk on Indian banking system has not been articulated properly. When interest rate goes up, both loans and investment portfolios suffer losses and also resource mobilization would become costly for banks. They have analysed interest rate risk of 42 major banks as at March 2002 and found that many banks have significant interest rate risk. Using discounted cash flows against different interest rate scenarios and also through stock market information these authors measured interest rate risks. Few banks have 'hedged' their interest risk and with scenario of 320 bps interest rate hike majority of banks in India would lose significant amount of their equity capital.

MEASUREMENT OF INTEREST RATE RISK

Effective management of interest rate risk (IRR) necessitates identification and quantification of risk. Various tools have evolved to measure interest rate risk and hedge them so as to reduce their adverse impact on bank balance sheet. Most widely used techniques for measurement of interest rate risk are: (1) Maturity Gap Analysis, (2) Duration and Modified Duration, (3) Simulation modeling and (4) Value-at-Risk.

Maturity Gap Analysis (MGA)

It is the simplest analytical technique for calculating IRR exposure. It distributes interest rate sensitive assets (RSA), liabilities (RSL) and off-balance sheet position into a certain number of pre-defined time bands according to their maturity (fixed rate) or time remaining for their next re-pricing (floating rate). A negative gap means that banks have more RSLs than RSAs. The gaps are multiplied by assumed interest rate changes to derive the Earnings-at-Risk (EaR). EaR broadly indicates the extent to which earnings can be impacted by interest rate changes.

Maturity gap measures the direction and extent of asset-liability mismatch. It is computed for assets and liabilities of differing maturities and is calculated for a set time horizon. This model looks at the re-pricing gap that exists between the interest earned on the bank's assets and the interest paid on its liabilities over a particular period of time. It highlights the net interest income exposure of the bank as a response to changes in interest rates in different maturity buckets. Re-pricing gaps are calculated for assets and liabilities of differing maturities. A positive gap indicates that assets get re-priced before liabilities, whereas a negative gap indicates that liabilities get re-priced before assets. The bank looks at the rate sensitivity of each asset and liability on the balance sheet. The general formula used is as follows:

$$\partial (NII)_i = \partial \{R_i (GAP_i)\}$$

NII : Net Interest Income,

R : Interest rates impacting assets and liabilities in the relevant maturity bucket

GAP : Differences between the book value of the rate sensitive assets and the rate sensitive liabilities.

Thus, with a change in the interest rate, the impact of the change on the net interest income of the bank can easily be identified. For banks, it is essential to benchmark their earnings and fix threshold limits beyond which hedging strategies can be devised. The gap analysis indicates IRR exposure of banks over distinct maturities and provides a cue to necessary changes in the portfolio.

Interest rate changes have a market value effect. The basic weakness with this model is that this method takes into account only the book value of assets and liabilities and hence ignores their market value. This method, therefore, is only a partial measure of the true interest rate exposure of a bank.

Variability of interest rate primarily depends upon various phases of business cycle and hence, for maximising NII, maturity gap model needs to be aligned with the different phases of business cycle.

Prosperity: During this phase, interest rate is generally at its peak. Therefore, banks should encourage fixed rate assets and floating rate liabilities. As interest rate is high, long-term fixed deposits should be avoided and assets and liabilities should be managed in such a way as to have a negative gap to take advantage of high interest rate environment.

Recession: During this phase interest rates start moving southward and hence, banks should try to get fixed rate loans, accept floating rate deposits for short-term and discourage long-term fixed deposits. To maintain their NII, banks should try to have a negative gap.

Depression: This phase coincides with low level of economic activities and interest rate, generally, at its beneath. To protect their NII, banks should sell their fixed rate assets. During this phase, banks should accept long-term fixed deposits at fixed interest rate and try to create floating rate assets. A positive gap during this phase is advisable for banks.

Recovery: Economic activities commence during this phase of business cycle and so also the revival of the interest rate cycle. Banks should create more rate sensitive assets at floating rate of interest and deposits at fixed rate. A positive gap with more assets than liabilities could be advisable for banks during this phase.

However, MGA features some limitations as under:

- It quantifies only the time difference between re-pricing dates of assets and liabilities. It fails to measure the impact of basis and embedded option risks.
- Gap report assumes that all assets and liabilities are matured or re-priced simultaneously.
- Gap also fails to capture variability in non-interest revenue and expenses, a potentially vital source of risk to current income.

Duration Gap Analysis (DGA)

Compared to the simple MGA, DGA matches the duration of assets and liabilities, instead of matching the maturity or re-pricing dates, and as such, is a more effective way of cushioning economic value of assets against IRR. Duration is a measure of the percentage change in the economic value of a portfolio, that will occur consequent to changes in interest rates. However, measurement of duration gap is much more complex compared to the simple gap method. Banks have the option of estimating the economic value changes consequent to changes in market interest rates by calculating the duration of each asset, liability and OBS position and weigh each of them to arrive at their weighted duration.

Difference between Duration of Assets (DA) and Liabilities (DL) is the bank's net duration. If DA > DL, then a decline in market interest rates is likely to increase the market value of equity (MVE). When the duration gap is negative (DL > DA), MVE increases when the interest rate increases and it decreases in the face of decline in interest rates. Using the duration model, it is possible to immunise the interest spreads of banks. If both assets and liabilities have same duration, they will immunise each other and hence, protect the interest spreads. In other words, setting the net duration gap at zero, interest rate risk can be eliminated. However, for optimising interest spreads, it is essential to link the net duration gap with the movement of interest rate cycle.

Duration analysis facilitates a comprehensive measure of IRR for the total portfolio, well recognising the time value of money. Its additive characteristic also enables banks to match total assets and total liabilities rather than matching individual portfolios. Duration gap provides an index of the interest rate sensitivity of various segments of the entire portfolio and hence, it is possible to estimate the aggregate duration gap of the bank. To protect the book value of the bank, the net duration gap (DGAP) should be fixed at zero. In other words,

$$DGAP = DA - \delta^* DL$$

where DA : weighted average duration of assets

DL : weighted average duration of liabilities

δ : ratio of liabilities to assets.

However, duration has also its own limitations as it assumes that there is always parallel shift in yield curve, which may not be so during the time of high upheaval in financial market.

After estimating duration for each bucket of assets and liabilities, it is necessary to estimate modified duration for 'stress testing and scenario analyses'. While duration is a static concept, modified duration is a dynamic one. Modified duration indicates the change in duration due to underlying change in interest rate. Modified duration along with the convexity enables banks to measure the effect of interest rate change on the portfolio loss/gain due to parallel shift in yield curve. Using the Talyore approximation series, a small change in yield, the possible change in price can be estimated by following formula:

$$\partial p/p = (\text{-ve})\ D^*\ \partial y + (1/2)^*\ C^*\ (\partial Y)^2$$

where D is the modified duration and C is the convexity correction:

$$D = (\text{-ve})\ (1/p)\ \partial p/\partial y$$

$$C = (\text{-ve})\ \partial D\ /\ \partial y$$

Using RBI guidelines for parallel shift in yield for different basis points for different zone, capital change for interest rate rise is estimated for investment portfolio.

In case of deposits/liabilities after estimating bucket-wise duration, modified duration is calculated following recent RBI's guidelines on ALM (2006). In case of commercial banks in India, deposits account for 95 per cent of liabilities. Hence, modified duration would be indicative in the sense that further rise in interest rate would affect cost of deposits.

However, advances, which constitute a significant part of assets, are affected by change in yield. After estimating bucket-wise duration of advances, modified duration is measured by considering respective bucket-wise yield of FIMMDA yield curve.

Simulation Modeling

Many of the reputed and fundamentally advanced banks take recourse to balance sheet simulation modeling for gauging the impact of interest rate movements on their earnings, spanning over different time horizons. Such a method eliminates the limitations of maturity gap and duration gap methods, by objectively and precisely mapping interest rate sensitivity. Being predominantly IT-enabled, simulation modeling provides cues regarding future course of interest rates, shape of yield curve, change in business activity and pricing and hedging strategies over a wide spectrum. Simulation modeling, by virtue of providing multiple strategic options, also proves to be an important planning tool, under both static and dynamic environs. However, its effectiveness depends on structure of the model selected, validity of assumptions, requisite IT support and quality of expertise handling the IRR affairs. Despite these methodological limitations, simulation modeling can be carried out for estimating the impact of interest rate change on net interest income under different scenario both through maturity gap model and Value-at-Risk model.

Value-at-Risk (VaR)

The limitations of assumption of parallel shift in yield curve make duration/convexity/modified duration redundant in exact estimation of impact of interest rate risk. In this context, it is generally advisable to use Value-at-Risk model for estimation of maximum loss for a given change in interest rate. However, the existing VaR model does not take into account the abnormal change/shift (beyond parallel shift) in yield curve and hence same model risk prevailing with normal VaR model. In this connection, Dharba (2001) used Extreme Value Method, which takes into account extreme events. Such events do not figure in normal parallel shift of yield curve, and estimate capital charge for market risk of investment portfolio of commercial banks in India.

Value-at-risk indicates the potential loss of a position/asset over a period of time with a given level of confidence. It is generally used for assets/segments of market/financial position, which are highly volatile in nature. VaR is mostly used for foreign exchange position, bond and equity market. It can be used for individual asset and also for the entire portfolio to arrive at the potential portfolio loss.

The adoption of portfolio risk profiling through VaR encourages new methods of hedging risk at the aggregate level rather than at individual asset level. Basel Committee has recommended VaR for banks holding complex mixtures of trading, hedging and speculative assets. Similarly, JP Morgan's proprietary version (Riskmetrics) provides time series of volatilities and correlations for traded financial instruments.

Assuming that price changes of financial instruments are jointly normally distributed, serially independent and have constant volatility, VaR is defined as:

$$VaR_i = V_i * (\partial V/\partial P) * \partial P_t$$

Where

V_i : market value of the position at time, i,

$\partial V/\partial P$: sensitivity of market value to changes in P (for example interest rates)

∂P_t: change in P, of the underlying asset, over time interval t.

VaR has greatest potential applicability in the area of trading risk (both bond, equity and foreign exchange markets). VaR limits can be set for entire trading operation and for each type of risk.

No doubt, Extreme Value Theory is more useful in estimating maximum loss, however, parallel shift in yield curve, generally causes maximum risk to interest rate change as abnormal shift in yield curve rarely occurs. BIS suggests the use of one year change in long dated paper (10 year paper) and it should be simulated by 200 bps for estimating VaR. From the Zero Coupon Yield Curve of Government Securities (from NSE), with an assumption of undiversified portfolio with one month holding period, this paper estimated the VaR risk banks' groups.

Interest Rate Risk : A Stock Index Approach

It is generally found that interest rate fluctuations, which affect bank's earnings are reflected in the stock price movement of the bank. Hence, stock price index also provides an avenue to estimate interest rate risk. In this paper, sensitivity of interest rate is observed against the return of Bank Index.

$$(R_s - R_L) = \beta + \lambda(R_M - R_L) + \in$$

R_L = Long-term risk free interest rate (Government Bond 10-year maturity)

R_s = Return on Bank Index

R_M = Return on Equity Market

'λ' indicates the sensitivity of interest rate change on stock price of the banks.

Data and Period of Study

The above empirical design is applied to the Indian banking system. The Indian banking system is divided into three broad categories namely Public Sector Banks (PSBs), Private Sector Banks (PVTBs) and Foreign Banks (FBs). RBI defined bucket-wise residual assets and liabilities for the financial year ended 2003-04 and 2004-05 are considered for estimation of interest rate risk. Data on assets and liabilities are collected from Indian Banks Association published annual data book on 'Banks in India' and other data are collected from National Stock Exchange and Bombay Stock Exchange websites.

RESULTS AND FINDINGS

Maturity Mismatches

Assets-liabilities mismatches are estimated across the Bank Groups for 2003-04 and 2004-05.

Cumulative Mismatches* (As at 31st March 2004)

	1-14 days	15-28 days	29 days-3 month	3 - 6 month	6 -12 month	1 - 3 years	3 - 5 years	Over 5 years
Public Sector Bank	-4.89	13.44	3.77	4.04	-6.95	-7.84	69.18	10.51
Foreign Bank	-4.72	14.17	4.27	4.81	-6.35	-7.41	71.48	11.15
Private Sector Bank	-4.94	13.18	3.59	3.77	-7.16	-7.99	68.36	10.28

*As a per cent to Total Outflows

Cumulative Mismatches* (As at 31st March 2005)

	1-14 days	15-28 days	29 days-3 month	3 - 6 month	6 -12 month	1-3 Years	3 - 5 Years	Over 5 Year
Public Sector Bank	-4.52	15.10	4.91	5.79	-5.59	-6.87	74.42	11.96
Foreign Bank	-4.90	13.38	3.73	3.98	-6.99	-7.87	69.00	10.46
Private Sector Bank	-4.85	13.62	4.81	6.23	-4.91	-6.08	81.08	13.66

*As a per cent to Total Outflows

Following salient features emerge from the analysis:

- The cumulative mismatches almost followed the similar pattern across the Bank Groups.
- All three Bank Groups have negative mismatches in the 1-14 Days, 6 month-1 year and 1-3 year buckets. These mismatches continued even in 2004-05 also.
- Significant amount of assets are created in 3-year and above for all three bank groups, both in 2003-04 and 2004-05.
- Short-term negative gaps indicate banks are not comfortable in managing short-term assets and liabilities.

- Nearly 80 per cent of assets are created above 3 years period, which indicates banks may face liquidity problems in the coming months.
- Assets-liabilities mismatches pattern indicate banks were prone to short-term interest rate fluctuations as they had locked significant funds in relatively long-term period.

Any change in interest rate would impact both assets and liabilities. Net Interest Income, because of change in interest rate, for each bucket, can be estimated through the mismatches of Rate Sensitive Assets (RSA) and Rate Sensitive Liabilities (RSL). With 25 bps increase in interest rate across the maturities buckets, the impacts on respective banks' groups is reported below:

Net Interest Income (Interest Rate increase by 25 bps)

Bank Group	2003-04	2004-05
Public Sector Banks	1109	1600
Private Sector Banks	255	768
Foreign Banks	114	115

Amount in Rs. crore.

An assymetry in the balance sheet emerges with the assets side of the balance sheet being generally immune to increase in interest rate because of competition. However, banks are forced to match any increase in the interest rates in the liabilities side. But rise in interest rate may call for more provisions on depreciation of investment portfolio, which is not accounted for in this estimate.

Duration Gap Analysis

Weighted average maturity of assets and liabilities, which is otherwise known as duration, is provided in the following Tables. From these Tables, following inferences can be drawn;

- Across the bank groups, duration of advances and deposits had increased except foreign banks group, for which it declined marginally.

- Duration of investment had declined across bank groups because of redemption, sale of long-term bonds and reduction of SLR investments.
- Modified duration had also reduced indicating the rising interest rate.

Duration Summary

Bank Group	Duration		Modified Duration	
	2004	2005	2004	2005
Public Sector Bank				
Advances	1.90	2.08	1.88	2.04
Deposits	1.89	1.91	1.87	1.89
Investments	4.52	4.19	4.06	3.99
Private Sector Bank				
Advances	1.89	2.04	1.84	2.77
Deposits	1.92	1.97	1.89	1.94
Investments	3.42	3.21	3.28	3.11
Foreign Bank				
Advances	1.78	1.64	1.74	1.58
Deposits	2.03	1.99	1.98	1.95
Investments	2.12	2.08	2.06	1.99

Duration Gap

Bank Group	2003-04	2004-05
Public Sector Banks	0.0339	0.0643
Private Sector Banks	0.1322	0.1506
Foreign Banks	0.0664	0.0529

As interest rate was increasing, bank groups had rightly positioned their assets and liabilities with positive and increasing duration gap. Private Sector Banks had highest duration gap both in 2003-04 and 2004-05.

Using the estimated Modified Duration, 'stress testing and scenario analysis' has been carried out across the bank groups. In an increasing interest rate environment, investment portfolio was put to stress testing for 50 bps and 100 bps interest rate hike and projected loss in investment portfolio across the bank groups is given in the Table below.

Projected Loss of Investment Portfolio

Bank Group/	2003-04		2004-05	
Increase in Yield	50bps	100bps	50bps	100bps
Public Sector Banks	10991	21357	11754	22789
Private Sector Banks	1974	3797	2240	4298
Foreign Banks	760	1462	808	1551

Amount in Rs. crore.

From the above Table, following inferences can be drawn:

All three bank groups incurred losses with rising interest rate. Public Sector Banks, with their large size of investment portfolio, incurred highest loss followed by Private Banks and Foreign Banks groups.

Value-at-Risk

Investment portfolio is divided into three broad residual maturities of 1 to 3 year, 3 to 5 year and above 5 year. Volatilities of monthly yield of above residual maturities are estimated for 2003-04 and 2004-05 by considering data for the last five years. For 1 to 3 year bucket, average yields of 1-year, 2-year and 3-year are considered. Similarly, for 3 to 5 year bucket, average yields of 3-year, 4-year and 5-year are considered and for above 10-year bucket, yield of 10-year papers are considered. As per the BIS guideline, volatility is estimated for 90-days holding period with 99th percentile of observed variation in yield. The average volatility in 2004 and 2005 were of the order of 108 bps and 129 bps respectively. The worst case of market-to-market losses are estimated as follows:

$$\Delta M_i = -\Sigma_{i=1} M_i\, d_i\, (\Delta y_i) + \tfrac{1}{2}\, \Sigma_{i=1} M_i\, C_i\, (\Delta y_i)^2$$

Where M_i = Total Investment in the ith Bucket

d_i = Duration of the ith Bucket investment

(Δy_i) = Shock to the ith Bucket investment using 99th Percentile

C_i = Convexity of ith Bucket investment portfolio

Value at Risk (Investment Portfolio)

Bank Group	2003-04	2004-05
Public Sector Banks	25777	31047
Private Sector Banks	4315	5520
Foreign Banks	1661	1992

Amount in Rs. crore.

Worst mark-to-market losses were estimated across the bank groups using the value-at-risk model. Rise in yield had impacted all bank groups and Public Sector Banks, with their highest exposure to Government Securities, had reported highest loss with the increase in yield.

Stock Market Index

The negative coefficient of sensitivity parameter, 'λ' indicates that the net return on Bank Index (net off risk free interest rate) as a function of return on Equity Index, will be more responsive with rise in risk-free interest rate.

Independent Variable	2003-04	2004-05
β	2.86 (16.08)	2.82 (15.06)
λ	(-ve)0.829 (8.16)	(-ve) 0.882 (9.16)
R^{-2}	0.64	0.892
F (1,50)	66.61 (0.001)	82.87 (0.001)

The above findings indicate that the rise in interest rate, though affecting the investment portfolio, has a strong bearing on return on Bank Index. The positive relationship of performance of Bank Index with risk-free interest rate also indicates the rise in Net Interest Income, particularly from advances, is strongly influenced by the Bank Index.

DISCUSSION

Interest rate risk exposes bank's financial position to adverse movements in interest rates. Excessive interest rate risk can pose significant threat to bank's earnings and capital base. Since

1970s, financial institutions accordingly developed countries have recognised interest rate risk and used different techniques to mitigate this risk. In the Indian context, interest rate risk is a recent phenomenon as financial markets were functioning in a regulated interest rate environment till 1993. Since 1993, the variability of interest rate has exposed banks' balance-sheets to unexpected risk. Hence, managing interest rate risk has become a focus area of commercial banks in India.

Interest rates, after bottoming out, have revised their cycle. Rising yield has hurt banks and many banks were forced to make huge provision for depreciation on their investment portfolios. Using various techniques, the study has found that Indian banks are very susceptible to interest rate risk. Maturity Gap analysis indicated that banking system in India is very prone to short-term interest rate instability. With high volume of funds locked at longer maturity, Indian banks may have to face asset-liability mismatches and liquidity crunch in the coming months with a 25 bps rise in interest rate across the maturity periods resulted in sizeable loss in Net Interest Income.

Duration analysis indicated that Indian banks were exposed to increase in interest rate. With large volume of investment in Government Securities, banks in India were susceptible to interest rate hike. With their largest exposure to Government Securities, Public Sector Banks (PSBs) in India, were huge losers of rate hike. 'Stress testing' through modified duration, revealed that Indian Banks could withstand an interest rate hike of 150 bps. However, beyond 150 bps, it would be difficult for Indian banks to make provisions for depreciation on investment portfolio. This finding makes it necessary for Indian banks, particularly Public Sector Banks, to reduce their exposure in Government Securities. The impact of yield volatilities at different time buckets was captured through VaR model. The worst mark-to-market loss was reported by Public Sector Banks because of their large exposure to Government Securities. Yield volatilities increased in 2004-05 and many banks were forced to take huge hits on investment portfolios.

The study had also found responsiveness of Banks' Equity Market Index with interest rate and with rising interest rate, return on Banks' Index was also increasing. This finding reveals that despite mark-to-market loss booked by investment portfolio, the performance of banks is influenced by rising interest rate.

CONCLUSION

With the removal of regulatory constraints on interest rates, the structure of interest rate is now market determined. Interest rates, after bottoming out, have revived their cycle and Indian Banking Sector is now under constant threat of interest rate risk. The time is now appropriate for Indian banks to develop and put in place appropriate techniques to measure interest risks. This necessitates aligning of banks' business with adroit risk management techniques. Banks need to evolve a comprehensive interest rate policy in keeping with the ALM framework. Banks need to segregate the entire balance sheet into different blocks so as to use different techniques of interest rate risk management. Risk limits should be fixed in a prudent manner so as to take advantage of market movements. Dedicated outfit for planning, estimating and regular monitoring and review risk management should be established. It would be prudent on the part of banks to reduce their exposure in Government securities. As a step towards interest rate risk management, during rising interest rate scenario, Indian banks should appropriately place itself with negative duration gap so as to take advantage of interest rate hike. RBI has advised banks to use Forward Rate Agreements and Interest Rate Swaps to hedge interest rate risks. However, for these types of instruments, there is no depth in Indian financial market. RBI has recently issued revised guidelines on ALM and advised banks to switch over to duration gap model from the traditional maturity gap model. The guidelines have called for estimation of modified durations for various assets and liabilities. Build up 'Investment Fluctuation Reserve' (IFR) would help banks to cope with potential losses due to rise in interest rate. Basel-II recommendations, which are likely to be implemented in 2006-07, call for a wider capital charge. Indian banks should be allowed to issue Tier-III capital so as to cope with capital provision for market risk. In sum, the issue of interest rate risk needs to be carefully monitored on an ongoing basis for the strength and resilience of the Indian banking system.

REFERENCES

Bae, S.C. (1990): "Interest Rate Changes and Common Stock Returns of Financial Institutions: Revisited", *Journal of Financial Research,* No. 13.

Booth, J.R. and Officer, D.T. (1985): "Expectation, Interest Rates and Commercial Bank Stocks", *Journal of Financial Research.*

Desmukh, S., Greenbaum, and Kanatas, G. (1983): "Interest Rate Uncertainty and the Financial Intermediary's Choice of Exposure", *Journal of Finance,* No. 38.

Flannery, M.J. (1981): "Market Interest Rates and Commercial Bank Profitability: An Empirical Investigation", *Journal of Finance,* No. 30.

Flannery, M.S. and James, C.M. (1984): "The Effect of Interest Rate Changes on the Common Stock Returns of Financial Institutions", *Journal of Finance,* No. 39.

Gilkeson, J., Hudgins, S.C. and Craig, Ruff (1997): "Testing the Effectiveness of Regulatory Interest Rate Risk Measurement", *Journal of Economics and Finance,* Vol. 21, No. 2, Summer.

Gilkeson, J.H., Sylvia, C. Hudgins, and Craig, K. (1997) "Testing the Effectiveness of Regulatory Interest Rate Risk Measurement", *Journal of Economics and Finance,* Vol. 21, No. 2.

Kaufman, G.G. (1984): "Measuring and Managing Interest Rate Risk: A Primer", *Economic Perspectives,* Federal Reserve Bank of Chicago, Jan/Feb.

Madura, J. and Zarruk E.R. (1995): "Bank Exposure to Interest Rate Risk: A Global Perspective", *Journal of Financial Research*, Vol. XVIII, No. 1, Spring.

Neuberger, J.A. (1991): "Risk and Return in Banking: Evidence from Bank Stock Returns", *Economic Review,* Federal Reserve Bank of San Francisco.

Patnaik, Ila and Shah, A. (2003): "Interest Rate Risk in the Indian Banking System", *Working Paper, ICRIER.*

Purnanandam, A. (2005): "Interest Rate Management at Commercial Banks: An Empirical Investigation", Research Article, Published by Ross School of Business, University of Michigan, May.

Quemard, J. and Golitin, V. (2005): "Interest Rate Risk in the French Banking System", *Banque de France: Financial Stability Review,* No. 6, June.

Sarkar, S.S. (2004): "Interest Rate Risk in the Investment Portfolios of the Indian Banking System", *Treasury Research Group of ICICI Bank.*

Sy, Amadou (2005): "Managing the Interest Rate Risk of Indian Banks' Government Securities Holdings", *IMF Working Paper,* No. 05/78.

Yourougou, P. (1990): "Interest Rate Risk and the Principal Depository Financial Intermediary Common Stock", *Journal of Banking and Finance*, No. 14.

Zimmer, S.A. and MaCauley, R.N. (1991): "Bank Cost of Capital and International Competition", *FRBNY Quarterly Review*.

Microfinance and Rural Non-Farm Sector: Thinking out of the Box

16

Debesh Roy

1. Introduction

The banking sector has grown both in depth and width since the nationalisation of commercial banks and formation of regional rural banks (RRBs). However, during the era of financial sector reforms, while the banking industry has made rapid strides in terms of profitability, financial viability and competitiveness, there are still persisting concerns that the banks have been unable to include vast sections of the society, especially the underprivileged ones, into their fold (Leeladhar, 2005). Thus, the Reserve Bank of India (RBI) has recently formalized a policy on financial inclusion, which is expected to provide banking services at an affordable cost to the disadvantaged and low-income groups. The earliest efforts in India towards financial inclusion, was the nationalisation of banks and the consequent spread of bank branches in rural areas. The access to banking services has increased considerably. This is reflected by the fact that the average population per branch has decreased from 64,000 in 1969 to 16,000 as at the end of March 2005. However, there are still some under-banked States in the country like Bihar, Orissa, Rajasthan, Uttar Pradesh, Chhattisgarh, Jharkhand, West Bengal, and some of the North-Eastern States. Further, various government sponsored anti-poverty programmes, *viz.* IRDP, SGSY, PMRY, SCP, etc. The Differential Rate of Interest (DRI) Scheme and the implementation of the SHG-Bank Linkage Programme have been instrumental in providing bank credit to the rural poor, who were earlier considered credit unworthy. The RBI has, therefore, urged banks to review their existing banking practices to align them with the objective of financial inclusion (RBI, 2005a).

Dispersed nature of agriculture requires dispersed agricultural banking, entailing a higher transaction cost, adversely affecting the profitability of banks. Banks may have to adopt different innovations in the credit delivery mechanism like hub and spoke model, satellite banking, etc., to increase the outreach to remove, or in any case, reduce structural inadequacies, particularly because net bank credit to agriculture was 12.5 per cent and 11.8 per cent for the years 2004-05 and 2003-04. In absolute terms, the ratio of agriculture credit to GDP was about 4.3 per cent and 3.5 per cent for the years 2004-05 and 2003-04. This is why, it is necessary for banks to explore alternative/ supplementary mechanisms of rural credit, such as, Self-Help Groups (SHGs)/Joint Liability Groups (JLGs), Micro Finance Institutions (MFIs), Non-Governmental Organisations (NGOs), Cooperatives, agent based banking, etc., for cost effective channels of credit delivery. Collateral issues of poor borrowers could also be effectively addressed through this mechanism. Monitoring and supervision of loans could also be outsourced by banks to the agri-clinics or to unemployed agricultural graduates on a fee based arrangement (RBI, 2005b).

Technological progress and technical efficiency are two important factors, which influence investment decisions of the farmers. Both these factors substantially depend upon the stock of information and knowledge available and its dissemination at the grassroots level. While research and development in agriculture increases stock of scientific knowledge, extension services facilitate dissemination of knowledge (RBI, 2005b). In order to enable farmers to increase farm production and productivity by adopting new and advanced technology, there is an imperative need to strengthen the extension network. However, it is generally observed that the existing government extension network is weak and ineffective. In this connection, farmers may be organized into Farmers' Clubs under NABARD's Farmers' Club Programme, to form a vital link between bank branches, Agriculture Universities, Krishi Vigyan Kendras, and research institutions on one hand, and the farmers on the other. NABARD reimburses maintenance expenditure of the clubs for three years and makes arrangements for training through 'Meet with Experts Programme'[1] and exposure visits for the club members. Farmers' Clubs can effectively function as extension agencies for dissemination of new technologies and as a vital link for 'Lab-to-land' projects. They also help bank branches in recovery of loans, identification of potential borrowers, and also inform farmers about various loan products and schemes of banks.

2. Innovation in Banks

The significance of innovation has been increasingly realized in the present day world (Sharma 2003, 2004, 2005a). Traditionally, innovation has been defined with focus on traditional concepts of industry research and development and the commercialization of new products and/or process technologies. But rapid changes now make it necessary to define innovation as "acceptance of and readiness to change across the organization, dedication to continuous improvement processes, willingness to experiment and explore novel ways, building new relationships and alliances, establishing new approaches to markets, channels, customers, pricing strategies and new and varied approaches to organization, measurement and performance measurement."

The history of the growth of financial development, particularly banking development, demonstrates that though banking industry underwent profound changes of consolidation, spread of electronic banking, etc., challenges remain. Sharma (2005) cogently argues that banks have much more to do in creating a robust culture of innovation to be relevant to consumers in terms of technology, quality, reliability, pricing, performance and support. Meeting the requirements of modern banking transactions in a far more global and synergistic context than ever before has driven home the significance of "innovate or perish" not only for success but in fact also for survival.

To be sure, important developments over the years like the SHG-Bank Linkage Programme, introduction of Kisan Credit Card and the Government of India's accent on doubling of agriculture credit over a period of three years (2004-05 to 2006-07) attempted to transform the process and pattern of rural credit in India. But bankers continue to be recalcitrant to promote the flow of credit to this sector, in any case to the desired extent, as borne out by RBI's successive reports on *Trends and Progress of Banking*. While this recalcitrance stems from the confluence of several forces and factors, mention may here be made of "information asymmetry", absence of requisite documentation of income, insistence on collateral security, an inadequate understanding of the rural scenario, the credit delivery system and the variety of activities subsumed under the broader agricultural category with variable cash flows based on the seasonality of the produce and the harvesting period. So, where do we go from here? What options do we have in propelling the growth of agriculture to a higher and more sustainable growth trajectory and usher in a 'second Green revolution'? Clearly, this is a task of massive proportions and requires synchronised measures. Towards this end, the option of sanctioning a flexible 'credit line' to the farmers instead of the conventional term loan and working capital could justifiably be explored. This credit line could be a function of size of landholdings, the nature of the financing activity and the collateral security available. This paper, however, does not make an attempt to examine such issues and confines itself to an analysis of innovations and initiatives in rural credit, especially those relating to microfinance and rural non-farm sector.

3. Microfinance Revolution in India

NABARD launched a Pilot Project on SHG-Bank Linkage in February 1992, which proved to be a revolutionary programme for attacking poverty through capacity building and empowerment of the poor. NABARD sees the programme as part of an overall arrangement for providing financial services to the poor in a sustainable manner and also as an empowerment process for the members of SHGs. The Committee on Banking Sector Reforms (RBI, 1998) recognized that the SHG-Bank Linkage Programme was an effective instrument to provide banking facilities to the poor, without subsidies and Government support. The Committee also appreciated the fact that the repayment record under this programme was good. It also recognized the need for banking policy to (a) facilitate evolution of cost-effective systems for banking with the poor, with satisfactory linkages; and (b) support scaling up of such efforts resulting in expanded outreach as well as high quality of loan assets. The Reserve Bank of India advised banks in February 2000 to mainstream micro-credit and extend the outreach of micro-credit providers. Micro-credit extended either directly or through any intermediary is reckoned as part of banks' priority sector lending. Banks are now free to prescribe their own lending norms. Micro-credit would form an integral part of their corporate credit plan and would be reviewed at the highest level every quarter. In view of its potential in the alleviation of poverty, banks have been advised to make all efforts for provision of micro-credit. Thus, microfinance can definitely prove to be effective in attacking poverty (Roy, 2005).

Having received a successful feedback on the implementation of the Pilot Project, NABARD in 1998 crystallized its vision for providing access to one-third of the rural poor through linking of 10 lakh SHGs by the year 2007. Accordingly, NABARD conducted a massive scaling up of training and capacity building awareness programmes for bankers, NGOs, Government agencies and rural volunteers in SHG promotion, nurturing, appraisal and financing. This massive initiative led to the bank linkage of more than 10 lakh SHGs by 31 March 2004, three years ahead of schedule. As on 31 March 2005, there were more than 16.18 lakh SHGs in the country, which were provided with bank loans. The Union Budget 2005-06 had set a target of 2.5 lakh SHGs for credit linkage during the year, which would lead to a cumulative credit linkage of 18.5 lakh. The progress of SHG-Bank Linkage Programme during the period 1992 to 2004-05 is indicated in Tables 1 and 2.

There has been a massive upscaling and spread of SHGs in the country during the period 1992—2005 (Tables 1 and 2). Further, while during the period 1992 to 2002-03, the number of credit linked SHGs increased by 7,17,360, the same increased by 9,01,116 during the two-year period 2003-04 to 2004-05. As on 31 March 2005, 35,294 bank branches have provided bank loans worth Rs. 6898 crore to 16.18 lakh SHGs, benefiting 242.5 lakh poor families. Average loan per SHG and average

Table 1: SHG-Bank Linkage Programme—Cumulative Progress

Period (end March)	SHGs financed	Bank Loan (Rs. Crore)
1992—99	32,995	57.1
1999—2000	1,14,775	193.0
2000-01	2,63,825	480.9
2001-02	4,61,478	1026.3
2002-03	7,17,360	2048.7
2003-04	10,79,091	3903.7
2004-05	16,18,476	6898.0

Source: Progress of SHG-Bank Linkage in India (various issues), NABARD.

Table 2: SHG-Bank Linkage Programme (Status as on 31 March 2005)

Sl. No.	Particulars	Cumulative as on 31 March 2005
1.	No. of SHGs linked	1,618,476
2.	per cent of women groups	90
3.	No. of participating banks	560
	i. Commercial Banks	48
	ii. Regional Rural Banks	196
	iii. Co-operative Banks	316
4.	Bank branches participating	35,294
5.	No. of States/UTs	31
6.	No. of districts covered	563
7.	No. of Partners	3024
8.	Bank loans (Rs. crore)	6898
9.	NABARD refinance (Rs. crore)	3092
10.	No. of poor households assisted (in million)	24.25
11.	Average Loan/SHG Rs.	42,620
12.	Average Loan/Family Rs.	3,044
13.	Model wise Linkage (Cumulative) (per cent)	
	i. SHGs formed and financed by Banks	21
	ii. SHGs formed by other agencies but directly financed by banks	72
	iii. SHGs financed by banks using financial intermediaries	7

Source: www.nabard.org

loan per family amounted to Rs. 42,620 and Rs. 3,044 respectively. The Union Budget 2006-07 proposed to increase the target for credit linkage of SHGs from 2.50 lakh during 2005-06 to 3.85 lakh SHGs during 2006-07. It also suggested that NABARD could open a separate line of credit for financing farm production and investment activities through SHGs (Chidambaram, 2006).

The SHG-Bank Linkage Programme has shown that group formation, savings and credit provide a mechanism to promote social development with income generating goals. Working through groups avoids individualizing and divisiveness of assistance programmes. Further, savings and credit schemes provide opportunities for people to generate income in their home areas and build their communities instead of migrating. SHGs provide opportunities for the rural poor to participate in the development process. They also provide opportunities for leadership development and for women to participate on equal basis with men. Moreover, group approach leads to economic independence for the poor, especially women. In case of women groups, income can accrue directly to women who often lack any source of income, and who would most likely spend additional income on improved nutrition and childcare having long ranging positive impact. The SHG movement has been found to be cost effective, and more and more people can be brought under sustainable developmental activities, within a short span of time. From the viewpoint of bankers, the SHG-Bank Linkage Programme has proved to be a cost effective business opportunity. Further, the average recovery of loans disbursed to SHGs has been found to be around 90-95 per cent.

The significant learning points of the SHG-Bank Linkage Programme in India have been to: (a) discover innovative methods of reducing the costs of intermediation; (b) leverage peer pressure to mitigate risks; (c) use Civil Society Organization (CSOs)/informal groups for need and capacity assessment; (d) incentivise lending and thrift by forming a pool in which the scales are favourable for internal lending which in turn keeps the poor away from money lenders; (e) involve and facilitate NGOs/CSOs to help banks to build up quality portfolios; (f) ensure proper utilization of funds available to groups which tend to function as self-monitoring units; (g) graduate from thrift to internal lending to consumption credit to micro-enterprises by using the group approach; (h) empower through collective decision-making, conflict resolution and other social activities; (i) help the poor and assetless to receive financial services through collateral substitutes; and (j) identify risks that can be managed by involving peer groups, NGOs/CSOs (RBI, 2005c).

4. Outsourcing Microfinance—An Alternative to the SHG-Bank Linkage Programme

ICICI Bank has been focusing on an alternative microfinance model, where direct lending to SHGs is avoided, as it has not been found viable by the bank. The bank felt that they must work with community-based organisations, which have intricate knowledge of clients and the geography in which they operate and are more aware of the needs of customers. Therefore, ICICI Bank signed up micro-finance institutions (MFIs) as intermediaries for micro lending. MFIs like Spandana, Share Microfin, etc., were mainly funded by private sector banks. The interest charged by these institutions to SHGs are around 24 per cent[2], compared to around 8-10 per cent charged by public sector banks and RRBs under the SHG-Bank Linkage Programme. The usurious nature of interest rates charged by MFIs, and the unethical practices in recovery of loans by them from SHGs has reportedly led to a number of suicides by SHG members in the State of Andhra Pradesh. The aggressive nature of the MFIs and the downward spiral of indebtedness are believed to have led to the suicides. The MFIs have also reportedly targeted the very borrowers who were members of SHGs promoted under the SHG-Bank Linkage Programme of the World Bank assisted Indira Kranti Pratham project (the erstwhile Velugu project) in the State.

Nevertheless, the MFIs experienced a huge surge in their business. Spandana, for example, saw its disbursements accelerate from Rs. 3 crore in 1997-98 to Rs. 300 crore in 2005-06, with a customer base of 8,00,000. Cashpor, also experienced growth in its loan portfolio from Rs. 26.3 lakh in March 1999 to Rs. 50.8 crore in March 2006, with a substantial increase in client base from 2,500 to 1,24,000.[3] The massive spurt in business of MFIs was possible due to large scale borrowings from a range of banks both in the public and private sectors, *viz.* ICICI Bank, UTI Bank, HDFC Bank, IDBI Bank, Oriental Bank of Commerce, ING Vysya Bank, Indian Overseas Bank, Canara Bank,

Development Credit Bank and SIDBI, foreign banks like Bank of Bahrain and Kuwait, Standard Chartered Bank, ABN Amro and Deusche Bank, as well as from various international agencies. Private sector banks and foreign banks have few rural branches. Hence, in order to fulfill their rural lending targets, these banks have adopted the outsourcing model of microfinance. However, large scale and unrestricted borrowings from multiple sources by the MFIs could lead to their bankruptcy and also result in huge NPAs in the books of the lending banks. There is also a myth[4] about high recovery percentage among SHGs under this model, as the MFIs have been found to provide fresh loans to SHGs by adjusting the old loans outstanding.

While there is no denying the fact that the MFIs have an important role to play in upscaling the microfinance programme, there are certain emerging issues relating to the regulation of MFIs, which need to be addressed. In this connection, an internal group of RBI made certain recommendations relating to the regulation of MFIs. While the group admitted that in terms of regulation and supervision of MFIs there are significant differences across the legal forms in relation to nature and extent of regulation and supervision, it concluded that a separate and exclusive regulatory and supervisory framework for MFIs may not be required for the present as bulk of the microfinance portfolio rests in the books of regulated entities like banks and NBFCs (RBI, 2005c). The group also recommended that non-deposit taking MFIs may attempt self-regulation by forming State level associations to evolve code of ethics, uniform standards of accounting practices and disclosures, empanel and train auditors, etc., with the assistance of NABARD and SIDBI. It also recommended that NABARD, SIDBI and major banks may consider promoting independent rating agencies by way of equity contributions.

5. Innovations in Microfinance

5.1 The International Experience

5.1.1 *Grameen Bank, Bangladesh*

Under the Grameen Bank model groups of five borrowers each are formed voluntarily. All members in the group are collectively responsible for repayment of the loans. Loans are made first to two members, then to the next two, and then to the fifth. These groups of five meet together weekly with seven other groups, so that bank staff meets with forty clients at a time. Further, if one member ever defaults, all members in the group are denied subsequent loans. The contracts take advantage of local information and the "social assets" that are at the heart of local enforcement mechanisms (Meier and Rauch, 2005). These mechanisms rely on informal insurance relationships and threats, ranging from social isolation to physical retribution, that facilitate borrowings for households lacking collaterals. The Grameen Bank has over two million borrowers, 95 per cent of whom are women, receiving loans totaling $30-40 million per month. Most loans are for one year carrying a nominal interest rate of 20 per cent (roughly 15-16 per cent in real terms). Under the Grameen Bank model regular repayments in small amounts are collected on a weekly basis. Regular repayment schedules screen out borrowers who lack discipline, and also give early warning to loan officers and peer group members about emerging problems. As the repayment process begins before investments bear fruit, weekly repayments require that the borrowers repay from their additional income source. Thus, banks effectively lend partly against the households' steady, diversified income stream and not just from the risky project (*ibid.*).

5.1.2. *Kredit Desa, Indonesia*

The Bank Kredit Desa system (BKDs) of rural Indonesia provides small loans (without collateral) to the poorest households, with an emphasis on petty traders. The innovation of the BKDs is to allocate funds through village level management commissions led by village heads. This works in Indonesia where there is a clear system of authority stretching from Jakarta down to the villages (Meier and Rauch, 2005). The management commissions build in many of the advantages of group lending while retaining an individual-lending approach. While the commissions are able to exclude the worst credit risks, they are relatively democratic in their allocations.

5.1.3 *Banking Correspondents, Brazil*

Unlike India, Brazil does not have a significant rural branch-banking network. A vast majority of the rural poor were cut-off from mainstream banking. In order to increase accessibility of banking services to the rural population, banks and regulators created a network of 'banking correspondents', which are small outlets with extended working hours that offered basic banking services. Under this arrangement banks are permitted to appoint a wide variety of institutions and entities as banking correspondents/agents, which are easily accessible to the people, e.g. drug stores, super markets, petrol pumps, small stores, post offices, lottery shops, etc. The Brazilian model is largely technology driven and uses kiosks and ATMs by such agents to accept payments, open accounts without a cheque book, take small deposits, provide micro-credit, sells savings and insurance (RBI, 2005c). Further, Post Office network and Post Office staff deliver banking services through Banco Postal.

5.1.4 *ACCION's Service Company Model of Latin America*

ACCION International, a microfinance resource institution working in the American continents, has promoted the 'Service Company Model' to expand microfinance operations. The Microfinance Service Company is a non-financial company that provides loan origination and credit administration services to a bank by way of sponsoring, evaluating, approving, tracking and collecting loans, for a fee. The loans themselves are on the books of the bank. This model has been successfully replicated by SOGBANK SOGESOL, in Haiti and Banco del Pichincha in Ecuador (RBI, 2005c).

5.1.5 *Teba Bank, South Africa*

Teba Bank, South Africa engages agents who are provided with hand-held mobile Point of Sale (PoS) devices. The wireless device has a built-in GSM modem, card reader and micro printer. The customers can use their debit card at the terminal to deposit or withdraw cash, make enquiry of balance and transfer funds. Physical cash can also be deposited with or disbursed by the agents (RBI, 2005c).

5.2 The Indian Experience

5.2.1 *Indira Kranti Pratham*

A unique poverty eradication programme Indira Kranti Pratham (IKP) is being implemented by the Society for Eradication of Rural Poverty (SERP)[5], in the State of Andhra Pradesh, through financial support from Government of Andhra Pradesh, Government of India and the World Bank. Out of 80 lakh poor families in the State around 69 lakhs (86 per cent) have been organized into SHGs. The poor women through disciplined utilization of funds and prompt repayment achieved an average repayment level of 95 per cent. In order to motivate the women SHGs to achieve 100 per cent repayment and to reduce their interest burden, the State Government introduced the *Pavala Vaddi* scheme wherein the Government ensures that the interest burden to the SHGs on the loans taken from the banks does not exceed 3 per cent. The interest paid by the SHGs over and above 3 per cent to the banks is reimbursed by the State Government to the groups. However, this incentive is available to SHGs, which have been prompt in repayment of bank loans. A community based recovery mechanism has been launched under this programme in 2006-07.

The unique institutional design of the IKP comprises the constitution of federation of all SHGs into Village Organizations (VO) and VOs into Mandal Samakhyas (MS) and MSs into Zila Samakhyas (ZS). The VO is a Community Based Organization (CBO) represented by all the SHGs in a village. The VOs have evolved into MFIs, which have mastered the best practices of microfinance. The State Government provides substantial fund support to VOs through MSs for on lending to SHGs. The VOs also access bulk loans from banks for on lending to the groups. They also provide many other services like monitoring the functioning of SHGs, audit support to the SHGs, preparation of household investment plans and micro-credit plans at SHG level and facilitate access to credit from banks to the SHGs. The VOs are federated at the mandal[6] level into MSs. From each VO, two representatives are nominated by the General Body to be the Executive Committee (EC) members of the MS.

The EC in turn elects five members as office bearers. The MS provides guidance and support to the VOs and plays an effective role in securing convergence with various line departments. In fourteen districts of the State MSs have federated at the district level as ZSs. In most districts the ZSs have taken up insurance programmes, *viz.* death and disability insurance. In two districts they have taken up cattle insurance and in two other districts they have taken up a unique health insurance scheme.

The IKP lays great emphasis on capacity building of SHGs, VOs, MSs and ZSs. Intensive, continuous training and capacity building have led to sustainability of the groups. The training consists of classroom sessions and cross visits to successful groups. In addition the capacities of SHG women have been developed to act as traders. These women are called Community Resource Persons (CRPs), and they spend time outside their villages to share their experiences and train new group members on the SHG/VO/MS norms and to develop with them the strategies for developing the host groups. This method of dissemination has enabled SHGs to emerge as strong groups.

Several major initiatives have been successfully taken up under IKP project towards women empowerment in the form of food security, health and nutrition, environment, etc. Some of these initiatives are as follows:

- **Community managed food security:** The SHGs in many villages have been trying to ensure that their members lift their entitlement of rice under PDS promptly and if any of the poor families is not in a position to lift its allotment, the SHG makes the payment to the dealer and enables the member concerned to receive the rice as per her entitlement. The member in turn repays to the group in weekly installments. The shortfall in a family between PDS allotment of rice and its monthly consumption is provided to the members on credit by the VO to the SHG.
- **Marketing at the doorsteps of the poor producers:** The SHG federations have enhanced returns to their producer members in selling their agriculture,

horticulture and forest produce at the village level by opening a procurement centre with quality control and marketing tie-ups.

- **Green initiative:** An initiative for non-pesticide management by SHGs is being undertaken in 24,000 acres of land in the State of Andhra Pradesh.
- **Community managed insurance scheme:** The ZSs in six districts of A.P. have covered more than 7 lakh poor women under an insurance programme where the premium collection and settlement of claims is managed by the ZS.
- **Community managed health and nutrition interventions:** The project has initiated interventions like health risk fund, community health activists, nutrition centres for pregnant and lactating mothers, medical care cover for SHG members by tying up with private medical college and hospital, life insurance run by ZSs, etc.
- **Initiatives for disabled persons:** The disability interventions have enabled more than one lakh persons with disabilities in rural areas to be organized and helped them develop their own livelihoods.
- **Gender interventions:** These interventions have been undertaken through counseling centres, *balika sanghams*[7], campaign against alcoholism, etc.
- **Convergence with all line departments and Panchayati Raj Institutions:** Various Government departments like Health, Education, Nutrition, Disability, Land Administration, Forest, etc., have been involving SHGs and their federations in implementing various activities of these departments. The District Collectors also play an active role in forging convergence between various line departments and SHGs and their federations. The SHGs and their federations also work closely with Gram panchayats, and each institution provides support to the other whenever required.

The IKP project has demonstrated that a systematic and holistic approach could make a significant impact on the livelihoods of the poor rural families, through various need based interventions and innovations. The model developed under this project could be replicated in other states, with suitable modifications as per regional or local needs.

5.2.2 *OBC Grameen Project*

Oriental Bank of Commerce (OBC) pioneered the innovative 'OB Grameen Project' in Uttaranchal and Rajasthan. Under this project, instead of the SHG members coming to the bank branch, the bank officials go to the groups on predetermined dates. This experiment could be replicated in other states and by other banks, as it saves the SHG members the trouble of visiting a bank branch several times before they are attended to by bank officials.

5.2.3 *The Partnership Model*

Popularised by new generation private sector banks, the 'Partnership Model' is a unique innovation, under which the MFI evaluates, recommends, originates the loans, helps in disbursal and subsequently tracks and collects the loans. The loans, however, appear in the books of the bank, instead of the MFI. This model has overcome the constraints of capitalization of the MFIs and the double exposure that the banks are exposed to (RBI, 2005c). For the services that the MFI provides a service charge is collected from the borrowers by the MFI. The MFI also provides First Loan Default Guarantee (FLDG) to the bank to a certain percentage (8-15 per cent) of the loan limit sanctioned in the form of security deposit with the bank so as to maintain its stake in the loan portfolio. As MFIs are reported to have found this deposit amount too large to mobilize, an experiment that has been worked out is that the FLDG amount is provided by the bank to the MFI as an overdraft.

5.2.4 *Pilot Project on Processor Cards and Branch Automation*

In order to demonstrate the concept of branch automation with specific reference to the use of memory/processor cards for SHGs and other clients, a pilot project has been launched in five branches of Sri Visakha Grameena Bank in Andhra Pradesh which would test the acceptability and adaptability of IT in rural areas as also to address MIS needs in rural banks. The project envisages the issue of processor cards to KCC holders and SHGs and also automation of book-keeping in SHGs, with a view to reducing paper work, saving time and improving efficiency of field workers (NABARD, 2005). The project components include provision of PCs in the selected branches, installation of information kiosk in one branch and issue of processor/memory cards to SHGs and KCC holders. The project has been extended to five branches of Krishna Gramin Bank, Gulbarga in Karnataka, in the second phase.

5.2.5 *Grain Banks*

A pilot project to facilitate monetization of savings and loans in kind and integration of the traditional approaches into the monetized microfinance system and also to enable the poor tribal population to access need based financial services and address their food and seed security concerns, has been launched in Thaumul Rampur block of Kalahandi district in KBK region of Orissa. The project involved the promotion of 25 SHGs and establishment of 3 Grain Banks at Silet, Sikerguda and Maltipada, covering about 100 households, with the support of an NGO Antodaya. The Kalahandi Anchalik Gramya Bank has been extending loans to the SHGs against the stock of grain and cash savings of the groups. The SHGs are expected to utilise the bank loan to procure grains when the price is low and for repayment of loan taken from the Grain Bank. With the successful implementation of the pilot project, ten Grain Banks are being established in Bastat and Kanker districts of Chattisgarh.

5.2.6 *Pilot Project on 'e-grama'*

A pilot project on 'e-grama' has been launched by NABARD in association with an NGO, for the establishment of 13 village information centres (e-grama) in Davangere district of Karnataka with the aim of equipping and enabling villagers and the rural poor with access to information. The technology integrated information networks cover areas like weather conditions, crop inputs, product prices, land records, etc. Further, services like book keeping of SHGs, printing, scanning, etc., are also envisaged to be provided (NABARD, 2005).

5.2.7 *Computer Munshi*

NABARD has provided grant assistance to an NGO, PRADAN, to train a skilled youth from a block/taluka/town as computer munshi, for maintaining SHG accounts, preparation of relevant reports for SHGs and bankers (at a cost). The computer munshi is equipped with a computer and software to serve 100 to 300 SHGs. The project is being implemented in four districts (nine units) Jharkhand and one district (one unit) in Orissa.

5.2.8 *Rural Volunteers as Book Writers*

Keeping in view the low level of literacy among members of SHGs and their heavy dependence on Self-Help Promoting Institutions (SHPIs) for record keeping, NABARD launched a pilot project for associating local rural volunteers as book writers for SHGs. This project, which is being implemented through five RRBs in two and three districts of U.P. and Bihar, respectively, aims to improve the regularity and accuracy in the maintenance of books of accounts and to explore the possible evolution of Management Information System (MIS) between SHGs and banks.

5.2.9 *Joint Liability Groups*

A major hurdle faced by small and marginal farmers, landless labourers and other rural poor, is their inability to provide collateral for availing bank loans. In order to address this problem, a pilot project on financing Joint Liability Groups (JLGs), has been initiated for developing effective credit products for mid segment clients, which reduce risks and transaction costs for banks and also introduce a greater degree of flexibility for the credit user to determine credit needs and priorities (NABARD, 2005). The JLGs under the pilot project comprise a group of 5-10 members, who offer an undertaking to the bank that enables them to jointly receive such amounts as deemed eligible by the bank for pursuing any activity—individually or jointly—as found suitable by the group. As collective guarantor for loans extended to individual members, by the financing bank, the group executes joint liability agreements, making them jointly and severally liable for repayment of loans.

5.2.10 *Social Clusters*

A microfinance model with a strong focus on maternal/child health and nutrition has been developed in Rae Bareli district of U.P. by an NGO Grameen Vikas Sansthan. The NGO has formed 100 SHGs with grant assistance from NABARD. The Catholic Relief Services (CRS) has provided maternal/child health and nutritional inputs to the SHGs through the NGO. The SHGs have demonstrated effective credit and thrift management and also the ability to shoulder the responsibilities for efficient community development. Accordingly, Social Clusters of SHGs have been formed (8-10 SHGs in one Cluster), to achieve enhanced performance in economic activities. The formation of social clusters is expected to be an effective strategy for bringing about holistic and demand driven development (Roy, 2005).

6. Expanding Outreach

While there has been a substantial expansion in the microfinance programme in India over the last decade, there is still a large section of the rural poor, especially in the Northern, Eastern and North-Eastern States, who are yet to be covered under the programme. While a large number of players, *viz.* banks, MFIs, NGOs, CSOs, individual rural volunteers, farmers clubs, as well as post offices have been engaged in the microfinance movement in the country, there are various issues which need to be addressed in order to increase manifold its outreach, and develop sustainable models of microfinance. An internal group of RBI suggested that linkages of CSOs/other entities with banks to expand the latter's outreach would require the development of two broad models, *viz.* 'Business Facilitator Model for Non-financial Support Services' and 'Business Correspondent Model for Financial Services' (RBI, 2005c). Banks need several activities/functions to be outsourced in order to increase transaction efficiency. These functions, which are integral to the 'Business Facilitator Model for Non-financial Support Services' may include (a) identification of borrowers and fitment of activities, (b) collection of applications and verification of primary information, (c) preliminary appraisal of credit based on standard norms set by banks, (d) marketing of financial products, (e) processing and submission of applications to banks, (f) promotion and nurturing of SHGs/JLGs, (g) post-sanction monitoring, (h) monitoring and handholding of SHGs/JLGs, and (i) follow-up for recovery of loans. The facilitators could be NGOs, farmers' clubs, individual rural volunteers, functional cooperatives, IT enabled rural outlets of corporate entities, postal agents, insurance agents and functioning panchayats, agri-clinics and agri-business centres, rural multipurpose kiosks and village knowledge centres, etc. Trained individuals and retired bank employees could also function as facilitators. In due course these volunteers could also be allowed to undertake financial activities under the 'Business Correspondent Model for Financial Services'. NABARD and several banks are involved in capacity building of SHGs, through Rural Entrepreneurship Development Programmes (REDP), Skill Development Programmes (SDP), followed by credit and market linkages.

Under the 'Business Correspondent Model for Financial Services' NGOs/CSOs/MFIs, as well as good working Primary Agriculture Credit Societies (PACS) could be leveraged as facilitators/correspondents to act as intermediaries to increase the outreach of banks in rural areas, and function as 'pass through' agents. In addition to the functions under the 'Business Facilitator Model', the correspondents would provide other value added services like (a) disbursal of small value credit, (b) recovery of loan, and (c) sale of micro-insurance, mutual fund, products and pension products (RBI, 2005c).

7. Sustainable Rural Development through Promotion of Micro-Enterprise among Matured Self-Help Groups—A Silent Revolution

There are more than 4.6 lakh SHGs in the country that are more than three years old. This may indicate the sustainability of the SHG movement. A large number of members of SHGs have been found to be availing loans for income-generating activities, once their consumption needs are addressed (Satish, 2005). The critical need of the hour is to promote sustainable development through micro-enterprises by SHG members. It has, however, been observed that the success rate of creating sustainable micro-enterprises is quite low. This could be due to the fact, that activities are selected primarily on the basis of the interest shown by individual members of SHGs, without taking into consideration the demand pattern in the market. Needless to say, taking up micro-enterprises with the intent of enhancing income level of the poor is a complex issue which needs a more holistic approach of appreciating skill levels, entrepreneurial spirit and dynamism, understanding markets, technology, etc. This task has to be handled with care in order to ensure that genuine concerns do not lead to failures of micro-enterprises and increased debt burden, leading to default. A need has, therefore, been felt to develop a hand holding strategy to enable the SHG members to graduate to the micro-enterprise stage (Roy, 2005).

The experiences of institutions like Bharatiya Agro Industries Foundation (BAIF), Development for Humane Action (DHAN) Foundation, Shri Kshethra Dharmasthala Rural Development Project (SKDRDP) in the promotion of micro-enterprises among SHGs, have highlighted the following issues:

- It is appropriate to introduce income-generating activities based on known skills, knowledge and resources.
- It is better to integrate with existing livelihood activities of group members.
- More emphasis needs to be laid on developing business skills than on providing backward and forward linkages.
- Micro-enterprise development is not a stand-alone activity, but requires a combination of factors to enable growth as a business entity.

- It is both efficient and cost effective to promote farm sector micro-enterprises because backward and forward linkages are locally available.
- Promotion of non-farm sector activities, particularly those in manufacturing sector, is a challenge for providing market linkages because significant sales turnover is required by each member to earn incomes which are even equivalent of minimum wages or to cross the poverty line.

Development of micro-enterprises among SHGs by tapping local skills, local resources and local markets could be a cost effective and sustainable model for rural development. Habits of thrift and credit have been developed among members of SHGs, and they are also in a position to meet their basic consumption needs. SHGs have also been borrowing from banks to meet their emergent needs as also their needs for engaging in income generating activities. Thus, at the microfinance stage SHG members become adept at rudimentary financial management techniques. Subsequently, there is a need for SHGs to graduate to the micro-enterprise stage. '3-M Model' (micro-planning, micro-enterprise and micro-marketing) developed by Marketing and Research Team (MART) could be an appropriate approach for developing micro-enterprises among matured SHGs. The market approach to micro-enterprise development takes into consideration demands of the market. Existing skills are matched with the availability of raw materials and infrastructure. The dynamics between demand and supply constitutes the market approach and is the key to detailed micro-enterprise planning. Micro-markets are local markets, e.g. rural *haats,* and village markets (shops, vendors and traders). They are important for micro-enterprise development as they (a) offer scope for products and services to be sold locally, making an enterprise self-reliant and locally sustainable, (b) allow scope for producers to directly understand consumer tastes and preferences, (c) prevent dependence on external marketing agency. Micro-planning involves mapping of local resources, infrastructure and skills, planning and developing linkages and networks with markets, banks and training institutions (Roy, 2005).

NABARD has identified nine districts, *viz*. Rae Bareli (U.P.), North 24 Parganas (West Bengal), Puri (Orissa), Panchmahal (Gujarat), Chandrapur (Maharashtra), Ajmer (Rajasthan), Kangra (Himachal Pradesh), Mysore (Karnataka) and Madurai (Tamil Nadu), in the country to implement a pilot project for promotion of micro-enterprises among matured SHGs. The idea is to develop a sustainable and replicable model for providing hand holding services to the members of matured SHGs for undertaking micro-enterprises. This would involve a holistic approach under which the '3M Model' would be put into practice. The project would be implemented through NGOs, who would act as Micro-Enterprise Promotion Agencies (MEPA). Appropriate linkages would be developed, involving training institutions, banks, suppliers of raw materials, marketing agencies, markets and other appropriate agencies. It is important to identify activities, which have adequate potential for development in a village, block or district. Further, the emphasis is more on skill upgradation in existing activites, both in the farm as well as non-farm sectors, rather than on imposing new activities on the SHG members.

The design of the pilot project focuses on identifying processes for: (a) preparation of village wise inventory for mature SHGs; (b) conducting village wise surveys for resource mapping through Participatory Method; (c) identification of the right type of micro-enterprise; (d) identification of matured groups for promotion of micro-enterprises; (e) building profiles of identified groups; (f) identifying groups/members who would like to work with the ongoing enterprises; (g) assessing nature of facilitation required at group level; (h) assessing training needs of group members; (i) hand holding/escort services required by the group members; (j) networking with various institutions for provision of identified facilities including training and backward and forward linkages; (k) role of various stakeholders; (l) the promotion of micro-enterprises is to be undertaken by one/two identified NGOs in a district; (m) the MEPAs are expected to adopt participatory methods for helping the group members in selecting the activity, imparting the right type of technical/skill building training, escort and hand holding services for backward and forward linkages including marketing, etc.

The challenge which emerges is the expansion in the vision of the SHG movement from microfinance to micro-enterprise development with the assumption that adequate physical and social infrastructure are created in rural areas, and technical, entrepreneurial, managerial and marketing skills are developed among SHG members. Meeting this demand would require concerted efforts and innovative initiatives on the part of all developmental agencies and stakeholders in the development process, including the SHGs. A holistic approach for developing micro-enterprises among SHGs, along with skill and technology development and upgradation and innovative marketing ensuring reduction in intermediation cost, could be the right recipe for sustainability of micro-enterprises. Such efforts where the rural poor are active partners in the development process could be instrumental in the attainment of sustainable rural development (Roy, 2005). While the pilot project on SHG-Bank Linkage led to the micro-finance revolution in India, it is hoped that the pilot project for promotion of micro-enterprise among matured SHGs would bring about a micro-enterprise revolution in the country.

8. Rural Non-Farm Sector

It has been widely recognized that there is a huge potential for income and employment generation in rural areas through the development of Rural Non-farm Sector (RNFS). Thus, reform in rural credit is incomplete without the promotion and development of RNFS. The term RNFS includes a wide spectrum of economic activities undertaken in the decentralized sector by artisans, craftsmen and non-agricultural labour in part-time activity (Sharma, 2005b). There is also a great scope for development of agro-based and food processing industries as the Indian economy is essentially agrarian in nature. However, the credit needs of this sector are not adequately met by banks. The share of the SSI sector in gross bank credit suffered a decline from 14 per cent to 8 per cent during the period end-March

2000 to end-March 2005. The SSI sector has, nevertheless, experienced a steady growth rate of bank credit from 6.04 per cent (2000-01) to 15.58 per cent (2004-05).[8] But this does not compare favourably against industry (medium and large), agriculture, other priority sector, wholesale trade and other sectors.

The foregoing analysis underscores the fact that there has been a lack of enthusiasm on the part of banks to finance the SSI sector (including RNFS). This is mainly due to the lack of availability of enterprising and skilled youth in the rural areas. There are also the problems of lack of collateral support and threat of NPA. Further, the experience of financing under Government sponsored programmes like Prime Minister Rozgar Yojana (PMRY) has not been very encouraging either. However, an analysis of NPA reveals that while the share of NPAs in the priority sector increased from 45.43 per cent at end-March 2001 to 49.05 per cent at end-March 2005 (in case of public sector banks) and the share of NPAs in agriculture increased from 13.87 per cent to 15.21 per cent, that of SSI sector declined from 19.44 per cent to 16.43 per cent.[9]

NABARD has been implementing various promotional progrmmes for the development of entrepreneurs through area based approach, and sensitization of stakeholders. NABARD had launched the District Rural Industries Project (DRIP) on a pilot basis during 1993-94 in five districts with the objective of demonstrating that intensive promotional activities under RNFS can create sustainable employment opportunities in the rural areas through enhanced credit flow to this sector. This project has since been extended to 103 districts of the country. The impact created in the districts covered under DRIP has revealed that there was a significant increase in credit flow and employment opportunities in these districts (NABARD, 2005a). Development of entrepreneurs through Rural Entrepreneurship Development Programmes (REDP), Assistance to Rural Women in Non-farm Development (ARWIND), creating a niche market for rural produce for women entrepreneurs (MAHIMA), strengthening of rural *haats*, and development of rural clusters are some of the interventions being carried out by NABARD for the development of RNFS.

SIDBI has also been implementing various projects for development of entrepreneurs through Rural Industries Programme (RIP). The RIP provides a cohesive and integrated package of basic inputs like information, motivation, training and credit, backed by appropriate technology and market linkages for the purpose of enterprise promotion.

It is also worth-mentioning that various public sector banks have collaborated in the establishment of entrepreneurship training centres (e.g. RUDSETI) in various parts of the country. In this context, the promoting banks concerned have the moral responsibility to credit link the entrepreneurs trained at these centres. There is also a need to expand the network of such training centres to all districts in the country.

With a view to addressing the genuine difficulties of SSIs in accessing bank credit because of their inability to provide adequate security, the Government of India launched the Credit Guarantee Fund Trust for Small Industries (CGTSI), with SIDBI as the nodal agency. The CGTSI guarantees 75 per cent of the credit risk of eligible lenders (member lending institutions), subject to a loan cap of Rs. 25 lakh and guarantee cap of Rs. 18.75 lakh per borrower.

The foregoing initiatives by NABARD, SIDBI and Government of India have the potential of boosting credit to the SSI/RNFS sector in a big way. It is for the banks to come forward to take advantage of the business opportunities created under this sector.

9. Conclusion

The SHG-Bank Linkage Programme has brought banking to the doorsteps of the poor, women and the weaker sections of the society. On this count alone this programme has been truly revolutionary in character. Various models and innovations have been developed in India and abroad. However, the one common thread connecting the various innovations has been the focus on empowerment of the poor and the women. In India the two most common models of microfinance have been the SHG-Bank

Linkage Programme and the Outsourcing model in the form of bulk lending by leading private and public sector banks, foreign banks, SIDBI, etc., to MFIs, which in turn on-lend to the SHGs. While the SHG-Bank Linkage Programme has been observed to be more sensitive towards the needs of the rural poor, the 'Outsourcing model' has led to the emergence of commercial oriented MFIs, which are functioning more as sophisticated money lenders than facilitators for the rural poor. While MFIs have an important role to play in upscaling the microfinance programme, issues relating to the regulation of MFIs need to be addressed. While separate and exclusive regulatory and supervisory framework for MFIs may not be required for the present as bulk of the microfinance portfolio rests in the books of regulated entities like banks and NBFCs, non-deposit taking MFIs may attempt self-regulation by forming State level associations to evolve code of ethics, uniform standards of accounting practices and disclosures, empanel and train auditors, etc., with the assistance of NABARD and SIDBI. It would also be pertinent for NABARD, SIDBI and major banks to consider promoting independent rating agencies by way of equity contributions. The banks and financial institutions providing bulk loans to MFIs, should also closely monitor and regulate the latter.

Various innovations in microfinance have evolved nationally and internationally. In this context the Indira Kranti Pratham project in the State of Andhra Pradesh has been found to be a holistic, well-planned and well-structured programme of microfinance. It has demonstrated that a systematic and holistic approach could make a significant impact on the livelihoods of the poor rural families, through various need based interventions and innovations. The model developed under this project could be replicated in other states, with suitable modifications as per regional or local needs. Other innovations worth replicating are pilot project on processor cards and branch automation, pilot project on 'e-grama', Computer Munshi Grain Bank, rural volunteers as book writers and 'OB Grameen Project'.

A major challenge which emerges is the expansion in the vision of the SHG movement from microfinance to micro-enterprise development with the assumption that adequate physical and social infrastructure are created in rural areas, and technical, entrepreneurial, managerial and marketing skills are developed among SHG members. A holistic approach for developing micro-enterprises among SHGs, along with skill and technology development and upgradation, and innovative marketing ensuring reduction in intermediation cost, could be the right recipe for sustainability of micro-enterprises.

Reform in rural credit is incomplete without the promotion and development of RNFS. There is a great scope for development of agro-based and food-processing industries as the Indian economy is essentially agrarian in nature. The credit needs of this sector need to be adequately met by banks. The role of NABARD and SIDBI in capacity building of entrepreneurs and bankers is critical in the development of RNFS/SSI sector. But here the rate of interest charged to the ultimate beneficiary needs to be carefully considered.

Banks, financial institutions, MFIs, Government departments and CSOs/NGOs need to be sensitized to activate financial inclusion, innovations and initiatives in rural credit, especially those relating to microfinance and rural non-farm sector, in a much greater measure. This is imperative to address the vast range of issues relating to socio-economic development in rural India.

NOTES

1. Training and Field demonstrations by experts in the area of agriculture and allied activites are arranged by NABARD for the benefit of Farmers Clubs.
2. It has been observed in the State of Andhra Pradesh that the effective rate of interest charged by the MFIs to SHGs is generally more than 24 per cent.
3. Source: *Business Standard*, 13 April 2006.
4. Based on discussions the author had with Mr. T.Vijay Kumar, CEO, Society for Eradication of Rural Poverty (SERP), Hyderabad.
5. The author acknowledges the fruitful interactions he had with the CEO and officers/field staff of SERP and members of SHGs, VOs and MSs in Warangal district of A.P.

6. Mandal is an administrative unit in the State of Andhra Pradesh covering a cluster of 30-40 villages.
7. This is a unique initiative under which minor girls are formed into SHGs. They meet regularly, save small amounts and discuss issues relating to education, environment, cleanliness, nutrition, etc.
8. Source: *Report on Trend and Progress of Banking in India*, RBI (various issues).
9. Source: *Report on Trend and Progress of Banking in India*, RBI (various issues).

REFERENCES

Chidambaram, P. (2006): *Budget Speech 2006-07*, Government of India.

Leeladhar, V. (2005): "Taking Banking Services to the Common Man—Financial Inclusion", *Commemorative Lecture* at the Fedbank Hormis Memorial Foundation at Ernakulum, December 2, 2005. www.rbi.org.in

Meier, Gerald M. and James E. Rauch (2005): "The Microfinance Promise", *Leading Issues in Economic Development*, Oxford University Press, 320-326.

NABARD (2005), *Progress of SHG-Bank Linkage in India 2004-05.*

Reserve Bank of India (1998), *Report of the Committee on Banking Sector Reforms* (Narasimham Committee II).

—— (2005a): *Report of the Internal Group on Regional Rural Banks.*

—— (2005b): *Report of the Expert Group on Investment Credit,* June 2005 (Chairman: Y.S.P.Thorat).

—— (2005c): *Report of the Internal Group to Examine Issues Relating to Rural Credit and Microfinance.*

Roy, Debesh (2005): "Sustainable Rural Development: Innovations in Microfinance and Micro-Enterprise Promotion", *Lucknow Management Association Journal*, Vol.1, No. 1.

Satish, P. (2005): "Mainstreaming of Indian Microfinance", *Economic and Political Weekly*, April 23-29, 2005.

Sharma, Manoranjan (2003): "Innovate or Perish—The Success Mantra", *BECON Conference Volume.*

—— (2004): "Centrality of Innovation for Banks", *Business Line*, August 31.

—— (2005a): "Innovation in Banks: Need to Push Full Throttle Ahead", *Professional Banker*, September.

—— (2005b): "Rural Non-farm Sector in India: Issues and Evidence", in Manoranjan Sharma (ed.), *Leading Issues in Indian Economy*, Atlantic Publishers and Distributors (P) Ltd., New Delhi.

Financial Inclusion in India

17

R.K. Anand

The banking industry has shown tremendous growth in volume and complexity in our country during the last few decades. Despite making significant improvements in all the areas relating to financial viability, profitability and competitiveness, there are concerns that banks have not been able to include vast segment of the population, especially the underprivileged sections of the society, into the fold of basic banking services. Internationally also efforts are being made to study the causes of financial exclusion and designing strategies to ensure financial inclusion of the poor and disadvantaged. The reasons may vary from country to country and hence the strategy could also vary but all out efforts are being made as financial inclusion can truly lift the financial condition and standards of life of the poor and the disadvantaged.

In the Annual Policy of the Reserve Bank of India for the year 2004-05, the Governor, Dr. Reddy observed: There has been expansion, greater competition and diversification of ownership of banks leading to both enhanced efficiency and systemic resilience in the banking sector. However, there are legitimate concerns in regard to the banking practices that tend to exclude rather than attract vast sections of population, in particular pensioners, self-employed and those employed in unorganised sector. While commercial considerations are no doubt important, the banks have been bestowed with several privileges, especially of seeking public deposits on a highly leveraged basis, and consequently they should be obliged to provide banking services to all segments of the population, on equitable basis.

In most developing countries, financial services, such as, saving accounts, credit from formal financial institutions and insurance is restricted to a large part of the population.

This is why the Secretary General of the United Nations stressed the need to make inclusive development as an integral element in the overall economic policy formulation. He quoted that "The stark reality is that most poor people in the world still lack access to sustainable financial services, whether it is savings, credit or insurance. The great challenge before us is to address the constraints that exclude people from full participation in the financial sector. Together, we can and must build 'Inclusive Financial Sectors' that help people improve their lives." Let us first examine the opposite term, i.e. Financial Exclusion.

1. Financial Exclusion

Financial exclusion in its broader meaning is the inability of the individuals to access a range of basic financial services on the grounds that:

(a) Financial access is either restricted or unavailable, or

(b) The Charges and prices of financial services are restrictive, or

(c) The beneficiary apprehends denial.

1.1 Reasons of Financial Exclusion

Insufficient **income**	Lack of **assets** whether physical or financial
Low **capabilities** due to lack of financial education, training or experience.	Negligible market **values**

1.2 Intensity of Financial Exclusion

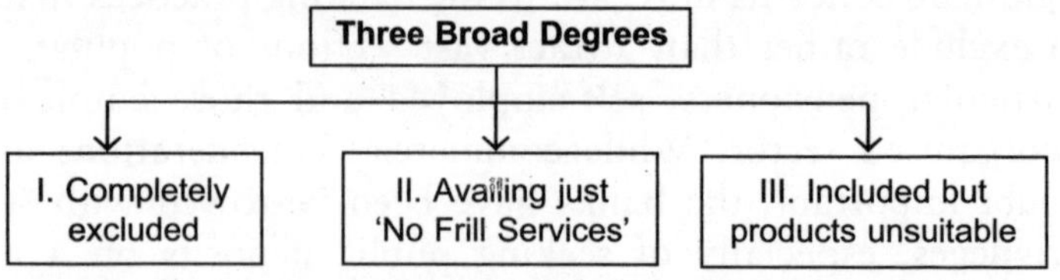

Consultative Group to Assist the Poorest (CGAP) estimates that between 2-3 billion people globally are still excluded from access to financial services with often the proportion of exclusion being more than 90 per cent in the Least Developed Countries.

UK's Basic Financial Model:

- Identification of 3 priority areas: access to banking services, credit, face-to-face money advice.
- Establishment of a Financial Inclusion Fund.
- 'No Frills' basic bank account.
- Post Office Current Account, Savings Gateway for low income employment.
- Community Finance Learning Initiatives.

A civil rights law, namely Community Reinvestment Act (CRA) in the United States prohibits discrimination by banks against low and moderate-income neighbourhoods. The CRA imposes affirmative and continuing obligations on banks to serve the needs for credit and banking services of all the communities in which they are chartered. In fact, numerous studies conducted by Federal Reserve and Harvard University demonstrated that CRA lending is a win-win proposition and profitable to banks. In this context, it is also interesting to know the other initiative taken by a state in the United States. Apart from the CRA experiment, armed with the sanction of Banking Law, the State of New York Banking Department, with the objective of making available the low cost banking services to consumers, made mandatory that each banking institution shall offer *basic banking account* and in case of credit unions the *basic share draft account*, which is in the nature of low cost account with minimum facilities. Some key features of the basic banking account are worth-mentioning here:

- The initial deposit amount required to open the account shall not exceed US $25.
- The minimum balance, including any average balance, required to maintain such account shall not exceed US $0.10.
- The charge for periodic cycle for the maintenance of such accounts to be declared up front.

- The minimum number of withdrawal transactions which may be made during any periodic cycle at no charge to the account holder must at least be eight.
- A withdrawal shall be deemed to be made when recorded on the books of the account holder's banking institution.
- Except, as provided below, an account holder shall not be restricted as to the number of deposits which may be made to the account without incurring any additional charge.
- The banking institution may charge account holders for transactions at electronic facilities which are not operated by the account holder's banking institution as well as other fees and charges for specific banking services which are not covered under the basic banking account scheme.
- Every periodic statement issued for the basic banking account should invariably cover on it or by way of separate communiqué maximum number of withdrawals permitted during each periodic cycle without additional charge and the consequences of exceeding such maximum and the fee if any, for the use of electronic facilities which are not operated by the account holder's banking institution.

1.3 Financial Exclusion—Indian Scenario

The India Economy has done well in the past decade and a half. However, more recently, during the last 3 years and in the current year, the average rate of the growth of the economy has been around 8%. But fears are now being increasingly expressed that our growth must not result in two Indias.

- The number of bank branches has grown eightfold from 8,187 in 1969 to 68,681 as at the end of 2005-06. The number of customers per branch declined fourfold from 64,000 to 16,000. However, during this period the total population of the country has also doubled (0.55 billion as per the 1971 Census to 1.03 billion as per the 2001

Census). Consequently, the extent of financial exclusion has not reduced significantly since 1969.

- In terms of regional dis-aggregation since 1991, population per bank office has increased in rural areas from 13,462 in 1991 to 16,650 in 2005 and, as expected, declined in the urban areas from 14,484 to 13,619 over the period. Three regions, North-Eastern, East and Central have higher population per office than the all-India average.
- It thus appears that in the last 15 years banking system has gone urban.
- Consequences of financial exclusion will vary depending on the nature and extent of services denied. It may lead to increased travel requirements, higher incidence of crime, general decline in investment, difficulties in gaining access to credit or getting credit from informal sources at exorbitant rates, and increased unemployment, etc. The small business may suffer due to loss of access to middle class and higher-income consumers, higher cash handling costs, delays in remittances of money. According to certain researches, financial exclusion can lead to social exclusion.

1.4 Reducing Inclusion (Widening Exclusion)

- Around 50% of our banking business is yet conducted in eight major cities—Mumbai, Delhi, Chennai, Kolkata, Bangalore, Hyderabad, Ahmedabad and Pune.
- Nearly 300 million people in our country are still below the poverty line.
- We rank in the bottom one-third of the countries according to the Human Development Index.
- In December 2003, 62% of all rural households (58% of farming households and 78% non-farming) did not have access to basic bank services.
- It is also estimated that about 12% of urban households do not have such access.

- Thus over 48% of all the households in the country remain excluded from the benefits of banking.
- 49% of the farm households receive credit from the institutional sources and non-institutional sources and the rest do not get credit and, therefore, there is exclusion of 51%.
- Dependence of farmer households on moneylenders has increased to 26.8% in 1991 from 17.5% in 2002.

Thus notwithstanding the expansion of banking, the formal credit system has suffered to have shrunk in rural and semi-urban areas during 1991 to 2006. This combined with the low growth in agriculture during the last decade seems to have widened the financial exclusion in the rural areas as shown in the graph:

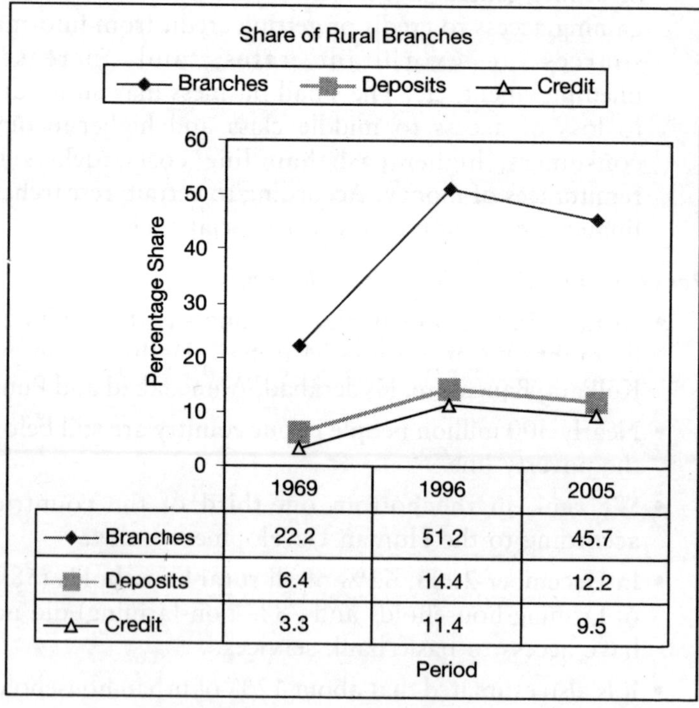

	1969	1996	2005
Branches	22.2	51.2	45.7
Deposits	6.4	14.4	12.2
Credit	3.3	11.4	9.5

Source: *Reserve Bank of India*

2. Uneven (Skewed) Financial Inclusion

The another serious aspect is its multidimensional 'Skewness' which is indicated below in Tables a-c based on database of 'The Situation Assessment Survey (SAS) of Farmers (59th Round NSSO), 2003'.

(a) Distribution according to marginal and sub-marginal farmer households:

Farmer households	Number (Million)			Per cent		
	Financially excluded	Financially included	Total	Financially excluded	Financially included	Total
Small/Marginal	40.27	34.70	74.97	53.71	46.29	100.00
Other than S/M	5.66	8.72	14.38	39.36	60.64	100.00
Total	45.93	43.42	89.35	51.40	48.60	100.00

The table shows that the marginal and sub-marginal farmers as a category constitute 83.9% of the total farmer households, at 89.35 million. Of these 53.7% (40.27 million) households were financially excluded. On the other hand, the farmer households other than small and marginal constituted 16.1% of the total farmer households, out of which 39.4% (5.66 million) households were excluded. This indicates that the exclusion is higher amongst marginal and sub-marginal farmers.

(b) Distribution of States as per the extent of Financial Exclusion:

Extent of Financial exclusion	States
Above 75%	Meghalaya, Arunachal Pradesh, Uttaranchal, Assam, Mizoram, Manipur, Jharkhand
50% to 75%	Bihar, Chattisgarh, Himachal Pradesh, Jammu & Kashmir, Nagaland, Orissa, Sikkim, Tripura, Uttar Pradesh
25% to 50%	Karnataka, Kerala, Madhya Pradesh, Maharashtra, Punjab, Rajasthan, Tamil Nadu, West Bengal,
Below 25%	Andhra Pradesh

The analysis of financial exclusion according to geographical spread revealed that in 7 states more than 75% farmer households were found to be financially excluded.

(c) *Distribution of size-class wise indebtedness of farmers' households:*

Size Class (ha)	Number			Percent (%)		
	Included	Excluded	Total	Included	Excluded	Total
Up to 0.40 ha	135820	169641	305471	44.5	55.5	100.0
0.41 to 1.00 ha	129211	154399	283610	45.6	54.4	100.0
1.01 to 2.00 ha	81920	78680	160600	51.0	49.0	100.0
Up to 2,00 ha	346951	402720	749671	46.3	53.7	100.0
201 to 4.00 ha	54409	39095	93504	58.2	41.8	100.0
4.01 & above	32882	17447	50329	65.3	34.7	100.0
Above 2.00 ha	37291	56542	143833	60.7	39.3	100.0
All sizes	434242	459262	893504	48.6	51.4	100.0

Table C indicates that an inverse proportional relation between size-class of land and non-indebtedness, i.e. the minimum size-class had the lowest inclusion.

3. Enhancing Financial Inclusion: Indian Perspective

In our country the Government has accorded high priority to the issue of overall inclusion in the development process through various initiatives such as the Rural Employment Guarantee Scheme, the Bharat Nirman programme, the Sarva Shiksha Abhiyan, and the like.

The Reserve Bank of India in its annual policy Statement of April 2005, while recognising the concerns in regard to the banking practices that tend to exclude rather than attract vast sections of population, urged banks to review their existing practices to align them with the objective of financial inclusion. In many banks, the requirement of minimum balance and charges levied, although accompanied by a number of free facilities, deter a sizeable section of population from opening/maintaining bank accounts. With a view to achieving greater financial inclusion, all banks need to make available a basic banking 'no frills' account either with 'nil' or very low minimum balances as well as charges that would make such accounts accessible to vast sections of population. The nature and number of transactions in such accounts could be restricted, but made known to the customer in advance in a transparent manner. All banks are urged to give wide publicity to the facility of such a 'no-frills' account so as to ensure greater financial inclusion.

The Government of India set up a committee with Dr. C. Rangarajan as its Chairman in June 2006 to examine the issue of inclusive growth. The Committee sets three requisites for the inclusive growth:

1. The economy needs to grow fast and include all segments to remain truly sustainable.
2. The pattern of economic growth must be such that it is labour intensive. It is in this context that an increasing emphasis on agriculture becomes relevant.
3. We need social safety nets and increase the expenditure on social sectors like primary health and primary education.

The Committee quotes that "There is a need to set in motion a virtual cycle of growth and inclusion."

4. Financial Inclusion Initiatives in India

In response to GoI and RBI/NABARD guidelines there are some developments during the current decade. These are:

4.1. Evolution of the 'Theory of 3 Pillars'

This holds that social transformation and inclusion of the disadvantaged would require to be based on the 'Three Pillars':

I. The State Government which would provide the framework for inclusion and implement fiscal measures to develop basic infrastructure to enhance economic and social capital.

II. The formal financial system represented primarily by banks which would provide savings facilities, efficient payment systems and low-cost credit.

III. Community Based Organizations and NGOs, which would catalyze local participation, formation of voluntary Self Help Groups and develop the linkages between the SHGs and banks.

A fourth facilitator in the process of transformation of the rural economy may be the Corporate Sector, which, for commercially strategic reasons and also in discharge of its Corporate Social Responsibility, has also took initiatives, e.g., the E-Choupal initiative of ITC, the Electronic Knowledge Delivery programme of the M.S.Swaminathan Research Foundation, etc.

4.2 NABARD's Initiatives

(a) The first SHG-Bank Linkage Programme was launched in 1992, which gathered momentum from 1999 onwards. SHGs have become a significant force. As we all know that there are today about 2.23 million SHGs with 32.96 million households covered and nearly 43,000 branches are involved. It has inculcated a savings and credit culture. **Among the States, Andhra Pradesh has been a pioneer in promoting the SHG-bank linkage programme.**

Issue: The SHGs need technical skills and marketing facilities, and not lowering the rate of interest or subsidies.

(b) As we graduate further we need to move to Facilitator model and the Correspondent model to supplement and not supplant the activities of commercial banks. NGOs can intermediate to make available banking services to small and marginal farmers.

Issue: There is an issue about the cost of credit. Worldwide experience shows that microfinance cannot be reached at a cost less than 20-25%. But somehow there is a mindset in India that 20% or 25% interest rate is an exploiting one.

(c) MFIs: The MFIs which are of recent origin may try to combine the good features of both pillar 2 and 3 by undertaking financial intermediation and providing livelihood support through local community participation.

Issues: The inadequacy of capital, instances of charging of exorbitant interest rates and highhanded approach for recovery by some MFIs, lack of a rating mechanism for MFIs and the need for training for NGOs and MFIs are the issues.

(d) RRBs: Regional rural banks are intended to serve a very different class of clients. In fact, they are intended to serve the people who are not clients at all.

Issue: It is important that the bank managements communicate with their employees and the trade unions to revive RRBs. The Regulatory control of RRBs is also likely to shift to NABARD.

4.3. RBI's Initiatives

The RBI has issued guidelines to significantly enhance the level of financial inclusion in a time-bound manner. The RBI's Annual Policy Statement of the year 2005-2006 urged banks to promote financial inclusion by opening 'no frills account', simplified 'KYC' procedure and reasonable bank charges.

Basic banking account ("No Frills"): In this context, with a view to achieving the objective of greater financial inclusion, all banks are advised to make available a basic banking 'no-frills' account either with 'nil' or very low minimum balances as well as charges that would make such accounts accessible to vast sections of population. The nature and number of transactions in such accounts could be restricted, but made known to the customer in advance in a transparent manner. All banks are advised to give wide publicity to the facility of such 'no-frills' account including in the local media indicating the facilities and charges in a transparent manner.

RBI advised the banks to make available a basic banking account with nil or low minimum balances and low maintenance and service charges. The procedures for opening "no frills" accounts have been simplified to enable the underprivileged sections of the society in both urban and rural areas to access basic banking services.

Further, in order to ensure that persons belonging to low income group both in urban and rural areas do not face difficulty in opening the bank accounts due to the procedural hassles, the KYC procedure for opening accounts has been simplified for those persons who intend to keep balances not exceeding rupees fifty thousand (Rs. 50,000) in all their accounts taken together and the total credit in all the accounts taken together is not expected to exceed rupees one lakh (Rs. 1,00,000) in a year.

Banks through the forum of SLBCs are targeting the districts. Palakkad District in Kerala recently became the first district to achieve 100% coverage for financial inclusion.

Issue: The change of mindset of bankers may take some time.

(a) **General-purpose Credit Cards (GCC):** Banks are offering revolving credit through the GCC facility at their rural and semi-urban branches. The GCC may be in the form of passbooks and will provide the rural customers ease in operations and a flexible source of liquidity.

Issue: Bankers need to be persuaded that 'All Poor are not uncreditworthy'.

(b) **SMEs:** These deserve to be encouraged more Total outstanding credit to SMEs is a little over Rs. 1,50,000 crore. Given the number of SMEs, the jobs that it creates and the fact that 40% of all the India's exports are products of SMEs, banks should lend more to SMEs.

Issue: This may require further simplification of procedure, cut down delay in sanctions and marketing support to make them self-sustaining.

(c) **Recent Initiatives:** The Reserve Bank has been adopting a **two-pronged strategy, which can be termed as 'Empowerment and Protection'.** As regards the former, financial inclusion is the first stage of the process. Simultaneously the concepts like Financial Literacy and Credit Counselling would also go in the same direction to help distressed borrowers and bring them within the fold of formal finance. As regards protection a Banking Codes and Standards Board of India and revised Banking Ombudsman Scheme have also been implemented.

Issue: Although these are in line with good global practices yet retraining and reorientation of bankers is required towards customer-centric environment.

5. What We can Do more

5.1. Cooperatives: Whatever be the goodwill and efforts of the Commercial Banks and the RRBs, the only way to extend farm credit to everyone is by a complete revamp of the cooperative structure. The Vaidyanathan Committee has also submitted a report addressing many serious problems faced by them. The second report dealing with the long-term credit is also received.

5.2. The 'Department of Posts' has also demonstrated its potential recently to become the hub for many activities and services for the financially excluded persons.

5.3. There emerges a consensus that the 'Attitude' must change, especially the attitude of human resources of RRBs and rural branches of other banks.

5.4. Institutional Measures: Like any complex machine the failure of any single component may cause the entire process to halt or even collapse, therefore:

- All participants must expect tangible benefit accruing in the long run.
- All participants must function together. There can be no success without synergy.
- The threshold to be crossed by the targeted sections to become free from the debt trap that they are already caught in.
- Banks to tackle the problem of identification of target population by using biometric technology.
- Banks and Government need to prioritize long-term planning as they may have little profit to gain in the short term.
- Banks need to develop a committed, specialized workforce, which will be at home in the environment in which they have to operate.

5.5. Bottom of the pyramid: As per the 2001 Census, 73% of the country's population resides in rural areas. The core issue of abject poverty requires that the problems of the class of marginal and sub-marginal farmers be addressed first. The second class of farmers is small farmers constituting about 40% of the farming community facing moderate exclusion. A safety net be built for this class of farmers offering:

- Assured wage employment during off-seasons—expansion of National Rural Employment Guarantee Scheme.
- Subsidiary occupations like animal husbandry, backyard poultry, small sheep units etc. (we have recently seen that suicides did not occur in families having subsidiary occupations, particularly dairy).
- The risk mitigation arrangements by way of crop insurance.
- Food security through grain banks etc.
- Subsidized irrigation facility

Conclusion

It is clear that execution of financial exclusion will require an approach in totality on the part of the banks in creating awareness about financial products, education, and advice on money management, debt counselling, savings and affordable credit. The banks would have to evolve specific strategies to expand the outreach of their services in order to promote financial inclusion. One of the ways in which this can be achieved in a cost-effective manner is through forging linkages with micro-finance institutions and local communities. Banks should give wide publicity to the facility of "no frills" account. Technology can be a very valuable tool in providing access to banking products in remote areas. ATMs cash dispensing machines can be modified suitably to make them user friendly for people who are illiterate, less educated or do not know English.

Banks would need to redesign their business strategies to incorporate specific plans to promote financial inclusion of low-income group treating it both a business opportunity as well as a corporate social responsibility. They have to make use of all available resources including technology and expertise available with them as well as the MFIs and NGOs. The bankers need to dispel the apprehension that financial inclusion is a losing proposition. This is in fact the business model that aims at the recruitment of customers for the banks where the present potential is less and the future potential is higher. It may appear in the first instance that taking banking to the sections constituting "the bottom of the pyramid", may not be profitable but it should always be remembered that even the relatively low margins on high volumes can be a very profitable proposition.

Financial inclusion can emerge as commercial profitable business. The real challenge lies in making an effort in taking turn once again towards the masses, which got excluded out of the Indian Growth Story, and the comforts allied to the same.

REFERENCES

SAS, NSSO 59th Round.

All-India Debt and Investment Survey (AIDIS), 2002.

Report of the Committee on Financial Inclusion with Dr. C. Rangarajan.

NABARD

18

Financial Inclusion of Farmers: Rajasthan Perspective

Rakesh Malhotra

ABSTRACT

Indian agriculture today faces an unprecedented crisis in sustaining the viability of its operations. There are serious problems in advancing the momentum of the green revolution. As evident from spate of humiliating suicides, the Indian farmer is at a highly vulnerable juncture. The Government has taken serious cognizance of the decay in Indian agro-economic rural fabric. Several initiatives have been contemplated, the foremost being financial inclusion of farmers. The paper, with particular reference to Rajasthan, attempts to examine the status of Indian farmers and their indebtedness in a proper historical and comparative perspective. An analysis reveals that institutional sources of credit have not been able to serve the farmers in India as was expected of them. Even today, after intrinsic efforts of expanding the outreach of formal financial sector in the nation, money lenders still play a pivotal role in dispensation of credit, their client base being equal to the client base of the banks in rural areas! Among the various states in India, in absolute terms, the number of farmer households was maximum in Uttar Pradesh and least in Sikkim. However, the incidence of indebtedness amongst the farmers was maximum in Andhra Pradesh and least in Meghalaya. The bulk of indebtedness lay in the bandwidth of less than 2 ha and most important non-productive credit need of the farmer was 'marriage'. It was interesting to see that in India, proportion of indebtedness was inversely related to the size of land holding. It was also seen that the farmers with land holding of more than 10 ha, had share of 0.8 per cent in total number of land holdings in the nation, albeit they held about 27.6 per cent of total loan accounts in the banks and accounted for almost half of the total loan amount given by the banks to farming community. While 'banks' were the major purveyor of credit to farmers in the country, in Rajasthan it was the 'money lender.' It was seen that the 'government' was major source of credit supplier in Sikkim, while 'cooperative societies' were the predominant supplier of credit to the farmers in Maharashtra. 'Banks' supplied credit to more than 60 per cent of farmers in Tripura. However, in case of Meghalaya farmers hardly got any credit from the banks! In Andhra Pradesh more than 53 per cent of the farmers had raised loans from 'money lenders'. Marked variations on account of 'caste' amongst the farming community to raise credit were also witnessed. The average amount of loan outstanding was Rs. 12,585 per farmer household in the country. Farmers in Rajasthan were able to raise more quantum of credit and were relatively more indebted than the farmers in other states. While Rajasthan had 5.44 per cent of total banking network of the country, Maharashtra had the privilege of having best banking network amongst the various states in the nation. It was further seen that not only the efforts in augmenting the outreach of banking sector in rural areas have been futile; but also the premise that by augmenting credit flow to farmers their cardinal problems would be ameliorated is misplaced. Probably, the solution to the vexed problem of Indian farming lies in designing a comprehensive 'livelihood approach' rather than merely resorting to fragmented initiatives.

ACCESS TO RURAL CREDIT: MACRO PERSPECTIVE

Despite massive expansion of the banking network and extensive dose of credit through various programmes for alleviating the rural poverty in the country, there are still persisting problems of inadequate outreach of institutional credit to the rural poor. It is evident that mere presence of a bank branch in the rural area cannot be construed as availability of credit to rural inhabitants. The formulation of special credit schemes or allocation of specific target is also grossly inadequate to ensure better 'access' of credit to the poor. Neither can the subsidies or subsidized credit, direct the flow of financial support to the most vulnerable class of the society. 'Access' in terms of credit is not merely a matter of physical reach but should also connote the notion of being able to reach, enter, understand and influence.

It is said "the availability of credit was not sufficient; it has to be converted into access or entitlement for the indigent section" (Veerashekerappa, 1994).[1] Dr. C. Rangarajan[2] in his keynote address observed "Greater access and sustainable flow of credit is critical for the empowerment of the poor." Despite a plethora of government sponsored programmes, wide banking network and steep increase in bank loans to the poor, timely and adequate credit, which are the main concerns of the poor, were not met by the formal financial system (De Silva and Deuby, 1992).[3] Foundation for Development Cooperation (FDC), 1995[4] observed "the financial services of the formal banking system had remained inaccessible to the majority of poor people in the rural areas in our country, as in several developing countries, forcing them to rely mainly on informal credit sources." With special reference to women, Lopez and March (1991)[5] concluded "women have a practical gender need for improved access to credit, and better financial knowledge."

In the Indian context, the absence of conveniently accessible and flexible products and services, simplified documentation and the insistence on collateral justify the poignant observation of the Report of the Agricultural Credit Review Committee of the RBI (1989): "the aim of serving the poor (through the banking system) has ended up by giving poor service."

All India Rural Credit Survey (ACRC) (1954)[6] showed that institutional credit accounted for hardly 7 per cent of gross requirement of credit by the village community. Of this credit, 3 per cent each was provided by government and cooperatives and about 1 per cent by the commercial banks. ACRC (1975) observed that the benefit of increased credit flow from the formal sector bypassed the relatively weaker section of the rural society. All India Debt Investment Survey of 1991 found that only 15.6 per cent rural households had borrowed from formal sources. Even the Rural Finance Access Survey (RFAS)[7] of NCAER and

World Bank carried out in two major states of India, Andhra Pradesh and Uttar Pradesh found that only about 21 per cent of rural households accessed formal loans. Chandra (1993)[8] drew a significant inference from his investigation in Punjab that "the increase in farm income is more due to borrowings from the informal sector than formal sector." He also concluded that, small farmers depended more on the informal sector than the others. In contrast, the study by Ambastha (1994)[9], found that the formal channel (institutional source) was the major purveyor of credit in the country. This study further revealed that the share of institutional credit increased from 12.2 per cent in 1951 to 61.2 per cent in 1981. Other investigations revealed that 58 per cent (Birthal and Singh, 1996)[10]; 60 per cent (Malhotra, 1997)[11]; and 50 per cent (Group Savings and Credit Management, 1998)[12] of the total rural households were served by the formal channel of credit. In contrast, Singh *et al.* (1998)[13] found that contribution of formal credit in total rural credit was as high as 85 per cent. Malhotra (2000)[14] in an empirical investigation in Rae Bareli district of Uttar Pradesh found that less than 0.5 per cent of female population and 3.5 per cent of male population in the study area were clients of banks. A similar study by Rao and Malhotra (2000)[15] in Varanasi district of Uttar Pradesh accentuated the inaccessibility of landless peasants to the funds of institutional sources as they lack adequate security/collateral to offer to the banks. It was also concluded by them that only 17 per cent of total surveyed households in rural areas were in the ambience of formal channel. In a study conducted by CmF[16] in 1604 rural households in 36 villages of 6 blocks in 5 districts of Rajasthan it was observed that banks provided about 24 per cent of credit needs in rural areas.

Table 1 shows the changing share of different agencies in providing credit in India over the last four decades.

Table 1: Percentage share of different credit agencies in cash borrowings of households

Credit Agency	Rural				Urban		
	1971-72	1981-82	1991-92	2002-03	1981-82	1991-92	2002-03
Government, etc.	3.1	4.2	3.9	2.7	10.0	7.9	6.2
Cooperative societies/ banks	14.9	26.3	25.7	28.0	18.3	21.9	22.0
Commercial banks	1.7	23.1	20.7	22.7	25.6	16.3	30.6
Insurance agencies		0.1	0.3	0.3	1.2	1.8	1.5
Provident fund		0.8	1.3	1.0	6.8	7.8	3.0
Financial corporations				0.6			8.4
Financial companies				0.8			2.5
Others			1.4	1.0		4.2	1.5
All Institutional agencies	***19.7***	***54.5***	***53.3***	***57.2***	***61.9***	***59.9***	***75.7***
Landlord	6.4	3.8	3.9	0.6	0.4	0.3	0.2
Agricultural money lender	18.7	9.7	8.1	9.6	0.8	0.6	0.6
Professional money lender	15.9	7.8	13.3	20.6	9.4	14.0	13.3
Traders	14.9	5.9	4.0	2.9	7.1	3.5	1.3
Relatives and friends	11.4	12.4	8.9	7.4	13.7	13.9	7.0
Others	12.9	4.7	4.2	1.7	6.0	5.1	1.8
All Non-Institutional agencies	***80.3***	***44.3***	***42.3***	***42.8***	***37.4***	***37.4***	***24.2***
All Agencies	**100.0**	**100.0**	**100.0**	**100.0**	**100.0**	**100.0**	**100.0**

Source: Report No. 502, Household Borrowings and Repayments, NSS 59th Round, GoI, 2006.

NSSO (2005) starkly revealed that the macro position of indebted farming households masked considerable regional variations.

This kind of macro-economic setting is not only disconcerting but also clearly undesirable. Professor C.K. Prahalad[17] has brought out that there is a huge market at what he calls "the Bottom of the Pyramid" (BOP). Manoranjan Sharma[18] has carried this point further by cogently arguing that there are huge business opportunities in financial inclusion. The poor are not a homogeneous mass with each group having its specific needs and absorption capacity for loans and other financial services. Hence, what is needed is development of the entrepreneurial pyramid for improving rural livelihoods on a sustained basis.

Table 2: Percentage of Indebted Farming Households by all sources of Loans, by sources of Loan and Distribution of Outstanding Loans by source, 2003

State	% of Indebted farming households in total rural households (All sources)	% of Indebted Farmer Households by Source of Loan		% of distribution of outstanding loan by sources	
		Formal	Informal	Formal	Informal
Andhra Pradesh	82	54	77	31.4	68.5
Arunachal Pradesh	6	14	103	26.9	73.1
Assam	18	15	88	37.5	62.6
Bihar	33	23	84	41.7	58.5
Chhattisgarh	40	66	56	72.4	27.7
Gujarat	52	63	49	69.5	30.5
Haryana	53	76	50	67.6	32.5
Himachal Pradesh	33	57	65	65.3	34.7
Jammu & Kashmir	32	9	94	67.6	32.3
Jharkhand	21	44	60	64.1	35.9
Karnatak	62	57	55	68.9	31.2
Kerala	64	96	40	82.3	17.6
Madhya Pradesh	51	64	66	56.9	43.0
Maharastra	55	92	30	83.8	16.2
Manipur	25	6	99	18.2	81.9
Meghalaya	4	2	97	6.0	94.0
Mizoram	24	33	67	77.3	22.6
Nagaland	37	20	79	68.8	31.1
Orissa	48	68	46	74.8	25.1
Punjab	65	58	70	47.9	52.1
Rajasthan	52	38	81	34.2	65.8
Sikkim	39	18	89	57.8	42.2
Tamil Nadu	75	59	67	53.4	46.5
Tripura	49	46	55	79.7	20.3
Uttar Pradesh	40	47	70	60.3	39.7
Uttarakhand	7	65	44	76.1	23.9
West Bengal	50	51	73	58.0	42.1
Group of UTs	51	42	71	59.0	41.0
All India	49	56	64	57.7	42.4

Note: Formal and Informal is more than 100 per cent because farmers borrow from multiple sources.
Source: NSSO (2005).

Rural Areas: It could be seen from Table 1 that in rural areas, there was marked increase in coverage of borrowing households from 19.7 per cent in 1971-72 to 57.2 per cent in

2002-03 by the institutional sources of credit with substantial increase occurring only in the eighties. There had hardly been any significant appreciation in augmenting the outreach of formal channel of credit since 1981-82. It was appalling to observe that there was an insignificant increase of only 1.3 per cent in outreach of banks (cooperatives and commercial banks together) in last three decades. This reflects the ineffectiveness of the banking system in increasing its client base, particularly in rural areas. It is also pertinent to note that coverage of commercial banks (including RRBs) had in fact declined from 23.1 per cent in 1981-82 to 22.7 per cent in 2002-03. This necessitates radical change in the approach of banking sector to serve rural India.

Amongst the non-institutional agencies, it was surprising to note that role of professional money-lender had in fact increased from 15.9 per cent in 1971-72 to 20.6 per cent in 2002-03. The money-lender was the biggest source of credit to rural inhabitant within the non-institutional category. In fact, the money-lender's client base almost matches the client base of banks in rural areas. All other categories of non-institutional agency had registered a decline over the period under report.

Urban Areas: The coverage of institutional sources of credit in urban India has expanded more than the growth in rural areas. The growth of banking sector in particular had been quite marked. Correspondingly the share of non-institutional sources in credit dispensation declined in urban areas of the country.

Indian Agriculture

Agriculture in India has come to be acknowledged as un-remunerative profession. Nevertheless, the population dependent on it still continues to be significant. The farming community in India constitutes more than 67 per cent of total population. Although agriculture's share in total gross domestic product (GDP) declined to about 20 per cent, it remains the single largest contributor to the well-being of the poor, sustaining over 70 per cent of the rural labor force, which predominantly includes farmers.

Indian agriculture is passing through a difficult time, which is widely acknowledged by major political parties, academia, administration and the government itself. There has been a plethora of initiatives by the government to address the challenges on this account, albeit incidence of spiral suicides of farmers in many states of the country has started to ring the alarm bells in the corridors of power. The spate of suicides since 1997-98 is considered a tragic manifestation of the deteriorating condition of the farmers. According to official statistics there were 8,900 suicides by farmers between 2001 and 2006 in the four states of Andhra Pradesh, Karnataka, Kerala and Maharashtra.[19]

The apathy of Indian agriculture by the Indian banks is accentuated by the fact that in 20 years from 1990-91 to 2005-06 the stipulated target of disbursing 18 per cent of net bank credit to 'agriculture' (under priority sector) has not been achieved even once. Further, the share of agriculture in total bank credit, which was 15.33 in 1990-91 declined to 11.1 per cent in 2005-06.

Thus, it should be quite appropriate and interesting to elicit the status of finical inclusion of farmers in India. This paper attempts to examine the status of the farmers and their accessibility to institutional sources of credit in light of the findings brought out by NSSO in its various reports with a focus on the position of Rajasthan in particular.

The National Sample Survey Organization (NSSO) has been conducting All-India surveys on Debt and Investment decennially since its 26th round (1971-72) in both rural and urban areas. These surveys generate basic quantitative information on assets, liabilities and capital expenditure in the household sector of the economy. The All-India Debt and Investment Survey (AIDIS), which was carried out as part of the 59th round of the National Sample Survey (NSS) during the period January to December 2003, was the sixth such survey conducted at the all-India level. Prior to 1971-72, two surveys namely 'All-India Rural Credit Survey' and 'All-India Rural Debt and Investment Survey' had been completed in 1951-52 and in 1961-62 respectively by the Reserve Bank of India (RBI) for rural areas only.

Indebtedness of Farmer[a] Households[b]

Table 3 illustrates the position of Rajasthan vis-à-vis the rural household scenario of India.

Table 3: Indebtedness of Farmers Households

For the year 2003

	India	Rajasthan	% to India
No of Rural House-holds	14,78,98,800	70,17,200	4.7
Number of Farmer Households	8,93,50,400	53,08,000	5.9
Number of Indebted FHH	4,34,24,200	27,82,800	6.4
Percentage of FHH Indebted	48.6	52.4	

Source: Report No. 498, Indebtedness of Farmer Households, NSS 59th Round, GoI, 2005.

It is estimated that there are about 15 crore rural households in the country; of which 4.7 per cent resided in Rajasthan. Rajasthan accounts for 5.4 per cent of total population and 10.8 per cent of total geographical area of the nation. The state has 5.9 per cent of total farmers of the country and 6.4 per cent of farmers who had taken credit (from any source) resided in Rajasthan. The data of indebtedness of farmers in absolute terms revealed that, while for all India the figure was 48.6 per cent; for Rajasthan it was 52.4 per cent. Evidently, in proportionate terms, there were more farmers in Rajasthan and greater

[a] Farmer: For the purpose of NSSO survey, a farmer is defined as "a person who operates some land and is engaged in agricultural activities during the last 365 days." By agricultural activities, it is meant the cultivation of field crops and horticultural crops, growing of trees or plantations (such as rubber, cashew, coconut, pepper, coffee, tea, etc.), animal husbandry, poultry, fishery, piggery, bee-keeping, vermiculture, sericulture, etc. It may be noted that persons engaged in agricultural and/or allied activities but not operating a piece of land are not considered as farmers. Similarly, agricultural laborers, coastal fishermen, rural artisans and persons engaged in agricultural services are not considered as farmers. It is also quite possible that during the reference period of last 365 days, a person could have left his entire land as 'current fallow' by discretion or due to natural situation or otherwise, such farmers are also excluded from the coverage of the present situation assessment survey.

[b] A group of persons normally living together and taking food from a common kitchen constitutes a household. Farmer Household: A household having at least one farmer as its member.

proportion of the same seemed to have borrowed money as compared to their counterparts in other states.

Among the various states in India, the number of farmer households was maximum in Uttar Pradesh and least in Sikkim in absolute terms. However, the incidence of indebtedness amongst the farmers was maximum in Andhra Pradesh and least in Meghalaya.

Indebtedness of Farmer Households by 'Source of Income[c]'

A farmer has different sources of income. These sources of income have been categorized into four categories by NSSO. The sources of income vary greatly across the length and breadth of the country. Table 4 shows the major sources of income of indebted farmers in the nation.

Table 4: Sources of income of farmers (in %)

For the year 2003

	India	Rajasthan
Cultivation	56.9	58.4
Farming Other than Cultivation	0.32	0.43
Other Agricultural Activities	0.41	0.31
Others	35.7	34.3

Source: Report No. 498, Indebtedness of Framer Households, NSS 59th Round, GoI, 2005.

The majority (56.9 per cent) of the farmers in the country, who had borrowed money, was engaged in the profession of crop 'cultivation.' However, in Rajasthan this category of farmers was more than the corresponding all India average indicating therein that more proportion of farmers in Rajasthan are indebted. It was seen that in North Eastern states of the country the indebtedness of farmer was primarily (more then 70 per cent) for crop cultivation.

The other source of income for the farmers is 'farming other than cultivation', which includes animal husbandry, poultry, fishery, piggery, bee-keeping, etc. This occupation covered merely 0.32 per cent of indebted farmers in the country. In Rajasthan

[c] The source which yields maximum income among various sources from which the household received any income during the 365 days prior to the date of survey.

this category was slightly pronounced (0.43 per cent) indicating therein that more farmers take to animal husbandry for their livelihood when compared to corresponding figures for all India. The third source of income for farmers is 'other agricultural activities' including horticulture and plantation. The proportion of the farmers under this category was 0.41 per cent for all India and 0.31 per cent for Rajasthan. Evidently, in Rajasthan lesser proportion of farmers depended on 'horticulture and plantation activities' when compared to similar data for all India. Apparently under horticulture and plantation there is greater requirement of water, hence farmers in the Rajasthan do not profess the same on wider scales. Among various states in India, Kerala was the state with the maximum proportion of indebted farmers engaged in professions of animal husbandry (14.1 per cent) and horticultural & plantation (10.1 per cent).

Indebtedness of Farmer Households by 'Size of Land' Possessed

Table 5: Farmers Households and Landholding (ha.)

For the year 2003

	Proportion of Land-holdings in India (in %)	Proportion of Farmers indebtedness in India (in %)	Proportion of Farmers indebtedness in Rajasthan (in %)
Up to 2 ha	83.9	79.9	63.6
2 to 4 ha	10.5	12.5	17.8
4 to 10 ha	4.8	6.4	14.1
More than 10 ha	0.8	1.2	4.5
	100	100	100

Source: Report No. 498, Indebtedness of Farmer Households, NSS 59th Round, GoI, 2005.

Average landholding in Rajasthan is highest (3.94 ha) among all states in the country (1.1 ha). The all-India scenario of land-holdings indicates that almost 84 per cent of landholdings were of less than 2 ha in size. Per capita landholding of more than 10 ha was seen in less than 1 per cent of total holdings.

An examination of the incidence of indebtedness among the farmers (Table 4) reveals that the bulk of indebtedness lay in the bandwidth of less than 2 ha. In other words, predominant proportion of the farmers, with small and marginal landholdings, had resorted to borrowing of money. Further, it was interesting to see that in India as the size of landholding increased, the proportion of indebtedness decreased. In Rajasthan the proportion of indebtedness for higher classes of landholding was more than corresponding figure for all India. Thus, it could be inferred that in Rajasthan more farmers of higher sizes of landholding resort to borrowing of money as compared to all India figures; whereas, in case of small and marginal farmers, the intensity of indebtedness in Rajasthan was less pronounced compared to the corresponding all-India averages.

Table 6 attempts to analyze the flow of credit outstanding according to size of landholdings.

Table 6: Loan Outstanding (in percentage)

For the year 2002-03

	Up to 2.5 acres (Small Farmer)	2.5 to 5 acres (Medium Farmer)	Above 5 acres (Large Farmer)
Landholdings	94.4	4.8	0.8
Loan Accounts	39.9	32.3	27.6
Loan Amount	23.3	25.8	50.8
Average Loan Amount (in Rs.)	17,869	24,455	56,220

Source: www.rbi.org & Report No. 498, Indebtedness of Farmer Households, NSS 59th Round, GoI, 2005.

An asymmetry in financing to farmers is clearly discernible with almost 95 per cent of farmers in India categorized as small farmers, but their share in total loan accounts in the banks was less than 40 per cent and their share in gross loan amount outstanding was around 23 per cent. Medium farmers comprised of less than 5 per cent of total landholdings in the nation, but had a share of 32.3 per cent in total loan accounts in banks, and 25.8 per cent in total loan amount outstanding from the banks. Ultimately, the large category of farmers have a share of 0.8 per cent in total landholdings in the nation, but held about 27.6 per cent of total loan accounts in the banks and accounted for almost half of the total loan amount given by the banks to farmer households.

As could be expected, the average amount of loan outstanding per account towards the farmers from the banks was seen to grow proportionally with the size of landholding!

Distribution of Outstanding Loan[d] by Purpose of Loan

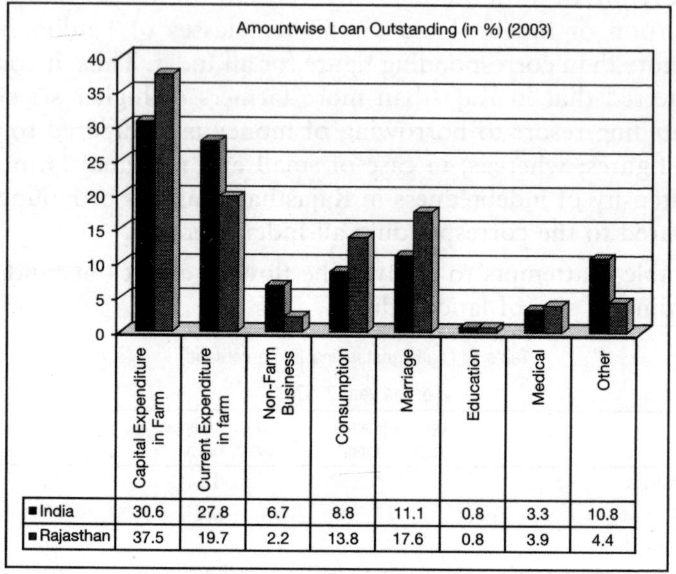

	Capital Expenditure in Farm	Current Expenditure in farm	Non-Farm Business	Consumption	Marriage	Education	Medical	Other
India	30.6	27.8	6.7	8.8	11.1	0.8	3.3	10.8
Rajasthan	37.5	19.7	2.2	13.8	17.6	0.8	3.9	4.4

Source: Report No. 498, Indebtedness of Farmer Households, NSS 59th Round, GoI, 2005.

There are various purposes for which farmer borrow money. The NSSO classified these purposes in eight different categories. The purpose 'capital expenditure in farm' was the prime reason of borrowing by the farmers on all-India basis. This purpose comprised of more than 30 per cent of total loans outstanding. The next major reason for which farmer raised loan was the 'current expenditure on farm', here again about 27.8 per cent of farmers had borrowed for this purpose. Credit for 'non-farm' purposes was raised by 6.7 per cent of farmers. Among the various consumption purposes 'marriage' was the prime need of credit requirement by the farmers, on the other hand

[d] Any liability which was taken in cash or kind is termed a loan, if the amount at the time of transaction was Rs. 300 or more. Loans taken from different sources are considered as separate loans. Even if two or more different loans were taken from the same source at different times, they were considered as separate loans.

'education' was the purpose for which least amount of loan was raised by the farmers. Hence, it could be deduced that most important non-productive credit need of the farmer in India was 'marriage', while he continued to neglect the 'education' needs of his family. Government and the financial sector should take cognizance of this *priority* of the farmer and design appropriate policies and financial products for him.

With reference to amount-wise loan outstanding in Rajasthan, many interesting facts emerge:

1. Farmers in Rajasthan had raised more quantum of loan for 'capital expenditure on farm' as compared to corresponding figures for all-India.
2. Farmers in Rajasthan seemed to have borrowed lesser amount for 'non-farm activities' when compared to their counterparts in all-India basis.
3. When compared to borrowing trend of farmers in all-India, the farmers in Rajasthan borrowed predominantly for 'marriage' (17.6 per cent) and 'consumption' (13.8 per cent) purposes. Evidently, the social rituals compelled the farmers in the state to seek more credit for these unproductive activities. It is the responsibility of the society and the State to arrest this tendency.

Table 7: Distribution of outstanding loan by purpose of loan (in %)
For the year 2003

Purpose	State with maximum share of expenditure		State with minimum share of expenditure	
Capital Expenditure in farm	Mizoram	80.7	Manipur	0.4
Current Expenditure in farm	Gujarat	50.3	Mizoram	0.0
Non-Farm Business	HP	29.0	Meghalaya	0.0
Consumption	Sikkim	20.4	Maharashtra	4.2
Marriage	Bihar	22.9	NE States	0.0
Education	Arunachal Pradesh	20.3	Many States	
Medical	Manipur	22.0	Meghalaya, Mizoram	0.0
Other	Arunachal Pradesh	41.1	Many States	

Source: Report No. 498, Indebtedness of Farmer Households, NSS 59th Round, GoI, 2005.

4. On an average, farmer in Rajasthan was borrowing more money for his health needs when compared to the corresponding data for all-India. Probably there is need for the State to be more proactive in ensuring better health support to the farmers.

It could be seen from Table 7 that there is wide variation in the pattern of credit needs among the farmers in different states of India. While farmers in Mizoram seemed to have availed loan primarily for 'capital expenditure on farm', the farmers in Gujarat have sought loan primarily for 'current expenditure in farm.' An extrapolation of this data with the cropping pattern, scales of finance, minimum support prices, etc. in the two states reveals interesting inferences. In Bihar, the farmers seemed to have heavily borrowed for 'marriage' purpose. Arunachal Pradesh is the state, where more than 20 per cent of loans availed of by the farmers was for 'education' indicating therein that the farmers in the state are eager to impart literacy to their wards. In Manipur, the farmers had borrowed substantial amounts for 'medical' purposes, indicating that the state had poor health services which need to be strengthened considerably.

Source of Loan (Amount-wise Outstanding)[e]

Table 8 gives a brief overview of the 'sources of loan' from where farmer raised credit. It could be seen from the same that 'banks' were the major (35.6 per cent) source of credit to farmers in the country, followed by the 'money-lenders' which were the source to the 25.7 per cent of farmers in the nation. The third major source of credit for the farmers in the country was the 'cooperative societies' which serve 19.6 per cent of the farmers in the nation.

Correspondingly, the scenario for the Rajasthan was quite different, wherein the 'money-lenders' were the major (36.5 per cent) source of credit to the farmers! This was followed by the 'banks', which had extended credit to the 27 per cent of the

[e] The data is based upon the 'outstanding amount' of the indebted farmer at the given point of time and not the number of indebted farmer households.

Table 8: Source of loan (Amount wise outstanding)(in %)

For the year 2003

Source	India	Rajasthan
Government	2.5	1.3
Cooperative Society	19.6	5.9
Banks	35.6	27.0
Money lender	25.7	36.5
Trader	5.2	19.2
Relatives & Friends	8.5	6.9
Doctor/Lawyer/etc	0.9	1.8
Others	2.1	1.4

Source: Report No. 498, Indebtedness of Farmer Households, NSS 59th Round, GoI, 2005.

farmers, followed by 'traders'. In a study conducted by CmF in Rajasthan it was concluded that most important source of credit is friend/relative (40 per cent) followed by money-lender which provide about 37 per cent of total credit and banks provide about 24 per cent of credit in rural areas. It was quite evident that in Rajasthan the formal financial institutions have not been able to extend their outreach to the farmers as extensively as compared to the banking network established in the other states.

Table 9: Source of loan (Amount-wise outstanding)(in %)

For the year 2003

Source	State with maximum share of Source of loan	
Government	Sikkim	34.8
Cooperative Society	Maharashtra	48.5
Banks	Tripura	60.5
Money-lender	AP	53.4
Trader	Sikkim	22.1
Relatives & Friends	Meghalaya	80.9
Doctor/Lawyer/etc.	Rajasthan	1.8
Others	Bihar	10.6

Source: Report No. 498, Indebtedness of Farmer Households, NSS 59th Round, GoI, 2005.

An analysis of the data compiled by NSSO for the country (Table 9), shows that the 'government' was major source of credit supplier in Sikkim, while 'cooperative societies' were the predominant supplier of credit to the farmers in Maharashtra. 'Banks' supplied credit to more than 60 per cent of farmers in

Tripura, albeit in case of Meghalaya farmers hardly got any credit from the banks! In Andhra Pradesh more than 53 per cent of the farmers had raised loans from 'money-lenders'. In contrast, in Arunachal Pradesh and Mizoram the farmers hardly drew any credit from the money-lenders. Sikkim was the state wherein 22.1 per cent of the farmers depended on 'traders' for their credit needs; in contrast in Meghalaya hardly 0.3 per cent of the farmers got financial assistance from the traders. It was also seen that in Meghalaya more than 80 per cent of farmers availed credit from 'relatives and friends', while in Haryana the least number of farmers depended upon relatives and friends for their credit needs.

Average Amount of Loan Outstanding

Table 10: Average amount of loan outstanding (in Rs.)

For the year 2003

	India	Rajasthan
ST	5506	12018
SC	7167	16708
OBC	13489	22009
Others	18118	18538
All	12585	18372

Source: Report No. 498, Indebtedness of Farmer Households, NSS 59th Round, GoI, 2005.

The average amount of loan outstanding per farmer household in Rajasthan *vis-à-vis* the all-India position is given in Table 10. While the national average of loan outstanding was Rs. 12,585 per farmer household in the year 2003, there were marked differences amongst the various categories of farmers with reference to amount of loan outstanding. The average amount of loan outstanding for a 'scheduled tribe' farmer was Rs. 5,506; that for 'other category' it was Rs. 18,118. Thus it could be inferred that 'general category' of farmers had availed greater amount of loan than the farmers belonging in 'backward classes.' In other words, this could also reflect the credit-worthiness of the farmer and his ability to raise loan. As far as the quantum of loan is concerned, the scenario for the Rajasthan was quite different from the national picture. The average loan outstanding in Rajasthan was Rs. 18,372 which was 46 per cent higher than the national average. Apparently farmers in Rajasthan were able to raise more quantum of credit and were relatively more indebted than the farmers in other states. It was also seen that the farmers in 'OBC category' had maximum average loan (Rs. 22,009) while 'scheduled tribe' farmer household had the least amount of average loan outstanding (Rs. 12,018).

Table 11: Average amount of loan outstanding (in Rs.)
For the year 2003

Category	State with maximum average amount of loan for respective category	
ST	Punjab	8495
SC	Rajasthan	16708
OBC	Kerala	33116
Others	Punjab	66147
All	Punjab	41576

Source: Report No. 498, Indebtedness of Farmer Households, NSS 59th Round, GoI, 2005.

The analysis of the data for the nation as a whole revealed that for 'scheduled tribe' farmers, the maximum average loan amount availed was that by the farmers in Punjab. In case of 'scheduled caste' farmers, it was the Rajasthan where average loan availed was highest amongst all the states in the country. In the case of the 'OBC' farmer households, Kerala recorded the highest average loan amount. And finally for 'other categories' of farmers, the highest average amount of loan outstanding was witnessed in Punjab.

Banking Network

Table 12: Banking Network in India
For the year 2004

	CBs	RRB	SCB	DCCB	SARDB	ARDB	PACS	Total
Number of branches	66163	14433	789	12128	1154	686	92103	187456
Percentage to Total	35.30	7.70	0.42	6.47	0.62	0.37	49.13	100.00

Source: www.rbi.org.

Table 12 brings out the broad picture of banking network in the country. It could be seen that country had about 1.87 lakh outlets of institutional credit in 2004. Numerically, PACS constituted more than 50 per cent of total network; however, they are construed to be fragile sources of credit suppliers in the nation (Bathla 2002[20]; Singh 2003a[21]; Singh 2003b[22]; Singh 2005[23]). Commercial Banks (CBs) are the prime source of supply of credit in India, in terms of banking network their share stood at more than 35 per cent amongst gross outlets of credit in country. This was followed by the Regional Rural Banks (RRB) structure.

Rajasthan has 5.44 per cent of total banking network of the country. There are about 4,800 bank branches and 5,400 PACS (Primary Agricultural Credit Societies) in the state. Among the various states in the country, Maharashtra had the maximum amount of formal credit outlets in the state. It had a share of more than 16 per cent of total banking network cf the nation. The state had more than 10,000 branches of banks, which was supplemented by more than 20,000 branches of PACS. Evidentially, the state has the best banking network in the country. In spite of this feature, the maximum suicides took place among the farmers in the Maharashtra. Hence, it could be inferred that merely existence of bank branches was not sufficient to address the credit needs of the farmers. There is an urgent need of appropriate financial product suitable to farmers to meet his credit needs.

Challenges Ahead

As per the NABARD[24], by the end of March 2006 about 5.90 crore Kissan Credit Cards (KCC) were issued, against estimated 8.9 crore farmer households in the country. This indicates that 56 per cent of farmer households have been covered by the banks in the country. Ground Level Credit (GLC) flow towards agriculture during 2005-06 was to the tune of Rs. 1,57,480 crore, which had almost doubled in the span of two years from April 2004. In spite of this, and also the personal intervention by the Prime Minister, spate of farmers' suicide, (particularly in Vidarbha region) in 2006-07 could not be contained and there are reports that as many as 67 farmers committed suicide in January 2007 alone.[25]

Hence, it is apparent that Indian agriculture is not only passing through turbulent times, but has also become unremunerative. The Government took a number of steps to mitigate the plight of farmers. One major policy thrust designed was *doubling of agricultural credit* in span of three years. Though the initiative itself is commendable, the premise of ensuring of credit to the farmers as panacea for all of their problems seems to be highly misplaced. Is the availability of the credit the cardinal reason for suicides by the farmers? Has the agriculture turned un-remunerative due to so-called high rate of interest charged by the banks on crop loan? Has the directive of providing credit at 7 per cent per annum solved the problem? Is the banking network insufficient to serve the farmers satisfactorily? Does the rural India need more bank branches? Are the present financial products adequate to meet the credit needs of the farmers? Is 100 per cent coverage of farmers by the banks the solution to all their problems? Is the amalgamation of regional rural banks of any positive consequence to the Indian farmer?

Even the Prime Minister, Dr. Manmohan Singh, in his inaugural address at 'Agriculture Summit 2006: Reforms for Empowering the Farmer' October 18-19, 2006, Vigyan Bhavan, New Delhi, remarked "What do farmers need—a lower rate of interest or reliable access to credit at reasonable rates? Is our existing institutional framework adequate for meeting the requirements of our farmers who are a diverse lot? Do we need to create new institutional structures such as SHGs, micro-finance institutions, etc., to provide improved and reliable access to credit? Or do we need to bring in money-lenders under some form of regulation?" Professor Mohammad Yunus, Nobel Laureate in his speech at *Centenary of Launch of Satyagragh* at Vigyan Bahawn, New Delhi on 29 January, 2007 persuasively argued that people are poor not due any of their reasons, but due to inadequate institutional framework provided to them.

No doubt credit is intrinsic for farmers, but is it the only prerequisite? Perhaps the most pronounced anomaly in the minds of policy-makers is that for development, credit is the prime mover! Access to credit is only an enabling factor, which needs to be supplemented and complimented by plethora of other initiatives, the foremost being the 'marketing linkages.' Financial inclusion alone cannot adequately transform the livelihood of the farmers. Hence, a multi-pronged approach is necessary to revitalize Indian agriculture.

Possible Alternatives to Augment Financial Inclusion

There could be a gamut of approaches to address the vexed issue of *Financial Inclusion* of Indian Farmer. Some issues, which could augment the access of financial services to rural masses, include the following:

A. Issues in Financial Sector

1. Financial Institutions need to have specific strategies for rural banking. Rural clientele need savings, credit, insurance and remittances products. The banking channel should endeavor to provide all of them under one roof.
2. The three important risks identified in agricultural lending are yield risk (or input-output risk), calamity risk and price risk. Banks will need to aim at minimizing these risks if they have to deliver affordable credit to agriculture.
3. Information systems for transparency need to be put in place, so that clients have faith and confidence in institutional credit system.
4. Performance standards for various banks with relation to service in rural areas particularly for the farmers need to be pragmatic, measurable and accountable.
5. Specialized 'Microfinance Credit Technology' needs to be placed in India so that the emerging sector is able to aptly supplement the efforts of formal channel of credit in serving the poor, particularly in rural areas.
6. A uniform banking/financial product for the entire country would obviously not work. Products need to be designed and packaged taking into account local culture, customs, language, literacy and social indicators. There is need to undertake 'market research' and work on 'new product development' for rural clients. Probably, hardly any research is going in to designing/refining financial products for rural clients.

Costing and Pricing with explicit advantage to rural areas needs to be brought about by the government.

7. Encouragement should be given to Business facilitator; Business Correspondent, MFIs; MFOs, MACS; Federation of SHGs; Kisan Clubs; etc. to play a proactive role in financial inclusion.
8. 'Information Technology' can play an important role in ensuring better access of financial products to its target clients. There is an urgent need to exploit this innovation in a more focused manner for rural services. All options, such as, mobile and satellite offices, rural ATMs, smart card and mobile phone based banking, use of intermediaries including SHGs, including post offices need to be explored for penetrating into the rural markets.
9. 'Capacity building' of bankers, particularly orientation of their mindset towards the rural clients needs to be undertaken.
10. 'Employee Incentive Systems' for bankers to work in rural areas and on achieving the defined goals should be put into place.
11. Total revamping of Lead Bank Scheme needs to be undertaken.
12. Recruitment of Staff should be allowed to RRBs.
13. 'Indian Post Bank' needs to be started in a meaningful manner.
14. 'Directed credit programmes' (with/without subsidy) should be dispensed with.
15. Institutionalization of Money-lenders, Pawn Brokers, *arhtis*, etc. should be explored.

B. Issues in Agricultural Sector

1. A post mortem of Green, White and Blue Revolutions needs to be undertaken in order to examine the reasons for relative success of various interventions.
2. An attempt to map of the soil health of India to provide tangible advice to farmers for viable farming.

3. Agricultural Research needs to be made professional and accessible to farmers at cost-effective manner.
4. Water management needs to be the pivot of Indian agriculture.
5. Encouragement should be given to cropping of dryland farming crops.
6. Pricing of farm produce needs to be administered in such a fashion that farming becomes a remunerative profession.
7. Agri-processing too needs to be strengthened.
8. 'Future trading' needs to encompass bulk of farmers.
9. Agricultural Insurance should be a result-oriented intervention. RKBY and *Vraksh Bima Yojana* need to be revisited.
10. Gender role in agriculture needs to be acknowledged and given sufficient role play.
11. Food security network for farmers needs to be evolved.
12. The focus of future plans and interventions should be for developing 'sustainable livelihood' rather than peace meal interventions.
13. There should be active participation of farmers in research and policy-making.
14. Flight of farmers from villages towards cites needs to be arrested, i.e. implement PURA.[f]
15. Public Private Partnership (PPP) models need to be explored to make farming a remunerative profession.
16. Propagation of Village Knowledge Centers is the cardinal need for supporting Indian agriculture.

REFERENCES

1. Veerashekerappa (1994); "Does Priority Sector Lending Help the Poor?" Kurukshetra, July 1994.

---

[f] Providing Urban Amenities in Rural Areas, is the concept proposed by Dr. APJ Abdul Kalam, Honorable President of India.

2. Rangarajan, Dr. C. (1994): Keynote Address Delivered at Indian National Workshop for Bankers on 31 January, at Mumbai.

3. De Silva, Donauts and Deuby, Vailla (1992): *Banking the Unbankable: Brining Credit to Poor;* Horizon India Books, New Delhi. Foundation for Development Cooperation *Best Practice of Banking with the Poor;* Brisbane, U.K.

4. Foundation for Development Cooperation (1991): *Best Practice of Banking with the Poor,* Brisbane, U.K.

5. Lopez, Euqemian Piza and March, Canadida (1991): "Gender Considerations in Economic Enterprises", *Report of the workshop held in Philippines,* Oxfam Gender and Development Unit, Women Resources and Research Centre, Oxford.

6. A Review of the Agricultural Credit System in India (ACRC) (1987): Reserve Bank of India, Mumbai.

7. Shylendra H.S. (2006): "Mainstreaming Microfinance for Poverty Alleviation: Need for a Proactive and Regulatory Framework", *Towards Sustainable Microfinance Outreach in India: Experiences and Perspectives*, NABARD, Mumbai, 178.

8. Chandra, Dinesh (1993): *Rural Credit—Role of Informal Sector*, Segment Books, New Delhi.

9. Ambastha, S.K. (1994): "Role of Co-operative Credit as a Source of Financing Agriculture in India", *Development Planning for Agriculture, Policies, Economic Implementations, Inputs Production and Marketing,* Mittal Publications, New Delhi, 265-275.

10. Birthal, S. Pratap and Singh, R.P. (1996): "Access of Rural Households to Institutional Credit: A study in Eastern Uttar Pradesh," *Agricultural Economic Research Review,* Vol. 9, No. 1, 21-35.

11. Malhotra, Rakesh (1997): *Policy Options for Augmenting Capital Formation from Livestock Sector in Uttar Pradesh,* unpublished Ph.D. thesis submitted to Lucknow University, Lucknow.

12. *Group Savings and Credit Management* (1998): A Study Commissioned by the World Bank under UP Sodic Land Reclamation Project, Bankers Institute of Rural Development, Lucknow.

13. Singh, S.P. and Mruthyunjaya (1992): "Impact of Short-term Credit on Income and Employment of Marginal and Small Frames of Aligarh district of UP", *Agricultural Economic Research Review,* Vol. 5, No. 1, 48-59.

14. Malhotra, Rakesh (2000): *Access of Rural Women to Institutional Credit: Issues and Alternatives,* Bankers Institute of Rural Development, Lucknow, 53-55.

15. Rao, D.S.K. and Malhotra, Rakesh (2000): *Demand and Supply linkages in Rural Financial Markets,* Bankers Institute of Rural Development, Lucknow, 27.
16. Brief note on the findings of the "Cash-Flow Study of Rural Households in Rajasthan", The study of Center for microFinance (CmF) under guidance of Prof M.S. Sriram IIMA.
17. Prahalad, C.K. (2004): *The Fortune at the Bottom of the Pyramid: Eradicating Poverty Through Profits*, Watson School Publishing.
18. Sharma, Manoranjan (2007): 'Financial Inclusion, Microfinance and SMEs-Business Opportunities', Leading Issues in Indian Economy, Atlantic Publishers and Distributors.
19. Suri, K.C.: "Political Economy of Agrarian Distress," *Economic and Political Weekly,* April 22, 2006, 1523.
20. Bathla (2002): *Institutional Credit in Indian Agriculture and Policy Options*, Occasional Paper 23, NABARD, Mumbai.
21. Singh, Surjit (2003a): *Institutional Finance in Rajasthan: Some Recent Trends and Concerns*, Working Paper, IDSJ, Jaipur.
22. Singh, Surjit (2003b): *Institutional Infrastructure and Institutional Finance*, in Bihar Development Report, Planning Commission, New Delhi.
23. Singh, Surjit (2005): *Agriculture Credit in the Post-Reform Period: Some Concerns*, Working Paper 145, IDSJ, Jaipur.
24. *Annual Report 2005-06*, NABARD, Mumbai.
25. *Times of India*, New Delhi Edition, 30 January, 2007.

Book Review

HIGH PRAISE FOR MANORANJAN SHARMA'S EARLIER BOOKS PUBLISHED BY ATLANTIC PUBLISHERS AND DISTRIBUTORS

LEADING ISSUES IN INDIAN ECONOMY

To know about the rural non-farm sector (RNFS), I turn to a piece by Manoranjan Sharma included in a book that he has edited, *Leading Issues in Indian Economy*, from Atlantic (*www.atlanticbooks.com*). "As RNFS is a microcosm of the economy, the withering of traditional arts and crafts as reflected in the precarious state of laheriya tie-dyeing of Jaipur, the folk-sarangi of Punjab, Paithani weaving of Aurangabad, kasuti embroidery in Karnataka, Chamba rumal embroidery in Himachal Pradesh, Farrukhabad silk printing in Uttar Pradesh, Toda embroidery in the Nilgiris, metal blockmaking in Varanasi, and so on causes concern", he writes.

Another chapter of interest is the one on 'shadow economy', by Amitabh Kumar, where he explains the Collard curve, on how tax revenue increases with administrative expenditure, but at a decreasing rate. Difference between the actual tax collection and the maximum possible yield can provide an estimate of the shadow economy, he says.

The book includes papers on financial sector reforms, globalisation, rural finance, exchange rate and so forth. Educative read.

The Hindu Business Line (HBL)

LEADING ISSUES IN INDIAN ECONOMY

During the pre-perestroika days, resource mobilisation was a major problem. In the post-liberalisation scenario, the Indian economy faces a different set of problems that relate fundamentally to structural changes. While resource crunch is no more an issue, its optimum deployment remains so. Several development-related problems need urgent attention. Infrastructure upgrading, investment in agriculture and manufacturing industry and fiscal reforms are only some of the issues. The contributors to this tome take a close look at these concerns as also come up with practical ideas for improving the economy's competitiveness. The essays in this collection are certainly illuminating.

The Tribune

LEADING ISSUES IN INDIAN ECONOMY

It is a unique effort on the part of Shri Manoranjan Sharma... written by renowned personalities on various aspects arising from implementation of reforms and present it in the form of a Book. The use of a Book like this is that it reflects opinions of different personalities, giving the readers a balanced perspective on the reform process.

First article is a comprehensive coverage of various aspects related to financial Sector Reforms in India. Reforms initiated in Banking, Securities, Foreign Exchange, Monetary Policy sectors were well documented. The performance of banking sector under various parameters was dissected scientifically to showcase the reflection of reforms. Shri Rakesh Mohan explained the complex subject matter in a simple and lucid manner. Indeed the article is a thorough coverage on financial sector reforms in India thus far.

In the second article on Understanding Globalisation Process, Shri Ameer Batcha has eloquently dwelt on different facets related to Globalisation Process. The article was put forth in three parts, covering the genesis, advancement and stabilization of globalisation process. Shri Ameer Batcha has analysed the entire gamut of globalisation process though the prism of Capitalism....

Various aspects involved in Integration of Financial markets in India with the world market are well brought out in the article written by Shri Arun Kumar Mishra and Shri A. Ramanathan. It is a wonderful article covering multitude of issues involved in integration process....

The impact of reforms on poverty is well brought out by Shri Debesh Roy. The facts and figures given as regards percentage of population below poverty line are thought provoking. The aspects related to poverty alleviation—issues and challenges are explained in a beautiful manner....

Agriculture for long has been the backbone of the Indian economy. India lives in villages and India derives its strength from its rural economy. The article written by Shri P. Satish titled 'Rural Finance: Issues and Perspectives' describes to the minutiae many issues related to the Agricultural Credit and also strategies/suggestions for growth of Agricultural Credit.... This is a very useful article.

The issues related to rural non-farm sector are thoroughly covered in the article 'Rural Non-Farm Issues and Evidence', by Shri Manoranjan Sharma. Non-Farm Sector is one area, which is not given its due in the overall scheme of things related to rural economy. I do not say Non-Farm Sector is panacea for all problems faced in rural economy, but I do say that if proper planning is put into this sector, it will solve the issues like rural poverty, rural unemployment, seasonal unemployment, etc.

The article on Exchange Rate, Food Price and Stabilization is actually a research paper prepared by Smt Ashima Goyal. In this article critical analysis was made on the working of current methods of price stabilisation. The article also makes factual analysis of exchange policy rule application in the nineties in India. This is a wonderful article taking into consideration the importance given for ensuring Food Security in India.

In the article 'Shadow Economy' written by Shri Amitabh Kumar, a very important topic of Shadow Economy was detailed. The central theme of the article is the measurement of the size of the shadow economy. Major methodologies in measuring shadow economy like Monetary approach, Discrepancy

Approach, Casual Approach and Direct Approach, are well explained. This article is basically a policy prescription aimed at precision in estimating the shadow economy and its impact.

Shri Ajit Kumar Singh made a critical assessment of Fiscal Reforms in his article 'Fiscal Reforms in India since 1991'. Important points like fiscal deficit, revenue deficit, primary deficit and monetized deficit are well explained. The critical analysis made on fiscal deficit tendencies in 1980s and 1990s is very useful one. The genesis of Fiscal Responsibility & Budget Management Legislation is highlighted. The highlight of the article is the major components of the unfinished agenda in fiscal reforms.

I strongly recommend this book to all students, banking professionals, economists, who are interested to know the intricacies involved in Reform Process and its implementation.

The Indian Banker

LEADING ISSUES IN INDIAN ECONOMY—AN ENLIGHTENING READ

.... The book under review 'Leading Issues in Indian Economy' edited by Manoranjan Sharma, Chief Economist and Deputy General Manager, Canara Bank has a complement of nine essays all authored by eminent writers and economists well versed with the subject, being extremely familiar with the milieu that they have chosen to deal with. Leading the pack is RBI's Deputy Governor, Rakesh Mohan with 'Financial Sector Reforms in India—Policies and Performance Analysis'. Authors Ameer Batcha 'Towards Understanding Globalisation Process', Arun Kumar Misra, Economist, Canara Bank and A. Ramanathan, 'Integration and Financial Markets in India', Debesh Roy, 'Impact of India's Economic Reforms on Poverty—Critical Issues and Challenges', P. Satish, 'Rural Finance: Issues and Perspectives', Manoranjan Sharma, 'Rural Non-Farm Sector in India—Issues and Evidence', Ashima Goyal, 'Exchange Rate, Food Price Stabilisation and Inflation', Amitabh Kumar, 'Shadow Economy—A Conceptual and Methodological Policy Frame' and Ajit Kumar Singh, 'Fiscal Reforms in India since 1991—A Critical Assessment' are the other contributors to the volume.

All the essays in the book have tackled the subject in a lucid manner shedding a lot of light on the developments over the years on the economic front.

In his introduction, Manoranjan Sharma harks back to the days after independence, highlights the progress and also visualises the road ahead for the country in several niche segments like agriculture, rural development and stresses the need to ensure a better distributive equity with a view to transforming the socio-economic milieu. The paper by Rakesh Mohan...dwells elaborately on the financial sector reforms, touching on aspects related to banking, debt market, monetary policy, forex, etc. and also evaluates the performance of various segments of the financial sector under the reform process. The essay on Globalisation discusses capitalism in its various forms and also narrates the conditionalities for reaping the benefits of globalisation.

The other articles in the book also make for enlightening reading covering a host of subjects like financial market integration, its impact on foreign economies, how it would work out in our country, etc., the impact of reforms on poverty, the success of poverty alleviation programmes, agricultural credit with case studies thrown in, the rural non-farm sector dealing with the role of FIs and banks in financing, exchange rates, inflation stabilisation of food prices, the meaning and concept of shadow economy, the various methodologies and approaches for estimating its size and a critical assessment of the entire reform process since 1991. The last article on reforms also discusses the salient features of the Fiscal Responsibility Bill, 2000.

The articles are all well researched and the authors' viewpoints are often corroborated with facts and figures lending an authentic touch to the treatises. The book's value is also enhanced as the contributions deal with the various aspects of the reform process, viewed from various angles and affords the reader a bird's eye view of the entire gamut of economic reforms. The book would be very beneficial to scholars and academics, business communities, policy makers and planners and would also be an interesting read for the general public too.

Shreyas

.... *Leading Issues in Indian Economy*...is an informative and insightful collection of well-researched papers, edited by Shri Manoranjan Sharma, Chief Economist, Canara Bank. The book contains papers by eminent persons, including Dr. Rakesh Mohan and other experts from the fields of academia and policy formulation. The issues debated are also fairly diverse, including implications of financial sector reforms, globalisation perspectives, integration of financial markets, poverty related issues, fiscal management and crucial aspects of rural India.

Dr. Rakesh Mohan, in his paper 'Financial Sector Reforms in India', has reinforced the contention that reform process has strengthened the health of the financial sector intermediaries, deepened financial markets and enhanced the instruments available in the financial system....

Shri Ameer Batcha's paper (Towards Understanding Globalisation Process) identifies a host of drivers for taking globalisation process to its logical end. The most important among them include changes in the mode of production, evolution in money and banking, advancement in science and technology, international trade and capital movement. The adjustment by the economy to the continuing change will also be not uniform. Such rigidities will not be confined to the labour force alone, but may also spill over to pricing of goods and services, monetary and fiscal policies. He also cautions about possible weaknesses in the financial system, which can dampen the spirit of globalisation. He forcefully argues that the stability of the financial system is the most important prerequisite to the success of globalisation.

Dr. A.K. Misra and Prof. Ramanathan's paper on financial markets' integration delves into the concept, attributes, experience of select countries, implications, measurement and policy issues of integration in the financial sector. The findings of their study clearly indicate that despite partial integration, Indian economy has been progressively integrating with the global markets. However, they have also brought out impediments, such as, political risk, transaction cost, taxation, capital control and imperfections in capital market.... The strength of the paper emanates from rigorous empirical investigation of the integration among various market segments, such as, the capital market, savings-investment, money and guilt markets in both domestic and international frameworks.

The fourth paper, 'Impact of India's Economic Reforms on Poverty', turns to the reforms process and offers a critique of its implications for the poor. While the first generation reforms have been able to increase the growth dimensions, the author demonstrates that the requisite percolation has not taken place because of the delay in second generation reforms and lack of required political will.... The successful implementation of the SHG-Bank Linkage Programme shows that the poor are bankable.... The success of micro-finance innovations in attacking both income and human poverty and ITC's innovative e-choupal project has important policy prescriptive implications for planners preoccupied with the task of advancing economic reforms and alleviating poverty.

P. Satish...has analysed in depth the issues and perspectives in rural finance, a topical area currently, both at the policy and operational levels. Apart from placing rural finance and the role of the banking system in a historical perspective, the author makes an incisive analysis of the viability of rural banking. He has also factored in a few case studies of banks at the domestic and international levels to corroborate his views on an ideal rural finance platform. Some of his prescriptions for improving the cause of the rural masses are quite apt in the present context. For example, he has advocated volume growth in banks' business to enhance viability of banks. Given the present state of rural finance, the author's suggestions, such as, greater technology orientation, minimum State intervention in the affairs of rural financial institutions and eliminating micro-management need to be seriously considered.

In the context of liberalisation, globalisation, technological upgradation, choice of technology and dynamics of growth, the criticality of the rural non-farm sector (RNFS), which significantly influences employment, industrial production and exports, has increasingly come to the fore. Despite its potential for transforming the socio-eco-political fabric of the country, RNFS is saddled with several problems. Shri Manoranjan

Sharma's paper situates RNFS in a proper socio-historical setting and provides a detailed road map for making RNFS an active ingredient for economic growth.... 'The retooling of the developmental strategy' for RNFS requires a fundamental reorientation of strategies and enhanced competitiveness through greater independence, flexible specialisation, modernisation, marketing synergies and customer focused intervention. Development of RNFS, through a direct assault on problems of poverty, unemployment and inequality, would undoubtedly be helpful in achieving the avowed goals of planning.

Professor Ashima Goyal...has analysed the intricate relationship between food security, exchange rate and price stabilisation. While food security is vital especially for low per capital income masses, a significant rise in food prices has serious consequences in hunger and deprivation.... Food prices can be stabilised by a rule that varies the nominal exchange rate to neutralise variations in world food prices. The level of domestic food prices and nominal exchange rates would have to be such that the real exchange rates are close to their sustainable levels. The author deserves kudos for working on an under-researched though important area.

Shri Amitabh Kumar's paper examines various facets of the shadow economy—a wide area of economic activity outside the pale of government accounting. Shadow economy refers to informal, block, clandestine and more commonly, to the parallel economy. Various methodologies to measure the size of the shadow economy constitute the major strength of the paper. The paper justifiably suggests a shift towards greater precision and analytical rigor in estimating the shadow economy to avoid a deleterious impact on macro-economic policies.

The final paper by Professor Ajit K. Singh makes a critical assessment of fiscal reform process since 1991 and dwells on the unfinished agenda therein.... The author's recommendation to target the services sector as a revenue generator on a much larger scale is eminently sound and sensible as services constitute well over 50 per cent of India's GDP.

With 150 works, including about a dozen papers at global Conferences, the Editor, Manoranjan Sharma is an influential thinker in development studies today. The papers are of a consistently high standard and each author makes some thought-provoking points and insightful observations. The book provides a close and careful examination of the discourses of economic reforms, globalisation, poverty, rural finance, non-farm sector, fiscal reforms through the lens of modernisation, structural transformation, growth and equity, sensitivity and pluralistic consciousness, producing a rich and multi-layered analysis of the contemporary Indian situation.

What is needed in today's world of rapid, often discontinuous change is not just an increase in the size of the cake but also a more even distribution of the slices for economic growth to promote "inclusive" growth and distributive equity. The Editor clearly reflects this concern in the identification of the subjects and their treatment. The book would stimulate informed debate and concrete action on economic development in general and the transformation of the Indian economy in particular. Consequently, the book would be of interest not only to the academicians and researchers, but also to the professionals, policy makers and even those at the helm of affairs.

Canbank Bimonthly Review

STUDIES IN MONEY, FINANCE AND BANKING

Post-liberalisation banking sector reforms have led to improvement in the performance of our capital markets. There is a symbiotic relationship between the size of financial markets and economic development. Organisationally dynamic and robust financial structure ensures a well-integrated economic growth. This book takes a critical look at, among other factors, the shifting paradigms of capital structure of banks, corporate restructuring and governance, etc. Useful for students of Economics.

The Tribune

STUDIES IN MONEY, FINANCE AND BANKING— AN USEFUL STUDY

.... In his detailed introduction to the volume of essays under the title 'Studies in Money, Finance and Banking', Manoranjan

Sharma, Chief Economist, Canara Bank, the editor of the volume discusses the recent trends, the strategic options and choices and several other matters of relevance. The essays, cover a whole gamut of subjects....

Bankers have a lot to gain from the contents of the book for almost all the articles are of particular relevance to them. There are two essays on the new Capital accord – Basel-II, viz. Capital Structure of Banks vis-à-vis Basel-II and Basel-II and its implications for Banks. While the former essay written by Sri N. Kantha Kumar, C&MD, Syndicate Bank and former ED, Canara Bank discusses various aspects like capital charge, determination of capital structure and the applicability of Basel-II in India, the latter etches in detail the accord *per se* delving into various intricacies and analysing how the accord would impact various functional areas of banks like profitability, risk management, lending patterns, etc. Also discussed in detail are the challenges under Basel-II and the imperative need for banks to raise capital in the event of a further tightening of capital adequacy norms.

The essay on Corporate Restructuring affords an objective view of latter day initiatives like Corporate Debt Restructuring (CDR), Asset Restructuring Companies (ARC) and also touches on the situation in various countries like UK, Korea, Malaysia etc. apart from the Indian experience. The functioning of the Asset Reconstruction Company of India Ltd. (ARCIL) has also been discussed....

Two of the essays in the book 'Steady Growth of Retail Banking in India—Issues, Policy and Strategy' and 'Rapidly Expanding Frontiers of Micro Finance: Assessment and Prospects' have been contributed by Manoranjan Sharma and both are of extreme relevance for banks as retail banking and micro finance have taken centrestage in the banking sector in the recent past. The topics have been dealt with extensively. The various avenues for retail banking available to banks and the increasing prospects for micro finance and Self Help Groups have been deliberated and a roadmap for banks vis-à-vis retail banking has been suggested. The other articles in the book 'Appraisal of Recent Interest Rates Policy', 'Reflections on

Corporate Governance in Banking Sector' and 'Non Performing Assets—A Threat to Stability' are also of topical interest and the authors have done well to delineate the various aspects involved in their dissertations. 'Studies in Recovery, Finance and Banking' should add a great deal to the knowledge levels of bankers.

Shreyas

Recent years have been characterised by wide ranging changes in the Indian economy. The Indian financial sector has been a focal area of on-going structural transformation. No wonder, then, it is important to understand the emerging contours, the cognisable dilemmas of the Indian financial system. The book attempts to take a long, hard look at the path traversed, persisting bottlenecks and the milestones ahead in enhancing the strength and resilience of the Indian financial system.

Various issues impeding the banking sector vis-à-vis developments in key real sectors and the associated challenges have been incisively examined in…'Studies in Money, Finance and Banking'.... The book features well-researched papers by eminent professionals in the field of banking research. The hallmark of the book is clearly traced to its successful attempt in effectively and meaningfully assimilating the perceptions of academia, research and the bankers themselves on topical issues.

The first paper in the book analytically dwells on the capital structure of banks against the backdrop of the Basel framework and the recent changes in the international financial architecture. Authored by Shri N. Kantha Kumar, a noted professional banker, the paper delves into the increasing vulnerability of the macro-economy and the banking sector and the significant bearing it has on the capital structure of the banks. Hence, he advocated a hard look on the fundamental weaknesses before attempting capital restructuring and adopt a system-wide approach....

Brinda Jagirdar, echoes similar sentiments about the imperatives on Basel II and has raised quite a few pertinent issues about the implications of Basel II on Indian banks....

.... Dr. Amarendra Sahoo in his well-researched paper 'Corporate Restructuring—Principles and Practices' has attempted to make a case for Indian corporates *vis-à-vis* the trends seen in other parts of the world. He strongly argues that although companies may fail because of incompetence, yet they may also fail because of constraints beyond their control....

.... Shri M. Ramaiah...brings out various international and national perspectives on the issue of corporate governance in the banking system.... He subtly substantiates such a view with evidence from the BIS Document on Corporate Governance, the Basel Papers on Core Principles and initiatives taken by the Hong Kong Monetary Authority. While investigating the Indian banking scenario, he raises a very pertinent issue that brings out the crucial issue as to whether corporate governance is compatible with public ownership that makes the system accountable to political institutions and not to the economic institutions or even the regulators.... The author also analytically scrutinises the recommendations made by the consultative group on Corporate Governance.

There is no gainsaying the fact that if the interest rate policy is to play its legitimate role in achieving the socio-economic objectives, there is a need to build up systematic analytical and empirical evidence in this context. The book...features a highly informative and illustrative paper that examines the recent policy of interest rate deregulation, with special emphasis on the soft interest approach and its ramifications in the social and economic spheres. The paper, jointly authored by Prof. L.M. Bhole and Pradyumna Dash, builds up a case for interest rates to bottom out at an appropriate level so that its adverse bearing on the macro economic fundamentals are kept to the minimum. The authors have comprehensively discussed interest rates in India in a historical perspective.... The reduction in interest rates has not helped to achieve the proximate (increased savings, investment and efficient resource allocation) and the ultimate (growth, stability and social justice) developmental objectives.... They have empirically established that higher (lower) interest rates encourage (discourage) investment. Similarly, soft interest rates have encouraged the savers to hold more of their savings in the form of currency and real assets, which is undesirable. For the banking system, the implications are even much more serious. The factors, such as, the high carrying cost of long-term deposits and NPAs, the loading of risk premiums on future accumulation of NPAs and the high operating cost in banks preclude further reduction in interest rates....

Shri Manoranjan Sharma...has succinctly summarised the perspectives of a professional banker and policy planner on the growing retail cult in the banking industry. He, in the first place, has attempted to dispel the misconception that retail banking and retail lending are on the same footage conceptually. Retail banking implies creation of product differentiation, be it in loans or deposits or ancillary services, by efficient service and matching competitive offerings in tune with distinctive needs and priorities of the customer. He has sort of scoped the retail market in India.... He has also acknowledged the important role played by the State governments in undertaking dynamic initiatives to further the retail market. He has underlined the importance of innovation in creating cutting edge solutions for the Indian banks....

Apart from dissecting the key value drivers and the role of bank credit in the housing arena, he has also questioned the clean chit given to retail loans as regards asset impairment is concerned. Consequently, he has recommended serious tracking of ground level movements of retail loans and introduction of risk containment measures. There is a compelling need for a rethink on striking a judicious balance between expanding business and adherence to well-defined policy and procedures. The author has also analysed the impact of retail lending on household indebtedness, citing the alarming proportions such a possibility has taken in many parts of the globe. Yet, the author cautions about the consequences of increasing indebtedness and the adverse impact on fundamentals like sustainability of private consumption and savings. While summing up, the author underscores the need for banks to invest in future while strengthening their core competence areas. He has singled out the non-urban segments as the most crucial driver of retail banking in the future.

Non-performing assets, notwithstanding the varied initiatives by the regulators and banks, continue to be a serious threat to a strong and stable banking system. The book...features a relevant paper, authored by Shri A. Karunagaran, examining NPAs as a potential threat to the stability of the Indian financial system.... He has shown cross-country evidence about the weakness of the financial system owing to pile up in NPAs and concomitant erosion in capital. Therefore, designing and implementing an appropriate NPA resolution strategy is a challenging, yet necessary task.... Government intervention coupled with strict enforcement of regulatory and supervisory benchmarks and focus on effective corporate restructuring are some of the remedial measures the author considers appropriate in the Indian context....

The concluding paper in the edited volume is contributed by Shri Manoranjan Sharma, on an issue as topical and relevant as the 'Rapidly Expending Frontiers of Micro Finance'. The higher cost of serving the rural power, as part of the ongoing socio-economic transformation, is a high risk and high cost proposition. Yet, the author demonstrates that such high cost is worth the pie in view of the emerging profile of the rural masses.... He, nonetheless, is realistic enough to conclude: "Despite the salubrious impact of micro-finance, it would be unrealistic to consider it as a panacea to all ills. It, perforce, requires other complementary interventions so as to make a perceptible difference to the teeming millions of the country."

Usually books on money, finance and banking look at issues either from the point of view of academicians or the practitioners and it is rare to come across books, which have a judicious mix of both academics and banking. The book under review represents the point of convergence of the best in academics and banking. It would, therefore, stimulate interest and research on various issues of considerable contemporary significance to the Indian financial system.

Canbank Bimonthly Review

Contributors

Y.V. Reddy, Governor, Reserve Bank of India.

Rakesh Mohan, Deputy Governor, Reserve Bank of India.

Rajesh Chakrabarti, Assistant Professor, ISB, Hyderabad, Andhra Pradesh.

Gaurav Chawla, Stern School of Business, New York University, New York, 10012.

M.B.N. Rao, Chairman and Managing Director, Canara Bank, Bangalore, Karnataka.

V. Leeladhar, Deputy Governor, Reserve Bank of India.

Manoranjan Sharma, Chief Economist, Deputy General Manager, Canara Bank, Bangalore, Karnataka.

Prakash Singh, Assistant Professor, Indian Institute of Management, Lucknow, Uttar Pradesh.

A. Karunagaran, Assistant Advisor, Department of Economic Policy and Analysis (DEAP), Reserve Bank of India, Mumbai, Maharashtra.

Biswa Swarup Misra, Associate Professor in Economics area in the Xavier Institute of Management, Bhubaneswar. The author is on lien from the Reserve Bank of India, where he is an officer in the Department of Economic Analysis and Policy (DEAP).

P.K. Raut, Deputy General Manager, Reserve Bank of India, Patna, Bihar.

M.S. Gopalan, Senior Manager, Canara Bank, Bangalore, Karnataka.

Atanu K. Das, Chief Economist, Assistant General Manager, Vijaya Bank, Bangalore, Karnataka.

A.K. Misra, Assistant Professor, School of Management, Indian Institute of Technology, Kharagpur, West Bengal.

Debesh Roy, Assistant General Manager, National Bank for Agriculture and Rural Development (NABARD), Regional Office, Kolkata, West Bengal.

R.K. Anand, Senior Manager, Punjab National Bank, Training College, Chandigarh.

Rakesh Malhotra, Deputy General Manager, Agriculture Finance Corporation, New Delhi.